A CONNECTED METROPOLIS

A CONNECTED METROPOLIS

LOS ANGELES ELITES AND THE MAKING

OF A MODERN CITY, 1890-1965

MAXWELL JOHNSON

UNIVERSITY OF NEBRASKA PRESS   LINCOLN

Portions of chapter 2 were previously published as "Borderlands Fortress: Newspaper Magnates, Preparedness, and the Rhetoric of Progress in World War I–Era Los Angeles," *Pacific Historical Review* 86, no. 2 (May 2017): 258–89. Chapter 4 contains song lyrics with credit to Upton Sinclair Papers, Courtesy Lilly Library, Indiana University, Bloomington, Indiana.

The University of Nebraska Press is part of a land-grant institution with campuses and programs on the past, present, and future homelands of the Pawnee, Ponca, Otoe-Missouria, Omaha, Dakota, Lakota, Kaw, Cheyenne, and Arapaho Peoples, as well as those of the relocated Ho-Chunk, Sac and Fox, and Iowa Peoples.

Library of Congress Cataloging-in-Publication Data
Names: Johnson, Maxwell, 1988– author.
Title: A connected metropolis: Los Angeles elites and the making of a modern city, 1890–1965 / Maxwell Johnson.
Other titles: Los Angeles elites and the making of a modern city, 1890–1965
Description: Lincoln: University of Nebraska Press, 2023. | Includes bibliographical references and index.
Identifiers: LCCN 2022045657
ISBN 9781496224323 (hardback)
ISBN 9781496236661 (epub)
ISBN 9781496236678 (pdf)
Subjects: LCSH: Los Angeles (Calif.)—Economic conditions—20th century. | City promotion—California—Los Angeles—History—20th century. | Los Angeles (Calif.)—Relations. | Elite (Social sciences)—California—Los Angeles—History—20th century. | Upper class—California—Los Angeles—History—20th century. | Men, White—California—Los Angeles—Attitudes—History—20th century. | Racism—California—Los Angeles—History—20th century. | Los Angeles (Calif.)—History—20th century. | Los Angeles (Calif.)—Social conditions—20th century. | Urbanization—California—Los Angeles. | BISAC: HISTORY / United States / State & Local / West (AK, CA, CO, HI, ID, MT, NV, UT, WY) | HISTORY / Social History
Classification: LCC HT325 .J646 2023 |
DDC 306.09794/940904—dc23/eng/20220928
LC record available at https://lccn.loc.gov/2022045657

Set in Adobe Text by Mikala R. Kolander. Designed by N. Putens.

To my parents—Lynn, Linck, and
Susan—and my wife, Whitney.

CONTENTS

ILLUSTRATIONS

ACKNOWLEDGMENTS

THIS BOOK WOULD NOT EXIST WITHOUT MICHAEL MCGERR'S CARING mentorship and tireless work on my behalf. From our very first meeting in September 2013, when he encountered an advisee who wanted to write "something about cities during the early twentieth century," Professor McGerr has been an exemplary advisor. He helped me to find a dissertation topic amid a forest of scattered thoughts and interests, demanded that I become a more careful, coherent writer, and then pushed me to revise the dissertation into a book. Such a generous professor with his time, I remain amazed at the degree to which he close-reads his students' and former students' work. (See the misplaced modifier in the last sentence? I'm sure he is already writing me an email about it). I am profoundly grateful for the opportunity to have worked with him over the course of a decade.

This project began as a dissertation at Indiana University, and I would like to thank the members of my dissertation committee (Wendy Gamber, Peter Guardino, and Ellen Wu) for their valuable contributions. Konstantin Dierks's history seminar fostered the first germ of what would become the dissertation. The Department of History's fellowship committee allowed me to make formative trips to Los Angeles during the earliest stages of this project and then supported me as I finished the dissertation. Thanks as well to the department's administrative staff, especially Alexia Bock, Becky Bryant, Nick Roberts, and Sarah Skinner, for all of their help.

After I graduated from Indiana University, various institutions and individuals allowed me to complete the book manuscript. Thank you to Culver Academies for its invaluable research support—Josh Pretzer was especially helpful in this regard. Gary Christlieb, Raegan Russell, Scott Sweet-Christian, and Tyler Yoder were all wonderful colleagues who sparked my thinking in new directions. A panel at the Western History Association Conference in 2021 encouraged me to revise chapter 3; thank you to Andy Aguilera for creating the panel and to Rachel St. John for providing important feedback on the paper. Over a period of four years, the University of Nebraska Press was wonderfully supportive of the project. Thanks especially to Bridget Barry for pushing me through from book proposal to finalized manuscript. Finally, thank you to Park Tudor School for its generous support of the project. Dr. Shants N. Hart was especially helpful in this regard.

Various archives and archivists have been indispensable to this project. Thanks especially to Mike Holland at the Los Angeles City Archives, who shepherded me through the collections on multiple occasions and located materials I never would have found without his help. His knowledge of both the City Archives and other repositories around the city is unmatched. Because of Mike's work, the City Archives is a jewel of the Los Angeles research scene. The staff at the Huntington Library pulled a huge volume of sources for me on a daily basis without complaint, even when I often returned boxes after looking at just one document. The library staff at California State, Dominguez Hills; California State, Northridge; Indiana University; the LA84 Foundation; the Seaver Center for Western History Research; Syracuse University; UCLA; and USC all answered many of my questions and made my research experiences easy and pleasant.

I would not have made it through graduate school without relationships formed at Indiana University. To Andy, Greg, Hannah, and Kyle: you guys are the best. Hannah Craddock-Mossman also provided crucial insight into the historiography of gender history, which proved invaluable as I revised the manuscript. Thanks as well to my friends in adjoining cities and states—Dustin, Kasey, Shane, Christina, Greg, Jasmine, Paul, Kristina, Jared, and Tessa—for providing such happy outlet spaces. To Clint and Mollie, my California family, thanks for your generosity during my research trips.

My love of history was sparked long before graduate school. I would like to thank my first great history teacher, Kathy Sabino, from Hamilton Central School, for nurturing those interests. Professor Andrew Rotter, at Colgate University, and Professors Henry Binford and Carl Smith, at Northwestern University, were all integral to my becoming a better historian.

My family has been wonderfully supportive throughout the process. To Ka, Peggy, Jan, Steve, Sarah, and Stephen: thanks for everything. My three parents—Linck, Lynn, and Sue—provided my earliest images of academic life and scholarship. Though they did saddle me with an unfortunate love of the humanities, they have made up for that oversight through their constant love for me. Finally, thank you most of all to my wife, Whitney. Even as she completed her own doctoral work, she listened to my ramblings about the American West. Despite her own commitments, she always thought about what I was saying and pushed me to critically expand my thinking on race and power in America. In the future, I will try to talk less about Los Angeles's dead, rich, white guys.

A CONNECTED METROPOLIS

INTRODUCTION
"The Damnedest Place"

SIMULTANEOUSLY A COMMAND POST OF THE AMERICAN EMPIRE AND an outpost utterly dependent on other places both national and global, Los Angeles has confounded observers for the last century. "The city and county of Los Angeles, Calif. consists of 4,071 square miles of rocks, sand and 'semiarid' land in the far southwestern corner of the U.S., virtually isolated from most of the country by dreary deserts and lofty mountain ranges," began *Life* reporter Roger Butterfield in his 1943 article "Los Angeles Is the Damnedest Place."[1] Yet, Butterfield noted, Los Angeles was an amazing success story: the fastest-growing and third-largest city in the United States, the second most productive industrial county in America, and the global center of the film industry. How did Butterfield explain such an unlikely rise? He felt its roots lay in boosterism, or in Butterfield's words, "selling sunshine to the world."[2]

American urban history is replete with studies of boosterism. From Chicago's development of its "hinterlands," to Kansas City's effort to gain railroad connections, to Seattle's embrace of a "Pacific cosmopolitanism" in the early twentieth century, scholars have exhaustively examined how economic and political leaders labored to sell their cities to the world.[3] Historians of Southern California have also focused on boosterism. To take one example, Paul Sandul finds a booster group in the "agriburb" of Ontario, California, that "saw the entire metropolis . . . or region (Southern

California) . . . as the stage in which they operated—and needed to operate."[4] Although the elites of Los Angeles often transcended nearby borders in their economic pursuits and lifestyles, the city stood as a focal point for their ambitions. "The metropolitan synthesis has drawn from too narrow a map of metropolitan space and the politics of growth," Andrew Needham writes in *Power Lines*, his study of energy consumption and the rise of Phoenix, Arizona. "Remapping metropolitan history at the regional level," he suggests, allows historians to more comprehensively examine cities and the "disruptions" created by urban growth machines.[5] *A Connected Metropolis*, therefore, seeks to "remap" Los Angeles's history at both the regional and national levels through the stories of the powerful businessmen, newspaper publishers, and public officials who propelled its growth from 1890 to 1965.

To be sure, historians of Los Angeles have struggled to depict the broad trends of the city's upper-class activism. They often defer to either a "sunshine" narrative of optimistic growth or a "noir" narrative of repressive social control.[6] But Los Angeles's upper class during the examined time period defied such easy categorization; it was malleable, transient, and variegated. "Mexican and Anglo-American landlords, transplanted Eastern and Midwestern entrepreneurs, and cinema and aerospace executives led different stages of urban development," Frederic Jaher argues in *The Urban Establishment*. "Each enclave contributed to the growth of Los Angeles but was unable to perpetuate its ascendance."[7] So who were these people? How might they be categorized? Jaher finds an "upper class" in Los Angeles, but the constantly changing composition of Los Angeles's wealthy, powerful group seems to resist such terminology. E. Digby Baltzell provides a more convincing term in his *Philadelphia Gentlemen: The Making of a National Upper Class*. "The *elite* concept refers to those *individuals* who are the most successful and stand at the top of the *functional* class hierarchy," he writes. "These individuals are leaders in their chosen occupations or professions; they are the final-decision makers in the political, economic or military spheres."[8] Baltzell's term *elite* guides my analysis, as does his simple definition of the term: individuals who lead their chosen fields at the upper echelons of the class structure. Not every person portrayed in *A Connected Metropolis* attained the same level of wealth, though all of them were powerful. Moreover, while the elite group may have changed composition over time, certain elite institutions, the Los Angeles Chamber of Commerce and Merchants and Manufacturer's Association most notably, remained powerful throughout the early twentieth century and fostered remarkable collaboration.[9] Still, whatever the broader applicability of Baltzell's formulation, it certainly describes Los Angeles's upper class in the twentieth century.

While many of those individuals and elite institutions engaged in boosterism, this does not fully explain the rise of the sprawling city. Indeed, boosterism is a relatively limited set of practices centered on the promotion of economic development, and Los Angeles grew from a remote frontier town in the 1880s to a global metropolis by the end of World War II because its elites moved beyond boosterism. Instead, they embraced and espoused a politics of connection, which revolved around efforts to tie Los Angeles to other places both tangibly and metaphorically. City leaders built tangible connections to secure, among other things, the water that irrigated Los Angeles's citrus farms and flowed through its sewers, the capital that funded its businesses, and the people who migrated from the Midwest to buy its houses. To build metaphorical connections, these men fiercely debated a series of questions. How should Los Angeles interact with other Pacific World and borderlands places? How receptive should the city be to new populations? And how much should it depend on federal power?

In its enormous growth and removed geographical location, Los Angeles essentially stands alone as a twentieth-century urban narrative, but the story's distinctiveness does not diminish its importance. A Connected Metropolis suggests that scholars should broaden their studies of boosterism to consider how urban leaders often looked beyond economic relationships to forge a comprehensive set of global connections. "New York was sui generis, a place set off from the rest of the country in many ways," Christine Stansell writes of early nineteenth-century gender dynamics in the Big Apple. "But if unique, New York was far from irrelevant to the rest of America: It was a historical stage writ large for encounters that reverberated across the rest of the nation."[10] Los Angeles's elite-driven politics of connection had a similar impact on the domestic and international spheres.

By the end of World War I, Los Angeles had achieved many of its boosters' dreams. Thereafter, Angelenos encountered and navigated, generally at the expense of marginalized groups, the ecological crises of the 1920s, the sociopolitical crises of the Depression, and the racial crises of World War II. City leaders understood that the Los Angeles area—its "rocks, sand and 'semiarid' land . . . virtually isolated from most of the country"—was not the obvious place for a major city to develop. They believed, then, that connections between Los Angeles and other places were all the more important. But Los Angeles elites were also willing to temporarily sever connections during times of perceived crisis. During World War I, for instance, two major newspapers amplified racist narratives about the susceptibility of Los Angeles to a dual Japanese-Mexican invasion and urged the city to become a "fortress." Using business and personal archives, newspaper articles, and popular media sources, I argue that the true story of Los Angeles's rise lies in the spectacular visions and rambunctious activism of a group of influential men dedicated to transforming a remote frontier town into a global metropolis.

As a group, the Los Angeles elites I discuss were white men who sought to work with other white men. American masculinity was in crisis at the turn of the century. Changes in industrial capitalism had created a middle class of white-collar white male workers who feared the implications of their loss of economic independence.[11] At the same time, the ideal of the New Woman also challenged traditional masculine dominance. As a result, many middle-class men tried to shift masculine norms away from conceptions of economic autonomy toward ideas of racial and sexual dominance.[12] Elites also worried about their masculinity; wealth might produce "the very effeminacy that was eroding manhood."[13] Some sought to shore up their masculinity through experiences in the "romantic wilderness."[14] Others promoted the "savage virtues" of brute strength and tenacity.[15] More broadly, elites formulated a hegemonic masculinity: habits and rhetoric meant to justify the supremacy of some men over others, and of men over women.[16] "Hegemonic forms of masculinity in modernity are historically derived from the growth of industrial capitalism and the growth of imperialism," scholars R. W. Connell and Julian Wood write.

"The bourgeois masculinities produced by these processes," they continue, had global similarities: "social conservatism; compulsory heterosexuality; integration with a family division of labor; strongly marked, symbolic gender differences; and emotional distance between men and women." Such hegemonic masculinity also held ties to local economic structures. "Men who were the bearers of these configurations of practice generally controlled the key industries in the local economy," Connell and Wood conclude, "so the locally hegemonic patterns of masculinity were typically integrated with the local patterns of capitalism."[17]

This analysis resonates in the history of Los Angeles. As historian George Chauncey writes, "The most powerful elements of American society decided the official maps of culture."[18] Though such official maps of masculinity did not necessarily determine social relations, elite culture sought to "police its own boundaries" regarding gender conformity.[19] For their employees, Los Angeles's business leaders "constructed within their company cultures a distinct new vision of white-collar manhood," historian Clark Davis writes. "They did this by arguing that white-collar tasks called for the very best attributes of manhood."[20] For themselves, in turn, Los Angeles's elites disseminated and performed a masculinity that was at once based on traditional norms of economic success and blended with new ideas about the "savage virtues." From martial discourse about the 1910 Los Angeles International Air Meet; to World War I–era efforts to encourage a manly, western preparedness in the region; to the 1920s desire to "tame" the Colorado River and bring its waters to the city; to the Depression-era campaign against "tramps," hegemonic masculinity lay behind much of the city's development. Manhood was a unifying force for Los Angeles's elites, and expressions of masculinity could emerge as much from moments of optimism as from moments of fear. In its capability to unite elite men in their connective work, masculinity was inextricable from the politics of connection. The elites profiled in *A Connected Metropolis* saw their masculinity as a significant factor in their success. They attributed to their masculinity a set of practices that, they thought, needed to be cultivated in Los Angeles and protected from dangerous deviants and outsiders.

Conceptions of whiteness also undergirded the activism of Los Angeles's elites. Historians have thoroughly documented how race divided Angelenos throughout the twentieth century.[21] City authorities often evoked racial hierarchies to police nonwhite bodies, initiating, in the words of historian Natalia Molina, "a long tradition . . . of tracing any blemish on the pristine image of Los Angeles . . . to the city's marginalized communities."[22] For elites, race thus became one tool in their toolbox of sociocultural negotiation and control. Often, they expressed their power by policing the mobility of nonwhite groups. "Mobility has been an active force in racialization over the twentieth century," Genevieve Carpio writes in her study of racialization in inland California. "Contests over movement have shaped racial hierarchies and regional attitudes towards a diverse set of migrant and resident groups."[23] Accordingly, during periods of upheaval—World War I, the Great Depression, World War II—elites emphasized the importance of creating and policing racial boundaries; they even depicted "Okies" as nonwhite, malicious outsiders. At other, more optimistic moments—the 1920s, the 1932 Olympics—elites temporarily diminished the importance of racial boundaries in the city. Generally, of course, they viewed Los Angeles as the "Nation's White Spot," in the words of historian Eric Avila. "Local boosters ensured that their version of the city myth appealed to whites only," he writes, "and acknowledged the presence of nonwhite peoples only to the extent of their capacity to provide cheap but invisible labor."[24] Nonwhites might augment the city's labor force or perceptions of its cosmopolitanism, but they were not viewed as full members of Los Angeles's civic culture. "The city fathers sent a clear message: social membership in the city would be reserved for whites only," Molina succinctly concludes.[25] Elites shaped their rhetoric, therefore, around notions of whiteness and labored to create tangible and metaphorical connections for the city on their own terms—privileging Anglo, capitalist, masculine power.

In their connective efforts, Los Angeles elites participated in a vibrant "infrastructure of ideas" about the city's connections. As the historian Carl Smith explains, the "infrastructure of ideas" could bring together "the ideas mainly of a small elite" engaged in a common goal.[26] "A city is as much an *infrastructure of ideas* as it is a gathering of people, a layout of streets," Smith writes in *City Water, City Life*, his study of urbanizing water systems. "A crucial component" of the urbanization process, he continues, "was the fashioning of a dynamic and conflicted imaginative as well as physical place."[27] Los Angeles elites ascribed to their growing city a set of ideas—about borders, connections, and gender—and created a civic rhetoric centered on positioning the city's development as a high-stakes, continually threatened venture. They worked these ideas out through collaboration with each other and communication with the public. "Since hegemonic groups can lead only by mobilizing the community to cope with the problems of its environment," Jaher writes, "social change may necessitate creating new institutions, norms, and goals and then coercing or persuading the community to accept these innovations."[28] Such men were by no means coherent in their beliefs. But, when some of them focused on a particular issue, they united in remarkable ways.[29] *A Connected Metropolis* argues that Los Angeles's white, male upper class often achieved a startling level of unanimity.

In examining Los Angeles's transformation through its elites, however, I do not subscribe to the "Great Men" theory of history, whereby a small group of "heroic" people accomplishes massive change.[30] To be sure, the individuals profiled in *A Connected Metropolis* fundamentally reshaped their urban environment and its connections. Sven Beckert defends such a focus on the most powerful members of society in *The Monied Metropolis*, his study of upper-class New York City during the nineteenth century. The upper class "had developed a distinctive sense of itself by the end of the nineteenth century," he writes. "And though it has become fashionable of late to de-emphasize questions of social power . . . the dramatically uneven distribution of economic resources allowed this small group of Americans to exercise an expanding power over the way people lived and worked."[31] While Los Angeles elites secured the city a major port, access to natural resources, and an Olympic Games, among other accomplishments, they were not "heroic." Throughout the first five decades of the twentieth century, local elites significantly damaged less powerful groups. During the 1920s, they robbed Owens Valley farmers of their water. During the Depression, they attempted to barricade the city from Dust Bowl migrants and crafted a vicious smear campaign to defeat Democratic gubernatorial candidate Upton Sinclair, who wanted to welcome such refugees. During World War II, they banded together to ensure the forcible imprisonment of thousands of Japanese Americans. *A Connected Metropolis* narrates the story of Los Angeles's ascent, the myriad costs of that ascent, and the embedded hierarchical and racist notions that lay behind it at each step. To an extent, my strategy is similar to that of Robert Caro in *The Power Broker*, his study of New York public works czar Robert Moses. "Robert Moses was America's greatest builder," Robert Caro writes. "But what did he build? What was the shape into which he pounded the city?" "In the evening of Robert Moses' forty-four years of power," Caro continues, "New York, so bright with promise forty-four years before, was a city in chaos and despair."[32]

In their discussions around and efforts to create connections, Los Angeles's elites broadly focused on three sets of relationships: local, transnational, and transcontinental. Local areas extended from the city's own boundaries to regional spaces. As the city annexed more territory throughout the twentieth century, city leaders struggled to incorporate new populations. To ensure the city's water and power supply, they looked to regional sites. The Owens Valley, an agricultural area two hundred miles to the north, was not particularly local. But city leaders such as William Mulholland, head of the Department of Water and Power, rhetorically tied the Owens Valley to Los Angeles, arguing that integrating the distant agricultural valley into the metropolitan water supply would be vital to the city's survival. In pursuing a broader policy of resource extraction, then, city leaders pursued connections on terms favorable to Los Angeles and often ignored the effects of their policies on partner populations. Debates about transnational connections focused on Los Angeles's Pacific boundary and the U.S. border with Mexico.[33] During the twentieth century, Los Angeles became defined by migratory "nodes of intersection" with Asia, Mexico, and Canada.[34] Sometimes, elites expressed fear of such transnational interactions—for instance, by promulgating long-standing racist ideas about a "Yellow Peril" that threatened the West Coast.[35] At other times, they hoped to spread the city's industries throughout the

Pacific World.[36] While globalization often clashed with nativism in the nineteenth century United States, in Los Angeles, borders seemed more proximate, even tactile.[37]

Finally, elites pondered to what extent they should pursue transcontinental connections. Angelenos referred to their community at various moments as "Southern California," "the Great Southwest," and the "Metropolis of the West." Los Angeles, the elites profiled here felt, needed to simultaneously interact with and distance itself from capital based in New York City and the federal government in Washington DC. Local booster Phineas Banning illustrates the importance of New York and Washington to late nineteenth-century Southern California. When he became a state senator in the 1870s, Banning fought to make Los Angeles a greater transportation hub and the San Pedro Bay, a few miles to the south, the city's sea outlet. Banning pressured Congress to ensure a first appropriation for port improvements in 1871. In 1873 he sold his stake in the Los Angeles & San Pedro Railroad to Collis Huntington's powerful Southern Pacific Railroad, based in New York, to ensure that Los Angeles would have a stop on the Southern Pacific's route from San Francisco to Yuma, Arizona. Banning's efforts, plus substantial monetary and land concessions from the city, put Los Angeles on a major railway line. Thereafter, the Southern Pacific continued to develop its interests at San Pedro. During the so-called Free Harbor Fight in the late nineteenth century, city leaders won a protracted battle against the Southern Pacific to locate a municipally controlled port at San Pedro. The Free Harbor Fight also depended on federal appropriations to dredge the San Pedro Bay and construct breakwaters there. Such triangular negotiations would continue to consume Los Angeles elites in the years ahead.

Beneath the politics of these three connection zones, which tended to surface particularly during times of perceived danger, lurked borderlands fears and aspirations. A concept first deployed by Herbert Eugene Bolton in his 1921 *The Spanish Borderlands*, the term *borderlands* has traditionally referred to the area of the southwestern United States bordering Mexico.[38] The Chicana theorist Gloria Anzaldúa, in her seminal *Borderlands/La Frontera*, contends that borders themselves connote fear. "Borders are set up to define the places that are safe and unsafe," she writes, "to distinguish *us* from *them*."[39] But the borderlands also offered investment opportunities for Los Angeles's elites. Beginning in the 1870s, American speculators made massive land purchases in northwestern Mexico. Newspaper magnates Harrison Gray Otis and Harry Chandler, of the *Los Angeles Times*, and William Randolph Hearst, of the Hearst publishing empire—all of whom feature prominently in the following chapters—bought undervalued land in the hopes of later selling it for a profit. Failing that, these men at least hoped to derive significant income from subdividing the land and renting it to farmers and ranchers.[40] At the same time, Anglo mining magnates looked to develop copper deposits in northern Mexico, especially in Sonora, bordering Arizona.[41] In Los Angeles's relationship with Mexico, historian Jessica Kim sees a borderlands "city empire," built by men such as Otis and Chandler. "Between 1865 and 1941," she writes, "Los Angeles and Mexico remained intertwined in the complex web of a city, its cross-border hinterland, and empire."[42] Borderlands discourse, then, could often reflect transnational concerns about the permeability of the nation's boundaries or the fertile development areas that lay beyond them. But during the Great Depression transcontinental concerns about unfettered domestic migration to California also sparked borderlands fears. The politics of connection, then, transcended borderlands discourse.

The elite project in Los Angeles depended on three factors: transportation technology, media companies, and public mobilization. Obviously, automobile culture came to dominate Los Angeles. During the 1920s Los Angeles County's inadequate roads outraged local boosters. By 1950, the city had become a "concrete utopia" of interconnected freeways.[43] Even before the automobile boom, Los Angeles depended on railroad connections and shipping traffic. Banning's efforts to secure for Los Angeles a place on the Southern Pacific line spurred the growth of the city. Midwestern migrants and vacationers flocked to Southern California throughout the early twentieth century, lured by advertisements telling readers of the region's beauty. For example, during the 1920s the All-Year Club, an Angeleno booster organization, touted the city's "cool summer nights" in newspapers across the Midwest.[44] Such travelers reached Los Angeles primarily by train. "Tourist Rush for Winter On: Rail Men Predicting Banner Year of Travel," announced one sample news article in the *Times* in 1925.[45] Once they arrived, Henry Huntington's Los Angeles Railway and Pacific Electric Railway, at the time the largest electric railway system in the world, connected Angelenos to each other and surrounding towns. Other visitors might arrive in Los Angeles by ship; Japan sent over 150 athletes to the 1932 Olympics in this fashion.

Transportation technology, then, allowed elites to plan for the future. They used print media outlets and motion pictures to disseminate specific visions of Los Angeles. The *Los Angeles Times* was probably the city's biggest booster. Led successively by Otis and Chandler, the newspaper emerged as a vociferously pro-business outlet that could dominate discourse. In its efforts, the *Times* was not alone. Hearst's newspaper, the *Los Angeles Examiner*, a competitor of the *Times*, also boosted Los Angeles. In the 1920s, when the motion picture industry relocated to Southern California, films also depicted the city as a model place in which to live.

But reliance on transportation technology and media outlets was not enough. For their vision to succeed, elites needed to mobilize the public to ratify or support certain measures. In the first five decades of the twentieth century, they urged Angelenos into action—to approve bonds issued to finance water and power initiatives, support a crackdown on unions, and purchase tickets to local events that would amplify the city's reputation, such as the 1910 Los Angeles International Air Meet and the 1932 Olympics.

Elite activism in Los Angeles, then, was expansive and multifaceted. Rather than writing a comprehensive history of Los Angeles's elites, however, I focus on how they shaped the city's connections to the outside world. Utilizing a case study approach, I especially focus on specific moments in the city's development when tensions over Los Angeles's connections, or lack thereof, emerged. I tie each movement to two or three contemporary figures who influenced the debates at hand. With the exception of chapter 1, each chapter encompasses roughly a decade. Chapter 1 discusses the long Free Harbor Fight from 1890 to 1910 and the rhetoric disseminated by publishers such as Otis, whose *Los Angeles Times* became a prominent port booster. After they gained federal support for the project, city boosters hosted the first major American airshow, the 1910 Los Angeles International Air Meet, which seemed to indicate the city's growing national prominence. Underneath boosterish confidence, however, lay distinct fears about the city's susceptibility to a future invasion. Chapter 2 picks up on that idea, as it details the World War I–era preparedness rhetoric of the *Examiner* and *Times*. Both newspapers disseminated fearmongering articles about the dangers of a purported dual Japanese-Mexican invasion. The two papers used preparedness to advocate postwar economic development. Chapter 3, primarily focused on the 1920s, details Mulholland's efforts to provide the growing city with a consistent water supply. He marshalled public support and federal appropriations to achieve his goals, but these efforts sparked backlash from Owens Valley farmers and local observers sympathetic to their plight.

Chapters 4 and 5 focus on the twin crises of the Great Depression and World War II in Los Angeles, respectively. During the Depression, Los Angeles elites embarked on four major efforts: fighting Mexican deportation, obstructing domestic migration, promoting the 1932 Olympics, and defeating Upton Sinclair's 1934 California gubernatorial bid. The era demonstrates a remarkable degree of collaboration in the elite rhetorical mission. Chapter 5 discusses Los Angeles's centrality to the World War II defense effort and the ramifications of the city's role in the minds of its leaders. "Total defense" led two progressive cosmopolitan politicians, Mayor Fletcher Bowron and Los Angeles County Supervisor John Anson Ford, to abandon their past ideals in order to intern thousands of local Japanese Americans.

Finally, the coda, "Where They All Are Headed," discusses the postwar era and growing challenges to the elite mission. Los Angeles elites experienced notable postwar successes, such as the 1953 election of Mayor Norris Poulson, who evicted a Mexican community in Chavez Ravine to build a baseball stadium for Brooklyn Dodgers owner Walter O'Malley and lure his team to Los Angeles. On the other hand, two 1965 events disturbed the Anglo elite mission. First, the 1965 Watts Rebellion underlined the degree to which African Americans—hundreds of thousands of whom had migrated to Los Angeles over the previous twenty-five years—chafed under segregation and assertions of white supremacy. Second, the Immigration and Naturalization Act of 1965 removed racial and national immigration quotas. Subsequently, the city would become a hub for documented Asian and undocumented Latin and South American immigrants. A reading of the *Times* during the postwar era illustrates how one elite media outlet tried to adapt to changing circumstances and maintain a sliver of control over the increasingly diverse, dispersed city.

At three places in the text, I provide "snapshots" of Los Angeles and its elites: in 1890, 1920, and 1940. The 1890 snapshot examines a real estate crash in the city and boosters' fears about its long-term prospects. The 1920 snapshot discusses two new industries central to the growing city: motion pictures and oil. Both industries demanded infrastructure improvement and lured to the city a new set of elites, men who would further pilot the politics of connection. The 1940 snapshot centers on a pivotal year for the Los Angeles aviation industry and municipal airport initiatives. City leaders finally succeeded in convincing voters to approve bonds to fund what would become Los Angeles International Airport. The local aviation industry also grew substantially during the time, as companies such as Douglas Aviation and North American Aviation won major federal military contracts. Collectively, the snapshots allow me to pan out and provide a broader historical context for the more focused case studies of individuals and institutions.

Overall, I reveal the longer arc of elite activism in the city and argue that scholars should expand their studies of Los Angeles and its power dynamics. Histories of the city's development have focused largely on later periods, primarily post–World War II.[46] In his examination of the historiography of Los Angeles, historian Scott Kurashige locates two turns: a post-1848 "white city" and a post-1965 "world city."[47] But the "world city" emerged out of the "white city," whose powerful leaders managed to establish tailored connections with the outside world. Those relationships have given the history of the city greater continuity than we have recognized until now. "Los Angeles has grown so fast that the Chamber of Commerce is no longer worried about getting new population, or even more industry," Butterfield wrote toward the end of his 1943 feature. "The Chamber maintains branch offices in Washington, Mexico City, and (in peacetime) half a dozen world capitals, and operates on an ever-widening economic and political scale."[48] Here lay emphatic evidence of Los Angeles's global reach. Though such expansion may have been unique to Los Angeles, it significantly affected other locales and populations. The forging of Los Angeles's connections also suggests how historians might research and produce more far-reaching urban narratives. "The time has come for the next urban history," A. L. Sandoval-Strausz argues, "one that analyzes U.S. cities in their transnational contexts."[49] *A Connected Metropolis* seeks not only to contribute to that historiographical movement but also to tie transnational contexts to regional and transcontinental initiatives.

Los Angeles's connective relationships did not just develop from boosterism; nor did they stand unchanged and uncontested over time. In March 1943, months after local Japanese Americans had been removed from the city, Mayor Fletcher Bowron took to the radio to chastise Angelenos for their behavior during an air raid drill the previous day. The city, he argued, was "one of the most vital, possibly one of the most vulnerable points in America." "Apathy on the part of such a large percentage of the people," he continued, "is the very serious thing."[50] Though Bowron's concerns were specific to the post–Pearl Harbor United States, his argument had echoed through the city for the previous fifty years. Los Angeles, city leaders maintained, was vital. It had potential to be the most powerful city in the American West. It might even stand alone as a Pacific World dynamo. But, city leaders argued, the city was also vulnerable. Culturally, its masculine identity might be undermined by changing economic and social currents. Domestically, it might attract undesired migrants. Internationally, it was situated at the confluence of potentially dangerous borderlands and Pacific World currents. In many ways, city elites manufactured these twin ideas and used them to shape a distinctive Anglo metropolis that stood, by the end of World War II, as one of urban America's most prominent success stories.

After World War II, the city's power dynamics grew more complicated. "Los Angeles is not what it was supposed to be," argues Avila.[51] Today, it is just 29 percent white. It is a diverse Pacific metropolis far removed from the minor, parochial city of the early twentieth century.[52] In 1900 Otis wrote to a friend that he envisioned Los Angeles becoming the metropole of a "Pacific Empire . . . a dominant subdivision of the mighty Republic."[53] His vision, far-fetched at the time, would largely come to fruition. Of course, Otis probably could not imagine the impact of such a transformation. So successful were the elites' previous efforts to secure nationwide and global connections for Los Angeles that a once small Pacific outpost became a supremely attractive conduit and landing place for people from around the world. Anglo elites ruthlessly shaped a city that would eventually escape their control.

SNAPSHOT
LOS ANGELES, 1890

AT LEAST LOS ANGELES HAD OUTPERFORMED WICHITA. IN MAY 1890, as a local real estate crash was wreaking havoc on the local economy, the *Los Angeles Times* took solace in the supposedly greater turmoil thousands of miles away. "Wichita, Kan., a city which enjoyed a phenomenal real-estate boom at about the same time that things were 'humming' in Los Angeles, is undergoing a similar experience to this city," the *Times* informed its readers. Both places, in fact, could be termed "paper cities, laid out in advance of population," only Wichita was "more so . . . in a business way . . . duller than the dullest."[1]

The crash caught Los Angeles at a crossroads between exaggerated contemporary expectations and past steady growth. Los Angeles's population almost quintupled from 1880 to 1890, as a sleepy frontier village of 11,183 became a rising community of more than 50,000, the fifty-seventh largest city in America.[2] In 1887 and 1888 local land values skyrocketed, and speculators swarmed to the city to gamble on its future. "Symptoms of feverish excitement were everywhere noticeable in Southern California," remembered local merchant Harris Newmark. "Selling and bartering were carried on at all hours of the day or night, and in every conceivable place."[3] In January 1888 the *New York Times* portrayed the boom through the story of one unnamed Connecticut migrant who decided to play the market. "She has, by a real estate investment near Los Angeles, netted a profit of over $5,000," the paper detailed. "The 'investment' she made amounted to $125, which was part payment upon $1,000 worth of land that for some remarkable reason suddenly spurted upward in market value to five times what she contracted to pay for it." In a letter she wrote home to her parents, the woman attributed her success to Los Angeles's strange culture. "Somehow the air out here sort o' makes everybody speculate," she told them, "and I couldn't help taking the chance."[4]

In reality, city leaders' careful efforts over the previous two decades to improve Los Angeles's infrastructure had fostered the real estate boom. In 1873, when only around eleven thousand people lived in the city, the Los Angeles Common Council, the predecessor to the city council, began to transform the city's hundreds of open canals, called zanjas, into a unified underground water network. The process took much longer than anticipated, but by 1890 most of the city's fifty thousand residents received their water through a closed public water and waste management system. During the same period, the council appropriated funds to build hundreds of new roads throughout Los Angeles and to repave many more.[5]

Transforming the built environment ensured greater Anglo control over the city. Racial tensions between Anglos and Mexican and Chinese Americans simmered from 1870 to 1890. In 1870 white residents rioted after rival Chinese gangs accidentally gunned down a local rancher in Chinatown.[6] Amid the ensuing massacre, a white mob set buildings ablaze and systematically tortured and lynched at least twenty Chinese residents. In 1879 the white populist Workingman's Party took control over the city council and tried to force many Chinese laundrymen and vegetable dealers out of business.[7] Sewer and roads projects largely excluded Mexican and Chinese neighborhoods and left these places with dirt roads and open sewers. City leaders demonized Calle de los Negros, a street near the downtown Plaza that became the center of Los Angeles's Chinatown, as a haven of sin and vice. In the summer of 1887, in an attempt to forcibly relocate Los Angeles's small Chinese population to a less central location, arsonists burned down much of the area. Though Chinatown remained, it shifted a few blocks away. City officials used part of the burned space to lengthen and expand Los Angeles Street, which had previously terminated at the beginning of Calle de los Negros.[8]

As late as 1885 over 90 percent of Los Angeles's thirty square miles was rural, and the furthest extent of developed residential and commercial property in the city lay only two miles from downtown.[9] Over the next few years, whites increasingly moved away from downtown to areas to the south and west, which boasted modern buildings and amenities.[10] "Many streets . . . that a half a dozen years ago were orchard land are now lined with fine modern residences," exulted the *Times* in December 1890, using rhetoric that would often be repeated over the next century. "Progress has laid her finger, and in every direction we have grown till we have a metropolis of which we may be proud and whose future greatness is assured."[11] The city's boundaries had not expanded, but white Angelenos were transforming rural farmland into residential space. By 1890 Los Angeles had begun to achieve some of its modern diffuse, segregated landscape.

Anglos also eventually took control over elite Angeleno society. During the 1830s—after Mexico gained its independence from Spain and the Mexican government moved to secularize Spanish missions—a group of approximately eight hundred Mexican Californians grabbed over eight million acres of land formerly held by the missions.[12] Large landholders formed a distinct ranchero elite; they raised massive cattle herds, displayed their wealth by building large houses and wearing expensive clothes, and ensured their power by fashioning themselves as Californios, a distinct socioracial class. Rancheros also built connections to international hide and tallow markets.[13] During the 1860s, however, rancheros—hurt by drought, a collapse of cattle prices, and rising tax rates—lost social, political, and economic power to a "new elite" of Anglo agricultural magnates and large-scale landholders.[14] By the 1870s Anglo migration to Los Angeles rendered Mexican Americans a minority in the city. Cristóbal Aguilar, who served as mayor of Los Angeles from 1870 to 1872, would be Los Angeles's last Mexican American mayor until 2005.

Most of the migrant Anglos who comprised the new elite had arrived in Los Angeles in their twenties or thirties from New England, the mid-Atlantic Coast, the Midwest, or Europe.[15] These men invested widely, but generally they focused on some combination of local agriculture, real estate, and banking. Born in Vermont in 1824, for instance, Ozro W. Childs migrated to northern California during the Gold Rush and then moved to Los Angeles after he failed to reap riches in the north. In Los Angeles Childs began as a merchant, expanded into real estate, and later dabbled in horticulture. In 1879 he helped found the University of Southern California alongside John G. Downey and Isaias W. Hellman.[16] Downey had been born in Ireland, and like Childs, had migrated to California during the Gold Rush before settling in Los Angeles. He served as the governor of California from 1860 to 1862 and later made his fortune in banking and real estate.[17] Hellman migrated to California from his native Bavaria a decade after Childs and Downey. Beginning as a dry goods dealer, he quickly moved into banking and real estate. With Downey, Hellman created the Farmers and Merchants Bank of Los Angeles, and, through his professional and personal investments, supported, among other initiatives, Otis's purchase of the *Times* and Henry Huntington's Pacific Electric Railway. Later in life, Hellman would move to San Francisco and become one of the preeminent financiers in America.[18] All three men, then, followed similar trajectories in Southern California. They also focused on similar types of investments related to Los Angeles's ascent. After Childs died in 1890, the *Times* published a glowing obituary, which illustrated especially well how contemporary Angeleno elites made diverse investments in a few crucial sectors and tied their own fortunes to that of Los Angeles. "For a number of years after he came to Los Angeles Mr. Childs was in the hardware business, but afterward purchased a 50-acre tract in the southeastern part of the city, and went into the nursery business," the paper narrated, "the city giving him in 1864 every block of land on Main street . . . except five, on condition that he should build a zanja, which he did." "In 1884 Mr. Childs subdivided his nursery tract," the obituary continued. "Besides these properties, Mr. Childs had large holdings in San Bernardino and San Diego counties, and this county . . . The total value of his estate is estimated at $1,500,000."[19]

As Childs's obituary showed, Los Angeles could provide opportunities for speculative gain, a lesson the broader public took to heart during the late 1880s. "A review of Los Angeles, without a glance at the characteristic features of the local real-estate market," concluded the *Los Angeles Times* at the beginning of 1888, "would be like the play of Hamlet, with Hamlet left out."[20] The newspaper surveyed the boom in a lengthy article four months later. "Everybody that could find an office went into the real-estate business. Doctors, lawyers and merchants shared the excitement," the paper claimed, "and some of them gave up their regular pursuits and pitched into real estate."[21] So quickly did real estate mania take over that the newspaper, a prominent booster outlet, warned its readers to be vigilant about potential investment opportunities. In April 1888 the paper decried "Confidence Men," who "have swarmed to this city from every known part of the world." Some grifters, the paper contended, targeted the vulnerable, especially middle-class women. Other grifters, the "high-toned real-estate swindler" in the words of the paper, tried to lure the rich into real estate deals from which the swindler might secretly profit. Confidence men would secure one price from the landowner, extract a high price from the wealthy purchaser, and pocket the difference. To deal with such crimes, the newspaper urged the formation of a "first-class vigilance committee," of the kind created by booming mining towns.[22] Los Angeles's rise, the paper feared, made the city vulnerable to outsiders.

Though it preached vigilance, the *Times* had not foreseen the risk of the ensuing real estate crash, one as spectacular as the preceding boom. Speculators drove prices to such a level that the bottom fell out of the market. The crash wiped out over $14 million in real estate in Los Angeles County from 1888 to 1889 and over two-thirds of all assessed land value by 1890.[23] While the editors of the *Times* seemed loath to cover the crash or its implications for Los Angeles, readers could still get a picture of declining fortunes in various news articles and letters to the editor. One March 1889 letter writer, for instance, defended M. L. Wicks, a bankrupt real estate speculator. In 1887 the *Los Angeles Daily Herald* had lauded Wicks as "one of the most live and progressive real estate men of Southern California . . . he owns nearly or quite all the land he offers for sale."[24] Two years later courts were foreclosing on much of that land, a worrisome situation for "S. Chivalry." "Wicks . . . is being pressed by some of his creditors," "S. Chivalry" wrote, "but these people seem to forget that by pulling him down, they are liable to do great damage to a number of dealers who have done much toward building up Southern California."[25] Five months later the newspaper profiled the fall of G. H. Simpson, a local official of the Pacific Coast Steamship Company, who had embezzled company funds to invest in the real estate market. "The dazzling rise in property values and the fortunes that were being made on every hand intoxicated Mr. Simpson," the article narrated, "but he did not get in right, and about the middle of this month the steamship company discovered that he was a defaulter to the amount of nearly $17,000." "He was unfortunate . . . in loading himself with real estate at boom prices just before the boom was to burst," Edwin Goodall, one of the company's founders, surmised.[26]

As the crash deepened, the newspaper even moderated its viewpoint on the city's prospects. In January 1890 one editorial praised "steady and solid growth" in various sectors, a far cry from the unbounded optimism of previous years.[27] In May 1890 another editorial, "Our Greatest Need—A Suggestion," asked Angelenos to recalibrate their outsized expectations for real estate and tourism and focus their efforts on promoting local agricultural initiatives. Remarkably, the editorial began by downplaying Los Angeles's exceptionalism. "Except in the rare cases of cities which are fortunately located at points where railroad and deep-water ocean traffic meet," the editorial argued, "all cities must chiefly depend for their growth upon the production of the surrounding tributary country . . . A city of the size of Los Angeles cannot expect to grow and prosper upon banks or tourists, or the sale of real estate at fancy figures."[28] Such an argument was prescient—local boosters would promote the city through its agricultural products in the decades to come. It was also misguided—the city would always benefit from tourism, and boosters, including Otis, would almost immediately try to transform Los Angeles into a railroad and deep-water connection site.

Los Angeles in 1890, then, was fragile, a place both unable to achieve the quick growth its boosters anticipated and one that had emerged over the previous twenty years into a western city worthy of investment. Certainly, the city did not seem to be a nascent global power in 1890. It did not have its own port, and local prospects to create one seemed dim. Though the Southern Pacific Railroad ran to Los Angeles, other railroads did not. The local water supply remained scant, and a much larger water supply would be needed to adequately provide for larger populations. Moreover, local elites could not achieve any of these goals by themselves; they would need to harness eastern capital and federal power. The *Times* could celebrate Los Angeles's growing population, but the city lagged behind minor urban centers in terms of population. Evansville, Indiana; St. Joseph, Missouri; and Lynn, Massachusetts, were each larger than Los Angeles, and San Francisco was almost six times as large.[29] The real estate boom had temporarily increased Los Angeles's population to at least sixty thousand and perhaps to eighty or ninety thousand, but those gains were transient, lost like the paper fortunes of contemporary speculators.[30]

Yet, local boosters continued to believe in the city's potential. By late 1890, just months after the nadir of the real estate crash, the *Times* again boasted about a transformed, exceptional Los Angeles, one poised for future progress. "Southern California has fairly entered upon a new industrial era," one editorial remarked. "This time there will be no craze, no wild speculation . . . The best that civilization hold [*sic*] shall yet be found here where summer never dies and harvests are eternal."[31] "As for the future, it lies in the hands of our citizens themselves," assured another editorial after Los Angeles officially broke the fifty thousand population mark. "We have resources in this section amply sufficient to support a city of half a million population."[32] Even so, major questions remained to be answered. Could Los Angeles escape the perils of "paper city" speculation in future boom times? How might Los Angeles's boosters lure a population of five hundred thousand people? Could they satisfy eastern demands and realize their own prerogatives? The 1890s battle between local boosterism and a national railroad would provide an initial test of elite Angeleno power.

COMMAND POST OR OUTPOST?

LOS ANGELES WOULD NOT REMAIN A SEMIDEVELOPED CITY FOR long. In the early 1890s the city quickly rebounded from the real estate crash and became increasingly distinguished by the ambitious aims of its boosters, who sought to position Los Angeles as the next great American city. Doing so would require outside capital and influence, especially from the railroads, which could transport agricultural goods from the city and migrants to the city, and the federal government, which could appropriate large sums to develop Los Angeles's port. In their quest to gain capital and influence, the city's boosters sought to achieve their goals without sacrificing Los Angeles's independence or their expansive vision for the city's future as a metropole. Eastern power brokers, on the other hand, did not wish to submit to the will of backwater boosters from a crude frontier town. The contingency and competition inherent to Los Angeles's late nineteenth-century rise can be best viewed in the lengthy, dynamic, and explosive battle between a regional power broker and a titan of national commerce.

On one side was *Los Angeles Times* editor Harrison Gray Otis, an aggressive city booster who resisted railroad domination over municipal affairs and saw Los Angeles as the epicenter of a future Pacific empire.[1] In 1900 he wrote a personal letter to a friend who would soon be arriving from the East to visit Los Angeles, or "God's Country," in Otis's words. "I would love to exchange views and 'swap yarns' with you, and tell you of my work and my conflicts and achievements modest though they be, and of my ambitions for the development . . . of this great Pacific Empire," Otis wrote, "destined to yet become perhaps a dominant subdivision of the mighty Republic."[2] In noting "my ambitions," Otis positioned himself as the hegemonic male Angeleno booster—someone who might emerge from "conflicts" with other men and help Los Angeles "dominate" other cities. In Otis's mind Los Angeles was hardly subservient to the East— its "empire" only demanded occasional governmental help and would eventually extend outward into the Pacific. The East of the United States needed to serve the West, not vice versa.

On the other side stood railroad magnate Collis Huntington, head of the powerful Southern Pacific Railroad, a man similarly devoted to expanding his power. Huntington's vision placed Los Angeles among other cities on the West Coast, at the edge of the Southern Pacific's realm—a crucial cog to be sure, but not a command post. San Francisco, Los Angeles's rival to the north, loomed much larger in Huntington's imagination than did Los Angeles.

In the last two decades of the nineteenth century, Otis and Huntington fought constantly—over political appointees, over newspaper coverage and railroad influence, and over the future of the Port of Los Angeles. The era thus came to be characterized by an ongoing battle between two elite figures: one who had embraced Los Angeles and settled there after his Pacific travels had ended and another who saw Los Angeles as a future outpost of western commerce but not an economic center. Their bicoastal conflict crested in the Free Harbor Fight, in which their disparate visions of the city's future clashed most ferociously. Huntington imagined that Los Angeles's best hopes lay in noncompetitive private development of a Los Angeles–area port connected only to the Southern Pacific Railroad. Otis and other proponents of a port at San Pedro sold the ideal that public port ownership could best spark municipal growth. Los Angeles, these boosters felt, only prospered because it resisted the Southern Pacific monopoly when possible. "The rapid growth of Southern California as compared with the rest of the State is undoubtedly largely due to the fact that for many years we enjoyed the advantage of railroad competition," a *Times* article concluded.[3] The Free Harbor Fight held significant stakes for men such as Otis. If the Southern Pacific won, Los Angeles's future seemed more limited, perhaps driven by eastern power and eastern capitalists rather than by the Angeleno elites who led the Free Harbor League.

In 1898, after Otis and public port boosters emerged victorious, they turned their attentions toward protecting the future port from the imagined threat of future military invasions. Los Angeles's destined Pacific empire, city elites felt, heightened the need for defense. In 1912 the Los Angeles Chamber of Commerce resolved that federal help would be needed to deter the foreign threats that would be drawn to Los Angeles if it experienced the progress it expected. "Whereas, by reason of the great extent of Southern California, its immense natural and artificial wealth and mild climate, Southern California offers a great temptation to oriental and other foreign powers whose population is pressing hard on the means of subsistence," the chamber's board of directors declared, "BE IT RESOLVED that this chamber favors steps to be taken to urge Congress . . . to establish in Southern California a mobile army post."[4] Such rhetoric also presaged fears about the violent overthrow of Los Angeles's Anglo, masculine norms. City leaders further fought to gain federal appropriations to develop the port and to formally merge Los Angeles with the coastal communities of San Pedro and Wilmington. Once the Panama Canal was completed, port boosters expected the city to achieve even greater economic benefits.[5] "As soon as the Canal is finished the ships of the world will come to Los Angeles Harbor," Walter Lindley, the president of the Los Angeles Chamber of Commerce, reported after visiting Panama in May 1912. "Los Angeles will begin a development that will surprise the world."[6] What might be called the "Long Free Harbor Fight," then, dominated elite attention from 1890 to 1915.

Aeronautics offered another path to municipal development. In 1910 the city hosted the Los Angeles International Air Meet, the first major airshow held in the United States.[7] Its promoters hoped that the meet might mark Los Angeles as a nascent power. "Nothing would draw to this part of the planet so many people or so much desirable publicity as a great aviation event on the scale proposed," the *Los Angeles Times* commented. "We can make Los Angeles loom up . . . promoting a science full of tremendous possibilities."[8] The aviation meet was one of three major airshows held in the United States—the others took place in Boston and New York—but local figures such as Henry Huntington seized upon the event as evidence of western exceptionalism and offered lucrative prizes in order to lure the participation of renowned fliers, such as Glenn Curtiss.[9] Lurking beneath optimistic pronouncements about the city's future, though, lay real fears about the Los Angeles's vulnerability as a connected Pacific command post.

The long-term promotion of the port and the short-term promotion of the plane in early twentieth-century Los Angeles centered on traditional booster themes featuring a faith in technology and mankind's capabilities. These developments collectively signaled that Los Angeles could become a global city—a center of commerce, industry, and tourism. Los Angeles's expansion, however, implied that Angelenos might need to further fortify their city. The potential threats only seemed to multiply as the city developed. In 1890 city boosters worked to distinguish Los Angeles from parochialism and eastern dismissiveness. By the end of the 1910 international aviation meet, the *Los Angeles Times* speculated about the future of this "now unprotected great city," susceptible to invasion.[10] What would happen if the "ships of the world," or the "ships of the air," arrived at Los Angeles's doorstep? The push and pull between expansion and seclusion would dominate much of the next half century.

Harrison Gray Otis: Transplanted Superbooster

Otis's life journey followed contemporary transcontinental currents.[11] Born in a small town in southeastern Ohio on February 10, 1837, the youngest of sixteen children of Stephen and Sara Dyer Otis, Harrison did not seem destined for such a mobile life. Stephen and Sara were farmers and staunch Methodists, and they named their sixteenth child after the early nineteenth-century Federalist politician Harrison Gray Otis. The previous Harrison Gray Otis not only amassed a fortune in law and real estate speculation but also obstinately shaped and defended the disastrous Hartford Convention, which discussed the possibility of New England seceding from the United States during the War of 1812.[12] The younger Harrison Gray

Otis would display similar ambition and pugnacity throughout his life. He began his newspaper career at fourteen, as an apprentice for a local newspaper owned by his brother. From there, Otis worked in different capacities for various printers nearby. He took vocational classes in Lowell and Columbus, Ohio, and in 1859 married Eliza Wetherby, whose father, a wool manufacturer, had founded Wetherby's Academy, one of the schools Otis attended. From there, Harrison and Eliza moved to Louisville, where Harrison became a staunch Republican, a political affiliation he would hold for the rest of his life.

With the outbreak of the Civil War, Otis, like many men his age, immediately enlisted. He served valiantly, was wounded at Antietam and later at Winchester, Virginia, and by 1864 had earned four promotions and became a captain under both Major General William Rosencrans and future president Rutherford B. Hayes. Discharged in August 1865, Otis began to exhibit the restlessness that would carry him across the nation. After a brief time running a newspaper in Marietta, Ohio, Otis moved into government bureaucracy, first as the official reporter for the Ohio House of Representatives and later at the Federal Government Printing Office and the U.S. Patent Office, both in Washington DC. By 1876 Otis sought even greater changes. A brief visit to California in 1874 piqued his interest in the state, and he quickly accepted a position as the editor of the *Santa Barbara Press*, a newspaper recently created by W. W. Hollister, another Ohioan who had migrated west in search of riches. Even after the move, Otis did not necessarily believe that his future lay in newspaper publishing. In fact, he hoped that his staunch support of Hayes in the 1876 election might lead to a prominent patronage post in California. Perhaps presaging Otis's later conflict with Huntington, however, Southern Pacific power brokers nixed Otis's appointment as the U.S. marshal of California in 1876, and Otis instead accepted the much less prestigious post of special agent of the Treasury Department for the Alaskan Seal Islands, a tiny group of twelve islands in the Bering Sea. In his position, Otis was responsible for antipoaching and alcohol control efforts.

The time away appears to have been a struggle for Harrison and Eliza, the latter of whom stayed in Santa Barbara with their three daughters and managed the *Santa Barbara Press*. When Otis resigned his post in 1882, the *Times* referred to Otis's work "in such an exile as the northern islands."[13] "There is hardly a sound afloat in Santa Barbara. Never was such dullness," Eliza wrote to Harrison in 1879. "After you get back perhaps you can find someone to purchase the Press, and then will shift it from our shoulders and be free."[14] Despite Eliza's hard work, the *Santa Barbara Press* suffered in Harrison's absence, and the Otises gave up control of the paper in 1880. Harrison returned to the mainland determined to fulfill his ambitions in a place that better suited him: Los Angeles, then just emerging from its violent, frontier past. In 1882 he became the editor of the *Los Angeles Times* and subsequently bought the paper in a joint partnership with local capitalist H. H. Boyce. In 1886, after Boyce and Otis's relationship soured over issues of labor and immigration, Otis raised enough money to buy out his partner. Undeterred, Boyce then created his own newspaper, the *Los Angeles Tribune*, a perpetual antagonist of the *Times* and a victim of many of Otis's attacks. Throughout 1890, in response to a blackmail case brought against Boyce, the *Times* referred to him as "Blackmailer Boyce," regardless of whether the article related to the case itself. "Boyce, the indicted blackmailer, the manager of a moribund organ, is like a rat whose last retreat is cut off," one editorial proclaimed. "He knows that the days of his venal organ are numbered."[15] Otis turned out to be correct. Beset by financial difficulties, Boyce sold the Tribune Publishing Company and moved to Boston later that year.[16]

From 1882 to 1910, Otis directed the *Times* with ruthlessness influenced by his military past. In addition to his previous Civil War experience, Otis served in the Spanish-American War as brigadier general of the United States Volunteers. From 1899 to 1902, after the war's conclusion, Otis's forces fought and won significant battles against Filipino forces during the Philippine-American War. Insisting on being called "Colonel" in later years, Otis named his houses "the Bivouac" and "the Outpost." Known to drill *Times* employees during labor conflicts, he kept fifty rifles and a number of shotguns inside the *Times* building, "the Fortress."[17] In 1912 Otis approved a notice to be sent "TO THE PHALANX: STEREOTYPING DEPARTMENT," which outlined departmental duties. "You have been provided with perfect working devices and good working conditions, and you are required to do your part in keeping them perfect," the notice concluded, implicitly comparing stereotyping machines to rifles.[18] Similar to other "jingoes," who upheld the necessity of the Spanish-American and Philippine-American Wars, Otis seems to have looked to war, and martial performance, as a "solution for [his] gender angst."[19] Just before Otis's death in 1917, he remained engaged enough at the paper to demand that a Mr. E. C. Orr be fired for "flagrant offenses, moral and otherwise."[20] Otis even placed a bronze eagle prominently on the *Times* building's façade, a testament to his patriotism, pugnacious character, and prominent conservatism. After a member of the International Association of Bridge and Structural Iron Workers bombed the *Times* building in April 1911, killing twenty people, Otis emphatically declared that the paper and its anti-labor mission would not be defeated. "O you anarchic scum, you cowardly murderers, you leeches upon honest labor," Otis proclaimed, "behold the stone image of the eagle that you could not reach."[21] In his work Otis accumulated enemies throughout the region, unions foremost among them. In 1915 the Los Angeles Typographical Union published an especially enraged rejoinder to Otis's anti-union activism. "H. G. Otis has hatred in his heart," began the pamphlet. Over the next twenty-four pages, the union laid out the long history of Otis's anti-union activism. "No palliation, no defense can be offered for [offenses] such as these," the pamphlet concluded. "God alone can forgive him."[22] After his return from war, therefore, Otis championed a hegemonic masculinity based on capitalist success, traditional gender norms, and martial expertise. Union members, to Otis, were cowardly "leeches," incapable of contesting his masculine dominance.

In addition to energetic, fastidious corporate leadership, Otis also displayed a keen business sense. By 1905 the *Times* stopped running advertisements on its front page and grossed over $1 million.[23] In 1916 an advertising rates book noted that the paper's daily circulation was 56,846 and its Sunday circulation 97,179, in a city of only 550,000 people.[24] Though the *Los Angeles Examiner*, a Hearst newspaper, had higher circulation numbers, the *Times'* $9 subscription price was higher than the *Examiner's* $8 subscription.[25] In 1900 the *Times* was the most profitable newspaper in the West and carried more advertisements than any other newspaper west of the Mississippi.[26] A letter Otis wrote to his daughter Marian and her husband, Harry Chandler, in 1914 is instructive in illustrating how closely Otis tied the paper to his legacy. The letter, later bound and published after Otis's death, conferred control of the *Times* to Marian and Harry on several conditions. Otis asked that they "preserve and protect" the tenets of the *Times'* journalism: respect for the government and the military, "industrial and all other forms of republican freedom," and "order in the state." He asked that they be faithful stewards of the *Times* as a business. Most of all, Otis made it clear how dearly he valued this asset. "Bearing in mind that *Truth* is the greatest thing in all the world, and *Duty* the first concern of good men and women, I enjoin the foregoing . . . practices upon you in the future conduct of the Los Angeles Times, because of my affections for you and for it," Otis wrote. "I enjoin you both to guard well your precious health, as well as the sacred trust now by me committed to your trusted and trustful hands and hearts."[27]

Beyond open shop activism and Republican politics, Otis devoted himself to municipal boosterism.[28] From his first experiences in Los Angeles, Otis had seemed optimistic about the city's future as the metropole of a future Pacific empire. In May 1875, after Harrison and Eliza toured California in preparation for their move west, Harrison sent the *Los Angeles Star* an account of his train journey back to Washington DC, which the paper subsequently published. Otis seemed preoccupied with the stark differences between West and East, "coming with quite sudden transition from a land of eternal summer not quite to a land of eternal winter, to be sure, but to one that strongly suggests Arctic life." If Otis only knew that he would soon encounter the true Arctic. Otis also reflected on the effects of California boosterism on the Midwest. "The facts which your enterprising people are spreading abroad relative to your noble State must be the means of doing her great good ultimately," he continued. "Thousands in the grasshopper-stricken districts of Kansas and Missouri must seek new homes and make a new start. Many of them will not stop short of the Pacific Coast."[29] A "land of eternal summer," propelled by migration from the East, would shape the broad contours of Los Angeles's future.

In 1888, at a meeting of local business leaders, Otis moved that those present create a permanent organization to support Los Angeles. That group, the Los Angeles Chamber of Commerce, began humbly, with a $5 initiation fee.[30] By the time of Otis's death in 1917, the chamber was the dominant center of boosterism in the city, a hub of elite activism perhaps unmatched in urban America. "The modern city of Los Angeles may be said to have entered upon its career in 1888, which was the very year that the Chamber of Commerce was founded," noted chamber member and city booster Charles Willard in his 1900 *A History of the Chamber of Commerce of Los Angeles*.[31] In 1906 Otis wrote a letter to journalist Kate Tannatt Woods declining an invitation to the Gentlemen's Night of the New England Women's Press Association. "I will not be able to be present, for I have much to do and am lingering in the glorious climate of California . . . instead of making myself a fool and rushing in where angels fear to tread, to wit; on the frozen veldt of New England's rock-bound shores, so to speak," he informed Woods.[32] Otis lightly mocked contemporary notions of East-to-West development, which emphasized the rough-hewn qualities created by frontier life.[33] The East, in Otis's view, was inferior and perhaps subservient to the West. Returning east would mean for Otis regressing to past days of "rock-bound shores." In Los Angeles he would create an empire.

Collis Huntington: Eastern Power Broker

While Otis traversed the outer U.S. territories, Collis Huntington conquered the country's middle. One of the "Big Four" railroad men in the West—along with Leland Stanford, Mark Hopkins, and Charles Crocker—Huntington worked throughout his life to dominate American railroads.[34] Born in 1821 in Harwinton, Connecticut, a small town just west of Hartford, Huntington was the sixth of nine children. The Huntingtons were a relatively impoverished farming family. Collis's father, William, a cantankerous, independent man, so angered local church leaders by disputing theological doctrine that they eventually excommunicated him. Later, the church investigated the household. Finding the children hungry and ill-cared for, officials took Collis and his brother Solon away from the family and sent the two boys to be apprentices with local farmers at the age of fourteen. From such inauspicious beginnings, Collis prospered. After a year with the farmer he began working for a neighbor, Phineas Noble, who ran a small general store in town. Collis impressed Noble by memorizing prices and calculating profits in his head, and Noble quickly made Collis a mobile peddler of goods in the area. Eventually, Huntington went into business for himself and traversed the East Coast, Midwest, and South, while selling wares from his wagon. In an article written several years after his death, even the *Los Angeles Times* expressed admiration for his journey from childhood poverty. "Collis P. Huntington started on his road to wealth as a peddler of clocks and watches," the paper wrote. "At 16 he went to New York City and with the little capital he had invested in a supply of watches and clocks, which he managed to buy cheap and in the course of time sold with profit to himself. Thus began what is known as the splendid Huntington fortune."[35] By 1844 Huntington was ready to lead a less transient existence. Solon had settled in Oneonta, New York, where he ran a general store. Collis paid Solon about $1300 and acquired half the company from his brother. He married Elizabeth Stoddard, a woman from Cornwall, Connecticut, and together Collis and his bride moved to Oneonta and spent the next five years building the business. Ever the rover, Collis expanded the store's business into New York City, where he sold goods on behalf of smaller stores and local farmers upstate.

Such relative placidity, though, was not to last for long.[36] With the Gold Rush in 1849, Collis and five other men from Oneonta traveled to the West Coast, where Collis planned to open an outpost of the general store and cater to miners there. After an arduous five-month long journey south, across mainland Panama and up the Pacific Coast, the men arrived in Sacramento in August 1849. In a later article, the *Chicago Daily Tribune* used Huntington's journey west to foreshadow his later career. "When Huntington went to the Golden Gate in 1849 by way of Panama he walked twenty times from one end of the isthmus to the other," the paper reported, "trading to make the capital by which fifty years later he was enabled to ride over 5,000 miles of railroad in his private car."[37] It was not an easy transition. For the next five years, Huntington's fortunes fell. The merchant life was particularly unpredictable in frontier Sacramento during the Gold Rush: supplies had to travel around Cape Horn or to be carried across Panama, the city had a particularly high crime rate, and heavy inflation played havoc with consumer prices, rents, and labor costs. The misadventures added up. Beset by financial difficulties, Huntington sold a portion of the firm to a recently arrived Floridian, Edward Schultz. In 1852 Huntington rented a building for himself only to see it burned to the ground. He then entered a series of unsuccessful partnerships in an attempt to alleviate his debt. Not until 1855—when Huntington partnered with the merchant Mark Hopkins, who had similarly arrived in Sacramento from the East in 1849—did Huntington begin to experience lasting business success. Huntington & Hopkins rapidly took over the market and reigned as one of the largest hardware stores on the West Coast.[38] The two men helped to launch the Republican Party in California, supported John C. Frémont's unsuccessful 1856 bid for president and then aided Abraham Lincoln's presidential candidacy in 1860. By 1861 Huntington and Hopkins were well-positioned economically and politically to finance the Central Pacific Railroad, which planned to build the western half of the transcontinental railroad. In their bid, Huntington and Hopkins partnered with fellow Sacramento businessmen Leland Stanford and Charles Crocker. Together, the four men would come to control western transportation.

Over the next five decades, Huntington would cement, often ruthlessly, his role as the foremost figure in western railroads.[39] A famously energetic and stout man—he stood over six feet tall and claimed at the age of seventy that he had only been sick once in his life, with dysentery in the early years in Sacramento—Huntington generally disdained anything not related to making money or gaining power.[40] "Bismarck's methods in diplomacy were C. P. Huntington's methods in finance," the *Los Angeles Times* noted after his death. "He gloried in conflict, and was a worthy antagonist. He neither gave quarter nor asked for it."[41] (The same description might have applied to Otis). In 1868 Huntington, Crocker, Hopkins and Stanford, the "Big Four," bought the Southern Pacific Railroad, which would merge with the Central Pacific in 1870 and eventually run lines from New Orleans to California. Together with the Union Pacific Railroad, the Central Pacific railroad completed the transcontinental railroad in 1869.[42] Huntington was also president and director of the Chesapeake and Ohio Railroad, which ran across Virginia and West Virginia. Without the other members of the "Big Four," Huntington personally developed the Newport News Shipbuilding and Drydock Company, connected to the Chesapeake and Ohio, which would eventually become the largest privately owned shipyard in the world. In 1890 Huntington ousted Stanford from the presidency of the Southern Pacific Company, a holding company for the Central Pacific and Southern Pacific, and took greater charge of the company's business. Huntington's growing fortune reflected his newfound responsibilities. At the time of his death, the *New York Times* estimated Huntington's fortune at between $25 and $35 million, with a $12 million stake in the Southern Pacific Company and $6 million in the Newport News shipyard.[43]

Huntington had a national vision. He anchored his businesses in New York but searched widely for investment opportunities. Perhaps the best illustration of Collis's tremendous impact on railroad development can be seen in the trip his nephew Henry Huntington made from San Antonio to New York City after Collis's death in 1900. The *New York Tribune* told its readers of Henry's "Record Breaking Trip." "Mr. Huntington was in Texas on Tuesday when the news of his uncle's death reached him, and his special train had right of way between New Orleans and Mobile," the paper reported. "Between these points the train covered 140 miles in 140 minutes, and between Mobile and Atlanta, 496 miles, the train made the distance in less than ten hours."[44] Collis had helped to develop a system that could carry Henry home quickly, and his fame was such that Henry had right-of-way on his journey.

Unsurprisingly, Huntington anchored his vision of future railroad development in the East and imagined that future development would spread from there. In 1899 he wrote a twenty-four-page letter to his financial agent, James Speyer, in which he recounted his career, mostly the building of the transcontinental railroad. At the end of the letter, Huntington discussed how his railroads had changed California, and its agriculture industry, for the better. "Before the advent of this great civilizing and wealth-producing agent, mining was the chief industry of California," Huntington claimed. "The construction of the railroad offered much cheaper and easier means of transportation to markets, and the ground was tilled and first devoted to the cultivation of cereals and fruits."[45] He moved from there to pontificate on the future of the Southern Pacific in California. "The people will sooner or later recognize that no other company can, or will, do more for the development of the industries and resources of the State than will the Southern Pacific Company."[46] To Huntington, the Southern Pacific had benefited and would continue to benefit California, but California was still subservient to eastern capital and civilization.

Huntington viewed California, then, as a prime investment opportunity, if not a future center of commerce. In 1862 Huntington had moved to New York City to serve as the Central Pacific Railroad's main lobbyist and advisor, but the focus of the company remained on California, especially after the Central Pacific Railroad moved from Sacramento to San Francisco in 1873.[47] Under Stanford's leadership, the Central Pacific acquired several railroads around Los Angeles in the 1870s, including the Los Angeles & San Pedro Railroad, which ran south to a proposed port site.[48] In 1886 the company sent its first refrigerated railcars, loaded with southern Californian citrus, across its lines to the East. Huntington continued these initiatives after he took power in 1890. In 1898 the company started *Sunset* magazine as its official outlet for promoting the West. By 1900 the company spent $400,000 annually advertising its routes throughout the region.[49] The Southern Pacific also continued to cultivate politicians who would be favorable to its cause. "Dr. John T. McLean, of Alameda, is here and says he wants to run for Congress," Huntington wrote to William H. Mills, one of the company's directors and its chief land agent in 1898. "If you could help him consistently I would like you to do so."[50] Economic and political influence allowed the Southern Pacific to advocate for its agenda in Washington and on the West Coast. As Huntington asserted power over the policies of the Southern Pacific, he increasingly fought with California boosters.

Civilizer or Octopus?

The Southern Pacific loomed large as a villain in late nineteenth-century Californian discourse. While the Southern Pacific did not always clash with Californian institutions—the railroad partnered with many boosters, including the Los Angeles Chamber of Commerce, to sell the West—to many Californians, the railroad often embodied a pernicious, monolithic image of corporate evil.[51] After the completion of the transcontinental railroad, Californians blamed the Southern Pacific for, among other things, its monopolistic control, high rates on agricultural freight, tying California to national economic panics in the 1870s, failure to promote widespread wealth, and the promotion of increased internal migration that threatened job prospects.[52] Certainly, the Southern Pacific was not omnipotent in California. In the 1890s a coalition of Californian newspapers, political leaders, and organizers defeated the railroad's effort to secure a cushy debt repayment plan for the enormous sums the Southern Pacific owed to the federal government.[53] Still, Huntington's political machine lobbied heavily at local and federal levels, and the railroad held enormous power over the public imagination. Frank Norris, the novelist and muckraker, harped on the Southern Pacific's power in his 1901 novel, *The Octopus*, about the battle between farmers and the railroad. "Because it can't be done . . . *You can't buck against the railroad*," notes one of Norris's farmers. "We tried it once, and it was enough to turn your stomach. The railroad quietly bought delegates . . . and did us up."[54]

After Huntington's 1890 takeover of the Southern Pacific, Otis's *Times* and William Randolph Hearst's *San Francisco Examiner* continued to portray the railroad as a despotic corporation. Even after his death, the *Los Angeles Times* dismissively referred to Huntington as "Uncle Collis" in its obituary and ensuing articles.[55] "[Otis] thought the railroad king dictatorial in his methods, particularly his opposition to the establishment of competing lines," the *Times* noted in 1900. "Almost from the beginning of his editorial management of The Times he has consistently and persistently attacked [Huntington] and what he represented whenever opportunity offered."[56] The paper further argued that California's population would have been 1 million larger without the undue limitations the Southern Pacific imposed on other nascent railroad lines.[57] In 1898 Mills wrote to Huntington about the "journalistic situation at Los Angeles," specifically the increasing power of Otis and Hearst. "I regret exceedingly the result at Los Angeles, which, combined with the present very unfortunate situation of affairs in San Francisco, weakens the position of the Company before the public very greatly," Mills wrote.[58]

The sporadic skirmishes between Huntington's Southern Pacific and Southern Californian elites exploded into a major conflict in 1890 over the location of Los Angeles's future port. The battle had roots in the modest development of the San Pedro Bay, a shallow mudflat twenty-five miles south of Los Angeles, which seemed ill-suited to a future as a center of ocean commerce.[59] Even after local businessman Phineas Banning successfully lobbied Congress to dredge the site to a depth of ten feet in 1871, San Pedro lagged behind other West Coast ports.[60] From 1871 to 1878, the port's total commerce only increased from fifty thousand tons to sixty-four thousand tons.[61] Under Leland Stanford's leadership, the Southern Pacific did add a "Sunset Route" line from San Francisco to Los Angeles and also hoped that its steamships might connect Los Angeles and San Francisco to Asia.[62] Boosters such as Otis hoped that San Pedro would become the city's port, a global economic hub. The Southern Pacific's work on behalf of San Pedro even led to a brief alliance with Otis, as the railroad initially supported San Pedro Port development.

The temporary peace was not to last. Under Huntington's leadership, the company moved away from its support of San Pedro. In 1890 a group of powerful national speculators, including the West Virginia coal magnate Stephen B. Elkins, founded the Los Angeles Terminal Railway. The new company operated a small network of lines that tied Los Angeles to San Pedro and other nearby communities, designed to one day connect to a larger line from Salt Lake City. The Terminal Railway also broke the Southern Pacific's monopoly at San Pedro and led to greater price competition for freight to and from the port. As a result, Huntington began to pursue a port monopoly at Santa Monica, a sleepy town fifteen miles west of downtown Los Angeles. Southern Pacific had owned some Santa Monica property since the mid-1870s and Huntington bought additional land to be added to the railroad's holdings. In Santa Monica, the Southern Pacific could be assured of a future monopoly, as the company owned a majority of the available property, and nearby mountains significantly reduced the amount of acreage over which a company might build a railroad line.[63] Huntington began constructing a railway line that required a three-hundred-foot tunnel through the mountains to the "Long Wharf" at Santa Monica, a dock that would eventually extend forty-seven hundred feet into the bay. The Southern Pacific, with the help of Huntington's congressional political machine, also began to seek federal appropriations to develop a port at Santa Monica. Boosters regretted the railroad's strategic shift. "The Southern Pacific showed every desire to assist in the effort to secure appropriations for San Pedro . . . when the presidency of the road changed from Senator Leland Stanford to Mr. C. P. Huntington," noted Willard.[64]

Otis's *Times* emerged as the major opposition to Huntington's Santa Monica initiative. The paper published a variety of letters to the editor that criticized Huntington's change in railroad policy. "[Huntington] has secured a vast tract of land a few miles west of Santa Monica, and will undoubtedly attempt to make it appear that there is no place as well adapted for a deep-water harbor as that . . . which happens to be located immediately in front of their land," wrote one reader.[65] Another letter claimed that Huntington was defying the will of god. "The Almighty made San Pedro a fine natural harbor, and the United States proposes to add the finished touches to His work," reader "Napoleon" began. "The Southern Pacific Railroad Company . . . proposes to set up a feeble opposition to Omnipotence at Port Los Angeles or Old Santa Monica."[66] More broadly, Otis's newspaper thundered that the Southern Pacific sought to retard Los Angeles's growth through monopolization. "The Harbor Question Is On," announced the newspaper in August 1892, in an article framing the debate as a question of public versus private development. "There is . . . a very strong sentiment against the appropriation of public money for the benefit of a private corporation," the editorial claimed. "The ocean front should be open to all common carriers."[67] "Let us have a deep-sea harbor for the people," demanded another editorial, as it urged Angelenos to "act broadly for the future."[68] The newspaper positioned the public as an underdog against a powerful corporate and political alliance. "Again and again have the people . . . won this harbor fight against the grasping greed of an unscrupulous foe," the paper declared in the midst of the struggle. "Again and again have they been robbed of the fruits of victory, even in the hour of triumph."[69] Even naming the conflict the "Free Harbor Fight" was a remarkable piece of advertising by Otis and other San Pedro advocates. According to such civic rhetoric, trade in San Pedro would not be truly "free" but instead mediated by influential city elites.

The battle between supporters of San Pedro and Santa Monica raged for the next decade.[70] First, the U.S. Senate's Rivers and Harbors Committee held hearings about the two sites and then presented a report favorable to San Pedro. Both Huntington and Otis testified for their respective causes. In 1893 and 1894 Huntington tried to persuade members of the Los Angeles Chamber of Commerce to support Santa Monica, but the body voted 328 to 131 for San Pedro.[71] Later in 1894 Huntington's congressional allies nearly passed a bill that would have given a $3 million appropriation to Santa Monica and only a $400,000 appropriation to San Pedro. The "double appropriations" issue divided Los Angeles newspapers and politicians alike. "If the money had fallen out of the skies, it could hardly have been more unexpected, for none of the California members of the House, nor the California Senators . . . had ever said one word about an appropriation for Santa Monica," noted Willard.[72] But the San Pedro single-appropriation interests emerged victorious. During the ensuing committee fight, U.S. Senator Stephen White (D-CA) fought for a new engineering report to determine the best site. In 1896 the congressionally appointed engineering board held seven days of public hearings in Los Angeles and heard testimony from thirteen expert witnesses in favor of Santa Monica and seventeen speakers in favor of San Pedro.[73] The board apparently agreed more fully with the second group of witnesses. In 1897 the board of five, the third to be convened on the issue, chose San Pedro.

Finally, in 1898 White, with the help of Otis and his activist Free Harbor League, overcame the last of the Huntington resistance. Congress officially chose San Pedro. For his work, White gained some renown in the city. Willard noted that White "was possessed of the brains, honesty, and courage that was needed at such a crisis."[74] After his death, the *Times* called White the "most distinguished son the State has produced in the half-century of her existence."[75] In December 1908, when city leaders unveiled a statue of the senator across from the downtown courthouse, the

Herald lauded White's efforts to "consistently and persistently put public duty before private politics."[76] That statue, eight feet tall and cast in bronze, now stands at the entrance to Cabrillo Beach in San Pedro, just north of the port White helped to gain for the city.[77] While Huntington was able to hold up the development of the harbor for two years, eventually the federal government began work at San Pedro, in Willard's words, "after the patience of the whole State . . . was exhausted."[78]

The Free Harbor Fight, then, revolved around two contrasting visions of Los Angeles's future. Huntington believed that the city's prospects were relatively limited—it would be subordinate to other, more prominent, metropolises. Otis propagated an expansive vision of Los Angeles's future. Anti–Southern Pacific articles sold well in a region predisposed to dislike the railroad, but Otis sincerely believed in Angeleno exceptionalism and Los Angeles's potential as a future metropole. The Free Harbor Fight had provided an important test of Otis's vision. Elites' subsequent challenge would be developing their newest gem and protecting it from dangers both real and imagined.

Protecting the Port

After the Free Harbor Fight, port development continued to depend on local public support for the project and financial appropriations from Washington. The federal government may have chosen to develop elites' preferred port site, for instance, but San Pedro and adjoining Wilmington were not yet part of Los Angeles. In the first years of the twentieth century, Otis's coalition worked to incorporate both cities into Los Angeles. In 1906 Los Angeles annexed the "Harbor Gateway," a five-mile strip of land connecting Los Angeles to the coast towns San Pedro and Wilmington, to satisfy a state requirement that only adjoining municipalities could merge.[79] Three years later, voters finished the job. On August 4, 1909, the citizens of Los Angeles and Wilmington merged by a vote of 13,739 to 221 in Los Angeles and 107 to 61 in Wilmington.[80] Then on August 12 the citizens of Los Angeles and San Pedro voted to merge by a vote of 11,587 to 109 in Los Angeles and 776 to 227 in San Pedro.[81] The port was now officially part of Los Angeles. Next, Los Angeles elites worked to develop their newest gem. As the Free Harbor Fight lagged in the court system, the Los Angeles Chamber of Commerce passed a resolution urging the federal government to create an even deeper harbor at San Pedro and fulfill Otis's dream of connected ocean and rail lines.[82] In 1911 the federal government began to dredge the bay to a depth of thirty feet and to widen its main channel to eight hundred feet.[83]

A deeper harbor, however, also sparked fears that Los Angeles might become a future military target. It is difficult to ascertain whether Los Angeles booster outlets truly feared an invasion at the turn of the century or whether they sought to use invasion rhetoric to justify greater appropriations. Certainly, the city's chamber of commerce did not uniformly advocate for American expansion, especially if expansion might threaten Los Angeles's own interests. In 1897 the chamber opposed the annexation of Hawaii on geographical and racial grounds. "We should . . . question the wisdom of annexation," one resolution posited, because of "the great distance of these Islands from the United States and the consequent difficulty and expense which would be involved in their defense and protection in case of war." "The enormous alien Mongolian population," the same resolution continued, "would be in some degree a menace to American labor."[84] More often, though, the chamber seemed to exaggerate Los Angeles's vulnerabilities to gain federal support. The McKinley administration clearly had Pacific ambitions; McKinley would later expand the U.S. empire into the Pacific by annexing Hawaii, Guam, and the Philippines after the conclusion of the Spanish-American War in 1898. The chamber, then, likely expected the federal government to be sympathetic to Los Angeles's Pacific concerns. In an 1897 resolution to McKinley, the chamber bemoaned the lack of Pacific Coast defense stations. "Whereas, the United States Government has withdrawn a portion of the forces of the regular army heretofore stationed on the Pacific Coast, and transferred the battle ship Oregon to the Atlantic" the chamber noted, "the withdrawal of these forces leaves a great portion of the Coast and Coast cities without proper protection from foreign invasion."[85] While the resolution did not directly reference the port, a deeper port would make it easier to station a protective fleet at Los Angeles.

Throughout the next decade, the Los Angeles Chamber of Commerce continued to imagine possible invasions. In late 1906 the chamber's Harbor Committee submitted a resolution to its board of directors about the need to lobby California's congressional delegation to secure federal port funding. "The entire coast of Southern California . . . offers a most inviting opportunity for hostile attack and invasion because of its unfortified condition," the resolution began. "The value if [*sic*] convertible material and property is so great as to invite such an attack."[86] The same qualities that had propelled Southern California's growth—the weather, industrial wealth—made the city a desirable target. These fears reappeared again in November 1911, when the chamber's Committees on Fortifications and Military and Naval Affairs sent the board of directors a lengthy report on the need for federal port fortification funding. The report imagined a foreign war plan to isolate the West Coast. "The enemy in possession of Los Angeles and all Southern California, controlling the railroads with the immense quantity of rolling stock, could push up the Coast, leaving an army to hold Southern California," the report surmised. "Southern California would be the future naval base in the event of war."[87] At the same time, the committees positioned Los Angeles as the key cog in the regional economy. "As Los Angeles harbor is a safe harbor in all kinds of weather, a foreign power would certainly take it without fortifications," the report noted, "the capture of Los Angeles would mean the fall of all Southern California." "More than half the wealth of Southern California is concentrated in Los Angeles County," it concluded.[88] The prospect of invasion was both terrifying and validating.

In addition to gaining naval appropriations, port activists also thought that the port needed to be protected from domestic and local opponents of their boosterish mission. The prospect of a Panama Canal, for instance, only increased port ambitions. Throughout its early history, the Los Angeles Chamber of Commerce fully supported the creation of any canal that would enable travel from the Atlantic to the Pacific. In the late nineteenth century, the chamber first supported the Nicaragua Canal, an often-speculated-about project designed to connect Lake Nicaragua to overland routes, thus bridging the isthmus. In January 1899 the chamber resolved that the

United States should try to complete a Nicaraguan canal and thereafter take full ownership of it. "The Canal would be of immense value to the people of the Pacific Coast," the chamber reasoned, "as it would afford greater protection to this coast in time of war, open new lanes of trade and commerce. . . . and multiply our resources and establish a shorter line of oceanic communication."[89]

After the United States instead pursued the Panama Canal project, and the latter neared completion in 1912, the chamber again burst into action with a series of resolutions meant to shape future canal policy in ways that might benefit public institutions over private enterprise. First, the chamber dispatched Lindley as a "special representative of the Los Angeles Chamber of Commerce to the Canal Zone, the Panama Republic and the Republic of Guatemala."[90] Then, in 1911 and 1912, the body passed three resolutions about two issues: canal tolls and railroad competition. Tolls, it opposed when levied "against American commerce and shipping engage in coastwise trade."[91] Railroads, the chamber worried, might buy a controlling interest in shipping and effectively stymie competition with transcontinental railroad lines. In July 1912 the board of directors prepared a document for its constituents about the two issues. After outlining the various resolutions it had passed, the board summed up its main argument. "The Board of Directors regard the matter of competition through the Canal as of vital importance," the board wrote, "and believe that there will be great danger to free competition if the trans-continental railway companies, with their enormous capital and power, are permitted to operate ships engaged in the coast-wise trade through the Panama Canal."[92] Anti-railroad rhetoric, of course, echoed the long history of California opposition to railroad rates, consolidated railroad company power, and railroad magnates such as Huntington. The board used well-honed antipathy for the railroads to fight for a version of free trade that would benefit and "protect" Los Angeles. The railroad companies would remain headquartered in the East, so they would not benefit Los Angeles to the same degree, and they might even harm the city by denying the port significant traffic. The logic of "free competition" in the resolution was similar to that of the Free Harbor Fight. The elite vision for Los Angeles demanded a port open to all businesses, controllable by public institutions—and therefore politically connected insiders—instead of specific private corporations.

The Long Free Harbor Fight, therefore, demonstrated the power of men such as Otis to shape the city's growth. Over twenty years, Free Harbor activists managed to develop ties to federal power and defeat a powerful eastern railroad and its local allies. They did so by crafting a persuasive set of rhetorical arguments, which emphasized both Los Angeles's potential and its vulnerabilities. Angeleno political figures may have exaggerated concerns about "hostile attack" in messages to the federal government, but that rhetoric was powerful and rooted in real concerns about the implications of Los Angeles's growth. The city's theoretical vulnerabilities would become even more tangible with the arrival of the airplane in 1910.

"The Playground of the World"

The Los Angeles International Air Meet, one of the events boosters hoped might bring greater publicity to Los Angeles, also brought underlying anxieties about expansion to the surface. While the meet promised to solidify the city's role as the "playground of the world," it also displayed to Angelenos the transformative capabilities of the airplane to reshape conceptions of space and time. In the wake of the aviation meet, the politics of connection would not seem so simple after all.

The meet holds an unheralded place in the history of early aviation.[93] After the Wright brothers took flight in 1903, global interest in flying grew substantially. In August 1909 Reims, France, hosted the Grande semaine d'aviation de la Champagne, generally regarded as the first international public flying competition. Over half a million people attended the Reims meet, which convinced two aviators, Charles Willard and Roy Knabenshue, to try to bring the next meet to Los Angeles during one of its mild winters.[94] Willard and Knabenshue contacted local promoter Dick Ferris, who functioned as the meet's CEO, and together the three men formed a stock company and surveyed different sites for the meet.[95] They settled on Dominguez Field, a space south of the city near San Pedro. There, they built tents to house aviators and their machines and a grandstand that could hold twenty-six thousand people.[96] Los Angeles newspapers grasped the moment's significance for the city. "The World Knows Now," announced the *Los Angeles Express* in the midst of the meet. The caption of a cartoon showed a personified globe looking at an "Atlas of the World." "Sure enough there it is in Southern California," commented the globe.[97]

Crucial to the meet's success, and to global recognition of the city, was the participation of Glenn Curtiss, an aviation pioneer who would eventually found much of the American aviation industry.[98] Curtiss was a creative, energetic man, irrepressibly driven to tinker and create. "Here was a man who began flying when human flight was regarded as an impractical dream," the *Washington Post* noted after his death. "Time and again the land-bound conservatives of those early days predicted for him a violent death. Yet he now dies at 52 in the serenity of a Buffalo hospital."[99] Like the Wright brothers, Curtiss had begun his career as a bicycle enthusiast. In the early 1900s he began to experiment with motorcycles and moved from there into aviation. The October 1924 cover of *Time* showed a mustachioed Curtiss staring confidently into the camera. The caption underneath read, "Handy at saving things."[100] In addition to piloting his own planes, Curtiss made major contributions to aviation technology. During his lifetime, he would generate numerous patents and found the first company specifically dedicated to manufacturing airplanes.[101] Curtiss was so successful that the Wright brothers sued him for a patent violation in 1909.[102] The court case would last for eight years, until U.S. officials asked both parties to settle, so it could use the aircraft in question for its World War I military operations. A 1955 article in the *Saturday Evening Post* on the increasing prominence of automobile seatbelts singled Curtiss out for his contributions to that innovation four decades prior. Apparently, after Curtiss interviewed one of the first airplane crash survivors, who had clung to the plane after mechanical failure, he "began to work at once for adoption of belts to keep fliers from being pitched out."[103] After Curtiss died of appendicitis in 1930, Congress awarded him the Distinguished Flying Cross for his work. Curtiss's impact, the congressional minutes noted, was so obvious "that it is not felt necessary to review his career at length."[104] Even the shortened profile that followed provided nine full paragraphs of Curtiss's achievements.

Curtiss became a major national celebrity after he won the Gordon Bennett Trophy at the Reims meet, a race among nations for fastest individual time trial around a roughly twelve-mile course. "American Flies Off with Grand Prize: Glenn H. Curtiss in a Wonderful Flight in Which He Smashes the World's Record for Speed, Wins International Cup of Aviation," gleefully announced the *Times*.[105] The course took Curtiss over fifteen minutes to complete, illustrating the infant state of aviation technology. Though Curtiss's victory enabled the United States to host the next Gordon Bennett race at Belmont Park in New York, where Curtiss would defend his crown, Los Angeles's organizers hoped to hold an interim exhibition where Curtiss might vie for prizes against other European and American aviators.[106] In a 1912 book Curtiss coauthored, *The Curtiss Aviation Book*—part autobiography, part forecast of the future of aviation—the aviator reflected on the importance of the Los Angeles meet. "The Pacific Coast, always progressive and quick to seize upon every innovation, no matter where it may be developed, had been clamoring for some time for an aviation meet," he wrote. "Sometimes it takes just such a public demonstration as the Los Angeles meet not only to spread the news of the general progress of mechanical flight, but to show the builders of aeroplanes themselves just what their machines are capable of."[107]

Henry Huntington led the effort to secure Curtiss's participation at the Los Angeles meet. Born in Oneonta, New York, on February 27, 1850, to Solon and Harriet Huntington, Henry had the good fortune to be Collis Huntington's nephew.[108] Beginning in his teenage years, Henry took an interest in business, supported by Collis, who saw Henry as the son he never had. In 1871 Henry began managing a West Virginia sawmill owned by his uncle. In 1873 Henry married Mary Alice Prentice, the sister of one of Collis's adopted daughters. Thereafter, the two men became even closer. After a series of other jobs working for his uncle, Henry moved to San Francisco in 1890 to take over the day-to-day management of the Southern Pacific Railroad. Over the next nine years, Henry helped to expand the railroad's routes throughout California, cut costs by slimming the Southern Pacific's workforce and limiting gifts of free passes over the Southern Pacific's lines, and achieved greater efficiency in day-to-day operations. After Collis's sudden death in 1900, Collis's opponents won the ensuing power struggle for control of the Southern Pacific Railroad and passed over Henry for the company presidency. Frustrated by his lack of power over company policy, Henry sold his shares in the Southern Pacific and moved to Los Angeles in 1902. His personal life also transformed dramatically during this time period. When Henry moved to Southern California, Mary Prentice Huntington stayed in San Francisco, and the couple eventually divorced in 1910. In 1913 Henry married his uncle's widow, Arabella Huntington, with whom he shared a passion for art and book collecting. Los Angeles then provided a distinct opportunity for Henry to reshape his life, separate himself to a degree from Collis's legacy, and create his own empire.

Once he moved to Los Angeles, Huntington began to participate in its elite society. He belonged to the Citizen's Alliance of Los Angeles, an anti-labor group.[109] He owned stock in the Southern California Edison Company, the power company involved in the Hoover Dam project in the 1920s.[110] He kept a twenty-five-cent copy of the *Etiquette of Yacht Colors* handy, "containing the yacht codes of the new international code signals, wig-wag, storm and weather signals, yacht routine, etc."[111] Unsurprisingly, given his belief in elite influence and the city's progress, from around 1906 to 1913 Huntington belonged to the Sunset Club, a Los Angeles men's boosterish social club. The club billed itself as unique in a time when men might join many different groups. "In this gregarious era the average man joins himself to many organizations," noted one organizational history, which named, among other groups, the Masons, the Los Angeles Chamber of Commerce, the Municipal League, and the California Club.[112] Yet, at the Sunset Club, one brochure maintained, "we are . . . our very selves. Once in each month for a few hours we are a big family of big brothers, living together in unity, eating and drinking and making merry together around the family table, free to talk and act as we really think and feel."[113] Members went on semiannual trips together: to far-flung places such as Santa Monica in 1902 and Santa Barbara in 1904. And, naturally, the group threw themed dinners. December 30, 1910, for instance, was "Oriental Night." "An Oriental ramble, headed by the Dragon, will reveal kaleidoscopic visions of color and a riot of sound," the invitation announced. "Incense-laden air, with nimble-fingered dingdo players and dainty, dreamy dancing queens . . . will delight the eye, tickle the ear, and ravish the nostrils."[114] By emphasizing "feelings" and exotic experiences, the club upheld ideas of "passionate manhood" that emerged in the late nineteenth century, centered on "manly passions" and primitive virtues.[115] Similar to other elites, Huntington expressed his masculinity via active participation in men's groups. Though Huntington left the club over a decade before his 1927 death, Sunset members saw fit to remember him in an eloquent obituary published in the *Annals of the Sunset Club: Volume III*. "With the passing of our fellow Sunsetter, Henry Edwards Huntington, Southern California has lost her greatest figure," the article began. "For generations the . . . Southland lay dormant and well-nigh unnoticed, until the magic power of his creative vision awakened them to flowing life and enkindled their activity."[116]

As Childs, Hellman, and Downey had done, Huntington amassed a network of interrelated businesses, each dependent on municipal growth and progress. Primarily, Henry focused on developing an interurban railway system. Henry's initial interest in such transportation seems to have been sparked by the associated needs of the Southern Pacific Railway. In November 1897 Collis wrote to Henry to ask him to purchase an electric railroad line between Pasadena and Los Angeles. "My impression is that if we could get hold of an electric road . . . it would be a good thing to do," Collis wrote, "as we could turn most of the quick passenger business on to the electric line and run many less trains on our heavy road than we are now running." "There ought to be considerable made by doing this business without competition," Collis concluded.[117] In 1901 Henry created the Pacific Electric Railway Company, which would grow into a complex network of streetcars, trains, and buses connecting Angelenos to each other and to surrounding counties. Huntington sold his interests in the Pacific Electric Company in 1910 to the Southern Pacific Railroad, but by the 1920s the Pacific Electric had become the largest streetcar system in the world and catalyzed land development around Los Angeles throughout this period.[118]

Henry Huntington probably saw the aviation meet as tied to those business interests in Los Angeles and embraced aviation as yet another facilitator of municipal growth. In 1909 he helped found the California Aviation Society, became its first president, and offered $50,000 to bring a major aviation meet to Los Angeles. "Mr. Huntington is head of vast interests in California," *Aeronautics* magazine informed its readers. "The object is to foster aeronautics and aviation throughout California as a sport and science."[119] Like so many of Henry's efforts, aviation could promote both Los Angeles and other companies in his empire. One ticket to the meet produced by the Pacific Electric Railway advertised the "Daily Contests in Speed, Distance and Endurance," "$80,000 in prizes," and "World's Biggest Balloons in Daily Flights." "See them FLYING," the ticket exhorted. Additionally, the bookmark informed readers that trips on the Pacific Electric Railways cost only thirty cents and ran every two minutes directly to the "Aviation Camp" at Dominguez Field.[120]

Huntington united with aviation promoters to sell the project, using a civic rhetoric that emphasized the meet's outsized stakes. The chamber of commerce passed a resolution supporting the contest. "The holding of such an exhibition and contest in midwinter would bring Los Angeles and its vicinity into world wide [sic] prominence, and if properly conducted, would greatly redound to the reputation and benefit of Southern California," its board of directors announced in November 1909.[121] Holding the meet in winter would show the world that Los Angeles was a year-round city, a place not affected by adverse weather conditions. In the weeks preceding the event, promoters nervously asked wealthy individuals to buy subscription shares to be paid back after the meet. One promoter even told the Aero Club of California that Los Angeles might gain over $5,000,000 in tourist revenue.[122] "Nothing has ever taken place in this city that will attract so much attention or give Los Angeles such widespread publicity as the flights that will take place next week," noted F. J. Zeehandelaar, the secretary of the Merchants and Manufacturers' Association, in a public letter that appeared in the *Times*. "Up to the present time only forty per cent of the amount necessary to carry out the meet has been contributed, and the committee appeals to those citizens . . . to come forward and send their subscriptions at once to the [M&M] headquarters."[123] When it arrived, ticket sales allayed such financial concerns; the meet was a momentous success. From January 10 to 20, 1910, over two hundred fifty thousand people came to see the events and marvel at newfound technological possibilities. Organizers earned over $137,000 in gate receipts alone, compared to just $115,000 in expenses.[124] Aviators competed for over $80,000 in prize money, a sum that the *Times* bragged was over double that awarded at Reims.[125] Organizers reserved over $40,000 alone for heavier-than-air aviation, while the rest of the money went to dirigible and balloon competitors. Some of the money went undispensed: for instance, a $10,000 prize for a nonstop cross-country balloon trip.[126] Aviators did cash in a variety of prize categories: highest altitude achieved, longest endurance, fastest start from ground to air, fastest speed achieved with a passenger on board, and most accurate take off and landings.[127]

During the meet, promoters told Angelenos to expect great things if the city grasped its opportunities. The city could expect its national and international reputation to grow. "More than ever before the aviation meet has emphasized the recognized fact that Southern California is the playground of the world," the *Times* asserted at the height of the meet. "We began by marking it the playground of America, but as we have become better known the idea has broadened . . . we have, everything considered, the finest playground upon this old ball." Going forward, the paper demanded that the city gain more events for its playground.[128] City newspapers also hoped the meet might have a lasting impact on youth. The *Times* reported on an "Aviation Day, Jr," a month after the games, during which various groups competed in categories similar to those of the senior meet, except played out with miniature airplanes. The *Times* described the perceived progression of technology with some wonder. "Long since did the youngsters graduate in automobiling . . . But, of course, autos are now merely used in transportation to and from aviation fields."[129] Two years later, the *Los Angeles Municipal News*—a short-lived, publicly owned, boosterish paper—urged the city onward in its efforts to "Teach Youth to Fly." "Annually, the 'young idea' is examined as to its progress in aviation, by a kite-flying tournament at one of the parks," the paper noted, "which in itself is a better show in many respects than the famous meetings of airmen at Dominguez field." The paper lauded the competitors, all of whom were boys, for designing miniatures with "size and lifting power."[130] Such masculine creations might propel the children to futures as productive members of masculine Los Angeles. The meet, then, seemed to augur progress and modernity. Much as the Port of Los Angeles had revolutionized the city's relationship to the world, the aviation meet might lure tourists to the city and spark creative impulses among its young people. If the city was already "the playground of the world," it might become a technological epicenter.

"The Aerial War Engine of the Future"

The meet's success and the optimistic cultural messages it generated, however, belied some significant unease about aviation and its effects. Flying was an intensely masculine activity, which could contribute to a new American manliness.[131] Aviators embodied American values, such as individualism and risk-taking, and might thrust America into a post-frontier future, distinguished by the "age of power and the machine."[132] And yet, early aviation was intensely dangerous. Aviation meets featured such frequent crashes that some writers speculated that many spectators attended the gatherings in order to see the carnage firsthand.[133]

Promotional material centered on portraying the 1910 aviation meet as both exotic and dangerous. A selection of postcards created for Aviation Week illustrates such dual themes. A card captioned "Greetings from California: We're All Up in the Air Out Here" showed a large balloon surrounded by airplanes, all of which hovered over barely visible mountains.[134] Another asked, "Los Angeles (The Angels): Why Shouldn't We Fly?" The accompanying image, which perhaps answered that question, showed an "angel," a baby with angel wings flying a plane, looking directly at the reader. Even more forebodingly, another postcard satirized the risks spectators took when they went to the meet. "We've Been to the Aviation Meet," the card announced. In the background a family exhibited the injuries they sustained as a result of the meet's popularity: the mother's purse was broken and dress ripped, the father sported a black eye as his arm lay in a sling and his foot in a cast, and even their small child walked with a cane as he wept with an apparently bruised mouth. Los Angeles's very success could be dangerous (fig. 1).

The national media echoed such ambivalence. One article, published in the *World Today*, detailed the author's experiences with aviators, whom he termed "Bird-Men." "To the average man, whose flying experiences are confined to the elevator in a city sky-scrapers, the aviation meet in Los Angeles in January was the strangest sight of a lifetime," Hamilton Wright wrote, echoing contemporary fears about the impact of white-collar work on masculinity. Still, Wright noted skeptically, "[Flying] looked easy and safe. 'A heap safer,' said a wiry cow-puncher who had come all the way from New Mexico, 'than one of those automobile things.'"[135] Similarly, *OutWest* profiled the meet under a glowing title: "The Noble Sport of Aviation." "Already we are beginning to feel a sympathy and a little contempt for our forefathers, whose dominion over the elements was so limited," reflected one writer.[136] The same article also detailed one of the horrific "great exhibitions" at the meet, a major injury suffered by one local aviator, Edgar Smith, who was injured by his own propeller. "The inert body was carried off the field, and those who saw the iron propeller, which was crumpled by the blow, supposed that the skull had been crushed," narrated the author. "This lad, however, seemed destined to add additional lustre to the sturdy tribe of Smith," the author continued, "for after lying in the hospital five days, he returned to the field . . . and once more tried to fly."[137] Such depictions echoed contemporary narratives of aviation as an audacious, masculine activity. By attempting again to fly, Smith demonstrated a similar spirit to that of men who pursued wilderness adventures to test their manhood.

Even more importantly, contemporaries during and after the meet seem to have grasped the future military uses of flight. Flying was not just a "fantasy" but a realistic option in the near future, one that might affect Southern California.[138] Sometimes, observers downplayed potential military uses of the airplane. One editorial in the *Times* claimed that airplanes in the future might only be able to carry small loads and might never be commercially viable machines.[139] More often, however, the *Times*

WE'VE BEEN TO
THE AVIATION MEET

/S 31

FIG. 1. Satirical postcards such as this illustrate the conflicted relationship between Angelenos and the 1910 international aviation meet. 1910 Los Angeles International Aviation Meet Collection, California State University, Dominguez Hills.

detailed engineers' efforts to gain military interest in their products. After the meet, Curtiss began to tour the United States. As he moved around, he began to show how planes and their inventors might operate in the future. In Atlantic City on July 12, Curtiss arranged a "sham battle," wherein he dropped oranges accurately from a height of three hundred feet onto the deck of a battleship. This, the Associated Press reported, "Proves Efficacy of Aeroplane in Warfare."[140] In December, Curtiss proposed to help train military officers in Southern California and to establish a military aviation center there. The government accepted his offer, and the fruits of Curtiss's labor became immediately evident.[141] In April 1911 one young man, Harry Harkness, flew from a military station near San Diego to deliver reports to a U.S. commander at the Mexican border. He returned to a joyous reaction from the assembled military figures. "Harkness, by his flight, demonstrated, with no doubt in the minds of the army officers here, the practical use of the aeroplane as a scout in time of war," one news article commented.[142]

At other times, observers went even farther—to link aviation to a potential invasion of Los Angeles via its port. The famous French aviator Louis

Paulhan sparked this discourse. On January 14, 1910, Paulhan took off from the Dominguez Airfield, ascended to a flying altitude of two hundred feet, flew over the cities of San Pedro and Wilmington, and completed a loop over the site of proposed federal fortifications at the harbor, before returning to wild applause from the gathered crowd. Paulhan had been in the air for thirty minutes, more than enough time for the *Times* to speculate on his flight's broader import. Two passages from the *Times'* detailed, two-page feature on Paulhan's flight especially stand out. First, the paper speculated about the flight's impact on civilian populations. "The population of Wilmington and San Pedro were [*sic*] thunderstruck when this queer creature shot above the horizon and whizzed over their heads," the paper reported.[143] Second, the paper contended that Paulhan's flight had changed the very tenor of the aviation meet when the Frenchman launched over a San Pedro lighthouse. "The menacing significance of his flight came like a flash to every one [*sic*]," the paper argued, "as he kept on to Point Firmin and passed, from the rear over the fortifications-to-be."[144] Aviation could conquer old technologies. Paulhan's plane "shot," "whizzed," and "swooped," while ships in the harbor could only "let out a groaning roar."[145] The newspaper's language further indicated gendered, sexualized fears about aging; the plane was youthful and "shooting" around; ships were old and "groaning." Aviation's ramifications suddenly became more apparent. If Los Angeles did not adapt to the new technology, it might be overtaken by virile nations to the south and west.

The image of Paulhan's flight over port fortifications had staying power, as well. The following December, the *Times* published two articles that linked flight to port concerns. One article expressed some optimism that planes might be used for defense purposes. The article opened with a relief map "of this now unprotected great city," which contrasted the mountains in the background with the flat land next to the bay. The image implicitly suggested that the harbor was ripe for the taking. Above that map was a picture of a massive airplane in flight. This plane, the paper hoped, might deter future enemies. In fact, the plane was not a mystery but an "Aerial War Engine of the Future That May Annihilate Foes Seeking to Enter the Country by the Los Angeles Gateway."[146] Land-based fortifications seemed almost naïve in their ambitions. The plane was now a border sentry. Another *Times* editorial, "Fortifications for Defense," furthered this point. Much of the editorial detailed the need for defense at the standard locations singled out by Los Angeles boosters: coastal cities and the Panama Canal. "The developments in projectiles, in armor plate . . . in torpedoes, in submarine navigations, and . . . in the science of aviation, have been so great," the editorial pointed out, "that it is difficult for even skilled army and navy engineers to determine what form such additional aids to fortifications should take." Or, more succinctly, "the inventions of tomorrow may cause us to discard the improvements of today."[147] Such an uncertain statement was a far cry from the chamber of commerce's optimistic declarations at the turn of the century.

The aviation meet, then, had altered some of the rhetoric about progress in Los Angeles. Aviation pioneers such as Curtiss and Paulhan disrupted ideas about a stable, well-defended port that would bring the world to Los Angeles. Paradoxically, bringing the world to Los Angeles during the meet vividly illustrated the perils of other, unconsidered future expansion. The ambivalent cultural discourse about geographic vulnerability, economic progress, and promotional success in Los Angeles might be best encapsulated in a comparison of contemporary aviation event promotional posters. The 1910 Los Angeles International Air Meet poster, titled "First in America," was cluttered—tens of planes soar over the mountains in the distance, the city and port in the mid ground, and tropical nature, accented by bright colors, in the foreground.[148] Three balloons float just under the planes. The closest plane shows its pilot waving his hat in the air as he passes overhead (fig. 2).

The image evokes wonder; the palm trees seem almost welcoming. But the poster's worldview is also chaotic. In contrast, two other posters—from a 1909 celebration of the Wright Brothers in Dayton, Ohio, and a 1910 meet in Rouen, France—are much more peaceful. The Dayton poster is pastoral; a lone plane flies over the lightly forested countryside. Its colors are more muted than those of the Los Angeles poster; it presents a calm scene (fig. 3).[149] The Rouen poster is similarly unpopulated. One plane flies over the city's skyline, its pilot waving to the gargoyles mounted

at the summit of a nearby church (fig. 4).[150] The smoke from factories below does not reach the man or his plane, and the muted gold of the sky is as calming as the Dayton poster's light greens and blues. As opposed to Los Angeles's poster, the Dayton and Rouen visions of future aviation development do not seem threatening. Flying has little direct influence on the people or places below.

Contemporary reactions to youth aviation similarly indicate the ambivalent feelings sparked by the meet. The same *Los Angeles Municipal News* article about the youth flying expedition also included a brief section on "Honors for Orientals." Much of the section was patronizing. "The Oriental school children . . . easily carry off the honors as the builders of wierd [*sic*] and unusual kites," the *Municipal News* noted. "Split bamboo and gaily painted silk paper is the material they work with. The American boys use heavier frames and cloth instead of paper."[151] Oriental kite-making, in contrast to the manly, practical American planes, was a "good, healthy amusement."[152] A question, however, lurked behind such patronizing prose. Like Lindley's "ships of the world" comment, what might happen if other, potentially hostile, populations grasped on to flight? After all, in 1909 Curtiss himself tutored a Japanese man named C. K. Knasu about the technology of flying. This "mysterious Japanese visitor," noted the *Times*, could not be trusted. In fact, the subheading of the article was "May Prove Menace."[153] *The Curtiss Aviation Book* itself detailed increasing Japanese interest in Curtiss's seaplane technology. "The fame of the hydroaeorplane has reached the Orient and a demonstration was recently given at Tokyo, Japan, for the benefit of the Japanese Army," Curtiss's coauthor, Augustus Post, wrote. "Curtiss has had several tryouts and has proved itself a success."[154] Flying, the *Municipal News* noted, was important so students could "keep abreast of the latest scientific progress, rather than to lag behind among the dry-as-dust ideas of bygone centuries."[155] Again, Los Angeles might easily be overtaken if its citizens were not adaptive and vigilant.

FIG. 2. The 1910 aviation meet poster, "First in America," presents a cluttered, semi-chaotic worldview. 1910 Los Angeles International Aviation Meet Collection, California State University, Dominguez Hills.

THE NATION, STATE and CITY
❧ WELCOME THE ❧
WORLD'S GREATEST AVIATORS

WILBUR WRIGHT.

ORVILLE WRIGHT.

✦ DAYTON, OHIO. ✦
JUNE 17-18-1909.

FIG. 3. Opposite: A 1909 Dayton, Ohio, aviation meet poster presents a pastoral scene. 1910 Los Angeles International Aviation Meet Collection, California State University, Dominguez Hills.

FIG. 4. Above: A 1910 Rouen aviation meet poster presents a peaceful landscape. 1910 Los Angeles International Aviation Meet Collection, California State University, Dominguez Hills.

Thanks to new technology, then, the world was arriving in Los Angeles—through its public harbor and through its events. Many different entities seemed optimistic about the city's future connections. Los Angeles seemed poised to become a center of global commerce and an enticing tourist destination. Otis's 1906 dismissal of "New England's rock-bound shores" in favor of California seemed prescient in the context of Los Angeles elites' success in gaining the city a successful port and luring a major world event there. Los Angeles seemed likely to capitalize on its connections to federal power and transform itself into a command post of a global economic empire. But, elites and elite institutions might wonder, what would happen if other nations, such as Japan, also advanced? What would happen if Angelenos got too comfortable? Already, the buoyant optimism about Los Angeles's global connections had butted-up against the vulnerabilities illustrated by the aviation meet. The politics of connections were contested even during relatively peaceful moments. Just four years later, a time of crisis would further upset such dynamics. The World War I years would coincide with increasing political instability in Mexico and spark fears of a dual Japanese-Mexican invasion. Connection during a time of war would not seem as enticing; borderlands fears would loom larger. Selling the city during this period would prove to be a much trickier proposition.

BORDERLANDS FORTRESS

LOS ANGELES WAS WEAK. RESTING PASSIVELY ON THEIR LAURELS,
Angelenos were oblivious to the malevolent forces amassing outside the city
gates—according to the city's newspapers, its denizens ignored the clear
threat that Japan and Mexico might sweep across Los Angeles's undefended
borders and defile the region. From 1913 to 1919, such messages detailing
an impending crisis dominated the pages of the two major Los Angeles
newspapers: the *Los Angeles Examiner*, controlled by William Randolph
Hearst, and the *Los Angeles Times*, controlled by Harry Chandler, Harrison
Gray Otis's son-in-law. Both newspapers staked their claims within the
political context of three security crises that dominated these years: the
escalation of Japanese-American tensions over China, a radical turn in
the Mexican Revolution, and World War I. In Los Angeles, World War
I intensified longstanding concerns about the state's borders, especially
the Pacific Coast. Mexican political instability combined with fears of a
so-called Yellow Peril to create the image of a dual menace threatening
the city from all sides.[1] The two newspapers continued to emphasize
these concerns even as external threats waxed and waned from 1914 to
1919. Indeed, neither the foiled 1915 Plan of San Diego, in which a Mexican revolutionary faction tried to gain support for a rebellion against
the U.S. government in the American Southwest, nor the Zimmermann
Telegram, an intercepted 1917 diplomatic cable from Germany to Mexico

proposing that Mexico invade the United States, fundamentally altered newspaper coverage.[2]

During this period of largely manufactured crisis, the *Examiner* and the *Times* urged two interrelated responses: collective preparedness and economic progress.[3] First, the papers argued that Los Angeles needed to prepare defenses both real and rhetorical—Angelenos should, for instance, support fortification of the harbor and in the process uphold the virtues of manhood. The city's chamber of commerce had pursued a similar line of argument a decade prior when it tried to make Los Angeles a naval hub, but the World War I crisis amplified the opportunity for invasion rhetoric to dominate public discourse. Second, such preparedness would ensure a prosperous future, in which borders would be opened in pursuit of free trade and Los Angeles would take its place at the forefront of American cities.

Generally speaking, then, both Chandler's *Times* and Hearst's *Examiner* propagated a vision in which secured borders might provide opportunities for the development of foreign commerce; in contrast, unsecured borders were dangerous. In light of this dynamic, the papers demanded that Los Angeles change, and Angelenos awaken, in order to preserve the city as an Anglo fortress. The construction of the city as a borderlands fortress, which entailed notions of masculinity, preparedness, and western exceptionalism, was not an end in itself. Rather, it was a reaction to Los Angeles's borderlands location and a precursor to economic expansion. Calling on both progress and preparedness, Los Angeles would assume an identity based on local industry, global trade, and regional boosterism.

World War I–era preparedness activism in Los Angeles, of course, had its roots in historical nativist trends. During the late nineteenth and early twentieth centuries, Californians increasingly worried about perceived threats from Asia. In 1882 Congress passed the Chinese Exclusion Act in response to growing anti-Chinese activism and violence in California. In 1907, after a rise in Californian nativism that linked Japanese immigration to racial dilution and diminished job opportunities for whites, the United States and Japan established the so-called Gentlemen's Agreement, whereby the United States would not restrict Japanese immigration if Japan would ban the further emigration of laborers to the United States.

During the 1910s the struggle over immigration between California and Japan intensified. The 1913 California Alien Land Law aimed to curb Japanese immigration by prohibiting alien immigrants from owning land and limiting their leases to three years.[4] The author of a 1916 book titled *The Japanese Crisis* cuttingly remarked, "[California] knows the old Japanese proverb 'Among flowers, the cherry, among men, the warrior,' and wonders whether the military ideals . . . are ascendant in modern times as in ancient."[5] Unfettered Asian immigration, some feared, might provide an opportunity for Japan to later carry out a military invasion. Immigrants might weaken California from within.

Around the same time period, Angelenos also encountered Mexican revolutionary ideals. From 1906 to 1907, and again from 1910 to 1911, Ricardo Flores Magón, the leader of the anarchist Mexican Liberal Party (PLM), lived in Los Angeles and published the radical newspaper *Regeneración* from an office downtown. Magón and his co-leaders were arrested multiple times in the United States on political grounds, as PLM supporters fought in the Mexican Revolution and also tried to influence events in Mexico from the United States.[6] World War I provided an opportunity for white elites in Los Angeles to capitalize upon long-standing racial tensions by linking a dual racial fear of Japanese and Mexican invasion to Los Angeles's progress. According to their logic, Los Angeles's borderlands location demanded preparedness to face both these threats, and preparedness, in turn, could create some of the infrastructure and popular engagement necessary to transform Los Angeles into a modern city.

The World War I period also sparked a temporary shift in Angeleno elites' relationship to the federal government. During the Free Harbor Fight and the debate over Panama Canal policy, local boosters had tried to court federal appropriations and support. During World War I the newspapers alleged that the government in Washington had abandoned Los Angeles. The preparedness discourse of the *Times* and the *Examiner* defined itself in opposition to the purportedly weak-willed nature of the federal government, the hegemony of the East Coast, and the ideology of national harmony. While eastern preparedness activists did not ignore external threats, their work focused on the domestic sphere and social reform.[7] In contrast, the Angeleno approach to preparedness, as exemplified in the *Times* and the *Examiner*, centered around the need to protect Los Angeles against social ills transmitted from abroad. The newspapers' vision entailed racial cohesion, strong masculine gender norms, and hierarchical social relations. Chandler and Hearst imagined that easterners and midwesterners would migrate to the West Coast to join their respectable, conservative coalition in the borderlands, a process well under way by the 1910s. Such migrants' travels would mirror Chandler's and Hearst's own journeys as successful eastern transplants to the West Coast.[8]

In their proclamations that Los Angeles was exceptional, poised to capitalize on internal migration, the *Times* and the *Examiner* read like other forms of typical urban boosterism from the time period that emphasized providence and uniqueness. But the papers moved beyond boosterism to assert that Los Angeles—vulnerable and feeble—needed to change.[9] The Democratic *Examiner* and the Republican *Times* were well suited for the role of dual manipulators of public fear. Though Hearst's and Otis's, or later Chandler's, political views frequently had put the papers at odds over the previous two decades, the papers sometimes disseminated similar, and mutually beneficial, messages about boosting and protecting the city. "It was a strange kind of competition," the historians Robert Gottlieb and Irene Wolt have argued, "encompassing one part war and one part accommodation."[10] Chandler and Hearst essentially formed the media wing of a powerful cabal that ruled Los Angeles during the World War I period. Having acquired power over the previous few decades, the newspaper magnates were now eager to express it.

Harry Chandler's Rise

Born in Landaff, New Hampshire, into a family of farmers on May 17, 1864, Chandler seemed unlikely to ascend to a place of power in a city on the opposite coast. In 1882 Chandler was set to begin his studies at Dartmouth College, but shortly after arriving on campus, he agreed to a dare that went wrong—he jumped into an ice-covered vat of starch, quickly developed pneumonia, and suffered severe lung hemorrhaging. Doctors told him he needed to move to a warm climate due to his badly damaged lungs, so in 1883 he traveled to Los Angeles. By 1884 he had found a job as a clerk with the *Los Angeles Times*, which was, of course, owned by Otis.[11] Over the next few years, Chandler rose in the hierarchy of the *Times*; in 1894, he married Otis's daughter Marian.[12] By the late 1890s it was clear that Chandler was the heir apparent to Otis, and indeed he took over day-to-day operation of the *Times* when Otis's health declined around 1905. Otis had gained fame as an emphatic public advocate for the conservative Republican causes he supported, including the open shop movement and American expansionism. Chandler's *Times* mirrored Otis's in many ways, perhaps most obviously in its fervent open-shop activism. In 1937, for instance, the *Times* published a series of articles criticizing Seattle labor leader Dave Beck and his work to create the Western Conference of Teamsters, a large, regional labor group. In November of that year, the paper published Chandler's personal defense of the *Times*' articles. "Your Mr. Beck's peculiar philosophies are negative of the Los Angeles credo, epitomized in type every day of the year at the head of the title page of the Los Angeles Times: 'Equal Rights—Liberty Under the Law—True Industrial Freedom,'" Chandler argued. "These principles . . . have built Los Angeles to the premier industrial and maritime shipping city of the Pacific Coast." "Would you have Los Angeles throw this all away?" he asked, echoing the city's existential civic rhetoric.[13]

The relationship between Otis and Chandler seems to have been warm and intimate. In light of Chandler's increasing responsibilities, Otis raised his son-in-law's salary to $3600 in 1905 and to $5000 in 1911.[14] In his 1905 letter to Chandler about the raise, Otis complimented Chandler's "ability, loyalty, integrity, zeal and devotion to duty" and told him of his "deep affection" for his son-in-law.[15] In his 1911 letter notifying Chandler about that year's salary increase, Otis briefly expounded on Chandler's true value to the *Times*. "My dear Harry: Your services are worth $10,000 a year to the Times-Mirror Co.," Otis wrote. "You do not get half that now. With my perennial good wishes and unvarying affection, I tender you herewith a half rate henceforth, to-wit, $5000 per year." The often fierce and domineering Otis concluded the letter with a gesture toward his own increasing frailty. "You are my strong right arm and I lean upon you," he revealed. "Very truly and affectionately yours, Harrison Gray Otis."[16]

A secretive and demanding man, Chandler devoted himself to two intertwined pursuits—personal economic gain and Los Angeles boosterism. He sought to promote the city as a moral, western outpost of Anglo Americanness. "[Los Angeles] has grown from a crude little frontier town into a great metropolis," Chandler recalled in 1941. "But another angle of the growth has impressed me more than anything else. That is the human angle."[17] Probably the most powerful man in the region by 1920, Chandler held major roles in founding most of the significant institutions in contemporary Southern California—the Ambassador and Biltmore Hotels, the California Institute of Technology, and the Hollywood Bowl among them. In the process, Chandler accumulated a fortune estimated to have been at least $200 million and perhaps as much as $500 million.[18] In 1914 he decided to move from his three-story Victorian home in downtown Los Angeles, where he and Marian had lived since 1903. In its place, the Chandlers built a mansion on five acres in the hilly Los Feliz neighborhood, about eight miles northeast of downtown Los Angeles. When completed, the 8,891 square-foot home boasted twenty-four rooms and views of sights as far away as Catalina Island.

While Chandler masked his investments behind shadowy economic partnerships, much of his wealth could be attributed to land development efforts.[19] A 1915 list of Chandler's company directorships listed, among other positions, seven land development firms, one mortgage firm, an oil company, and a water company.[20] In 1909 Chandler and Otis paid $2.5 million to buy 47,500 acres from the rancher Isaac Newton Van Nuys in the San Fernando Valley, northeast of the city. The developers' newly formed Los Angeles Suburban Homes Company set about turning the land into the largest subdivision in the area. "The center of our tract is about nine miles from the City limits of Los Angeles," the promoter and developer H. J. Whitley wrote about the Van Nuys tract. "The climate has all the well known [sic] Southern California characteristics, in fact is almost identical with that of Los Angeles, with the possible exception of less fog," he argued. "It will no doubt be the policy of the Company to encourage buildings . . . for high-class dwellings," he further promised prospective buyers.[21] Three current towns—Van Nuys, Reseda, and Canoga Park—emerged from the former ranch.

Outside of the United States, Chandler seemed more willing to relax his class standards for development. On his Mexican land holdings, organized as the Colorado River Land Company, Chandler pursued a policy of limited initial investment to drive down purchaser costs. "You will remember that it was determined that the Company would not improve any land nor install any of the canal systems necessary to irrigate the land cultivated but would grant leases at a very low rental . . . for the first few years," Colorado River Land Company official W. D. Davis wrote to Chandler in April 1920.[22] One 1919 four-year lease agreement between the company and two Japanese farmers for a property in Mexicali restricted the lessees to agricultural use of land and told them to "deal directly" with a local water company for irrigation services.[23] Such a policy of limited initial investment, another employee wrote to Chandler in 1920, would ensure long-term gains, "the great advance that I am positive is going to take place in the value of our holdings."[24] Finally, some of Chandler's fortune depended on the use of U.S. military power to ensure his holdings in Mexico and elsewhere, a political stance that would ally him with Hearst during the World War I era.

William Randolph Hearst's Evolution

While Chandler moved his way up the ladder of the *Times*, Hearst dabbled in print media, art collecting, politics, and film. He could do so because he was born into wealth. After his expulsion from Harvard in 1885 due to a series of academic and social misadventures, including sending engraved chamber pots to his professors, Hearst took over the *San Francisco Examiner*, which his father owned. An ambitious figure who, like Chandler, displayed a certain aversion to public performance, Hearst began to expand his media holdings. In 1895, four years after his father's death, Hearst's mother gifted him $400,000, which Hearst used to buy the *New York Journal*. He subsequently engaged in a famous circulation war with Joseph Pulitzer and his newspaper, the *New York World*. In the mid-1910s, Hearst started a short-lived film studio, the International Film Service, which produced comic strips, films, and newsreels.[25] His drive to create a media empire based on sensationalism, nativism, and expansionism would not abate.

Hearst's political ambitions fostered a distinct set of foreign policy ideas, which emerged over the course of a political career of mixed results. Though he served in the U.S. House of Representatives from 1903 to 1907, Hearst perennially failed to achieve the higher elected offices that he craved. After a series of electoral defeats in New York and a failed 1904 presidential campaign in California, Hearst launched the *Los Angeles Examiner* as a populist, pro-labor competitor to the *Times*. Hearst's politics combined a variety of seemingly conflicting stances—anti-corporate populism, economic expansionism, isolationism, and jingoism. While he opposed the U.S. entry into World War I and the League of Nations, he advocated U.S. imperial ambitions in Latin America and demanded greater recognition of the Yellow Peril from Asia.[26] Of course, Hearst's public twentieth-century foreign policy stances also served his own financial interests. "Mr. Hearst has been saying things about his Americanism for almost fifty years," wryly commented the writer Hamilton Basso in a 1935 *New Republic* article. "He started the Cuban war because he was a patriot. The mere accident that the circulation of *The New York Evening Journal* passed 500,000, while that of *The Morning Journal* jumped 200,000 in six weeks, meant nothing to him. Nothing at all." "Mr. Hearst is boss and he's going to stay boss— just as long as he can," Basso concluded. "He has an awful lot at stake."[27]

By the late 1910s Hearst was spending more time on the West Coast and began to build the mansion that would be known as Hearst Castle on his 250,000-acre estate in San Simeon, California, between Los Angeles and San Francisco. The castle vividly illustrated how Hearst wished to display his entry into elite Californian society. From 1919 until 1947 builders constructed more and more of the castle as Hearst intermittently lived there. Today, the estate comprises four separate residences, the largest of which, Casa Grande, is 68,500 square feet and includes 38 bedrooms, 42 bathrooms, and 30 fireplaces.[28] Like Henry Huntington, Hearst assembled a major art collection at his new home. "A number of sensational purchases were made by A. Arnold, an agent said to be representing William R. Hearst in the latter's provisioning for his new mansion in California," noted a *New York Tribune* article about a New York art sale in May 1924. On Hearst's behalf, Arnold purchased two ceilings from a Spanish palace for $9,050, an altar piece for $1,850, twelve lanterns for $2,880, "and a large sixteenth century iron gate, for $3,000."[29] In July 1929 the *New York Times* published a lengthy article on Hearst Castle, "A Renaissance Palace in Our West." Though the land had been in the Hearst family for many years, Hearst "recognized the possibilities of the place for week-end and occasional longer vacation retirements from his Los Angeles and San Francisco offices." So, he decided to build the estate on a scenic hillside. "When one is more than halfways [*sic*] along the climb the colored summit comes suddenly into view ... brightening against the California sky," Duncan Aikman narrated. "Out of its richness rises the white side-wall of a palace which might have been the Apennines villa of some Renaissance grand ducal seigneur." Inside, Hearst had begun to display his art collection. Outside, "it occurred to Mr. Hearst that his guests might be entertained with a collection of beasts usually to be found only in public parks and circuses," Aikman continued. "Eagles flap their wings from tree-high cages near the Casa Grande and from an enclosure a little in the rear tigers and bears roar their welcome."[30] Such extravagance demanded a serious investment. Hearst spent around $10 million on the mansion and was later forced to sell some of his acquisitions, including the exotic animals, when his media empire declined in the 1940s.[31] By building such a remote, exotic estate, Hearst not only flaunted his wealth but also proclaimed a masculinity based on his domination of nature. During the World War I era, Hearst was beginning his transition to a full-fledged West Coast activist. If not an Angeleno, Hearst certainly was becoming a Californian with serious interests in Southern California.

Threats to the South, Threats to the West

Though the two men took significantly different journeys into the elite Angeleno class, Chandler's and Hearst's financial interests led both of them to disseminate fearmongering articles about Japan and Mexico. Both men held significant estates in Mexico—Chandler in Baja California and Hearst in Chihuahua—that were important parts of their economic and personal legacies.[32] In 1915 a federal grand jury indicted Chandler for attempting to overthrow the provincial government of Baja California, insert leaders more favorable to U.S. interests, and thereby retain his ranch in the face of Mexican land reform efforts.[33] The ranch was well worth keeping; a later article in the *Saturday Evening Post* estimated that it produced $18 million worth of cotton in 1919.[34] After Chandler's death, an article in *Newsweek* judged Chandler's land to be symbolic of his "Midas touch."[35] For Hearst, who had inherited his land from his father, the mining mogul and U.S. Senator George Hearst, the land held both sentimental and economic value.

The Mexican Revolution threatened to disrupt Chandler's and Hearst's land interests. As various rulers temporarily took over Mexico in the 1910s, revolutionary forces continually attacked Chandler's estate in Baja California and Hearst's in Chihuahua.[36] Pro-American president Porfirio Díaz left the country under duress in 1911; his exit was followed by the short tenures of Francisco Madero and Victoriano Huerta. Venustiano Carranza overthrew Huerta in August 1914, which especially worried Chandler and Hearst because Carranza advocated widespread land reform. Efforts in that direction in fact culminated in article 27 of the Mexican Constitution of 1917, which specified that "only Mexicans by birth or naturalization and Mexican companies have the right to acquire ownership of lands, waters, and their appurtenances, or to obtain concessions for the exploitation of mines or of waters."[37] Both Hearst and Chandler demanded that the United States interfere in the Mexican Revolution—to prevent Carranza's land reform efforts from succeeding and to promote Mexican revolutionaries who were more amenable to American business interests.

While Chandler and Hearst held fewer personal interests in Japanese policy, they still wished to influence Angeleno attitudes toward Japan, albeit in different ways. If Hearst was known for his anti-Japanese sentiments, Chandler had a more ambivalent relationship with Japan. He opposed the 1920 Alien Land Law because he relied on Japanese labor to cultivate land he owned. Nevertheless, through the *Times*, Chandler propagated fearmongering regarding potential invasions on both the Mexican and

Japanese fronts.[38] Though he did not hold explicitly anti-Japanese views, Chandler used the potential susceptibility of Los Angeles's coastal borders to demand more comprehensive preparedness policies. Hearst's and Chandler's conception of a Japan-Mexico menace, then, fit with the notion of an expanded, hemispheric "transborder Yellow Peril," in part influenced by Japanese migration to Mexico, that the historian Eiichiro Azuma has applied to early twentieth-century California.[39] By publishing editorials and tailored news articles, Chandler and Hearst stood poised to counter the purported Japanese and Mexican threats through the print media, as their newspapers sought to convince Angelenos of the active threats posed by the Japanese and Mexican governments in tandem.

To be clear, the *Times* was not nearly as anti-Japan as the *Examiner*, and the former sometimes served as a voice of moderation regarding Pacific affairs. For instance, in 1916, after Japan elected a new premier, the *Times* published an editorial by the Japanese journalist K. K. Kawakami, titled "Will Japan Fight?" "You may rest assured that he will never assume rash measures in handling foreign affairs of the empire, least of all questions involving the United States," Kawakami wrote.[40] At other times, however, the newspaper broadcast the opinions of Americans who viewed Japan as a menace to be reckoned with. In 1915 the *Times* showcased a lengthy interview with Orville J. Nave, the chaplain of the Grand Army of the Republic.[41] Nave, who lived in Los Angeles, felt that the "weakness of a democracy" that did not allow America to force its citizens to prepare left the country open to naval attack from Japan. Japan, in contrast, was "young and virile . . . acting with the swiftness of an eagle after his prey." America's Pacific defenses made it "as helpless and defenseless as poor, humiliated China," Nave declared. Such rhetoric sounded similar to the depictions of "groaning" ships during the 1910 international aviation meet. Without American preemptive preparedness, Nave thought, Japan would easily take over the lucrative oil fields and railways in Southern California.[42] Nave was not alone in expressing this opinion in the pages of the *Times*. "Jap Invasion Is Predicted," announced the headline to a 1916 article about the views of the activist Henry Wise Wood.[43] In 1916 *Times* columnist Harry Carr railed against "pacifists" who downplayed the threat from Japan, when, in his opinion, the Philippines and Hawaii were in grave danger. Carr ended his argument on a dark, ambiguous note. "Nobody knows how many Japanese soldiers there really are in Mexico," he concluded. "Or under what conditions they are there."[44]

The *Times* expressed significantly more hostility toward Mexico. An editorial from 1916 titled "Our Duty in Mexico" argued that America should "at the first aggressive act of Mexico . . . march our forces at once into Chihuahua, Sonora, and Lower California, take possession of them and stay there until the last bandit shall be shot or hanged or driven southward and peace and order completely restored."[45] Such order, another editorial hypothesized, might be achieved by establishing "an American Protectorate" over parts of northern Mexico. An occupation would control the criminal element: "The banditti who have ravaged the border . . . would be driven out or exterminated."[46] In 1917 the *Times* warned its readers to prepare for full-scale invasion. "We have abundant and overwhelming evidence that we are about to be invaded and attacked," one editorial noted. "Don't wait for the attack . . . Guard the border, of course, but move the border many miles southward, plant the Stars and Stripes there and keep them there!"[47] When a government report revealed the Plan of San Diego in 1919, the *Times* proclaimed across its front page that the report "Exposes Carranza's Plot to Seize Border States."[48] To the *Times*, violations of the border posed a profound crisis for the Southwest.

The *Examiner* agreed with the *Times* about the reality of the borderlands crisis. Often, the *Examiner* imagined Japan and Mexico together as an overwhelming invasion force that would subvert American gender norms. In response to the Zimmermann Telegram, the *Examiner* published an editorial declaring that if America were defeated by an alliance of Germany, Japan, Mexico, and possibly Russia, "Mexico would take our southwest and restore it to barbarism" and "Japan would take the Pacific Coast and devote it to Oriental ideals and standards."[49] In this scenario, Los Angeles's geographic location would be especially alluring to the Japanese: "On the rich Pacific Coast, the most favored and the most fertile part of the whole United States, the blood-red sun of Japan would shine in oriental splendor . . . over a teeming and thriving Japanese united

Eastern Asia."[50] According to the *Examiner*, this "Japanese united Eastern Asia" would emerge because Angelenos had not viewed the Pacific Rim with appropriate alarm. Such rhetoric echoed a longer American cultural tradition of portraying Asian men as dangerous sexual deviants.[51] As the link between "fertile" and "teeming and thriving" illustrates, the *Examiner* equated its prediction of a borderlands doomsday with a pseudo-sexual defilement of western virtue. Limited preparedness threatened not only American sovereignty but also American manhood.

Hearst also did not limit his apocalyptic rhetoric to real-world scenarios. In 1916 his film company produced *Patria*, a fictional "preparedness serial" about Patria Channing, the only heir to a set of munitions factories. She was, according to the film's promotional materials, "custodian of the $100,000,000 Channing Fund, secretly accumulated to assist in American defense in case of foreign aggression."[52] Based on the novel *The Last of the Fighting Channings*, *Patria* depicted a conspiracy between Japan and Mexico to steal the Channing fortune and invade the United States.[53] The *Los Angeles Examiner*, along with other Hearst newspapers such as the *San Francisco Examiner*, published chapters from the novel every Sunday and, as figure 5 shows, urged readers to "READ This Story Here—Then SEE It in Motion Pictures." The film was so racially inflammatory that President Woodrow Wilson asked Hearst's company to remove *Patria* from circulation. As Wilson stated, "it is extremely unfair to the Japanese and I fear it is calculated to stir up a great deal of hostility."[54] Undeterred, Hearst continued to widely market *Patria* and serialize the film in his newspapers.

The last chapter of the film's serialization particularly engages the themes of preparedness that were central to fears of borderlands invasion. After she defeats the evil Baron Huroki, chief of the Japanese Secret Service in America, Patria ruminates on the future:

She foresaw quite clearly what would happen within the next few days and weeks. The storm of popular indignation; the massing of troops along the border; the interchange of diplomatic amenities; the studiously polite disavowal of Huroki and all his alleged invasion . . . the simmering down of popular interest; the return of the common apathy;

FIG. 5. Chapters of *Patria* appeared in the *Examiner* and illustrate gendered invasion fears in World War I–era Los Angeles. *Los Angeles Examiner*, April 1, 1917.

the renewed reign of lethargic indifference to the need for "preparedness" . . . And so she began to understand that the victory of the day was but a barren one.[55]

The story's ambivalent end note suggests the constancy of perceived threats and the temporality of sensationalism. Media coverage could not be the only vehicle for change; its effects were too fleeting. Instead, the media needed to promote substantive preparedness, which would follow from sensationalism.

Just one of many racist preparedness films produced around this time, *Patria* in particular addressed the American Southwest and Pacific Coast. The *Examiner* warned that the film's very specificity gave it credibility. One article about *Patria* proclaimed that it was a work of "prophetic genius." The article went on to state, "When the proper moment arrives Japan will strike without giving us warning."[56] The *Examiner* argued that the West Coast would be hindered by geography because "the great cities on the Pacific, the fertile lands of Washington, Oregon, and California, are fenced off from the eastern section of the United States."[57] Again, the paper implicitly connected agricultural "fertility" to sexuality; again, western men would have to fight to protect their manhood. Collectively, the *Examiner* argued for an Angeleno identity based on the construction of tangible defenses and the concretization of internal order. In response to *Patria*'s prophesy, the *Examiner* and *Times* undertook a multipronged campaign for preparedness.

Preparedness, Los Angeles Style

In Hearst and Chandler's view, the fortification of the Port of Los Angeles was a necessary response to such threats. After Los Angeles annexed the harbor town of San Pedro and obtained federal appropriations to expand the port, its shipping grew by 600 percent in the 1910s.[58] A *Times* article in 1913 proudly called the port "A Mecca of Ocean Carriers."[59] On April 14, 1917, the *Examiner* treated its readers to some of the first pictures of the harbor defenses at Fort MacArthur, which was built by the U.S. government and overlooked San Pedro Bay. The *Examiner* succinctly declared, "This Battery Is Ready for Business."[60] The next day the paper printed plans for a $12 million expansion of the harbor that would render it "not only one of the best equipped and most efficient of the nation's trade gateways, but provid[e] also for its adequate defense."[61] In May 1917 the *Examiner* further termed the plan a "Huge Project of Defense," and prominent Angelenos endorsed the project.[62] Ironically, these plans seemed to undercut the paper's previous exposition of the comprehensive defenses around the harbor. For example, in a 1915 article about the defenses at Fort MacArthur, which were termed "impregnable," the *Times* informed its readers that Major Raymond of the U.S. Corps of Engineers "urges larger quarters for the military post at the harbor, declaring the present holdings are inadequate."[63] Both the *Times* and the *Examiner* simultaneously upheld the vitality of the port's fortifications and urged further improvements. As the Los Angeles Chamber of Commerce had realized a decade previously, preparedness could boost infrastructure.

Other military fortifications, the papers contended, could save Los Angeles if an advancing force landed. "Mighty Agitation Is Needed to Get Protection for Southern California," Harry Carr, the anti-pacifist *Times* columnist, announced in one article. To deter the Japanese threat and protect the new port fortifications, Carr called for a complement of mobile troops posted in Southern California. "There is not on the whole North American continent a more vulnerable place from a military standpoint than . . . the land that we know as Southern California," he continued. "In view of this situation it is a joke for Congress to hand us this little fort and stop there."[64] On the morning of April 8, 1917, just two days after the United States declared war on Germany, the *Times* answered a series of rhetorical questions in a wide headline that filled the page: "Is Los Angeles in Real Danger of a German-Mexican Attack by Land? No; From Japan? No." To explain its confidence, the paper offered its readers an illustration of "home guard defense districts" within the city, a proto-martialization of the metropolis that would protect it.[65] The city would be divided into nine sections, each with a separate commander. Troops and barricades were generally concentrated at the boundaries of the city, further emphasizing Los Angeles's own borders, apart from the national ones.

Plans of defense went hand in hand with a demand for greater military training. In a 1915 editorial titled "Preparedness," the *Times* stressed the need for "a considerable increase in our regular Army" and "preparation for organizing, disciplining, and equipping a large reserve force of volunteers."[66] The calls grew louder after Mexican revolutionary general Pancho Villa's forces killed fifteen Americans in Columbus, New Mexico, in 1916 and the United States failed to apprehend Villa in Mexico during the subsequent Punitive Expedition.[67] In response, the *Examiner* published an editorial titled "Failure of Militia in Mexico Crisis Shows Need of Universal Military Training in This Country." The article argued that military training would ensure economic efficiency and proper masculinity. "[America's failure] indicates that America is like those fat and flabby nations of history which have been from time immemorial the victims of leaner, but better prepared countries," the *Examiner* warned.[68] Such gendered rhetoric consistently appeared in the pages of both newspapers. During World War I, both the *Examiner* and the *Times* trumpeted Los Angeles's enlistment numbers and enrollment drives. The *Examiner* encouraged enlistment by printing a cartoon titled "The Feminine Heart Loves a Uniform," in which a young woman stares at a soldier instead of her boyfriend.[69]

Articles in the *Examiner* and the *Times* espousing military preparedness emerged in tandem with the national preparedness movement led by Leonard Wood and Theodore Roosevelt. Wood, a general and former chief of staff with the U.S. Army, pressured the government to initiate universal military training in 1915. He even created a model training camp for wealthy civilians in Plattsburgh, New York, that exposed the rich to the rigors of outdoor exercise and military drilling. The camp, where enrollees trained intensively for six weeks, served forty thousand men in 1915 and 1916.[70] Wood, as historian Michael Pearlman has argued, designed Plattsburg to enforce an ideology of "ascetic discipline" that might trickle down to the lower classes and promote class and sectional unity. While Roosevelt, stymied in recent political ventures, had different priorities in mind, he held a similar ideology. After U.S. entry into World War I, Roosevelt urged President Wilson to allow him to create a volunteer division of men, from every state and social class, in order to generate sectional and social harmony.[71] (The *Examiner* had similarly imagined an opportunity for social harmony through military discipline, which the paper claimed would result in the "democracy of the poor man's son sleeping and marching and eating beside the rich boy, all for the sake of their common country.")[72] Through such ventures, Roosevelt sought to remedy a rising crisis of masculinity amid the "female invasion" of the economic and political spheres.[73] As the United States increasingly industrialized in the late nineteenth century, elite men such as Roosevelt resurrected frontier values such as self-reliance, as they bemoaned the loss of purportedly crucial aspects of American masculine culture.[74] "For them," Richard Slotkin writes, "the problem of a closed Frontier is not the lack of economic opportunity but the loss of those conditions that allowed their class to acquire the virile character that entitles and enables them to rule giant corporations of a modern nation-state."[75]

The values the *Times* and *Examiner* preached, about the discipline and manhood that might be produced by military training, were similar to those preached by Wood and Roosevelt. Indeed, the two newspapers often argued that an Angeleno masculinity forged out of frontier values such as personal responsibility and hard work could deflect foreign threats. At other moments, however, the papers took pains to separate Los Angeles's values from those of the East. Indeed, more often than not the *Times* and the *Examiner* presented Los Angeles as exceptionally western. In an editorial about migration to California, the *Times* wished that, rather than heading to California, radicals would go east toward Washington and Woodrow Wilson. "California invites the blooded stock of the country to come here and keep coming," the paper announced. "For drones and scrubs and the I.W.W. she has no use. She invites them all to join Coxey's Army and go to Washington and call on the Princeton schoolmaster."[76] Again, the federal government served as a useful rhetorical foil. In the editor's view, those "radicals" were lazy, demanded handouts from the government, and therefore did not belong in Los Angeles. "Drones" rejected frontier virtues of individualism. Kelly Lytle Hernández has shown that city leaders, including Otis through the *Times*, had previously (from 1880 to 1910) led a mass incarceration effort targeted at poor white male transient workers. The "tramp panic" eventually made Los Angeles the largest per capita imprisoner in the United States.[77] Just four years later, the *Times* returned to its rhetorical campaign against lower-class "scrubs," presumably reminding its readers that the city could not afford to let down its guard in the face of a new threat. The two newspapers, then, did not trust Americans as a whole to sustain a masculine frontier culture. Only the "blooded stock" should come to Los Angeles and aid preparedness.

Frontier masculinity, if properly deployed toward military training, would protect Southern California in the event of an invasion. A 1916 editorial in the *Times* titled "PREPARE!" assured readers that "the stalwart manhood of Los Angeles, which today will march through our streets, would, if the necessity should arise, form an army adequate for the defense of California [from Japan] when sufficiently drilled and adequately equipped."[78] Such an imagined crisis would have profound implications.

In its own pages, the *Examiner* detailed what might happen if defense failed: "The new world would be for the yellow races, with their different standards, their different purposes, their different principles, their hatred of the white race and all of its works and ways."[79] The papers advocated a new form of preparedness, based in Los Angeles and founded upon middle-class sensibilities, which rejected "tramps," to protect Southern California from border threats.

A debate in the *Times* about sports further elucidated the notions of gender inherent to Angeleno progress. In April 1917 the *Times* reprinted a short piece by cultural commentator Chauncey Thomas from the magazine *Outdoor Life*. The article, titled "America Is Effeminate," began with an arresting set of juxtapositions: "If we are to thrive as a people we Americans must have more boxing and less baseball, more leather and less lace, more drilling and less dancing, more artillery and less alimony, more men and fewer Miss Nancy's."[80] Thomas associated powerful men with militaristic activity and social power. Effeminate men, by contrast, relinquished power to women through their weakness. According to the *Times* and the *Examiner*, California needed to uphold respectable masculinity and conservatism. Only then would the city's security be ensured, paving the way for progress.

Woodrow Wilson's Preparedness Skepticism

In part, both papers blamed President Wilson, acting as a symbol of eastern power as a whole, for what they viewed as his dangerously inactive borderlands policies. A 1913 editorial, written as part of an attempt by the *Times* to convince the president to formally recognize the government of Mexican president Huerta, charged that Wilson's inaction in this respect threatened U.S. interests in Mexico. "Wilson is posing as an egoist of monumental proportions, and is making it harder for those of our countrymen whose lives and whose property are endangered by the Civil War in Mexico," the article argued.[81] In 1917, in the midst of negotiations between the United States and Japan about China, the *Times* again lamented Wilson's lack of control over foreign policy. "The Wilson administration is not framing a Far Eastern policy," the paper maintained. "It has received one framed and delivered with charges prepaid."[82] In 1917 a *Times* editorial argued that Wilson should not lift the U.S. embargo on the transportation of arms to Mexico. "Certainly every one of our commanders on the border knows," the paper insisted, "that arming Carranza's soldiers is only arming Villa's bandits."[83] Such anti-Wilson rhetoric from the paper is not surprising, because the president was Chandler's and Hearst's avowed enemy, and the *Times* was a Republican publication. But the rhetorical choices of the *Times* and the *Examiner* revealed a distinctive local worldview. Even as eastern migrants and ideals influenced the city, the newspapers argued, Los Angeles would be in the future superior to eastern cities because it promoted frontier masculinity and preparedness, strength instead of Wilson's weakness. Los Angeles elites had become more confident in the city's future as a place partially disconnected from eastern capital and federal power.

Wilson stoked Angeleno antipathy by following a calculated policy of limiting direct American intervention in Mexico. The president had certainly inherited an unstable political situation in Mexico, in part precipitated by U.S. involvement in that country's internal affairs. In February 1913 Huerta's allies first forced Mexico's President Francisco Madero and Vice President José María Pino Suárez to resign and then imprisoned them. Three days later, a soldier named Francisco Cardenas assassinated Madero and Suárez as he was transporting them to prison. In a personal diary entry, Paul von Hintze, the German ambassador to Mexico, wryly indicated his skeptical view of Madero's "protection" in the hands of Huerta's government. When Hintze demanded that he be allowed to protect a German secret agent named Felix Sommerfeld from Mexican authorities, "[The government] suggested bringing [Sommerfeld], guarded by police, to Veracruz."[84] "Obviously," Hintze remarked, "this method proved not necessarily safe, as has just been demonstrated by the murder of Francisco Madero . . . This only increased my concern."[85] Originally unbeknown to Woodrow Wilson, Henry Lane Wilson, the U.S. ambassador to Mexico under William Howard Taft, was complicit in the coup. Lane Wilson, who opposed Madero on the grounds that his tenuous grasp of power endangered U.S. business interests, threatened Madero with U.S. military intervention and urged him to resign. Afterward, Lane Wilson secretly encouraged Huerta to carry out a coup and assured him of U.S. diplomatic recognition.[86] President Wilson eventually fired the ambassador in July of that year.[87]

Thereafter, while President Wilson did not want to recognize Huerta's government, which he viewed as undemocratic, he hesitated to take definitive action in Mexico. After firing Lane Wilson, he decided to send John Lind, the former governor of Minnesota, to Mexico as a new "special envoy." The president instructed Lind to "demand immediate cessation of fighting, early and free elections, and Huerta's departure."[88] Though Lind's mission ended in failure just a few months later, his dispatches from Mexico sparked a vital conversation in the upper reaches of the federal government. This conversation, which generally dismissed the viability of any transborder Yellow Peril, illustrated the ways in which Wilson, Lind, and Robert Lansing, Wilson's secretary of state, acted to limit U.S. involvement in Mexico, even at the cost of American business interests there. During World War I, then, the federal government acted in ways contrary to the two newspaper magnates' interests in Mexico.

Lind was perhaps a surprising choice for the position of special envoy to Mexico. He had gained stature as something of a maverick politician. Swayed by the Democrat William Jennings Bryan's presidential campaign speeches, Lind left the Republican Party in 1898 and won election as governor of Minnesota on the Democratic and Populist tickets. In 1912 he helped to secure Wilson's nomination at the Democratic Convention. In his role as special envoy to Mexico, Lind dismissed a potential Japan-Mexico alliance. Japan and Mexico had a relatively warm history; the 1888 Treaty of Amity, Commerce, and Navigation established equal diplomatic and economic relations between the two countries, and Japanese officials were welcomed in Mexico under the Huerta administration.[89] However, after meeting with two Japanese military officials, perhaps to determine if they posed any threat, Lind assured the White House that "there is not the slightest danger that the Japanese will ever become popular with the masses of the Mexican people." Later in the same memo he mocked the susceptibility of the United States to the Japanese "bugaboo," an image that carried cultural power in California.[90] According to Lind, Japan and Mexico might threaten some of the United States' international interests, but neither government posed any serious security risk. Lind went as far as to write to Wilson that the Mexican people could be trusted to create a democracy. "They have come into contact with the people of the United States to a great degree," Lind maintained, "and they appreciate and sympathize with our government."[91] Most of all, Lind asked the president to look to northern revolutionaries such as Pancho Villa and Venustiano Carranza as representatives of the democratic will of the Mexican people. Regarding Villa, Lind reported, "He is the highest type of physical, mental, and moral efficiency . . . he has absorbed a very considerable amount of 'culture' in the past three years."[92] In Lind's view, both Carranza and Villa would be just rulers because they had absorbed democratic ideals from the United States. To Chandler and Hearst, in contrast, these northern Mexican revolutionaries posed a tremendous threat through their close proximity to the weak border.

Wilson did not always agree with Lind, but he generally pursued a policy of limited border action at odds with policies demanded by interventionists like Chandler and Hearst.[93] On August 27, 1913, Wilson gave a "Message on Mexican Affairs" to a joint session of Congress, in which he announced that Lind had been sent to Mexico. "All the world expects us in such circumstances to act as Mexico's nearest friend and intimate adviser," Wilson declared, as he promised U.S. aid.[94] Even when Wilson violated his own decree, he maintained a belief in paternalistic social reform. On April 21, 1913, Wilson sent U.S. marines to Veracruz to seize a customs house and enjoin Huerta's resignation. This action inspired a Mexican artillery attack, which in turn pushed the United States to send its fleet into the Veracruz harbor and to land troops to occupy the city, in part to block Huerta from receiving German arms.[95] Two days later, when the fighting ended, 17 Americans and about 150 Mexicans had been killed.[96] "Washington seems to be trying now to find a formula for the events that avoids [the] word 'war' and its existence," noted Paul von Hintze.[97] The United States occupied Veracruz until November, when the United States and Mexico reached a diplomatic agreement at the Niagara

Conference after Carranza took power. Months before a diplomatic agreement was reached, Hintze revealed on April 29 that "Woodrow Wilson is very relieved by [Huerta's] offer of mediation."[98] Thereafter, Wilson avoided direct involvement in Mexico while simultaneously trying to aid anti-Huerta revolutionary efforts.[99]

Wilson's resolve to avoid direct involvement in Mexico was put to the test two years later during the Punitive Expedition. The expedition ended in military and diplomatic failure, and the United States withdrew its forces under pressure from Carranza in 1917. For all that, as a Wilson biographer has noted, "Wilson resisted intense pressure to go to war in Mexico."[100] Even Wilson's decision to call up the National Guard in 1916 in response to the Villa threat did not incite conflict but instead likely helped to enforce a temporary peace on the border.[101] Wilson employed a "container" policy toward the border—he would keep Mexican problems in Mexico and try to indirectly influence the results of that country's revolution.[102] Such a tactic was at odds with the *Examiner*'s and *Times*' desire for an American invasion. Even as the border area stood as a contested site of constantly changing war aims and alliances, Wilson struck a middle ground between nonintervention and self-determination. Carranza, for instance, likely had a role in creating and trying to carry out the Plan of San Diego.[103] During the Punitive Expedition, U.S. intelligence forces, apparently with the full knowledge of General John Pershing, even recruited Japanese agents to assassinate Villa by poisoning his coffee.[104] Still, despite constant opportunities to engage with events in Mexico, Wilson limited direct U.S. involvement in the Mexican Revolution.[105]

Wilson formulated a similarly ambivalent foreign policy toward Japan. By 1917 Japan had extended its power over certain parts of China, and the United States was concerned that the Open Door policy would be violated.[106] Japan and the United States eventually signed the 1917 Lansing-Ishii Agreement, which recognized Japanese "special interests" in China but did not fully resolve the extant disagreements.[107] Lansing considered the preservation of the status quo to be "the most important to American interests."[108] Neither Wilson nor Lansing proposed military intervention in China or direct action against Japan. In fact, Wilson resisted direct intervention in the Pacific in the face of activist military advisors who urged him to go to war. When military leaders such as Leonard Wood and Admiral Bradley Fiske attempted to convince the president of the "probability" of Japan attacking the Philippines and Hawaii in 1913, Wilson angrily rejected their arguments and demanded that the Navy adhere to a "policy of nonprovocation" toward Japan.[109] (Of course, the *Examiner* and *Times* had also argued that Wilson should prepare America for an attack). The Office of Naval Intelligence continued to monitor the situation in Japan, and military officers repeatedly moved equipment and troops to U.S. holdings in the Pacific, sometimes without Wilson's knowledge, until the end of World War I.[110] Nevertheless, Wilson discounted any threat of a dual Japanese-Mexican menace, especially as it related to the mainland United States and potential targets such as the Port of Los Angeles.

There was, then, a monumental gap between Chandler and Hearst's view of the border and that of Lansing, Lind, and President Wilson. Two documents that Lind kept in his files illustrated this discrepancy. First, a brief, undated, and unsourced report in Lind's papers contained remarkable allegations of treasonous activity by Hearst and Chandler to unsettle the Carranza government:

> The most recent movement has been the sending of money, etc., to Villa. This is handled by Roy Offutt, of Los Angeles, who works actively with Harry Chandler, of the Los Angeles Times, who is in close touch with Hearst in the anti-Mexican work, in order to save the 3,000,000 acres of land in the northern part of Lower California which his father-in-law, General H. G. Otis, obtained on a faulty title under the diaz [*sic*] regime.[111]

Regardless of their veracity, the charges asserted in Lind's document linked the two major Angeleno media magnates as complicit in violating U.S. neutrality and nonintervention in Mexico.

The second document about Chandler and Hearst that Lind kept in his files was a speech dated October 9, 1916, titled "Peace and War." In the speech, Lind propagated a noninterventionist worldview explicitly at odds with that of Chandler, Hearst, and other interventionists. "They clamor for 'preparedness,'" Lind thundered. "They have tried to plunge this country into a hysteria of fear that we are going to be thrown into war with Germany or England or Japan." He went on to single out "American 'investors' in Mexico" as "millionaires" who use "every instrument they control—their money, their newspapers, their magazines . . . all their 'dark and devious ways'—to bring about 'intervention' . . . And all for what? Profits! Privilege profits!"[112] To Lind, preparedness was a manufactured crisis designed to benefit elite men. To Chandler and Hearst, who worked together discursively and perhaps even in their real-world actions, such hysteria was warranted.

The gulf between Woodrow Wilson's foreign policy prerogatives and those of Chandler and Hearst, therefore, indicate that Los Angeles's emerging, distinct identity as a western fortress was not just rhetorical. The two newspaper publishers collaborated to shape both a cultural movement and civic rhetoric devoted to preparedness and municipal infrastructure projects. They imagined a future in which Los Angeles would not be subservient to eastern interests but could follow its own path or even shape federal policy to benefit the Pacific Coast. Though Wilson resisted their efforts, the World War I era preparedness campaign initiated a process that would eventually enable efforts such as Japanese internment during World War II.

Preparedness Enables Progress

For Chandler and Hearst, the border needed to be fortified not only to make Los Angeles a safe, removed entity on the West Coast during the war but also to allow Los Angeles's industries to spread beyond metropolitan boundaries after the conflict. If Los Angeles were secure from external threats, the business community could promote expansion without fear that expansion might make the city vulnerable to attack. In late December 1916 the *Los Angeles Examiner* treated its readers to a "California Preparedness and Progress Edition" of the newspaper. On the first page, a man clad in a toga looked into the distance while leaning on a pillar inscribed with the word "Industries." The first article outlined the "epochal record of industrial achievement for Los Angeles and the environing metropolitan district." The ensuing pages documented various accomplishments such as expansion of the oil fields and the harbor district that made Los Angeles the "Metropolis of the West."[113] Boosterism did not just entail promoting the city without regard to the drawbacks of expansion. Instead, the *Examiner* and the *Times* advocated for a narrative of progress for Los Angeles based on a concept of transnational regionalism and secured through preparedness. The two newspapers told Angelenos to expect that their work during wartime would allow the city to become a dominant western command post in the decades to come. Preparedness was a gateway to progress.

Paradoxically, the *Times* and the *Examiner* grew more confident as Carranza gained more power in Mexico. In February 1917 the Mexican Constitutional Congress ratified the Mexican Constitution, and Carranza became president of Mexico in May of that year. On June 23, 1917, the *Times* confidently decreed that "the United States is Mexico's Friend." The *Times* assured its readers that Japan would have no power in Mexico: "Such an invasion of Mexico by the Orient, whether warlike or peaceful, will never happen, for . . . the United States, under its doctrine of pan-Americanism, will be called on to assist in solving the problems of life for all our southern republics."[114] Such a change in the newspaper's tone, from alarmist to sensible, was profound. The preparedness work the city had accomplished, according to the *Times'* narrative, had enabled pan-Americanism. In fact, the paper's assurances sound similar to those of Lind and Wilson—invasion rhetoric was no longer needed. In November 1917 the *Times* forecast Carranza's overthrow. "Mexico has been going steadily to the devil ever since Porfirio Diaz was exiled in 1910," the paper argued. "Now it is Carranza's turn to go, and no tears will be shed either north or south of the Rio Grande when he departs."[115] The *Times* envisioned a return to the economic profits gained under Díaz. Though Carranza would not leave office until 1920, the *Times* clearly felt more confident that the Mexican government would accept U.S. interests in the country and excise any militaristic rhetoric. Fears of invasion had largely dissipated.

The *Examiner* was even more exuberant than the *Times* about the future. In addition to the "California Preparedness and Progress Edition," the paper published multiple editorials in 1917 and 1918 detailing various vital projects to be undertaken in the city. In May 1917 it urged the citizens of Los Angeles to approve the harbor expansion plan in order to gain a U.S. naval base. "The LOGICAL place," the *Times* maintained, "because of available oil supply; because of good railway connections . . . because of the currents of commercial shipping that will flow in this direction—is Los Angeles."[116] The article cited the parts of the city most susceptible to invasion—the oil fields and the harbor—as crucial components of the Los Angeles's future. In November 1917 the *Examiner* called the proposed harbor a "Great Link with All the World's Commerce."[117] The port was now a protected economic asset.

A series of articles in the *Examiner* in 1918 illustrated the extent of the paper's entrepreneurial spirit. Titled "Los Angeles after the War: The Pacific Coast Industrial Center," the series outlined multiple ways in which Los Angeles could achieve that designation. Two of the articles—"Feeding the People" and "Bringing the World's Shopping Here"—especially demonstrated the newspapers' changing tenor from fearing borderlands invasion to invoking borderlands opportunity. "Feeding the People" demanded that Los Angeles create an industrial structure capable of employing one million people.[118] The *Examiner* then imagined that, after Los Angeles became an industrial hub, it would become a conduit for global "shopping": "Note the great foreign ports of Europe, Asia, Africa, Oceania, South America, and America and . . . note the comparatively shorter distance to many of these ports than the distance from New York or other Atlantic and Gulf ports."[119] In *Patria* the distance between Los Angeles and New York had necessitated preparedness and propagating an image of the government as a removed, uncaring foil. After the war, the same distance would guarantee economic progress. According to the papers, this vision of free trade was only possible if Los Angeles fortified its internal borders in order to grow from fortress to global metropolis.

Two editorial cartoons published by the *Examiner* provide a fitting summation of the discursive transition in both papers. In one, Uncle Sam looks up from Washington at a man and a woman in the sky who stand over the City of Los Angeles. The woman, shown in figure 6, holds up a lamp that lights the land in California. Below them, an oil derrick burns smoke onto Baja California in Mexico, which is inlaid with the word "Progress."

In the great forward movement along the paths of intellectual and material achievement the men and the women of Southern California challenge the admiration of the whole country

FIG. 6. This cartoon, which linked preparedness to progress, also illustrates a prevalent contemporary narrative of Angeleno exceptionalism. *Los Angeles Examiner*, December 27, 1916.

The woman, akin to a modern Lady Liberty or an updated version of the "progress" figure in John Gast's 1872 painting "American Progress," shifts the standard narrative of American east-to-west development. The cartoon's caption reads, "In the great forward movement along the paths of intellectual and material achievement the men and the women of Southern California challenge the admiration of the whole country."[120] According to the cartoon, with appropriate preparedness Los Angeles would act as a city upon a hill for the rest of the United States and extend its light of progress to Mexico. In a sense, then, Lind was correct in his assessment that the basis for preparedness was "Profits! Privilege profits!"

In June 1917 the *Examiner* crowed that "Southern California Is Calm—Confident—Patriotic" because the paper had helped to build up its "splendid spirit" amid war. A cartoon accompanying the article, figure 7, shows a muscular hand holding a shield up to protect the City of Los Angeles, replete with stacks of large coins and dollar signs in its streets, against ghoulish "Calamity Howlers" attacking the region from beyond its borders. Inlaid on the shield are the words "Editorials," "Special News Articles," and "Sanity."[121] This evocative image demonstrates the many ways in which border rhetoric could be used. The *Examiner*, after all, was itself a "howler" throughout much of the World War I era. After the war, when Los Angeles's borders were safe, the city might again pursue profits.

The two cartoons were prescient, as Los Angeles city leaders pursued a broader economic relationship with Mexico, and the world, almost immediately after World War I. In 1920 Álvaro Obregón forced Carranza out of power and tried to gain American investment by reassuring businesses that the economic climate in Mexico would be favorable to their interests. In 1923 Obregón signed the Bucareli Treaty, which essentially annulled article 27, the land reform section, of the Mexican Constitution. The *Examiner* had called for similar legislation five years previously, arguing that Carranza's decree about land reform "practically confiscates the oil land holdings of British and American citizens in Mexico and gives to the Kaiser more military assistance than if Mexico were able to send him a million dollars."[122] Obregón's policies also pleased the *Times*—although its writers believed that "Uncle Sam could have no confidence in Carranza," they urged the United States to "extend a helping hand to Obregón with the assurance that it will be received in good faith."[123] In December 1920 the *Times* recommended a future partnership between Southern California and Mexico for the development of the latter's natural resources, on the basis of "fair co-operation."[124] As in the *Examiner*'s cartoon, the *Times* imagined that Los Angeles could spark Mexican development.

After Obregón's ascension to the presidency, Chandler continued to try to influence Angeleno and national policy toward Mexico. In February

HOW A CRITICAL SITUATION WAS CHANGED INTO SAFETY

Southern California Is Calm —Confident —Patriotic

The Advantage of Printing Uncensored News

FIG. 7. In 1917 the *Examiner* declared that it would defend Los Angeles from "calamity howlers," a change from its previous policy of outlining the city's vulnerabilities. *Los Angeles Examiner*, June 17, 1917.

1922 he appeared at a meeting of the board of directors of the Los Angeles Chamber of Commerce and urged it to pass a resolution favoring U.S. recognition of Obregón's government.[125] In March the chamber formally passed a resolution "which was the result of the committee's deliberations and its conference with Mr. Harry Chandler." The resolution favored policies similar to those urged by the *Times* during the previous decade. "Whereas the people of Southern California and of other territory adjacent to the Mexican border realize fully the necessity and desirability for friendly and intimate trade . . . with the people of the Mexican Republic," the resolution proclaimed, "THEREFORE BE IT RESOLVED that the Los Angeles Chamber of Commerce believes that the time is now opportune . . . [to] bring about the recognition of the Republic of Mexico by our government."[126] After the fortress had been secured, Los Angeles elites could again look abroad for economic gain.

More complicated, Los Angeles's relationship with Japan played out over a longer chronology. In 1920 California was in the process of passing a new

Alien Land Law, which strengthened the 1913 law and prevented Japanese immigrants from owning land. Those who supported these draconian provisions hoped that they might eventually stop Japanese immigration altogether.[127] Montaville Flowers, a nativist political commentator who resided in Los Angeles, developed the logic behind postwar anti-Japanese sentiment in his 1918 volume *The Japanese Conquest of American Opinion*. "'Peace hath her victories no less reknown'd than war,'" Flowers opened his monograph, quoting the English poet John Milton. "Japan is now trying to secure possession of that weapon."[128] In Flowers's view, Japan would deploy its weapons toward a variety of harmful aims including "the removal of restrictions on immigration; the rights of naturalization, American citizenship, and of intermarriage with the white race; the overthrow of all anti-Asiatic land legislation in the Western states; the rapid acquisition of this land."[129] Those aims, which Flowers intended to combat, echoed wartime fears and the anxiety central to the plot of *Patria*. According to Flowers, western territory and Anglo manhood would be forcibly overtaken by virile Japanese settlers. However, Flowers found greater threat in surreptitious Japanese propaganda than in the prospect of a dual Japanese-Mexican military invasion. *The Japanese Conquest of American Opinion* paralleled more traditional Yellow Peril fears of unmitigated immigration and declining American job prospects. Though contemporary commentators were much less likely to proclaim the importance of future economic ties with Japan, wartime preparedness had moderated the fears central to *Patria*.

"Progress" in Mexico did not accompany "progress" in Japan, but Chandler's and Hearst's rhetorical work during wartime influenced the postwar narrative regarding Los Angeles's modernity. The two magnates' efforts suggest that in Los Angeles the borderlands concept was malleable, especially in the hands of elites who were constantly on the move. Rather than broadcasting their personal fears, the two men's newspapers frequently used Los Angeles as an experimental propaganda zone. The speed and ease with which the *Examiner* and *Times* shifted their discourse indicates the broad way in which borderlands rhetoric might be invoked over time to advocate new forms of expansion or control over other populations.

The World War I period crystallized the tension between expansion and retrenchment that had played out in discussions of the port and the aviation meet. The location of Los Angeles was a vital component of the policies proposed by the *Times* and the *Examiner*. The newspapers consistently argued that Los Angeles's history was inextricable from the transnational history of Southern California: the city's distinct geographical position at the confluence of multiple borders required that Angelenos recognize both the potential gains that might be achieved through economic relationships with Japan and Mexico and the vulnerabilities that might be unearthed in pursuit of them.

If city elites chose to pursue broader connections, contemporary Los Angeles provided significant opportunities for further development. By 1920 Los Angeles would grow substantially, to a population of about 576,000, making it the tenth largest city in the United States.[130] But Los Angeles was still a developing town, even a frontier town, its success sometimes more aspirational than real. One 1916 *New York Times* article seemed surprised by "Lower California's Unusual Charms." "The influx of tourists from the East to Southern California this year is finding in Los Angeles and Southern California even more pleasures than in former years," the article reported, singling out "a vast improvement in city and country scenic beauty, accommodations, and attractive investments."[131] Eastern power brokers, both the federal government and prominent media outlets, did not take Los Angeles particularly seriously as a developing metropolis. To them, Los Angeles seemed to be a parochial backwater. Still, Chandler and Hearst believed that wartime preparedness had laid the ground for the city's impressive future. Indeed, industrial progress, commercial speculation, and pervasive optimism characterized Los Angeles throughout the 1920s. The discourse of fear propagated by the *Examiner* and the *Times* contributed to modernist boosterism and aided postwar economic expansion.

SNAPSHOT

LOS ANGELES, 1920

ON JANUARY 1, 1920, AT THE DAWN OF A NEW DECADE, THE *TIMES* expressed glowing optimism about the city's future. "Growth in population, wealth and production, further development of resources and the establishment of new industrial and agricultural enterprises made the year 1919 one of the greatest in the history of the Southwest," began one multipage article on January 1, 1920. "The Great Southwest . . . is a tremendous national asset, whose wonderful resources have even yet been only lightly drawn upon."[1] Six months later, a poem published in the *Times* referred to Los Angeles as a "Radiant queen . . . In a dreamland of beauty, an empire of good."[2] "There isn't a city in America where so many big things are in sight as are in sight here," yet another editorial, titled "The City of Wonder," claimed. "There isn't another city on the map in which a dollar would rather venture."[3] "The City of Wonder" description proved to be durable. "Los Angeles . . . the Wonder City of the United States is the most talked of city on the continent," concluded *Los Angeles Today*, a publication of the Los Angeles Chamber of Commerce, in 1922. "Indeed, its fame has spread all over the world."[4]

The real estate panic of 1890 had caught Los Angeles at a crossroads, but the end of World War I solidified the city's place as a nascent American metropolis. The 1920 census determined that Los Angeles's population was 576,673, which made it the tenth largest city in the United States and the biggest city west of St. Louis.[5] The population growth accompanied an increase in the city's square mileage. In 1900 Los Angeles encompassed forty-three square miles. By 1910—after adding, in addition to several smaller tracts, 34 square miles in the 1909 annexation of San Pedro and Wilmington communities and 15 square miles when the city consolidated with Hollywood and East Hollywood in February 1910—Los Angeles had more than doubled to 101 square miles. By 1920, thanks in large part to the city's 1915 consolidation with the San Fernando Valley, 170 square miles, Los Angeles contained 364 square miles of territory.[6] If city boundaries had once enclosed the original downtown pueblo area and a few small surrounding tracts, by that same year Los Angeles sprawled twenty miles inland to the northeast, twenty miles west to various ocean communities, and twenty-five miles southwest to San Pedro and Wilmington.[7] Throughout, Los Angeles remained a largely white city. The 1920 census identified 94.8 percent of Angelenos as "white," 2.7 percent as "black," and 2.4 percent as "other."[8]

As it grew, Los Angeles lured two new industries: motion pictures and oil. In 1923 the erection and immediate popularity of the famous Hollywood sign signaled that the motion picture industry ran through Southern California. By 1930 total capital invested in major motion picture companies would reach $850 million.[9] Early films set in Los Angeles broadcast a specific vision of the city to the world. The satirical 1923 *Souls for Sale*, for instance, told the tale of Remember Steddon, a rural farm girl who jumps off a train to escape a murder attempt by her new husband. Early in the film, a movie director discovers the stranded Steddon in a California desert and takes her to Los Angeles to recuperate. She eventually gets a role in one of the director's films, but the man turns out to be just as dangerous as Steddon's ex-husband. In the climactic scene, the director endangers his actors by burning a circus tent and using wind machines to send the flames higher, but Steddon survives and completes her performance.[10] *Souls for Sale* portrayed Los Angeles as a place that did not take itself too seriously, one that encouraged freedom and ambition.

Oil shipping and production also boomed in the area. During the first few years of the 1920s, discoveries in Newport Beach, Huntington Beach, and Long Beach to the south, and Inglewood to the west made Los Angeles the Saudi Arabia of its time.[11] "Oil in quantities undreamed has rewarded the efforts of the prospectors," commented the *Times* in 1921.[12] In 1923 Los Angeles's three major oil fields constituted 80 percent of California's oil production.[13] The perceived environmental and social degradation fostered by the oil industry's growth so upset novelist and social activist Upton Sinclair that he published *Oil!* in 1926. Loosely based on the life of Southern California oil entrepreneur Edward L. Doheny, the novel detailed the rise and fall of James Arnold Ross Jr.[14] "Not since the world began had there been men of power equal to this," remarks Ross's son early on in the novel. "And Dad was one of them."[15]

The career of the real-life Doheny serves as an excellent illustration of how a new class of elites amassed control of local growth industries from 1900 to 1920. By 1920 traditional elite occupations—publishing, finance, and real estate, among them—were dominated by an "Old Guard" of men who had accrued significant wealth in the early twentieth century and then passed it on to their sons or in-laws, such as the Otis to Chandler transition at the *Times*. The newer growth industries, especially motion pictures and oil, remained open to people who were not born into wealth.[16] Upward mobility in growth industries would continue to characterize Los Angeles for the next few decades. "Successive stages of growth," Jaher argued, "brought the insurgence of new elites."[17] These men found fortune in Los Angeles but did not necessarily tie their prospects to municipal progress. "Insurgency," in fact, benefited from and further developed Los Angeles's connections to transcontinental and transnational capital flows.

Doheny had limited success before he arrived in Los Angeles. Born in Fond du Lac, Wisconsin, in 1856, Doheny graduated high school at age fifteen and found work with the United States Geological Survey. In his position Doheny traveled from Kansas to the Dakotas before leaving government work to prospect for gold in the region in 1875. Failing to make his fortune in gold, Doheny traveled south to New Mexico, where he eventually left prospecting work, passed the bar examination, and practiced law for a year in 1889. In 1890 Doheny moved with his first wife to Southern California, where he again failed in a gold-prospecting venture that this time left him penniless at age thirty-four. Not until 1892, at age thirty-six, did Doheny begin to make his fortune when he drilled for and found oil on a small plot of land he had bought near downtown Los Angeles. Over the next four years, he added another eighty-one wells throughout Southern California to his growing empire. Combined, they produced 350,000 barrels of oil. In the mid-1890s, in a deft, farsighted move, Doheny vastly increased oil demand when he convinced the Atchison, Topeka, and Santa Fe Railroad to switch its fuel source from coal to his oil.[18] By the twentieth century Doheny had a firm grasp on the oil industry in Southern California, investments that would only grow more profitable in the age of automobiles. He continued to develop oil fields in Southern California and added major international properties to his portfolio. Doheny's Pan American Petroleum and Transport Company drilled one of the most productive wells in the world in Tampico, Mexico, and developed fields in Columbia and Venezuela. By 1920 Pan American was the largest oil company in America.[19] Doheny's personal life too was based in Los Angeles and connected to points beyond. In the early 1900s he bought a mansion in Chester Place, a gated community near the University of Southern California. Doheny eventually donated over $1 million for the university to build a library in honor of his deceased son. At the same time, he owned a home in Manhattan and an enormous yacht named *Casiana* that traversed the Caribbean and Atlantic Oceans; his club affiliations included memberships in the Atlantic Yacht Club of Brooklyn, the Columbia Yacht Club of New York, and the New York Automobile Club.[20]

Unlike previous Angeleno elites—men such as Ozro Childs, John G. Downey, and even Otis—who tied their fortunes to Los Angeles's municipal development, Doheny tied his to a specific, modern commodity that he might extract from and sell in Southern California. Doheny clearly sensed the importance of Southern California extractive sites and markets. In 1925 he wrote a guest column for the *Times* on "The Perpetuity of Our Vast Petroleum Yield." In the future, Doheny encouraged readers to continue to use oil in large quantities. "I consider California secure in relying on its present source of fuel for industrial and automobile purposes for generations to come," he concluded.[21] When he died, in 1935, Doheny left an estimated $100 million fortune gained mostly through oil, a sum that had purportedly been much higher before the Great Depression.[22] In its 1935 obituary the *Times* lauded Doheny for his devotion to oil. "The fortune he himself amassed is secondary to the service he performed for the people of California," eulogized the paper, "in helping to demonstrate and realize upon the enormous possibilities for adding to the resources of the State in their vast underground reservoirs of what today is the life blood of all nations."[23] Doheny was an Angeleno, but he was a forward-looking, modern figure who did not limit himself to opportunities based in the city. Rather, he sensed that Los Angeles would grow in ways that could increase his own fortune and power.

To ensure such growth, city boosters sought to continue developing the infrastructure necessary to sustain exponential growth. "In its position of metropolis of all the West . . . Los Angeles must keep constantly alert," the *Times* proclaimed in 1920, echoing World War I–era preparedness rhetoric. "Provision for a future of magnified demands is imperative."[24] In 1890 Otis's *Times* had lamented that Los Angeles was not "fortunately located at points where railroad and deep-water ocean traffic meet."[25] By 1920 the city was a transcontinental and global hub. Two major rail stations—La Grande Station, the home of the Atchison, Topeka, and Santa Fe Railroad and the Union Pacific Railroad; and Central Station, home of the Southern Pacific Railroad—served travelers from across the United States.[26] In 1911 Los Angeles's various urban and interurban electric railways merged and became the Pacific Electric Railway Company. The largest electric railway system in the world, the Pacific Electric ran over more than one thousand miles of track inside the city and to points beyond, such as San Pedro, Redondo Beach, and Santa Monica.[27] After the Panama Canal opened in 1914, the Port of Los Angeles had also grown quickly. A 1921 editorial described in glowing terms how "each day ships laden with the products of the world steam into port either from the Panama Canal and the south [or] from the treasure laden lands of the Orient."[28]

Finally, the *Times* urged the city to commit to improving driving conditions in Los Angeles County. After Henry Ford's moving assembly line began production in 1913, Angelenos were quick to embrace the automobile. In 1920 one *Times* article promoted Los Angeles and its liberating car culture through Lura Anson, a "charming society girl," and minor actress. "Miss Lura Anson Thinks a Buick and Los Angeles Is Hard Combination to Beat," announced the headline. "The motor car has given the California girl the distinction of being the leader of all her sisters in outdoor activities," the article continued. "With her auto she goes to the golf links, the beach, or over difficult roads to the mountain camps with a freedom and independence that have made her wholly self-reliant. The automobile is the modern emancipator."[29] Though it might be an "emancipator," the driving culture also furthered traditional gender norms—in such depictions, upper-class women, economically supported by men, were free to embrace a life of leisure in Southern California. As they drove more often, many Angelenos demanded a comprehensive road improvement program. "I believe the one outstanding disgrace of Los Angeles is the condition of its streets," wrote one outraged citizen to the *Times* in 1922. "No more can Angelenos brag of their good roads."[30] The problem certainly had not escaped political leadership. In a 1919 *Times* article, Jonathan Dodge, chairman of the Los Angeles County Board of Supervisors, decried the state of Los Angeles County's thirty-five-hundred-mile road system, only sixty miles of which were concrete pavement roads.[31] Infrastructure advocates had some success. Voters passed county highway construction bond issues of $25 million in 1915 and $40 million in 1919.[32] A comprehensive overhaul to the city's road system, however, would prove more elusive in the years ahead.[33]

In addition to transportation networks, a friendly labor market, boosters felt, would secure Los Angeles's place as a nascent industrial city. By 1910 Los Angeles had gained some acclaim as the United States' preeminent anti-union, "open shop" city, a reputation many elites wished to preserve through media activism and extralegal violence. Open shop advocates especially detested the International Workers of the World (IWW) because the union had some success organizing dockworkers at the Port of Los Angeles.[34] In the 1910s dock workers struck multiple times in San Pedro, with and without the help of the IWW. In 1912 twenty-five "wobblies" even briefly shut down the harbor before their strike collapsed.[35] The federal effort to stamp out the IWW and other radical labor unions during World War I by using the 1917 Espionage Act curtailed labor actions in San Pedro, but local elites and city authorities did not succeed in eradicating pro-labor sentiments in San Pedro entirely.[36] After World War I, the IWW continued to try to achieve better working conditions for harbor laborers. The *Times* decried labor stoppages in June 1919 and November 1919, though authorities quickly broke both strikes.[37] "Thousands of men are on strike at the shipyards," the newspaper commented in June. "The radical elements of the . . . I.W.W . . . have opened their campaign for the reduction of this citadel of industrial freedom."[38]

By 1920 open shop advocates were ready to stamp out union activity in San Pedro using any means possible, and the confrontations came to a head in 1923. On April 25 the San Pedro IWW chapter sparked a national walkout of dockworkers opposed to the 1919 California Criminal Syndicalism Act and its utilization against labor unions, especially against members of the IWW. On May 1, 1923, the chapter issued a strike call, which seven hundred workers followed. Over the next ten days thousands more people began to attend the strikers' mass meetings, and their picket lines eventually closed the port to daily business. Alarmed by the national attention the strike had gained, city leaders dispatched hundreds of policemen to secure the docks and arrest prominent leaders. Damaged by the leadership vacuum and the strength of the city's response, the strike collapsed by the end of May. Thereafter, the Los Angeles police, the press, armed vigilantes, and the KKK joined forces to expel the IWW from San Pedro; by the end of 1925, this goal had been achieved.[39] For its part, the *Times* placed anti-union sentiment at the heart of Los Angeles's rise. "Los Angeles has achieved with justice the repute of being the freest city in the freest land under the sun," commented the paper in August 1920. "Free labor and labor that would be free gravitates to Los Angeles from every corner of America. Union labor and those that stand for it . . . naturally seek San Francisco."[40]

Los Angeles elites, then, seemed to have little to fear in the decades to come. "The industries that we have constitute a solid foundation for further growth," claimed the *Times* in 1919. "Los Angeles is well on the way to manufacturing supremacy."[41] The city's demographic and physical growth seemed to ensure direct prosperity for those wisely invested in growth sectors and indirect prosperity for anyone who might benefit from Los Angeles's role as a growing commercial hub. New industries, boosters felt, would flock to the city, drawn by its friendly labor conditions and comprehensive transportation system. Migrants would follow the industries. The next twenty years, however, would demand answers to two major questions. First, could Los Angeles provide for even greater growth, reaching a population of a million and beyond? Second, was growth always a good thing? A new set of elites, many of whom occupied positions outside of traditional power structures, would try to answer these questions and further secure Los Angeles's place as a growing metropolis.

"VIRTUALLY ON THE EDGE OF A DESERT"

IN HINDSIGHT, LOS ANGELES SEEMS TO HAVE GROWN EASILY DURING the 1920s.[1] By 1930 the population had doubled from 576,673 to 1,238,048, a figure that made Los Angeles the fifth largest city in the United States and the first Western city to have a population larger than 1 million.[2] By the end of the 1920s Los Angeles County made up almost 39 percent of the entire population of California.[3] Spreading northward and southward, the city had annexed forty-five communities over the preceding ten years, totaling eighty square miles of territory.[4] As the 1930s began the *Los Angeles Times* reflected on the great progress the city had made over the previous decade. In the first two days of 1930, the newspaper repeatedly boasted of the city's great success in four areas: agriculture, the attraction of new residents, general economic activity, and the harbor.[5] Los Angeles's demographic changes especially excited one man, the author Edgar Lloyd Hampton, whose article "The Great Migration: And Where It Will Lead" filled three full sheets of the paper. He singled out internal migration's impact on Los Angeles industry and infrastructure. "The result of this concentrated movement," he wrote, "is clearly apparent in the figures. The factory era began in 1900 with an output of $15,000. By 1920 this yield had reached $788,652,885. In 1923 it passed the billion-dollar mark and has continued steadily upward . . . [now] the yearly manufactured product exceeds $1,300,000,000." Hampton saw only future success, driven by "the movement of eager, restless people . . . driving persistently, increasingly, onward toward the west."[6]

Expansion, however, had severely challenged the city in ways seemingly forgotten by boosters such as Hampton as the 1920s ended. Most notably, city leaders had struggled to secure Los Angeles's future water and power supply. In 1910 the completion of the Los Angeles Aqueduct, city boosters felt, signaled the end of water shortages. During the fight over the aqueduct, returning to the common themes of its civic rhetoric, the *Times* had preached a constant fear of drought in its pages and assured its readers that the aqueduct would be vital for the city's future.[7] The end product, which used $26 million in public bonds, carried water over two hundred miles from the agricultural region of the Owens Valley to Los Angeles. By 1920 the Los Angeles Department of Water and Power (DWP), led by metropolitan water pioneer William Mulholland, was already pursuing additional water sources in the Owens Valley and further afield.[8] In 1926, even as Owens Valley farmers rioted against the theft of their water supply, Mulholland spoke at a waterworks convention about the "Proposed Aqueduct from the Colorado River," part of the Boulder Dam project. He spent much of the speech making Los Angeles's case for the project. Mulholland noted the city's issues stemmed from its location. "The city of Los Angeles is virtually on the edge of a desert," he argued. "You may go in any direction from the city . . . and you will find the desert before you go very far;—the arid, grinning desert."[9] Therefore, Mulholland argued, the city needed the Boulder Dam (later renamed the Hoover Dam when work began in 1930); it could not exist any longer on the "old water supply," especially not with the desert at its doorstep.[10] Water extraction from other areas, Mulholland felt, could secure Los Angeles's future in the midst of an inhospitable location.

Mulholland's efforts culminated in Los Angeles's victory over Owens Valley farmers in the California Water Wars, the triumphant completion of the Boulder Dam, and the calamitous failure of the St. Francis Dam, part of the Los Angeles Aqueduct system, which killed over four hundred people when it ruptured in 1928.[11] The growing city, therefore, presented fundamental challenges to those who wished to ensure a prosperous future for Los Angeles. With connections, boosters such as Mulholland argued, Los Angeles might endlessly grow. Without such connections, harmful as they might be to extractive sites such as the Owens Valley, Los Angeles might disappear. The DWP and its media allies hid their self-interests behind a comprehensive depiction of Los Angeles as threatened by its environment, necessitating a masculine taming of the wilderness. Unlike World War I, the solution was not to create a fortress. Instead, boosters tried to harness public activism and federal funding to extend Los Angeles's aqua-imperial tentacles hundreds of miles to the north and to the east.[12] The contested 1920s exposed the legacies of Los Angeles's thirty-year rise. One such battle—the World War I–era fight for preparedness—had ended in triumph, with a city prepared to grasp the opportunities presented by the 1920s. The next—how to control growth and its effects—would consume elite actors for the next two decades.

William Mulholland: Water Booster Extraordinaire

Today, William Mulholland is a controversial figure.[13] Is Mulholland perhaps Noah Cross, the villain of the 1974 film *Chinatown*, head of a vast conspiracy to steal water rights for the city of Los Angeles? Or is he Hollis Mulwray from the same film, the dedicated civil servant undone by the actions of others? Or even Claude Mulvihill—the policeman in *Chinatown* who acts as the muscle behind elite actions?[14] For much of his life in Los Angeles, though, Mulholland was peerless, the creator god who gave continued life to Los Angeles through his water projects. "Be it resolved . . . that the memory of our chief William Mulholland be forever preserved, which will be done by his deeds and achievements in . . . pioneering the development of the city of Los Angeles," read a resolution of the Los Angles Water and Power Employees' Association after Mulholland's death in July 1935.[15]

Like so many others, Mulholland followed a migrant's path to Los Angeles, but his journey was more disjointed and itinerant than most.[16] Born in Belfast, Ireland, in 1855, the fourth child of Hugh and Ellen Mulholland, Mulholland spent much of his life on or around water. Mulholland's mother died when he was seven, and, after his remarried father severely beat him for receiving low grades at age fifteen, Mulholland ran away and enlisted in naval service. In 1874, after four years at sea, Mulholland stepped ashore in New York City. He found work on shipping vessels in the Great Lakes, in a timber camp in Michigan, and with a transient wagon team that traveled the Midwest fixing clocks and other mechanical appliances. In 1876 William settled in Pittsburgh with his brother Hugh, who had also emigrated from Ireland. There, they joined an uncle, who had previously moved to America, and his family. A tuberculosis outbreak forced the entire family to decamp for California just two years later. Lacking the funds for the voyage, Hugh and William tried to stow away on a ship, but they were caught and ejected from the vessel near Panama. Similar to Collis Huntington, Mulholland encountered some difficulties in crossing the Isthmus of Panama. The brothers eventually hiked the fifty miles across the isthmus and then signed up to work on a ship headed for Mexico. From there, the two men took another job aboard a ship to San Francisco. They finally traveled south to Los Angeles in 1877. "It was 1877 when William Mulholland rode into Los Angeles on horseback," detailed a 1939 pamphlet published by the DWP. "The man who later was to be accorded nationwide recognition for his engineering genius started his career as a common laborer."[17]

Mulholland quickly became inextricable from the major moments in Los Angeles's water history. Having decided within a month of landing in the city that frontier Los Angeles was not the place for him, Mulholland set forth for San Pedro to find a ship out of the harbor. On his way, he met Manuel Dominguez, the grandson of a major Spanish land grantee, who asked him to help him dig a well on the property. The water business interested Mulholland. "The first well I worked on changed the whole course of my life," he recalled in one 1925 profile that appeared in the *Western Pipe and Steel News*. "Right there I decided to become an engineer."[18] In the 1870s, Angelenos received their water from zanjas, a system of open ditches that ferried water from the Los Angeles River to houses and agricultural fields. After a brief period prospecting in Arizona with Hugh, William returned to Los Angeles and took an apprenticeship as a deputy zanjero, essentially a ditch tender, under Fred Eaton, who ran the Los Angeles City Water Company (LACWC), a private, for-profit corporation that had gained a controversial, and cheap, thirty-year lease on Los Angeles's water rights in 1868.

Over the next decade, Mulholland moved up the ranks of the LACWC and became its superintendent in 1886 when Eaton left to become the head engineer for the City of Los Angeles. In 1890 Mulholland, then thirty-five years of age, married Lillie Ferguson, fourteen years his junior. The couple moved to a home on Sixth and Cumming Streets in Boyle Heights, near downtown Los Angeles and just south of the University of Southern California. The marriage seems to have been a happy one. William and Lillie had seven children together before Lillie's premature death of cancer in 1915.[19] In 1920, befitting his increasing status and wealth, Mulholland moved his family five miles west to a large home on Saint Andrews Place valued at $30,000 in 1930.[20] Mulholland also owned a six-hundred-acre ranch in the San Fernando Valley, just northeast of the city, a massive property for a public servant.[21] The water pioneer certainly drew a large salary. In 1909 the city gave Mulholland a raise to $15,000, an hourly rate over ten times greater than that of relatively highly paid unionized cement finishers in the city.[22] Mulholland was less a public servant and more a member of the elite who happened to work in a public industry.

Mulholland's driven nature propelled many of Los Angeles's major water initiatives. In his writings and public statements, he made a compelling case for Los Angeles's water future and the vital necessity of his department's work. At the conclusion of World War I, Mulholland asked the Board of Public Service Commissioners, which governed the DWP, to press on with new water projects. "The time has arrived . . . when the needs of the works, due to the growth and development of the City, will require that little or no attention be paid to increased costs," he wrote. "The rapid growth of the City will not brook any suspension of the expansion of the Water Works."[23] In a 1920 article he authored for *Public Service*, the monthly bulletin of the Los Angeles Department of Public Service, Mulholland further argued that water engineers needed to plan for exponential growth. "Many of our prominent and enterprising citizens in the past have attempted predictions as to the City's future growth," he wrote, but "there is not a single instance . . . in which they have not been surpassed in realization."[24]

In the early twentieth century, Mulholland embarked on the project that would in many ways define his life. City officials, led by then-mayor

Fred Eaton, opted out of the contract with the LACWC in 1898 and began sustained efforts to take public control of the Los Angeles River's water supply. In 1901, after three years of acrimonious litigation, the city agreed to buy the waterworks from the LACWC company for $2 million, supported by issuing public bonds.[25] Mulholland acted as a negotiator between the city and LACWC and an expert witness in the many legal hearings held on the value of the LACWC's holdings. The city rewarded Mulholland with the head superintendent job for the newly formed DWP in 1902. Mulholland then set his sights on a much larger project—securing municipal water from a more stable source than the flood-prone Los Angeles River. He settled on the Owens River, far to the north and east of the city, between the Death Valley and Sequoia National Parks. There, he planned to build an aqueduct for Los Angeles.

The Imperial Aqueduct

The story of the Los Angeles Aqueduct has been told and retold, litigated and relitigated, at length in the historiography of the city. In each version, Mulholland emerges as a single-minded planner, relentlessly devoted to providing water for future Angelenos.[26] Mulholland sensed that Los Angeles would grow a great deal in coming decades and launched a preemptive plan to solve a future problem, subsuming naked self-interest into a narrative about the city's survival. In 1912 Mulholland wrote a pro-aqueduct editorial for *Real Estate News*. "Water in this fever region," he wrote, "is the magic fluid with which unremitting and untiring Labor has moistened the desert and out of the desert a garden has come forth."[27] The moral debate about the aqueduct should not obscure just how efficiently Mulholland completed such a major project.[28] From 1902 to 1905, Mulholland and Eaton, aided by Federal Bureau of Reclamation agent Joseph B. Lippincott, bought up water rights and land around the Owens Valley. In 1905 Angelenos approved a $1.5 million bond measure to begin further land acquisition in the Owens Valley and to plan construction. Two years later, voters approved a much larger $24.5 million bond issue to finance construction of the aqueduct, and Mulholland's crews began their monumental work. From 1907 to 1913, a crew of at times as many as

6,000 men built 215 miles of cement aqueduct, including over 50 miles of tunnels, a structure that transported water by gravity alone, one of the great engineering accomplishments of the twentieth century. "Under [Mulholland's] leadership an army of 5,000 men labored for five years so that the Los Angeles of today could be possible," a 1939 pamphlet commented. "He successfully completed within the original time and cost estimates the most difficult engineering project undertaken by any American city up to that time."[29] The builders overcame local political turmoil, including an investigation into allegations of corruption and mismanagement. In 1908 Mulholland called preliminary work on the project "appalling in its magnitude and expense."[30] Still, when Mulholland's crews completed their labor on November 5, 1913, the city hosted a celebration in the San Fernando Valley. Mulholland opened the gate of the aqueduct for the first time, the Catalina Military Band played the "Star Spangled Banner," and the Board of Public Works officially transferred the aqueduct to the Public Service Commission.[31]

As in many other moments in Los Angeles's history, federal power became vital to the aqueduct's development. When Owens Valley farmers realized the scope of the purchases, they began legal action against the city, arguing that city officials hid their true identities and did not reveal the extent of the water rights they planned to take; they further pressured federal officials to complete a proposed reclamation project in the Owens Valley. The Owens Valley farmers' case reached the executive branch, where a cadre of federal advisors, sympathetic to the Los Angeles cause, convinced Theodore Roosevelt to side with Los Angeles.[32] Federal power had again sustained Los Angeles's growth; the anti-Washington "borderlands fortress" did not last for long.

Many Los Angeles elites benefited from Mulholland's work, sometimes to the detriment of other localities. Lippincott became assistant chief engineer of the Los Angeles Aqueduct. Eaton bought some Owens Valley land for himself, hoping to sell it back to the city at a later date for a large profit. A syndicate of speculators, led by some of the most prolific businessmen in the city's early history—streetcar and land developer Moses Sherman, Henry Huntington, Otis, and Chandler—who knew about the project in advance, irrigated a planned real estate development in the San Fernando Valley and made a huge profit.[33] "Mr. J .B. Lippincott . . . in collusion with Los Angeles politicians and financiers, conspired to destroy the Owens Valley project in favor of a big land promotion scheme in San Fernando Valley," alleged the *Gridiron*, an Owens Valley–allied newspaper based in Los Angeles, in 1931.[34] Los Angeles annexed much of the San Fernando Valley in 1915, adding to the wealthy burgeoning metropolis. Even San Fernando Valley farmers eventually protested the deal.[35]

Time after time, Angeleno boosters linked the aqueduct's completion to a prosperous future. During the fight to secure the 1905 bond measure, the *Times* had preached a fear of drought in its pages and assured its readers that the aqueduct would be vital for the city's future.[36] "STUPENDOUS AQUEDUCT PROJECT WILL MAKE LOS ANGELES GREAT" announced a typical headline in June 1907.[37] "The Water Is Coming," assured the paper two months later. "When Owens River flows into the San Fernando Valley reservoirs, there will be water for Los Angeles and all of her neighbors."[38] In 1906 Mulholland tried to assure W. J. Washburn, the president of the Los Angeles Chamber of Commerce, that water would never again be an issue after the aqueduct was completed. "I feel confident . . . that the water supply of the City will not become inadequate in advance of the completion of the Owens River Conduit, after which our water troubles, let us hope, will be settled for all time," Mulholland wrote.[39]

Thereafter, the DWP adeptly linked the aqueduct to Los Angeles's progress at every turn. Mostly, the department detailed its triumphs over an unforgiving environment. "The snow waters from the High Sierras, brought to our city by the Aqueduct, have builded [*sic*] Los Angeles into the metropolis of the West," wrote Mulholland in 1925. "Without Aqueduct water this amazing growth would have been impossible."[40] Angelenos had based conceptions of the city's exceptionalism on its growth—the shocking idea that a city of midwestern transplants located in a semiarid climate with no natural harbor might become the urban power of the West Coast. Such conceptions were also gendered—Los Angeles's victory over its environment proved the prowess of its masculine ideals. The aqueduct was a crucial step on that path. Whether or not the city needed the water in 1905 was immaterial. City leaders always imagined a time when the water *would be* needed. The "Great Migration" to Los Angeles seemed to be the city's destiny.

After he completed the aqueduct, such logic led Mulholland to quickly set his eyes on further water projects. The aqueduct began to provide the city with electricity in 1917, when the DWP built its first hydroelectric power plant forty miles northeast of downtown Los Angeles. In 1920 the city added a second power plant. Beginning in the early 1920s, a little over five years after the completion of a project meant to provide water for generations, Mulholland began to warn city leaders of Los Angeles's susceptibility to drought. "With the continued rapid growth of the City," he related in his 1922 annual report, "the work of the Department for the future will necessarily have to expand to keep up with the requirements of the consumers."[41] In 1924 a city board of engineers agreed with Mulholland's assessment. "Continued growth of the community coincident with the occurrence of a series of wet years might make a shortage of water unapparent," they wrote. "At the first recurrence of a series of dry years, however, an acute shortage would result if an additional water supply is not provided."[42]

As he had done a decade prior, Mulholland called for greater extractive connections. Amid a "hysteria" at the DWP about Los Angeles's growth issues, Mulholland tried to extend the city's water holdings and encroach even farther into Owens Valley's agricultural regions.[43] After Los Angeles voters resoundingly rejected an effort to secure water rights to the McNally Ditch—one of the oldest Owens Valley irrigations cooperatives, which stretched over fifty-four thousand acres—via bond issue, the city negotiated with individual farmers and bought options on over 80 percent of the available land for over $1 million.[44] Later in 1923 the city paid Owens Valley power brokers Leicester Hall, William Symons, and George Watterson to help purchase more land from other irrigation cooperatives.[45] One statement of 1923 land purchases made by the city showed that forty-two individual farmers sold properties ranging from 28 to 1380 acres to Los Angeles authorities.[46]

Los Angeles's imperialism pushed Owens Valley residents to the breaking point. By 1924 the valley's crop production had declined by 50 percent.

Over sixty farms closed in 1923 alone.[47] The Owens Lake ran dry. Beginning in 1924 Owens Valley residents resorted to violence as a means to bring the water controversy to public attention. On May 21, 1924, a group of forty men in Bishop, eighty-seven miles northeast of Fresno, stole dynamite from a Watterson storehouse, perhaps with George Watterson's knowledge, and blew a hole in the aqueduct.[48] On November 16, after negotiations over reparations for the farmers' ruined land failed, a group of ranchers took control over the Alabama Gates, which controlled the flow of water into the aqueduct, and diverted the water into the Owens River. Over the next few days, as many as eight hundred people joined the rebellion—a group big enough to deter local authorities from intervening. "AQUEDUCT IS SEIZED; LOS ANGELES WATER TURNED INTO RIVER: Sixty Owens Valley Raiders Take Possession of Gates and Defy the Sheriff," declared a front-page story in the *New York Times*.[49] The paper informed its readers that the "Fight Began 20 Years Ago," a "feud" that could not be resolved.[50] Los Angeles now had a national public relations problem.

Into this chaotic scene entered the Los Angeles Chamber of Commerce, which aimed to quell the violence and preserve the city's national reputation. Los Angeles could not afford to lose public or federal support for its growth initiatives. In July, after the first acts of sabotage, the chamber's board of directors hosted a special committee of members who had traveled to the Owens Valley. The board passed a cautious resolution urging the creation of an "exempt zone" of land the city would not purchase.[51] In December the board discussed a report from its Reclamation and Power Development Committee, which asked that "an equitable and just adjustment be made to protect the interests fairly both of the City of Los Angeles and of the property owners in Owens River Valley." The board also debated "whether or not at this time publicity should be given this action."[52] As evident in these maneuvers, the chamber valued a peaceful completion of negotiations without further embarrassing flare-ups.

In the summer of 1927, after another series of dynamiting, the chamber sent a new delegation to the Owens Valley. The produced report narrated a series of dramatic scenes. Towns lay deserted, to disastrous effect. "There are no people there; the schoolhouses are closed; stores have disintegrated . . . The farm houses have been pulled down or hauled away, and a few have been burned," the group reported. Moreover, Los Angeles authorities were actively presiding over this dystopia and creating a fortress there. "The aqueduct, when you come down at night," the report noted, "looks like a battle front in a moving picture . . . a spectacular scene, but it is distressing to think we are spending $50,000 a month there in an American community, to stop criminality." The report complained that ongoing militarization reflected badly on the community—a "disgrace to us"—and then outlined the need for some degree of reparations.[53] Here lay the chamber's worries in a few short pages. The Owens Valley was unstable, and Los Angeles's costly overreach reflected badly on city leaders. Better to settle than have the story gain national traction. Here, media connections between Los Angeles and the outside world posed a public relations threat.

Owens Valley resistance from 1924 to 1927 came to be known as the California Water Wars. Farmers' actions contributed to narratives about the Owens Valley as an uncontrolled place, but nothing farmers did seemed to move Los Angeles officials to action. In response, Owens Valley residents and their allies entered the public relations fray and aimed to create connections of their own. Newspapers such as the *Owens Valley Herald*, the *Bishop Index*, and the *Inyo Register* published muckraking pieces designed to expose how elites were taking advantage of middle-class Angelenos and Owens Valley residents alike.[54] Journalistic help arrived from outside the Owens Valley as well. Andrae B. Nordskog ran one such newspaper, the *Gridiron*, "California's Fighting Newspaper," out of Los Angeles. Nordskog, a failed opera singer and political reformer who would later run as the vice presidential nominee of the Liberty Party in 1932, grew attached to the plight of Owens Valley farmers and their fight against what he saw as entrenched elite Angeleno interests.[55] He even called the DWP "Power-Drunk," criminally tied to the "'Boss Rule' gang" he alleged controlled city politics.[56] Nordskog's dispatches from the Owens Valley attempted to enlighten Angelenos regarding the effects of Mulholland's water boosterism. Though Nordskog did not change the course of the conflict, his involvement forced the DWP to defend itself against substantive accusations of harmful conduct.

In May and June 1927, after ranchers resumed their dynamiting campaign and destroyed portions of the aqueduct on five separate occasions, Nordskog traveled to the Owens Valley to inform his readers about events on the ground. "Those of you in Los Angeles, who think it is only a handful of unreasonable men in Owens Valley who are trying to blackmail our city into submission, should change your minds," he announced in his first report. He went on to detail how "every man, woman and child . . . are in accord on the matter of wanting the City of Los Angeles to make amends for having ravaged the efforts of the pioneers whose lives have been spent in making a veritable God's country out of what was previously a desert waste."[57] Ironically, Nordskog used a Mulholland-like rhetoric of conquering nature in his writing: Angelenos, he insisted, were not the only people who had fought nature to create new urban possibilities. One week later, after yet another dynamiting, Nordskog lamented the inaction of Los Angeles water authorities, whom he termed dangerously "stubborn."[58] In July he criticized the advertising efforts of the DWP. "They should spend money for water and not for self-justification literature," Nordskog argued. "The propaganda that is being fed to the people of Los Angeles . . . about the great prosperity of Owens Valley is based on the most unfounded falsehoods ever dreamed of."[59] He further outlined the "devastation"—of farms, of wealth, of people—all initiated by Los Angeles's greedy pursuit of water rights.[60] In contrast, city officials such as Mulholland, he alleged, "got wealthy on their holdings in San Fernando Valley."[61] Finally, on July 8, Nordskog presented an arresting set of rhetorical questions. "Why this devastation of beautiful farms? . . . Why this breaking up a valley family of happy people? Why this expenditure of millions of taxpayers' money for lands and water rights that are wholly unnecessary?" he asked. The answer, of course, was "BUREAUCRATIC BOSS RULE."[62] Nordskog challenged the elite power structure of Los Angeles by unearthing new knowledge for the public. He fought against city leaders who relied on print media boosterism and carefully staged advertisements, and in doing so proved himself a challenger to the Angeleno boosters, someone who upheld the sovereignty of a space boosters wished to conquer. Grassroots activism, then, threatened to derail city leaders' control over hinterland extraction sites.

As is evident from Nordskog's critique, Mulholland's DWP disseminated its own version of events. Even as the Los Angeles Chamber of Commerce and the *Times* urged Mulholland to negotiate with the ranchers and purchase their lands at fair rates, the DWP obstinately argued that its work brought progress to both Los Angeles and the Owens Valley. Such an argument can be best seen in one pamphlet the department produced during the water wars. "Owens Valley and the Los Angeles Aqueduct," published in 1925, sought to answer "charges against the aqueduct and its management." "Fame of the Los Angeles aqueduct has spread round the world," began the pamphlet. "When it was completed in 1913 . . . [m]ountain ranges had been pierced, forbidding deserts spanned, to bring water over a distance of 250 miles and make possible the amazing growth of the city."[63] The aqueduct had similarly provided benefits to the Owens Valley—rising land values, tax revenue from Los Angeles, a railroad, and improved highways among them.[64] Contrary to the chamber of commerce's position, the DWP maintained that its extractive connections provided real value for Owens Valley residents.

Mulholland and his allies also fought for the creation of additional one-sided connections. In 1924 W. P. Whitsett, a mining and real estate entrepreneur who had helped Chandler and Otis to market their Los Angeles Suburban Homes Company and would later serve on the board of the DWP, spoke in front of the chamber of commerce. Whitsett asked the group to support tourism in the Owens Valley.[65] "In our own High Sierra country are over 2,000 lakes, forests unsurpassed in beauty, mountain meadows and streams," he argued, "almost undiscovered, with no better road than a desert trail, and an impossible railroad . . . undeveloped in the backyard of the greatest tourist city of the world."[66] Apparently ignoring that the Owens Valley was over two hundred miles away from Los Angeles and hardly lay "undiscovered," Whitsett urged "friendly co-operation" to develop roads and other tourist infrastructure. Tourism, he imagined, might lure as many as fifty thousand tourists, who would buy supplies, pay for guides, and spark higher employment levels. He thought his planned Owens Valley park might even achieve higher goals. "While they mingle together, those from the North and those from the South, in God's great out-door domain . . . new friendships will be born and broadened until they will finally encompass the grandeur of California as a whole."[67] Whitsett apparently convinced the chamber. "The members of the Board of Public Service were assured that the Los Angeles Chamber of Commerce was sincerely interested in the move and would lend its heartiest cooperation," noted the board of directors' minutes.[68]

Whitsett was not alone in planning a tourism-based future economy for the Owens Valley. One guide to its Inyo and Mono Counties called the area "The Open Sesame to Nature's Treasure House."[69] The cover of the June 1926 issue of the *Intake*, the DWP's magazine, exhibited a picture of cliffs in the Owens River gorge, with the caption "Our Own Little Grand Canyon."[70] The last statement is perhaps the most indicative of Angelenos' mindset in promoting Owens Valley tourism. The city had built connections to the valley, and so, elites imagined, city leaders should control and remake the region. Formerly wild forests might become stable business enterprises. For those remaining Owens Valley farmers, this effort must have seemed to be the cruelest irony: first Angelenos endeavored to decimate the landscape, then they tried to repackage its natural beauty for even further profit.

In the end, Los Angeles won the water wars. In August 1927, when the chamber of commerce was worried enough about violence in the area to send out a delegation, the Inyo County Bank—owned by Wilfred and Mark Watterson, nephews of George Watterson—collapsed. A subsequent audit revealed that the two brothers had been siphoning money from the bank to their own businesses and those of ranchers in need in the Owens Valley. The bank closed, the brothers spent over five years in San Quentin State Prison, and the final resistance to Los Angeles's aqua-imperialism fizzled.[71] In 1931, after a California Senate investigation into the water rights situation, Los Angeles bought much of the remaining property for sale in the region.[72] The history of the Los Angeles Aqueduct and the California Water Wars, then, demonstrates the scope of Los Angeles elites' power. Owens Valley farmers had little power over federal policy and little ability to shape media narratives, beyond limited acts of resistance by publishers such as Nordskog. The "wars" were really a series of skirmishes with a predetermined winner. Mulholland shaped the DWP into a public agency capable of remarkable acts of creation and destruction. Today, Los Angeles encourages some tourism by permitting outdoor recreation on much of its 310,000 acres in the area, but the Owens Lake is mostly dry and agriculture is essentially nonexistent.[73] Ironically, however, after all of the infighting, the propaganda, and the ruined communities, the Owens Valley water source was not enough for the thirsty metropolis. A new prize lay much farther east.

Taming the Colorado River

In the early 1920s city leaders turned their attention to the Colorado River.[74] Running over fourteen hundred miles from northwestern Colorado to the Gulf of California in Baja California, the river has sustained some form of life since the Clovis civilization inhabited part of New Mexico over twelve thousand years ago. For much of American history, the Colorado River was thought to be an uncontrollable flood risk, meaning the river could not provide water or power to a broader swath of the southwest.[75] By the beginning of the twentieth century, this mindset had begun to change, however. In the late 1890s developer William Beatty and engineer George Chaffey built the fourteen-mile Alamo Canal to divert part of the river's flow just north of the Mexican border to agricultural areas in the Imperial Valley, in south-eastern California.[76] In 1902 Los Angeles's Edison Electric Company sent Lippincott to survey the Colorado, in the hopes that the company might dam the river. Lippincott pronounced the project unfeasible and Edison Electric abandoned its plans. In the early 1920s the federal government became interested in a dam on the river to control flooding and generate electric power. After additional surveys, the Federal Reclamation Service settled on Black Canyon as the most favorable site, on the Arizona-Nevada border, just thirty miles southeast of Las Vegas. For the rest of the decade, Los Angeles water advocates fought to connect the Boulder Dam to the city. The project, they claimed, would demonstrate the city's masculine triumph over the unruly wilderness and cement Los Angeles's prosperity.

The Boulder Dam relied on federal appropriations to a greater degree than any other project in the city's prior history. First, dam proponents sought a major congressional appropriations bill to finance the estimated $165 million cost. California congressman Phil Swing, who represented Imperial and San Diego Counties, first proposed such a bill in 1922, and Congress held hearings on the matter throughout the decade. In 1924, at the first hearing, Mulholland articulated his desire to not only purchase enough power from the dam to make the project profitable but also to divert water from the dam to Los Angeles for domestic use.[77] "Today, only thirteen years after the completion of the aqueduct . . . we find our city rapidly approaching its second million in population, and we are already completing plans for a second much great water project," reasoned Mulholland in a 1928 article for *Community Builder* magazine.[78] As the decade progressed, Los Angeles leaders continued to influence the Boulder Dam project. From 1924 to 1926, anti-dam activists, including power companies and those with significant Mexican land holdings, succeeded in delaying proceedings. While Swing proposed the bill three separate times, only on the third try, in 1927, did the proposed legislation advance from committee to the congressional floor. The Swing-Johnson Bill, cosponsored by California Progressive senator Hiram Johnson, barely passed both houses of Congress, and President Calvin Coolidge signed it into law on December 21, 1928.

The appropriation provided for construction of the Boulder Dam, an arch gravity marvel standing over seven hundred feet tall and six hundred feet wide at its base; the downstream Imperial Dam; and the All-American Canal, which ferries water from the Imperial Dam eighty miles into the Imperial Valley. In 1928 California established the Metropolitan Water District (MWD), a public conglomerate that still provides water to its twenty-six member cities and water districts, including Los Angeles. Armed with a $220 million bond issue, the MWD paid the Bureau of Reclamation to build the Parker Dam, 150 miles downstream of the Hoover Dam on the Colorado River. The MWD then built the Colorado River Aqueduct to take water from the Parker Dam to Southern California. Once finished in 1939, the Colorado River Aqueduct stretched 240 miles from the California-Arizona border. Today the aqueduct provides water to eighteen million people, and Los Angeles and the Metropolitan Water District collectively purchase over 40 percent of the power the Hoover Dam produces.[79]

Unlike other endeavors in Los Angeles's history, the Hoover Dam projects did not unite city elites.[80] Harry Chandler and the *Times* especially opposed the Swing-Johnson Bill because it contained funding for the All-American Canal, which would divert water just before the Mexican border.[81] Chandler still owned his ranch in Mexico and feared that irrigating it might become much more difficult if U.S. officials dammed the Colorado River. Connections to the Colorado, then, would hurt Chandler's own interests; Los Angeles's elite group was still malleable, susceptible to changing power dynamics. Chandler banded together with the private power companies, such as Edison Electric, and engaged in a thinly veiled propaganda campaign opposing the project. Perhaps the most potent attack the *Times* made was that the Hoover Dam project was an overreach of local power that might crush private enterprise. Here, the *Times* turned traditional arguments in favor of federal power on their head. "The Public Service Commission, led by their little coterie of municipal ownership jobbists, has conceived the notion that Los Angeles should build the dam and reap the profits, shutting out everybody else," alleged one 1923 article.[82] In 1926 the *Times* broadcast at length the fears of Elmer Leatherwood, a Utah congressman, who warned of the "Increase in Federal 'Paternalism'" that might accompany development of dam power.[83] The dam, the paper claimed, amounted to an anticompetitive power grab by municipal water advocates and as such threatened to diminish Los Angeles's independence.

Similar to the Free Harbor activists of the past, pro-dam forces united to shape a narrative based on protective public mindedness. The progressive municipal ownership advocate John Randolph Haynes boosted the dam.[84] William Randolph Hearst's newspapers got behind it. Southern Californian public servants, including the mayors of San Diego and Riverside, formed the Boulder Dam Association to lobby on behalf of the project and public ownership. In 1927 the *Boulder Dam Association Bulletin* tried to reject claims that the project would be "socialistic." "We are not advocating Government ownership per se, nor are we seeking to thrust Government into business," one article claimed. "There is not water out there in the Colorado that is not NOW owned and beneficially used, and STORAGE, immense STORAGE is the only way to get more water, and we do not ask for any DONATION—we pay back every cent, should do so, can do so and will."[85] Around 1928 Chandler apparently changed his mind on the subject. Drawn by the potential economic gains he might realize if Los Angeles grew even further, he asked *Times* writers to ameliorate their tone toward the Boulder Dam project.[86] In general, against the backdrop of Chandler's temporary opposition to the project, it is remarkable the degree to which Mulholland and his allies succeeded in their public dam campaign.

As he had done during the aqueduct campaign, Mulholland stressed that the project was necessary for Los Angeles to survive. Only the Hoover Dam, he argued, would provide enough power and water to ensure Los Angeles's future prosperity. In 1921 Mulholland contributed to a DWP pamphlet designed to educate readers about the Boulder Dam. "Los Angeles is fast reaching the limit of supply of power from the aqueduct plants," he wrote. "The Boulder Canyon project on the Colorado River, then, is where Los Angeles must look for its future supply of power."[87] In his 1925 annual report, Mulholland revealed that Owens Valley water alone would not sustain the city and outlined "the absurdity of getting additional water by building another aqueduct from that source." "Our only recourse," Mulholland maintained, "is for us to keep pressing the work in connection with the contemplated additional supply from the Colorado River."[88] DWP's advertisements similarly tied extractive connections to Los Angeles's survival. "OUR WATER SUPPLY MUST NOT FAIL," preached one pamphlet issued before a water bond election.[89] Another pamphlet told citizens to "Prepare for the Next Million population" by passing the bond issue.[90]

Often, the DWP used cartoons to convey its message. A 1925 cartoon in the *Intake* showed a musclebound Uncle Sam setting the Boulder Dam into place with the aid of a worker shoveling "legislative cement." Above him, the words "unlimited hydro-energy" floated in a cloud, all overseen by a godlike figure on top of the cloud.[91] In December another *Intake* cartoon showed Mulholland in a Santa Claus outfit placing a new doll, labeled "Actual Starting of Work on the Colorado Aqueduct" into a stocking. Below him, discarded, lay another doll, "The Present Aqueduct: Patched and Battle-Scarred but Still in the Ring!" "From the looks of the gift I brought to this little girl some years ago, this new one will be appreciated," commented Mulholland-cum-Claus.[92] Finally, a 1930 *Intake* cover presented readers with two options seemingly modeled on Mulholland's "Virtually on the Edge of a Desert" speech five years prior. One half showed an aqueduct leading to a burgeoning Los Angeles skyscape. The other, sans aqueduct, showed a dry desert. "This—or—This?," asked the cartoon, captioned "Los Angeles Cannot Survive without Water" (fig. 8).[93] The stakes were again monumental. Taming the surrounding wilderness demanded the Colorado aqueduct project. As Owens Valley farmers were fighting to for their farms, then, the DWP was already dreaming of new, purportedly vital, gifts for the city.

Similar to its work to rhetorically tie the Panama Canal to Los Angeles, the Los Angeles Chamber of Commerce sought to integrate the Colorado River into the city and region writ large. In 1925 the chamber reprinted and publicized a statement its president, Richard W. Pridham, made before the Senate Committee on Irrigation and Reclamation. "Such a dam will . . . create a reservoir of water to serve Los Angeles and other communities of the Southwest whose rapid growth will soon vitally need this as a dependable source of supply," Pridham argued. "It is a great economic waste to allow the flood waters of the river to spend themselves in the Gulf of California when by impounding them they can be made productive of great wealth."[94] Mulholland and others, then, argued that one-sided extraction would provide benefits to Los Angeles, the extraction site, and the nation.

The Colorado aqueduct project also hinged on the idea that conquering wilderness was an essentially masculine effort, akin to early aviation endeavors or martial preparedness. The DWP kept in its archives a pamphlet, possibly produced by the department, of an article written by the author Herbert Corey, titled "Boulder Dam: A National Opportunity to Turn a Menace into an Asset."[95] "The Boulder dam is being planned to command the meanest, most savage, wickedest big river in the world," Corey wrote. "It has been as uncontrollable as a storm at sea. It drowns valleys as easily as it pulls men down in its swirls."[96] In 1930 the *Intake* gleefully announced, "Boulder Dam Opens New Era: Great American Desert About to Be Conquered."[97] Irrigation and reclamation had long

been central to the regional identity of the American West as a site where man needed to remake the environment to ensure his survival.[98] The *Intake*'s rhetoric also echoed a long cultural association of irrigation with masculine fantasies of controlling nature.[99] Similarly, Mulholland created a male-dominated bureaucracy in the DWP, promoting a work culture that easily propagated the idea that it was man's duty to tame the "most savage, wickedest big river in the world."[100] Similar to World War I–era ideas in the *Examiner* and *Times* that preparedness would ensure Los Angeles's safety, the DWP argued that the manly act of controlling the dangerous Colorado River would ensure Los Angeles's future.

Hollywood similarly endeavored to show Americans how conquering the wilderness might promote masculinity and prosperity. In 1926 Samuel Goldwyn's *The Winning of Barbara Worth* illustrated to audiences nationwide the potential benefits of damming the Colorado River. Based on Harold Bell Wright's 1911 best-selling novel of the same name, *The Winning of Barbara Worth*, a silent film, told viewers about early 1900s attempts to irrigate the Imperial Valley—southeast of Los Angeles, on the Mexican border, where Chandler owned land and which the All-American Canal irrigated. Bell told his story through a love triangle between Barbara Worth, Abe Lee (a cowboy), and Willard Holmes (an eastern engineer).[101] "Sunk into the Earth like a great molten bowl, lay the desert—unconquered Empress of the Wilderness—beautiful—mysterious—merciless . . . A tawny siren, whispering promises of a Paradise beyond—crushing out the lives of men in its poisonous embrace," announce stills at the opening of the film. Goldwyn went to major lengths to accurately portray the film's desolate setting. He filmed in Black Rock Desert in Nevada, near the border with Oregon, and built a replica town of "Barbara Worth" to serve as a set, complete with a mess hall and a 185-foot well to serve the tent city he erected to house the cast and crew. One day, a sandstorm blew away the "Barbara Hotel."[102] All told, Goldwyn spent over $1 million on the film.[103]

FIG. 8. Cartoons such as this one illustrate the DWP's use of desert imagery to promote its own initiatives. Image of cover of "Water," *Intake* 7, no. 5 (May 1930), Los Angeles Department of Water and Power Records, Los Angeles City Archives, box C-1504.

The film's story revolves around Mulholland's rhetorical mainstay: geo-graphical peril. Barbara's parents both die of exposure in the first minutes of the film while trying to cross the California desert. Jefferson Worth, a speculator who dreams of irrigating the barren Imperial Valley with water from the nearby Colorado River, discovers Barbara during his own jour-ney across the desert and adopts her. From there, the film moves ahead fifteen years. Jefferson Worth has formed the small town of Rubio City with his traveling companions—including Abe Lee and Lee's father—but his dream of an irrigation project has not come to fruition. The region is "desolation still unconquered," in the words of the film. Hope arrives with the appearance of two easterners: James Greenfield, an entrepreneur, and Holmes, his stepson. Greenfield proposes to finance a project to irrigate part of the desert. Holmes supervises the building of a dam on part of the Colorado River to provide water to Greenfield's newly created town, Kingston. Greenfield makes a fortune by raising prices in Kingston, but he refuses to reinforce the dam. Jefferson Worth's crew and Holmes both warn Greenfield about a coming flood; Greenfield promptly fires them all for insubordination. Worth moves his family and friends away from Kingston to higher ground, where they create the town of Barba.

The personal and geographical crises come to an emphatic denoue-ment at the end of the film. Lee and Holmes dramatically save Barba from Greenfield's efforts to deny it capital from local banks by con-vincing another wealthy eastern capitalist named Cartwright to invest. Immediately thereafter, a heavy rainstorm overwhelms the dam and the flooding destroys Kingston, but not Barba. "Our battle with the River has just begun," Holmes tells the assembled men of Barba after the flood. "We've got to drive it back and hold it there—the future of this Valley is in our hands!" Apparently, they are quite successful in the next few years. "And Holmes won!," one of the final stills announces. "The river, arch Enemy of Man, became his servant . . . The sun-blistered wasteland had become a second Eden." Along the way, Barbara, played by Vilma Bánky, has to choose between Lee, played by Gary Cooper in his first role, and Holmes, played by Ronald Colman. She chooses Holmes, and the final scene of the movie shows Holmes driving through the vibrant, pastoral landscape of the irrigated Imperial Valley and returning to his home, where he embraces Barbara and their newborn daughter. Such a narrative sounded very similar to the DWP's advertisements. In both, Californians had to wage an existential war against the desert and the uncontrollable Colorado. Failure ensured extinction, but success might create Eden.

The film told a specific story about western connections to the outside world. Greenfield and Holmes are easterners, unprepared for the desert's rigors. An early scene shows the two men stranded in the desert because their car cannot make it over the poor roads. Barbara Worth and Abe Lee, meanwhile, have no trouble helping the easterners on horseback. By the end of the film, Holmes is a westerner. He rides a horse with ease, summons the men to battle the Colorado River, and works to create an agricultural paradise in the Imperial Valley. The West has transformed Holmes into a more masculine figure, one capable of remaking nature. Early on, Greenfield's greed, an expression of his insidious eastern character, threatens the whole irrigation project. "I'm really only the engineer for a soulless corporation bent on making big money quick," Holmes tells Barbara. Later, after Jefferson Worth has led his followers to Barba, the men call him "the saviour of the desert." Cartwright, another eastern capitalist, does save Barba. But he does so only after Holmes convinces him to invest, using a language of western masculinity and by outlining western virtues. "Fight the Colorado river and whip it!," Holmes urges Cartwright, who has arrived in the Imperial Valley on a vacation. "You can save a people from ruin, make millions for yourself and build a new Empire here." Connections, then, were useful, at times vital, but they were to be pursued on the West's own terms.

Media outlets certainly picked up on the film's regional lessons. "The story revolves around the ambitions of a desert capitalist," remarked one article in the *Washington Post*. "To accomplish his purpose he brings from the East a cold, calculating financier who sees nothing in the dream of the desert king save more gold to be added to his already swollen horde."[104] Locally, the *Los Angeles Times* lauded the film's portrayal of western predicaments and solutions. Harold Wright Bell had loosely based his novel on the 1908 Colorado River Flood, which significantly damaged the Imperial Valley. In 1926 the newspaper seemed eager to apply the film's lessons to future irrigation endeavors. "The romance of the winning of the West," argued one editorial, "is the epic of the triumph of mind over matter, the conquest by strong sinews and intrepid spirits of the dragons of the flood and the desert." "Great is the film," concluded the article, "because it is a true portrayal of the winning of the West. What was done in the Imperial Valley visualized what is being done elsewhere, and, more important still, what can be done."[105] Another editorial argued that the film could be revolutionary in encouraging further water initiatives. "'Uncle Tom's Cabin' played a leading part in bring home to the American people the necessity for the abolition of slavery," the article noted. "Perhaps an equally important part may be played by 'The Winning of Barbara Worth' in firing the imaginations of the American people and impressing upon them the importance of reclamation and flood control as a national issue."[106]

Similar to the California Water Wars, the effort to build the Hoover Dam and secure its output for Los Angeles demonstrated the power of Mulholland and the DWP to shape local and federal policy. Mulholland could count on support from allies in print media and Hollywood to promote his plans. The pro-dam campaign articulated a worldview that Los Angeles was vulnerable to geographical disaster. In order to resist the environmental forces that sought to undo the city's progress, Los Angeles needed to remain vigilant and develop the extractive connections that had propelled its past ascent. The constant need to build, however, was also dangerous. Mulholland's paranoia about the city's future would lead him to catastrophe.

"Anchoring Dams in Rotten Mountains"

If *The Winning of Barbara Worth* preached concerted, measured development, the 1928 St. Francis Dam disaster illustrated the effects of wanton, impetuous irrigation projects. The story of the disaster demands a brief background sketch. Essentially, the crisis emerged from Mulholland's long history of stubborn water negotiations. In 1905 Fred Eaton—Mulholland's former boss and the mayor of Los Angeles when the city made its water a public utility—bought a parcel of land in the Long Valley, just north of Bishop, as a speculative ploy.[107] He then offered the city a permanent easement on part of the land for $450,000, so the DWP could build a hundred-foot-high dam in the future, a deal Mulholland reluctantly accepted. By 1920 Mulholland was ready to begin building a dam on Eaton's property in an effort to better control the flow of the aqueduct, provide Owens Valley farmers with some mandated water rights, store excess water, and provide hydroelectric energy.[108] Mulholland now wanted to build a dam at a slightly different section of the property at a height of 140 feet. Eaton again tried to make money off his investment and asked for an additional $900,000, a demand he quickly raised to $1.5 million and then $3 million when Mulholland balked at the price. Infuriated, Mulholland cut off negotiations altogether and decided to build a dam in the San Francisquito Canyon—forty miles northwest of Los Angeles, hundreds of miles south of Bishop, and adjacent to two preexisting Los Angeles hydroelectric plants. Los Angeles secured the necessary permits for the land in 1923, construction began in 1924, and the dam opened on May 4, 1926.[109] When completed, the dam rose 185 feet above the canyon floor, only the second concrete gravity dam the DWP had built.

In his rush to design and build the dam, Mulholland disdained the opinions of expert engineers. From 1926 to 1928, as the concrete settled, several cracks appeared in the St. Francis Dam, and it began to leak around its base in February and March 1928.[110] Mulholland came to inspect the dam on the morning of March 12, 1928. He concluded that the leakage was minor and the dam was in good condition. That very night, the dam catastrophically ruptured. Underneath the base, water permeated the relatively unstable mica schist upon which Mulholland had built. Around midnight, the pressure built to such a degree that the entire east side of the dam collapsed. In under an hour, both the east and the west sides of the dam had washed well downstream, and a flood of over 1 million cubic feet per second of water surged through the canyon, killing everyone in its path.

It is hard to overstate the damage caused by the dam's collapse. The flood immediately killed the dam keeper and his family, who lived in a house near the structure. From there, the torrent continued, killing those who lived in the hydroelectric compounds as well as some San Fernando ranchers. By 1:20 a.m. the flood hit the town of Kemp, just north of the San Fernando Valley, by 3:00 a.m. it continued on to Santa Paula, just east of Oxnard, and by 5:30 a.m. the water completed its fifty-mile journey to the Pacific Ocean. Four hundred forty-one people died in the carnage, as over twelve billion gallons of water swept over them.[111] "Many of the bodies," the *Times* reported on May 15, "will never be recovered as scores are known to have been swept out to sea, while many more must be buried from three to six feet deep in mud and debris."[112]

The St. Francis disaster abruptly ended Mulholland's career. Until the end of his life, he believed that a terrorist dynamited the dam in action perhaps related to the Owens Valley water wars. Subsequent studies have shown, however, that the dam failed of its own accord, a harrowing result of the hubris Mulholland often displayed in pursuing his water ventures. Mulholland quickly resigned from the DWP, though he stayed on as a consultant for the department, and he died in 1935, just a year after Eaton had passed. The two men reconnected after the disaster, brought together by their shared relation to the tragedy and their diminished reputations.[113] The propaganda network Mulholland had created did allow him to live out the rest of his life in relative peace, separated from the DWP but not particularly demonized. In April 1928 a lengthy coroner's inquest of the matter concluded that Mulholland was in error for his reckless selection of the site and building on unstable ground. "It is the belief of this Committee that the dam failed because it rested on a defective foundation," simply concluded the 1928 engineers' report requested by the Los Angeles City Council.[114] In general, however, the report, as well as a concurrent coroner's investigation report, exculpated Mulholland. The authors of both documents instead blamed systemic flaws that allowed Mulholland to gain so much power. The city's newspapers also declined to cover the investigations to any great degree or to place blame on Mulholland alone. Sometimes, the papers even blamed other forces, such as the supposed Owens Valley dynamiters. "It is plain that [Mulholland] was dictated to by circumstances not under his control," argued a *Times* editorial, "among them the desirability of providing a large water storage near the city in view of possible damage to the Aqueduct."[115]

The St. Francis collapse muddied the politics of connection; one-sided extraction could have dangers. Reactionary populist minister Robert Shuler—who preached to large crowds from his downtown church, published his own newspaper, and owned a popular Southern California radio station—railed against the calamity in *Bob Shuler's Magazine*. "Every cent spent effectively by the tax payers in protecting our valleys from floods is a merited investment," he wrote in 1929, "but that does not mean that our supervisors should anchor dams in rotten mountains and thus endanger the lives of thousands of our people."[116] While Shuler did not mention Mulholland by name, he clearly referred to him. Shuler agreed with the idea of "protecting our valleys," but he believed that the city's infrastructure developments had gone too far, that they were being pursued with little contemplation. Instead of shoring up Los Angeles's environmental vulnerabilities, Shuler argued, Mulholland's projects had endangered Angelenos.

Mulholland had fostered a growth mania, built on the image of Los Angeles at the edge of a desert. Mulholland's masculine vulnerability ideology was integral to Los Angeles's efforts to build the Los Angeles Aqueduct, defeat Owens Valley farmers in the California Water Wars, and ensure that the Hoover Dam would benefit the city. Such rhetoric also, however, consumed the DWP and led to the St. Francis disaster. If the crisis were so dire, contemplation and excessive planning could harm the city. Rapid infrastructure development contributed to an aura around Mulholland. During the 1920s, he seemed to be an unstoppable force. In one evening, the logic that had propelled his career forwards—that the environment threatened Los Angeles—unmade him. Paradoxically, for a man who was obsessed with "taming" the West, the St. Francis disaster was so damaging because the dam itself built up the water's potential energy and made its current more severe when it ruptured.

While Mulholland's career came to an ignominious end, Angelenos did not doubt for long the importance of positioning the city at the confluence of extractive connections. When the Hoover Dam began sending power to Los Angeles in 1936, the city held "ten days of tribute to electricity" to mark the occasion. On its first night, October 10, city leaders erected a series of massive lights around Los Angeles, one on top of a tunnel overlooking downtown, "a light so powerful that its rays will burn the clothes off an individual at half a mile," according to the *Times*. The light illuminated a parade commemorating Southern California's history, the paper further noted, "designed to accentuate the progress forward from primitive conditions to the latest word in modernity."[117] In the newspaper's estimation, over one million people attended the first night's festivities, "with an exuberance and spontaneous feeling that has not been observed since the demonstration the day the World War ended."[118] "We celebrate not only the greatest power plant on earth," former representative Swing noted in his speech to the crowd, "but also the conquest of the Colorado. It is no longer the master. It is now the servant of man."[119] Here lay evidence of Mulholland and the DWP's vulnerability rhetoric once more. Mulholland had died the year before, but his ideas continued to shape Los Angeles's development. The city needed to be protected from its environment. Progress depended on conquering the world around Los Angeles and tying tributary areas to the city.

The problems of Los Angeles's environment in the 1920s, moreover, grew out of the city's successes in luring migrants to the city. Increasing population—the Great Migration that Hampton had extolled at the beginning of the decade—sparked a need for water and power development. In 1924 Roger M. Andrews, vice president of the Los Angeles Citizens National Bank, gave a speech to the local Optimists Club in which he asked city leaders to curtail some internal migration to the city. "Los Angeles has made the mistake of inviting too many people to the party," Andrews claimed. "It is high time we dropped everything else and put our house in order." The only solution, Andrews felt, was to catalyze new industrial development. Then, and only then, Los Angeles "will have the pick of the country's best and most virile workers when we can offer permanent opportunities for employment."[120] It was not a question of luring just any migrants; only "virile," manly migrants could propel the city's further growth. Such comments were remarkable amid a municipal climate that encouraged constant, faster growth in all sectors. City boosters demanded that men such as Mulholland solve Los Angeles's environmental issues and disprove an environmental determinism that suggested Los Angeles should not be a major American city. Of course, Andrews's concerns about encouraging domestic migration would also seem prescient one decade later. The Great Depression would only exacerbate the problems of accelerated growth. And city elites would look at the same problems and contemplate a drastic step—closing the city's borders in a time of turmoil.

THE PERILS OF EXCEPTIONALISM

ALTHOUGH THE GREAT DEPRESSION AFFECTED LOS ANGELES LESS
severely than it did eastern cities, Los Angeles was not immune to the
impact of the economic crisis. In January 1931 a local man wrote to the *Los
Angeles Times* lamenting the state of municipal real estate. "Through the
official acts of the officers of the city we have had between 4000 and 5000
foreclosures in the last year," wrote T. A. Sloan. "Most of these foreclosures
have been caused by high taxes and heavy assessments."[1] Apparently, it
was easier for Sloan to blame the government than a growing economic
collapse for his financial issues. When Angelenos lost their housing, some
were forced to live in the fetid inner-city slums.[2] Most struggled both to
find work and to psychologically cope with this reality. For example, in
May 1932 the *Los Angeles Times* discussed the Angelus Temple's welfare
efforts.[3] "'Work Test' Cuts Breadline from 600 to Thirteen," announced the
Times, as it lauded the organization's efforts to single out the "deserving"
poor.[4] The temple did so by giving men identification cards, designating
them as either able or unable to work, which many men supposedly tore
up. It apparently never occurred to authorities that those receiving aid
might not want publicly to display their status as failed breadwinners amid
a national crisis of masculinity.

Los Angeles relief agencies illustrated the impact of local unemployment
during the first years of the Great Depression. In 1932 alone, the city's

Department of Social Services recorded fifty-six thousand applications for help, an increase of 42 percent from the previous year.[5] The department's annual report for 1933 showed an increase of 74 percent in the number of transients cared for—ninety-seven thousand cases overall.[6] At the end of 1933 the department reported spending over $630,000 on charitable endeavors, including over $144,000 for the "relief of destitute women" and $320,000 for "[h]ospital, medical and clinical care of indigent children," a collective increase of 41 percent from the previous year.[7] To put this in perspective, the Unemployed Cooperative Relief Council of Los Angeles, a nonprofit relief group, bought 2,940 pounds of bread on January 31, 1933, for just $29.40.[8] $630,000 was a significant commitment.

Los Angeles relief agencies further buckled as domestic migrants increasingly arrived in California. With the state unemployment rate hovering around 30 percent in 1933, Los Angeles elites began to worry about the impact of such "indigent migrants" on the city's budget.[9] From 1935 to 1940, roughly ninety-six thousand people from the Southwest moved to Los Angeles.[10] Upon arrival these "Okies" began to symbolize the Depression writ large.[11] They settled by the thousands in federal transient camps, tent cities, and makeshift urban shelters nicknamed Hoovervilles after the president many blamed for federal inaction during the Depression. Beyond relief expenditures, city leaders feared the social impact of transiency. In October 1934 city councilman Darwin Tate introduced a resolution intended to push transient camps to the outskirts of Los Angeles, on the belief that transiency threatened the city's civilized norms. He first outlined the problems with locating camps near traditional housing markets. "It is the experience of authorities that the gathering of large numbers of persons with only temporary accommodations for living is a distinct menace to the peace and tranquility of residential districts," he wrote. Therefore, he hoped that the city would "declare as a matter of policy that such transient unemployed camps of barracks . . . be confined to the industrial zones."[12] The resolution only stalled after being sent to the city's attorney for a report on its legality.[13]

The flipside of such anxieties might be best viewed in a petition from the city council to the Works Progress Administration (WPA) one year later, asking that the agency eliminate some of the requirements for Angelenos to receive aid.[14] Namely, the council argued that homeowners with limited home equity, or whose homes were under water financially, should be able to accept WPA positions, even though the national guidelines did not permit homeowner participation. The resolution specifically mentioned "needy home owners and holders of equity in this community."[15] When the WPA declined to change its policies, the council began to lobby the federal government to impose change from above. Three years later, the city council even directly petitioned Franklin Delano Roosevelt, who demurred.[16] To the city council, home ownership in Los Angeles, the opposite of transiency, was linked to morality; homeowners should not be punished while indecent tramps received aid. In 1935 the federal government ended the Federal Transient Service, which had provided welfare to around seventy thousand people in California.[17] The withdrawal of federal support only amplified local calls for protection from prodigious migration.[18] When three hundred fifty thousand Angelenos needed public assistance in 1935, migrants became an unwanted, racialized minority.[19]

The Great Depression, then, unearthed the dangers inherent to elites' four-decades-long advertising project. From 1890 onward Los Angeles elites had proclaimed that their city was exceptional, and its enormous growth over that time lent some credence to their argument. During the 1930s exceptionalism became dangerous. If employment was no longer a given, migrants might sap the city of its wealth instead of fueling its growth. The elite mission—to create a dominant Pacific metropolis—depended on hegemonic masculinity, manageable migration, and unbridled capitalism. Threats to the three pillars of this vision underpinned the real fear about the viability of the project during the Great Depression. The decade revealed the paradoxes created by Los Angeles elites' past boosterism and provides a glimpse into the diverse and malleable activism propagated by elite actors and institutions in a time of crisis.

As Chandler and Hearst had allied during World War I, various Los Angeles elites collaborated to use the Great Depression as an opportunity to improve their city. Four narratives highlight their labor: an attempt to resist Mexican repatriation, a decade-long fight to deter domestic migration, efforts to sell the 1932 Olympic Games, and the campaign to defeat Upton Sinclair's 1934 California gubernatorial bid. With the exception of deterring internal migration, elite activism was especially pronounced in the first years of the Depression. The activists' work largely centered on achieving control. Mexican laborers, elites argued, should not be deported because they were controllable; however, migrants from within the United States were citizens and therefore dangerous. The Olympics, in turn, could exhibit temporary, liberal cosmopolitanism. Most dangerous, Sinclair threatened to fundamentally alter the state's economic structure and to permanently subvert elite control. Collectively, then, these efforts illustrate the extent of fear about Los Angeles's fate amid global economic meltdown.

In 1931, concerned by escalating white male unemployment, the federal government began to deport Mexican aliens who lived in Los Angeles County, home to roughly 168,000 Mexicans.[20] Led by Charles P. Visel, the Los Angeles city coordinator of Herbert Hoover's Emergency Committee for Unemployment, the Mexican "deportation drive" eventually forcibly transported over two thousand people, some birthright U.S. citizens, out of the country and caused many others to leave the area in fear.[21] The Los Angeles Chamber of Commerce, and in particular the head of its Agricultural Department George P. Clements, opposed federal efforts to put quotas on Mexican labor or to deport Mexicans during the Depression. For his part, Clements was not necessarily motivated by altruism. "There is no labor in the United States capable of doing the work for which [Mexican labor] is in demand and for which he is so suitably fitted," he protested in a letter to the California Congressional Delegation in 1927. "Since this source of labor is alien," Clements continued, "it is controllable."[22] Clements's rhetoric depended on notions of Mexican labor as compliant and emasculated in the face of elite, male control.

Simultaneously, the chamber opposed domestic migration to California. "Is it possible to expect these people—white Americans who will anticipate American standards of living—to be satisfied with the conditions which the agricultural practices of the state of California impose in labor needs?" the chamber asked in a 1936 letter. "Will they be adaptable to rough industry and public utility requirements, and if not, who is going to take care of these people?"[23] Mexican laborers were "suitably fitted" to poor living and working conditions, but American migrants, Clements worried, would want to be well-treated. Attempts to give domestic migrants "American standards of living" could overwhelm the state's relief agencies.

At the same time, Los Angeles hosted the 1932 Olympic Games, a moment that cemented the city's status as a growing economic power. Upper-class members of the Olympic Planning Committee, including real estate mogul William May Garland—who served as president of both the Planning Committee and the Community Development Association (CDA), which spearheaded the Olympic bid—and film mogul Louis B. Mayer, hoped to amplify Los Angeles's prestige.[24] Garland hoped that the Olympics could show the world "sincere evidences of friendship on every side that the citizens of Los Angeles are thrilled by your presence and are happy because you are their guests."[25] Similarly, the official report of the 1932 Olympic claimed that "here was a great happy family of forty nationalities putting the politicians of the world to shame."[26] Such language reflected a western, boosterish cosmopolitanism in the early twentieth century, which focused, in the words of historian Shelley Sang-Hee Lee, on "the dynamism and possibilities of international crossings," centered "explicitly on *place*."[27] Los Angeles could be a cosmopolitan center, even in a time of crisis, because the Olympics embodied a controlled cosmopolitanism: short-term, bounded by a distinct "village," and mediated by national committees. Los Angeles, then, was less the head of a permanent "happy family" and more the host of a world's fair.[28]

The narrative of Los Angeles as a "happy family," flawed as it was in 1932, would only grow more complicated as the Depression deepened. Upton Sinclair's 1934 gubernatorial campaign especially sparked the ire of Chandler, Hearst, and Mayer. Sinclair premised his campaign on "production for use," a proposal to eliminate private markets by enabling the unemployed to farm California's unused agricultural areas and run its unused factories. Under his End Poverty in California (EPIC) plan, California would confiscate farms and factories, implement a progressive income tax, and guarantee old-age pensions. In the Democratic primary on August 28, Sinclair stunned his rivals by sweeping to a landslide victory over George Creel, the former World War I propaganda czar.[29] The *Los Angeles Times* blamed Sinclair's primary win on "hordes of interlopers" who took advantage of a "trick primary law."[30] As a result, Mayer led a modern media smear campaign, perhaps the first of its kind, to discredit Sinclair.[31] Asked about domestic migration in September 1934, Sinclair told the press, perhaps in jest, "If I'm elected Governor, I expect one-half the unemployed in the United States will hop the first freights for California."[32] Over the next month, the *Los Angeles Times*, as well as many other California newspapers, excoriated Sinclair for his remark. Weakened by such negative publicity and by a third-party run by Raymond Haight that drew votes from Sinclair's campaign, Sinclair lost the general election to Frank Merriam by over two hundred fifty thousand votes.[33] Sinclair's campaign highlighted contemporary debates about borders, connections, and expansion in Los Angeles. The candidate also broadcast a very different image of California's, and Los Angeles's, future geosocial role. To Sinclair, California should bridge its borders and welcome outsiders. To Mayer and others, California should be prepared to dynamite those bridges in uncertain times.

How did one small, homogenous community sell a vision in which Los Angeles's citizens should both welcome national and international visitors to the 1932 Olympic Games and demand a short-lived "Border Patrol," or "Bum Blockade," headed by Los Angeles Sheriff James Davis, to keep out domestic migrants in 1935?[34] How did they craft a nuanced plan for Los Angeles during crisis based on temporary inclusivity and comprehensive restriction? Each outcome depended on specific members of elite society and their contributions to various municipal and regional institutions—the Los Angeles Chamber of Commerce, the CDA, and the local Republican Party, among them.[35] Cooperation was also integral. Clements, for instance, supported restricting internal migration, Harry Chandler and Louis B. Mayer participated in the Olympic project, and Garland ran the local Merriam campaign. Men such as Chandler, Clements, Garland, and Mayer illustrate the cooperation and creativity at the heart of the elite rhetorical mission, one continually grounded in the image of Los Angeles as a connected yet threatened city. "Sinclair Invites Mob

Rule in California," one *Los Angeles Times* article announced. "Impossible Schemes for Socializing State Would Leave It at Mercy of Jobless Hordes Expected."[36] As a result of Depression-era fear, Los Angeles elites made the remarkable decision to sever some of the national ties that had contributed to the city's rise. Controllable connections would be pursued. Dangerous connections demanded walls.

Resisting Mexican Deportation

George P. Clements both fit into the standard elite Angeleno trajectory and defied it. Born in Canada in 1877, Clements moved to Michigan at the age of seventeen and later became a doctor in Nebraska. Similar to Chandler, ill health forced Clements to move to Los Angeles in 1902, where he took up farming and land speculation. He bought a hundred-acre farm in Riverside, about sixty miles southeast of Los Angeles where he not only grew alfalfa and citrus fruits but also started a small tree nursery.[37] Later, Clements bought additional land in Riverside, as well as two farms in the Imperial Valley.[38] Clements developed a keen interest in scientific farming; the *Times* credited him with introducing the Klondike Watermelon to the area, improving windbreaks on farms, and coining the term "raincrop."[39] Unlike Chandler, Otis, and many others profiled in previous chapters, Clements supported the Democratic Party and served on its county committee in the 1910s.[40] "Despite the many honors which came to him in later life, Dr. Clements always liked to consider himself first as the ally of the dirt farmer," a *Los Angeles Times* obituary read.[41] Clements's social conscience extended to conservation activities and Native American relations.[42] In 1930 he decried the status of the Bureau of Indian Affairs in an article for the *Times*, one of many he wrote for the newspaper on a variety of topics. "Lo the Poor Indian," Clements wrote, as he demanded reform of "the old rotten and poisonous consignment of bureau brutalization, parasitism, and pork-barrel and job-holding graft that has come down the years through a 'century of dishonor.'"[43] The next year, Clements expressed similar outrage about planners who were "Butchering California's Landscape" to make way for highways and urban development.[44] After his death, a former colleague wrote to the *Times* lauding his commitment to preservation. "I . . .

learned much of his philosophy, which was, 'God-created resources do not belong to one generation except to husband and preserve for future generations,'" wrote Byron Blotz. "An expanding organization carrying the name of George P. Clements would be constructive if adopted on a nationwide basis," Blotz continued. "I should like to become a member of such an organization."[45]

A four-page article in the 1940 *Saturday Evening Post* similarly depicted Clements as an eccentric, driven man who was devoted to conservation. "The doughty doctor's tactics in public debate are pretty baffling," wrote Frank J. Taylor, "Years ago, through illness, he lost his hair and his hearing. An unruly wisp of hair eventually returned . . . but to hear he relies upon an earphone connected with an amplifier in a little black box with a switch on it." "After firing a verbal bombshell," Taylor continued, "the doctor invariably reaches into his little pocket. 'Deafness is a great asset,' he explains slyly. 'I can tell my side of the story, then turn my old box off.'"[46] Beyond such antics, Clements clearly saw a need for Angelenos to reform their water use habits. Taylor termed Clements "A Heretic in the Promised Land," who often provided a needed dose of reality about Los Angeles's climate situation. "Today the doctor is convinced that the ebullient Southern Californians are doing just about everything they can think of to destroy their prodigiously fertile land in the most expensive way, and he never overlooks a chance to say so," the article continued.[47] Clements agreed with Mulholland that Los Angeles lay in an ecological crisis zone but disagreed that the solution was to pull more and more water from elsewhere. In fact, Clements opposed both the Hoover Dam and the Colorado River Aqueduct.[48] Clements defied elite Angeleno society at other times as well. "When [Mexican revolutionary leader Álvaro] Obregón came into power," Taylor narrated, "he was induced to invite the doctor down as guest of the government to advise on adapting crops to soils on the great estates they were dividing . . . among them the haciendas of his fellow Californians, Harry Chandler and William Randolph Hearst." Tellingly, Clements also called contemporary commercialism "a parasite growth on agriculture." "Nobody else ever said anything like that on Los Angeles Chamber of Commerce stationery and stayed on the pay roll," concluded Taylor.[49]

Nevertheless, as Clements became more interested in farm labor policy in the 1920s and 1930s, his recommendations easily meshed with those of the broader membership of the Los Angeles Chamber of Commerce. In 1917 Clements joined and remade its agricultural department, which he then managed for over two decades.[50] In his leading role on the Agricultural Committee, Clements shaped the chamber's position on Mexican immigration and rural labor. During the Depression, Clements spent much of his time opposing outside intervention in the agricultural labor system. In 1935 he wrote to a colleague at the chamber to express his idea that urban relief wages were too high and did not force the unemployed to seek labor in private industry.[51] "Every official . . . that I met on my two days survey in Kern, Tulare, and Kinds Counties . . . informed us that at the present time there was a job for every able-bodied man willing to work," he reported after a 1937 trip to regional farming communities.[52] Accordingly, Clements resisted federal intervention in the labor market. In such instances, Clements's agricultural interests converged with the interests of the chamber in controlling relief expenditures. Both sides agreed that laborers were flooding Los Angeles and disrupting the regional labor market.

When it came to Mexican labor, then, Clements set out to uphold farmers' rights against Visel's federal power.[53] Visel, the federal official who led the Mexican deportation drive, tried to secure the chamber's support for Mexican deportation in early 1931. "It is estimated that there are between 20,000 and 25,000 deportable aliens of various nationalities in this district," he wrote to the Crime and Unemployment Committee of the chamber in early January. "These people are committing a crime by simply being here. They are holding jobs which are most sorely needed by our citizens."[54] Visel thought he could reduce crime "if some method could be devised to scare these people out of our city."[55] Accordingly, the federal official began directing raids of public spaces in Los Angeles for supposed illegal immigrants. On February 26, 1931, Visel's agents arrested four hundred people in a raid heavily publicized by Los Angeles newspapers.[56] Very few undocumented immigrants were detained. The value of the raids lay in the terror they inspired in the Mexican community. "Fugitive Aliens Seized in Drive: Thirteen Taken in First of Raid Series," read one headline in the *Los Angeles Times*.[57] Visel also publicly urged any undocumented immigrants to leave of their own accord to save themselves from an arduous deportation process.[58]

As Visel continued his raids into the spring, the Los Angeles Chamber of Commerce tried to reassure the Mexican community of its safety. "We assume it unnecessary to call the attention of our Mexican friends to the fact that they should in no wise [sic] be influenced in leaving . . . because of idle rumors,"[59] announced a statement released by the chamber's board of directors in May. Behind the scenes, the chamber tried to reason with Visel. In late January, the organization's secretary sent him one of Clements's position papers on the importance of Mexican labor to the region. "We must be careful to see that in our desire to help our own white citizens we do not overlook our citizens of other races who have just as much claim on our consideration as our American-born people," noted the chamber in its cover letter.[60] Though the federal government distanced itself from Visel's work in June, by then Hoover's appointee had significantly damaged Mexican-Anglo relations in the city.[61] Privately, Clements expressed his objections to all forcible Mexican repatriation, as the federal government was not the only actor engaged in such activities. Alongside Visel's deportation campaign, the Los Angeles Board of Supervisors initiated its own effort to fund the transportation of thousands of Mexicans back to Mexico in the spring and summer of 1931.[62] After he toured a train transporting over one thousand people back to Mexico, Clements complained about the falsehoods Angeleno officials told to those on the train. "Most of them had been told that they could come back whenever they wanted to," he wrote in August. "I think this is a grave mistake, because it is not the truth."[63] Moreover, Clements worried about the fate of American-born children on the train, who would not be able to return to the United States without a birth certificate and other scarce documentation.[64] Clements rued the loss of Mexican laborers he viewed as valuable assets to the regional economy, as they were cheaper than American workers and did not demand the same standards of working conditions.

Clements's discussion of supposed racial purity at other moments in the 1920s and 1930s more fully illuminates his worldview regarding Los

Angeles and its surrounding borders. In December 1927 Clements issued a report on Mexican laborers, which he divided into three groups: the "ruling class," the "riff raff," and, the largest group, the "Mexican peon." While Clements believed that the "riff raff . . . found along the railroads and in the Mexican cities . . . should never be permitted to cross the border," he had high praise for the "peons." "They are clean, healthy and frugal," Clements insisted. "They are honest, they are generous to a fault . . . they have no idea of time or money or values as we know them . . . It is this class of people who come to the United States to sell their labor for American dollars."[65] On the one hand, "peons" were naturally uncivilized. On the other hand, they would not pose a danger to white civilization or take advantage of the borderlands. Unlike portrayals of the supposed Japanese-Mexican menace during World War I, Clements claimed that "peons" did not threaten Anglo manhood—they did not even understand the value of money. In Clements's mind, such people were backward, but their backwardness made them pliable and trustworthy.

Clements also defended Mexican immigrants by denigrating other groups. The prospect of increasing Puerto Rican immigration and employment especially worried him. In 1917 the Jones-Shafroth Act had granted Puerto Ricans United States citizenship. The Great Depression generated renewed anti-American protests in Puerto Rico and a renewed discussion of the island's status (in 1936 U.S. Senator Millard Tydings unsuccessfully attempted to pass a bill that would allow for Puerto Rican independence).[66] Clements seems to have been deeply involved with the contemporary political discussion about Puerto Rico. In a series of speeches and letters beginning in 1926, he repeatedly outlined what he saw as the differences between Puerto Rican and Mexican laborers. Clements began to develop his arguments in a 1926 speech at the Annual Conference of the "Friends of the Mexicans," held at Pomona College. While railing against quota laws, Clements singled out "The Porto Rican Negro" for special attention.[67] "It is said that there are a million available workers to be obtained from Porto Rico—a number of them have already been brought into the state of Arizona," Clements noted, but "in my estimation it is a dangerous experiment . . . he is an American citizen and in coming becomes a fixture. You cannot deport him."[68] Mexican laborers might be deported if they misbehaved, but unfortunately (at least in Clements's mind), Puerto Ricans had rights.

In 1929 Clements expanded his attack on Puerto Rican immigrants. In a remarkable letter to the Chamber of Commerce of the United States signed by the Los Angeles Chamber of Commerce, but clearly penned by Clements himself, Clements raised the possibility of a racial apocalypse if federal authorities excluded Mexican labor from America.[69] His dystopian vision is worth quoting in full.

> If we cannot get the Mexican to supply . . . casual labor, we have but one place to turn—the Porto Rican negro or as he is commonly known, the 'Portuguese Nigger', a hybrid with all the vices of his progenitors and few of the virtues, thin lipped, straight nosed, frequently red haired, blue eyed and freckle faced, naturally indigent, naturally vicious. I do not think I need to stress the biological problem, particularly in California and the border states, where so many of our people are dark skinned. He is an American citizen, and once coming to us becomes a real social problem as well as adding to our American negro problem . . . Picture to yourself these 186,000 California farmers, the highest type of agricultural people in the world, living ideal rural lives to the greater part isolated, with 150,000 hybrid negroes tramping all over the state. Is there any wonder we want to keep our Mexican labor?[70]

Just a few weeks later Clements again warned that "casual laborers of this hybrid negro" would "overrun" California if allowed to do so.[71] Mexican laborers, in contrast, were relatively harmless "peons" who would submit to the will of farmers.

The idea of control—of keeping "our Mexican labor"—illustrated the extent of gendered concerns about white masculinity amid hordes of "hybrid negroes." To Clements, Los Angeles stood in a precarious position, which demanded that farmers be allowed to control their own labor force. Risking otherwise would recklessly endanger the region's racial purity. Clements's rhetoric echoed portrayals of Puerto Rican migrants as dangerous beasts during debate over the Jones Act in 1917.[72] His fears of the "biological problem" also echoed World War I–era depictions of a rapacious Japanese invasion in films such as *Patria*. To Clements, social order needed to be tightly controlled by local elites, not by removed Washington bureaucrats. Los Angeles could not afford to ignore borderlands threats that threatened to displace white supremacy. As the Depression enveloped the nation as a whole, Clements also called for California to cut itself off from the nation—to create protonational barriers and migration regulatory structures on the state's eastern border.

Deterring Domestic Migration

The desire to protect Los Angeles from dangerous others also lay behind the city's chamber of commerce's opposition to domestic migration to California. Much of the discussion about migrants took place between the chamber's Unemployment Committee and its board of directors. As early as 1931, the board discussed a report from the Unemployment Committee on "considerable difficulty with respect to the undesirable transients," which demanded, in the Committee's mind, universal transient registration and the creation of a municipal work camp.[73] As the Depression progressed, the chamber continued to press for aggressive incarceration and expansive surveillance.

In the early years of the Depression, the rock pile made up the first part of the chamber's protection plan. The rock pile—a mound of large rocks that prisoners were forced to break into small pieces, with no constructive purpose—had long held a place in American and Angeleno carceral history.[74] In the twentieth century, large-scale prisons, or "Big Houses," evolved in part from Southern "plantation prisons," which primarily imprisoned African American men and forced them to work on chain gangs. Like their predecessors, Big Houses demanded that inmates submit to punishing labor designed to maintain order.[75] The rock pile was a more gratuitous version of the chain gang—prisoners who worked on them did not even produce public goods.[76] As Kelly Lytle Hernández has shown, Los Angeles authorities placed rock piles on penal premises during the "tramp panic" of the early 1900s.[77] Other cities and states—including New York—moved toward prison philosophies of "punishment without labor" after World War I. Los Angeles city leaders returned to an older ideal during this time of crisis: unproductive labor could act as a deterrent to would-be offenders and convince inmates to behave once they returned to civilian life.[78] The "tramp panic" of the Great Depression again sparked the creation of a racialized other—in the form of the "vagrant," the "Okie," or the "bum." "If every bum were offered work, most of them would be weeded out," commented a *Los Angeles Times* editorial. "There is nothing like a rock pile to cure vagrancy."[79] Because homelessness was deeply gendered during the Depression, "bums" connoted images of deviant men, significantly more dangerous than Mexican "peons."[80] Unlike "peons," tramps were white and should have held American capitalist values. In resisting work and rejecting traditionally masculine roles, the *Times* surmised, they deserved to be punished.

Over many months, the Los Angeles Chamber of Commerce further pursued punitive action toward migrants. At a meeting in late November 1931, the board enthusiastically agreed to participate in a state-wide group dedicated to planning "a number of concentration camps . . . near the border, to which could be sent those arrested on vagrancy charges to be put to work on rock piles in order that California might not be the dumping ground for the indigent from all the other states."[81] The board also requested a rock pile in Los Angeles as an emergency measure.[82] In fact, the chamber's municipal blueprint called for two different rock piles. One would be for vagrants who submitted to "voluntary" labor for four hours a day in exchange for room and board and the other a stockade for those who refused to submit to the "voluntary" camp.[83] The board essentially recommended "carrot or stick" options to combat dangerous racial deviants. Because "bums" were nonwhite deviants, in the board's mind, they should be treated as though they were Mexican "riff raff."

State border protection made up the second part of the chamber's threefold plan. On October 28, 1931, the board of directors began a "serious discussion of the question of influx of undesirable transients into California," a conversation that would continue for the rest of the decade.[84] To combat the threat, the chamber first called for the registration and documentation of all "indigent unemployed appealing for charitable assistance," to thwart welfare fraud and enable surveillance.[85] Because not all who applied for welfare were out-of-state migrants, registration would enable the incarceration of external indigents. In 1933 the Committee on Unemployed Transients even recommended federal action to establish concentration camps for transients throughout the United States.[86] They did not succeed in this attempt, but the effort indicates the degree to which Los Angeles elites wanted to separate California from the rest of the United States. To them, severing connections would enable future prosperity.

National policing was the final step in the chamber's plan to deter migration. Here, the organization asked the federal government to express greater control over local populations. One 1934 resolution asked that the federal government work with railroad companies to prevent migrant travel.[87] Assistant City Attorney Newton J. Kendall issued a similar report, which the *Times* publicized, alleging that "the transcontinental railroads . . . permitted transients to travel without interference."[88] Clements personally felt that potential migrants should be detained at home, before transiting for Los Angeles. In 1937 he wrote a long letter to Congressman Jerry Voorhis, who represented Los Angeles County in the House of Representatives. Clements suggested to Voorhis that the government establish work camps in California for some migrants and return other migrants, including families traveling together, to their home states. "Taking all things into consideration," Clements wrote, "the thoughts that we have suggested would . . . discourage transients from other states from piling up in California."[89] Work camps could act as a deterrent to potential migrants. As late as 1939 Clements wrote to the California Chamber of Commerce to detail his concerns about the "embarrassing" state of migration. "The only way it can be checked," Clements argued, "is an endeavor by the states from which the migrants originate . . . to hold them."[90] Imprisoning would-be migrants in their home states indicated Clements's view that the United States was not a collective entity, dedicated to mutual progress. Instead, California was different; California was threatened. Therefore, the federal government should take significant steps to protect it.

Eventually, the Los Angeles chamber got part of its wish when, for a few months in 1936, Los Angeles Sheriff James Davis moved his forces to the California border to forcibly expel prospective transients. The chamber of commerce had called for a "border patrol" as early as October 1931, but local and state authorities were previously loath to implement such measures because of the negative publicity that might ensue.[91] On February 3, 1936, Davis posted 126 of his officers at various major car and railroad state border crossings.[92] "If we wait until these thousands of indigents scatter over the 460 square miles of incorporated Los Angeles the Police Department can have little control over them," reasoned Davis in a *Times* interview.[93] Termed both the "Foreign Legion of Los Angeles" and the "Bum Blockade," the officers stopped poor families, searched trains, and generally enforced a fascist, amorphous standard of policing built on class and racial concerns. "It has turned back thousands of vagrants and potential criminals, it has arrested a number of wanted men, it has caused a great exodus of indigents," the *Los Angeles Times* happily noted. Any opposition to the patrol, the *Times* continued, would only enable "an attempted invasion . . . [by] swarms of two-legged locusts."[94] While Davis abandoned the border patrol in April—after the ACLU challenged the blockade in court and the patrol's operation became unsustainably expensive—the chamber urged him on at each step. On March 12, 1936, the chamber's board of directors invited Davis to its weekly meeting and asked him to report on the state of the border patrol. "It was quite evident from information obtained from all sources that this movement is of extreme benefit to California," remarked the secretary in the minutes.[95] Afterwards, the chamber petitioned Governor Merriam to make the patrol a permanent, state-governed force.[96] Even after the state's attorney general contacted the chamber a week later to inform them that the border patrol was likely illegal, the board did not abandon its support of Davis's work.[97] In late October, months after the border patrol had ceased operation, the board held a discussion on its lobbying efforts and instructed its Governmental Affairs Committee to ask Davis "what plan he had for patrolling against hoboes."[98] As late as September 28, 1939—the day after Warsaw surrendered to Nazi forces and the day before Nazi and Soviet officials partitioned Poland—the board held a meeting to discuss the "indigent problem" in California.[99]

The chamber clearly felt that the specter of impoverished migrants threatened the Anglo, masculine, middle-class identity that the organization had sought to nourish and protect in Los Angeles. During the Great Depression, Okies were thought to be more menacing than Japanese or Mexican laborers. The chamber linked its plans for transient work camps to a racialized vision of proper policing. The board's activism, then, manifested Chandler and Hearst's World War I–era rhetorical fortress in Depression-era Los Angeles, this time directed toward internal enemies. By attempting to sever California's connections with the rest of the United States, the board sought to defend Los Angeles against insidious migrants, who posed a threat similar to that of potential Japanese and Mexican invaders during World War I. During the Depression, preparedness demanded a comprehensive surveillance program and more powerful carceral institutions.

Clements's resistance to indigent American migrants eventually collided with his work defending Mexican transients. In 1939 Clements published an angry review of Carey McWilliams's seminal *Factories in the Field*, an exposé of California agriculture. In *Factories in the Field*, McWilliams criticized the farm labor system, which he termed "farm fascism," and called for a new agricultural structure. "What has long been termed 'the farm labor problem' in California may be said to date from the introduction of intensive farming with the attendant requirements for an abundance of cheap, skilled, mobile, and temporary labor," McWilliams wrote.[100] Clements presumably agreed with this point and presumably detested McWilliams's solution: "a basic change in the type of ownership and a breaking up of the large estates."[101] In response, Clements sought to isolate the purported flaws in McWilliams's analysis of California agriculture. After outlining the geographical particulars of California that in Clements's mind demanded the existence of large estates, Clements moved on to a discussion of transient labor. In part, Clements blamed white laborers who had made it "impossible for the transient Mexican to find work." As he had with Mexican laborers years previously, Clements divided white laborers into three groups: "chronic itinerants," "crackers," and "the remnants of the American pioneers." "Chronic itinerants" were clearly not welcome. "Crackers," like the Mexican "riff raff," "constitute a health menace to the state." Pioneers, while "the best type of our American people," would not be able to assimilate because there was not enough labor to go around.[102] Mexican transient labor, then, was the only solution for California. Well after the worst years of the Depression in California, Clements felt that California needed to be protected from migrants, liberal thinkers like McWilliams, and even "the best type" of American laborers. California, in his mind, should exist to serve those who could succeed there. Openness might imperil Los Angeles. Connections might be dangerous.

Selling Mediated Cosmopolitanism

If openness were merely temporary, though, and offered substantial economic and sociopolitical rewards, city leaders would rush to throw back the gates. During the Depression, Los Angeles held one of the most successful modern Olympic Games, an event dedicated to the rhetoric of international cosmopolitanism at every turn. The games emerged after a fourteen-year elite-led effort to mark Los Angeles as a global power. Through the work of the Community Development Association and its leader, William May Garland, Los Angeles staged a remarkably popular, and profitable, Olympics amid a global depression. The 1932 Olympics, then, demonstrate the effectiveness of elite collaboration at vital moments in the city's history. The Olympics also demonstrate the continuing narrative of manufactured, mediated openness that dominated elite activism and discourse throughout the decade.

Staged from July 30 to August 14, 1932, the Tenth Olympiad exhibited the fruits of city boosters' past work.[103] "Los Angeles was a city emerging from its western hick town raiment in the summer of 1932 when the Olympics put it on the world map," noted a 1984 retrospective.[104] To be sure, Los Angeles was not a "hick town" in the early 1930s, but the games marked an important step in solidifying the city's global connections. During the Olympics, over 1,300 athletes from 37 nations competed in 117 events across 14 sports. While over twenty-eight hundred athletes had participated in the 1928 games, held in Amsterdam, only three fewer nations took delegations to Los Angeles, a surprising statistic in light of the Depression and the great distance traveled by participants. Japan sent 157 athletes, the second-largest Olympic delegation, behind only the United States. India sent nineteen athletes, including its dominant, gold medal-winning men's field hockey team. On July 30 over 101,000 people gathered to watch the opening ceremonies in the Los Angeles Memorial Coliseum, which had been constructed in the early 1920s with events such as the Olympics in mind.[105] In the end, attendance at the various sites spread throughout the city topped 1.3 million, an average of over seventy-seven thousand visitors per day. Ticket sales alone brought in $1,483,525.25 in revenue, which allowed organizers immediately to repay a $1 million state bond issue and end up with a $200,000 surplus.[106] On the final day, as over eighty-seven thousand people watched the closing ceremonies, the famed sportswriter Grantland Rice felt moved to comment upon the games' place in history. "As the chorus of farewell faded out across the Pacific, the Olympic torch turned from flame to darkness," wrote Rice, "The greatest of all Olympic Games had come to the closing curtain."[107]

Similar to the 1910 Los Angeles International Air Meet, the 1932 Olympics effort did not always appear destined for success. Into the spring months preceding the games, organizers struggled to attract local and national interest in the Olympics and confirm the participation of many European nations. In March the *Times* reported that organizers were asking Los Angeles residents to "lend their co-operation in an intensive letter-writing campaign urging friends and relatives in other parts of the country to attend the big international event here this summer."[108] "In William May Garland's later years," remarked sportswriter Al Stump, "the chief organizer spoke of haunted nights, of waking to the nightmare of . . . opening the festivities to 10,000 kids, some pensioners and the LAOC's creditors."[109] In an effort to promote the games, officials supported substantial marketing campaigns. The All-Year Club of Southern California, a local booster group dedicated to selling Los Angeles nationally, reminded "Easterners" that the games were not often held in the United States. "Come early and stay late . . . Remember, this is a *year 'round* vacation land," urged one statement.[110] To lure people to the Olympics, the Union Pacific Railroad published a brochure advertising the valuable experience of attending the games. "Because of its international character, the tenth Olympiad confers an honor upon the entire nation," the brochure noted. "Los Angeles will undoubtedly be one of the most cosmopolitan cities in the world during the two weeks while the Olympic Games are in progress."[111] The publicity seems to have worked. "In an astonishing turnaround during the week of July 11–18, business exploded," narrated Stump. "Where few takers had been, 35,000 seats were sold in one seventy-two hour [sic] period."[112]

As the summer progressed, local elites continued to coordinate their efforts.[113] The *Times* informed its readers in late July that "Things Are Looking Up" in Los Angeles. "Estimates of the All Year Club ... are that the Games will bring at least 325,300 visitors who will spend $37,581,000 or more," the *Times* commented. "The city has accommodations for some 392,000 transients."[114] These "transients" weren't the malicious kind—the poor Okies, the indigents—but the good kind—those willing to spend money, those who would leave in a month. Other booster groups joined in. *Touring Topics*, the magazine of the Automobile Club of Southern California, devoted much of its July edition to informing visitors about the "Southland and its wonders."[115] For their part, Hollywood studios arranged for major motion picture stars to visit the Olympic Village.[116] On August 6 Mayer hosted a luncheon and tour of his studio for delegates from thirty nations.[117] Overall, the Olympic effort succeeded emphatically. "Considering the economic climate," the same 1984 retrospective ruminated, "Los Angeles' success reads like a fiscal fairy tale today."[118]

The effort to secure the 1932 Olympics for Los Angeles had begun in 1918, when community leaders began to mobilize among themselves. Garland later remembered the effort to gain his participation:

> Some time in 1918 . . . I was visited by five publishers—Harry Chandler of the Los Angeles Times; F. W. Kellogg representing the Los Angeles Evening Express; Guy B. Parham, representing the Los Angeles Herald; M. H. Imsen, representing the Los Angeles Examiner, and H. B. R. Briggs, representing the Los Angeles Record. They stated to me that, for the first time in the history of Los Angeles, the newspaper publishers had arrived at the determination to become united on everything that had to do with the upbuilding and advancement of Los

Angeles . . . They enlarged their plan by suggesting that they add about twenty, or twenty-five representative business men . . . and complete an organization which would be known as the Community Development Association.[119]

The Community Development Association grew into the leading sports booster association in the city, an exemplar of Los Angeles elites' cooperative and political skills. The CDA also created the Olympiad Committee of the Games, which included CDA members such as Briggs, Chandler, and Garland.[120] One of the group's first projects was building a suitable athletic facility for the city to hold major events. In 1919 the CDA announced its plans to build a privately funded facility that would eventually pass into public hands. When the CDA finished the Los Angeles Coliseum in 1923, in Exposition Park near the campus of the University of Southern California, it had cost $772,000 and could seat 75,000 people.[121] The coliseum became the centerpiece of Los Angeles's Olympics bid. In 1923 Garland successfully lobbied to be appointed to the American Olympic Committee. In that role, he became close friends with Pierre de Coubertin, who had initiated the effort to revive the Olympic Games in the 1890s and served as president of the International Olympic Committee from 1896 to 1924. In 1923 at the IOC's meetings in Rome, Garland, backed by Coubertin, secured the 1932 Olympics for Los Angeles in an uncontested bid process. Garland stressed the importance of making the games a global event. "I addressed the body," Garland recalled, "and told them that . . . if the games were to be truly international in character they must be held in other parts of the universe."[122]

Garland was a prescient choice to lead the CDA. Born in Westport, Maine, in 1866, he eventually migrated to Chicago. In 1890 Garland suffered a hemorrhage severe enough that his doctor ordered him to move to the West Coast. Arriving in Los Angeles, Garland took a job at the Pacific Cable Company, where he saved up enough money to buy a piece of property—the first of many.[123] W. M. Garland Company came to dominate Los Angeles commercial and residential real estate. A sample article in 1912 announced that the W. M. Garland Company was handling the sale of "200

Lots and 50 Acreage Sites" in Beverley Hills, for which there was a one-hundred-person waiting list.[124] As Garland's real estate empire expanded, he held the presidencies of, among many other groups, the Los Angeles Realty Board, the National Association of Real Estate Boards, the Los Angeles Athletic Club, the Automobile Club of Southern California, and the 1932 Olympic Organizing Committee.[125] A fervent Republican—Garland wrote to Coubertin after the election of Calvin Coolidge in 1925 that "the Republican Party . . . remains overwhelmingly in power, representing the conservative, safe and sane element of our citizenship"[126]—Garland gained local adoration from other elites. Upon his death in 1948, the Los Angeles City Council adjourned to honor his legacy, and the *Los Angeles Times* mourned the passing of the "pioneer Los Angeles financier and civic leader."[127]

Garland believed that the modern Olympic Games held the capacity to promote peace and understanding around the world. In May 1923, a few months after Los Angeles had been selected as host for the 1932 games, Garland asked Coubertin to write a letter to the citizens of Los Angeles about the Olympics. "I would have you set forth clearly what 'Olympism' means and what it stands for; what message it carries to the world . . . as a potential factor in the encouragement, maintenance and preservation of peace," he wrote.[128] In his closing message at the games, subsequently printed in the *Times*, Garland reflected on the broader impact of the competition. "Although you depart from us," Garland remarked, "we feel in a sense that each one of you leaves with us something of his or her spirit; something which will live on with us through the years as an Olympic heritage."[129] That heritage provided "a tolerance and understanding . . . that could be achieved in no other way . . . the greatest single force for world peace that has ever been known."[130] Much as Whitsett had felt that an Owens Valley park might provide positive connections between California's north and south, Garland believed the Olympics might provide positive connections around the world. Accordingly, the 1932 Olympics promoted three policies and ideals designed to promote openness: the Olympic Village, shared fiscal responsibility, and Los Angeles as the future center of "New Olympism."

The 1932 Olympic Village inaugurated a tradition that survives to this day. Built on roughly three hundred acres of land near Culver City loaned by the family of deceased real estate speculator Lucky Baldwin, the village housed all male athletes at the games, while women were given accommodations in a hotel.[131] Five hundred fourteen-by-twenty-four-foot cottages housed the athletes, who ate in one enormous, communal dining room.[132] Building the village allowed organizers to significantly cut down costs for participating nations. National Olympic committees paid only two dollars per athlete per day for food, lodging, and transportation and were thus able to afford travel costs.[133] Most importantly, the village provided organizers a useful image of cosmopolitan sportsmanship.

"Turbaned Tornadoes Hit Village as Indian Men Arrive," announced the *Times* on July 10, 1932. The article, which outlined how the Indian field hockey team was prepared to dominate the games in "the city of many tongues," was just one of many dedicated to exploring the Olympic Village and informing readers about the wonders found there.[134] Sometimes, especially in describing non-European athletes, the articles denoted arrivals in surprisingly militaristic language, perhaps revealing some underlying tension behind the facade of local harmony. The New Zealand team "invaded" the village when it arrived, while a second group of Japanese arrivals was described as "reinforcements" who "stormed" the premises.[135] Even the German delegation was deemed to be an "army."[136] Mostly, though, the *Times* wrote of curiosities—of "caballeros," of dueling scars on the bodies of German athletes, of the purple patent leather shoes worn by one Australian athlete and which prompted the village shoe shiner to shake his head in amazement.[137] Collectively, the articles indicate a desire to create an Olympic melting pot. The effects of the village might spread to the host city. The *Times* noted the salubrious benefits of the games on the "foreign colonies" of people who lived in the city—Brazilians, Germans, Japanese, and Swiss among them.[138] The Olympic Village, then, functioned as a kind of theater for Angelenos to view other cultures in a safe, bounded environment. The athletes were exhibits, similar to those one might find at a museum or a world's fair. They would not pose a significant threat to the stable, masculine metropolis.

Promotional literature created around the Olympics also linked openness to the games' frugality. The organizers envisioned that their organization might unite athletes and attendees under a banner of shared determination to navigate the global crisis. "The record of our city's conception of its responsibility . . . discloses one fundamental and guiding principle," noted the games' official report. "To adhere strictly to the Olympic ideals . . . Not a single note of commercialism was allowed to permeate the consummation of the task."[139] While the extent of "commercialism" is debatable, the organizers certainly harped on the steps they took to ensure the financial viability of the games. Single tickets cost one, two, or three dollars. The pricier events were the Opening Ceremony, certain rowing competitions, and an exhibition of American football played between select college players from both coasts.[140] Of course, anticommercialism only extended so far. John C. Porter, the mayor of Los Angeles, urged the committee to allow children free admission, but organizers charged them fifty cents apiece.[141]

Furthermore, commercialism could be linked to professionalism, the antithesis of the amateurism the games promoted. At the Opening Ceremony, Coubertin extensively discussed the amateur ideal and the trend toward professionalism, "a vicious influence because of the pernicious cycle which it engenders and to which it inevitably leads."[142] That cycle might wield its destructive power on society. A "Souvenir Book" prepared by the organizing committee announced its "confidence in the child of modern Olympism to overcome the disintegrating influences rampant in mass society throughout the human family."[143] Amateurism implied open competition; amateurism might heal the world.

Finally, organizers presented Los Angeles as a node of future Olympic activity, the epicenter of humanitarian sportsmanship.[144] Garland imagined such a future in one of his letters to Coubertin. "If you care to speak of this Pacific Coast as one of the future centers of the New Olympism, so much the better," Garland wrote, not so subtly indicating his hope that the IOC would grant Los Angeles the right to host future Olympics.[145] Other organizers picked up on and reproduced Garland's idea. In a lengthy article for the *Los Angeles Times*, Maynard McFie, the vice president of the games' organizing committee, related to readers the history of the ancient Olympic Games before turning to 1932. The article depicted a flattened globe—two intersecting circles—with Los Angeles in the middle and lines running to and from it. "Los Angeles, the Olympic City in 1932, is centrally located with reference to the rest of the world, as shown by the map above," the caption noted.[146] The image appeared very much like a shipping map or one of the idealistic portrayals of the developing Port of Los Angeles. Here, it would be a good thing if the currents of the world led to Los Angeles.

At the Opening Ceremony, Robert Sproul, the president of the University of California, concretely summarized contemporary elite discussions of cosmopolitanism and connections. Sproul gave the dedication address and benediction, which he titled "The Same Great Pattern." That pattern, Sproul argued, was the trend of positive exchange initiated by the first Olympics in Greece. "The land of Greece was open to the East, and so her people were able to draw unto themselves the treasures of Asia, and, adding them to their own, to recreate them into a civilization which after the long procession of the centuries, still profoundly influences all the world," Sproul began. The 1932 Olympics might do the same, Sproul thought. "We, too, are neighbors of Asia and to us today are open those self-same opportunities to give, to take, and to recreate," he surmised. "May we not fail to emulate the example so nobly set for us and prove ourselves not wholly unworthy of this our environment, of these our opportunities."[147] While Sproul's vision of being a good neighbor was perhaps more accommodating than that of the organizers, he perpetuated their rhetorical talking points. An open Los Angeles could influence world affairs, and cosmopolitan experiences would enlighten its citizens. Of course, the Olympic Games were also a safe atmosphere. The event operated under preexisting structures and did not threaten to disrupt local hierarchy. Best of all for men such as Garland, the games could be sold as anticommercial even as Los Angeles reaped the tourist profits.

The Threat of Governor Sinclair

City leaders threatened to deactivate Los Angeles as an economic node, however, if Upton Sinclair's gubernatorial campaign succeeded. For his part, Sinclair was hardly the man to back down from a war of words.[148] Though he was born in Baltimore in 1878 to an upper middle-class family, his parents' fortunes considerably cratered when his father became, in the words of one biographer, "a periodically unemployable alcoholic" shortly after Sinclair's birth.[149] Thereafter, Sinclair's family migrated to New York City and occasionally back to his aunt's Baltimore home in particularly hard times. By the time Sinclair graduated from City College in 1897, he desired to become a writer. His first forays produced a series of eight pulp fiction novels centering on young men in the military. In his production phases, Sinclair would dictate as many as eight thousand words per day to two full-time stenographers. Around 1900, determined to fulfill grander self-expectations for his literary career, Sinclair increasingly distanced himself from pulp fiction and embarked on a successful career penning serious, sometimes exaggerated works about big business and its societal effects. Criticizing modern society similarly led him to embrace a series of "fads"—sexual abstinence, raw food diets, refraining from alcohol consumption, and occult rituals, among others. Sinclair moved with his wife to Pasadena, California, in the 1920s, where he would live for much of the rest of his life. In California, he embraced, in his words, "an open-air life," in a community he termed "a parasite upon the great industrial centres of other parts of America . . . smug and self-satisfied, making the sacredness of property the first and last article of its creed."[150]

In his work, Sinclair took aim at injustices perpetrated by those true believers in the "sacredness of property." An avowed socialist—he unsuccessfully ran for the House of Representatives and the Senate on the Socialist ticket in 1920 and 1922 respectively—Sinclair often harped upon class concerns. In 1906 Sinclair spent six months investigating Chicago's meatpacking industry. He intended the novel he produced, *The Jungle*, to inform readers about the destructive class relations produced by industrial capitalism. Instead, Sinclair's readers seized upon his depiction of factory sanitary conditions, and the novel eventually led to the passage of the 1906 Meat Inspection Act and Pure Food and Drug Act. Most relevant to Sinclair's 1934 gubernatorial campaign was his 1919 *The Brass Check*. Sinclair divided his nonfiction exposé of the American journalism industry into three parts: "The Evidence," "The Explanation," and "The Remedy." Throughout the book he criticized the sensational gossip produced by Hearst's papers, but he focused on Los Angeles media outlets in particular at the end of "The Evidence." "I have lived in Southern California four years," Sinclair wrote, "and it is literally a fact that I have yet to meet a single person who does not despise and hate his 'Times.'"[151] Sinclair criticized the *Times* for its conservative bent, salacious gossip, and general lack of "journalistic integrity."[152] Another chapter, titled "The Daily Cat-And-Dog Fight," discussed relations between the *Times* and the *Examiner*. The *Examiner*, Sinclair felt, "is entirely commercial, its fervors are for the local industry of 'boosting.' It has an especially annoying habit of disguising its advertisements so as to trap you into reading them as news."[153] The competition between the two papers, Sinclair argued, injured civil society. "It is impossible to get the news of world-events in Southern California without having [the two newspapers'] greed and spite thrust upon you," he argued.[154] During Sinclair's gubernatorial campaign, California newspapers so attacked Sinclair that he produced a pamphlet, *The Lie Factory Starts*, seeking to debunk the papers' depictions of him.[155] The deplorable state of journalism in Los Angeles, Sinclair felt, diverged greatly from the ideal of cosmopolitan openness.

Even though Sinclair had once dismissed the Los Angeles area as populated by "retired elderly people, whose health has broken down," he had assimilated to a certain degree into Angeleno elite society by the early 1930s.[156] Sinclair and his wife Mary Craig Kimbrough settled in a home in a tree-lined section of Sunset Avenue in Pasadena, a wealthy suburban town northeast of Los Angeles and adjacent to San Marino, where Henry Huntington had built his mansion. The couple also owned a formerly foreclosed mansion in Beverly Hills, to which he sometimes retreated during the campaign.[157] An avid tennis player, Sinclair played at the Live Oaks Tennis Club and the Valley Hunt Club, both fashionable Pasadena institutions, but his socialism barred him from further socialization with the conservative members there.[158] Instead, he gained entrance into the town's liberal elite group, whose members included King Gillette, the razor mogul.[159]

Therefore, it might have confused some Los Angeles elites to learn of the radicalness of EPIC. Even by the standards of early twentieth-century populism, Sinclair's plan stands out for its ambitious, uncompromising aims.[160] Capitalism, Sinclair told an audience at the Shrine Auditorium in Los Angeles on the eve of the 1934 Democratic Primary, "has served its time and is passing from the earth."[161] He outlined EPIC in the 1933 volume, *I, Governor of California, and How I Ended Poverty*, a fictive imagination of his campaign and governorship. "I say that if it was right for our forefathers to turn out King George III of England and his governors and officials," Sinclair imagines telling an assembled crowd on the eve of the election, "it is equally right for the people of California to take back at least part of the resources which have been stolen from them by three generations of wholesale graft, speculation, and monopoly."[162] In *I, Governor*, Sinclair goes on to resounding victory in the general election and sets about implementing his plans. He purchases private property for workers' "colonies," passes a massive bond issue, and convinces California's citizens to take money from private banks in order to purchase the bonds.[163] Notably, Sinclair only spent one chapter of the book, out of six, discussing implementation. In the last chapter, "Victory," he pans through California. Poverty has become extinct—except for one "religious hermit who lived in a cave"—and EPIC is spreading throughout America. The public runs the newspapers, which contain no advertisements. Though in his imagination Sinclair had won on the Democratic ticket, at the end of *I, Governor* the Democratic and Republican parties are now marginal outliers, while the Socialist Party is "active and powerful." As a result, "The people had lost their fear of the State . . . It was no longer the incarnation of selfishness, an instrument of repression of exploiting classes."[164] More than any other part of Sinclair's plan, this vision of an expansive, welcoming state bureaucracy sparked a panoply of attacks. Though he was wealthy and connected, Sinclair opposed the Los Angeles elite mission. Similar to the way in which Andrae B. Nordskog had fought against one-sided extractive connections in the California Water Wars, Sinclair argued that the city should not cut itself off from the United States in order to preserve hierarchical capitalist structures. Nordskog and Sinclair were

THE PERILS OF EXCEPTIONALISM

very different in one crucial aspect, however: Sinclair had a great deal more power. Nordskog was a minor newspaper publisher; Sinclair was a national figure, who had fought for years against economic injustice. Sinclair had defeated the political establishment once in the Democratic primary, and he seemed poised to take advantage of contemporary economic upheaval and sweep into the governor's office. He was a very real threat to local elites.

Though the anti-Sinclair campaign was multifaceted, Louis B. Mayer directed its progression. Born Lazar Meir in the northern Ukraine on July 12, 1884, Mayer embarked on a trajectory that embodied the standard migrant journey to Los Angeles, except on a much grander scale.[165] The Mayer family fled from Russian pogroms in the mid-1880s to Boston, via England and New York. After a few years spent on Long Island, the family moved to New Brunswick, Canada, around 1892, during which time Lazar Meir became Louis Mayer. As a child, Louis searched the street salvaging anything that he could for resale, especially looking for scrap metal for the family business. By the age of fifteen, he took over the business from his father and began to travel throughout northeastern Canada and the United States. In 1904 the nineteen-year-old Mayer moved to Boston, where he moved into the theater business. In 1914 he started a film distribution company, the American Feature Film Company. His success in that venture—propelled by his prescient purchase of the New England rights to *The Birth of a Nation*—prompted him to pursue film production, and he moved with his wife and children to Los Angeles in 1918.

Mayer was able to command the nascent motion picture industry in relatively little time. In 1924 Mayer's Metro Pictures merged with Goldwyn Pictures and Marcus Loew's chain of theaters to form Metro-Goldwyn, shortly renamed Metro-Goldwyn-Mayer. MGM would come to dominate the industry and produce such famed films as *Ben Hur* and *The Wizard of Oz*. A determined, controlling man, Mayer ruled as a "feudal lord," hated, loved, and feared. As a glimpse into his character, one Mayer biography opens on the executive breaking up a marriage in order to provide a wife for the actor Van Johnson and thereby hide Johnson's homosexuality.[166] "Study men and women more assiduously than books," he advised readers of the *Times* in 1930. "The day of the 'one man' business has passed forever."[167] While this may have been true—Mayer depended on the producer Irving Thalberg during many of MGM's most successful years—Mayer made MGM as much of a "one man business" as possible. At his funeral in 1957, more than two thousand people gathered at Wilshire Temple to mourn.[168] "It was [Mayer's] vitality and foresight during most of his career which enabled the film industry to become a tremendous world influence," noted an obituary.[169]

Mayer was no stranger to Republican Party activism. Historian Steven Ross has referred to him as "The Man Who Brought Hollywood into the Republican Party."[170] He served as a delegate to the 1928 and 1932 Republican National Conventions, as a result of which he became close friends with Herbert Hoover and chaired the California Republican Party from 1932 to 1933. From 1928 on Mayer increasingly tied Los Angeles to Washington through the actors, studios, and showmanship at his disposal. In the 1932 elections Mayer began to make and disseminate fake "newsreels," which were partial toward Hoover.[171] He did the same in the 1934 gubernatorial election. MGM produced a series of newsreels involving "interviews" with Sinclair supporters. The reels shocked viewers with the knowledge that Sinclairites dressed like bums, spoke glowingly of communism in foreign accents, and stated their intentions to move to California for EPIC.[172] Combined with Mayer's personal distaste for Sinclair's socialism—when Sinclair had worked on an adaptation of his *The Wet Parade* with MGM, Mayer refused to allow the author and his wife visit the studio until the film made a profit at the box office—Mayer had means, motive, and opportunity to obliterate Sinclair's campaign.[173]

While Los Angeles elites at first dismissed the seriousness of Sinclair's candidacy, opposition quickly coalesced after his primary victory. During the general election campaign, Los Angeles transformed into a center of elite political activism. In September, a group led by Chandler and Mayer quickly pledged $50,000 to defeat Sinclair.[174] Led by Mayer, movie studios garnished employees' paychecks for "donations" to the Merriam campaign. The actor Billy Wilder later remembered how he tried to protest the $50 garnishment on a $250 paycheck. When Wilder asked why he wasn't able to make his own donations, he was told "the house is burning down . . . That son of a bitch Bolshevik Sinclair must be stopped."[175] Warner Brothers announced a month before the election that it was temporarily "suspending" a $350,000 expansion pending the voting results.[176] The head of United Artists forecast that the entire film industry would move to Florida if Sinclair prevailed.[177] Other groups joined in as well. Alarmed by Sinclair's threats to confiscate private land, the California Real Estate Association attacked the candidate. Garland himself directed the Merriam for Governor Campaign.[178] On Election Day, the Los Angeles Chamber of Commerce demanded that member businesses close their doors and canvass for Merriam.[179] Most of all, the print media declared war. The major newspapers in California—the *San Francisco Chronicle*, the *Oakland Tribune*, the *Sacramento Bee*, Hearst's *San Francisco Examiner, Los Angeles Examiner*, and *Los Angeles Herald-Express*, and Chandler's *Los Angeles Times*—smeared Sinclair with information taken directly from the Merriam campaign.[180] Each day, the newspapers ridiculed Sinclair for his utopian ideals. They also harped on the danger he posed. "Is This Still America," asked one August editorial in the *Times*, continuing, "Either we take the Red path; or we close that gate right now—forever."[181] The theme of "gates" and other border imagery would be central to both campaigns' discourse. The rhetoric of "closing the gate" sounded very similar to the borderlands fortress idea of the World War I era. Sinclair was a threat on the same level as a dual Japanese-Mexican invasion of the southwestern United States.

The two campaigns most often disagreed in a language that reflected different visions about California's geosocial role. Sinclair's speeches, letters, and campaign literature openly discussed his views. The anti-Sinclair campaign relied on more impersonal editorials and leaflets, which implicitly foretold a darker future if California became more open. Notably, Sinclair embraced California exceptionalism in many of his speeches, the same exceptionalism that boosters feared would lure too many migrants to the West Coast. Largely, he focused on the geographic and technological factors that would allow the state to prosper amid the Depression. On August 2, a few weeks before the Democratic primary, Sinclair addressed a statewide audience for the first time over radio. "Why do we have to have poverty in our golden State, with millions of acres of fertile land?," Sinclair asked rhetorically. "There is only one thing that can be done, make it possible for the unemployed to produce from themselves."[182] Ten days later, he claimed that modern technology should produce equality. "We have invented marvelous machines which are capable of pouring out wealth in a golden flood," he argued. "We no longer have to get rich by robbing our neighbor—we can get rich by using our own creative powers."[183] If one removes the "robbing our neighbor" line, Sinclair sounds very much like a California booster.

The Sinclair and anti-Sinclair campaigns diverged the most about issues relating to social activism, migrants, and borders. Both Sinclair and his enemies agreed on the revolutionary ideology inherent to Sinclair's vision, but the two campaigns tried to slant their depictions of Sinclair's aggressive undertones. For his part, Sinclair never shied away from militarism. He named his future farms "colonies," after all. EPIC's letterhead image showed a honeybee in flight with its stinger out over the EPIC motto, "I Produce—I Defend."[184] Sinclair's campaign songs evoked a battle taking place in the state. "There's something in the air / Crowds rushing here and there / They're gath'ring ev'rywhere / See how their banners flare / For justice they declare . . . When we elect Sinclair," read the opening verse from one song.[185] "Hail to our chief who in triumph advances / Hail to our chief and his conquering clan / He is our leader in planning 'End of Poverty,' / Which surely will be done thru his Epic Plan," read another.[186] Here, militant activism was a good thing. The muscular energy of the Sinclair campaign dovetailed with the era's challenge to masculinity. As America's corporate culture fractured during the Depression, a "uniform ideal of male success," which connected economic advancement to masculinity, broke down as well.[187] Such campaign songs harkened back to older forms of masculinity, based on physical labor and determination. By calling for its manly "crusaders" to "conquer," the campaign not only addressed the contemporary crisis of masculinity but also challenged elites' hegemonic masculinity. Sinclair pledged that his supporters might regain their manhood via participation in EPIC.

Anti-Sinclair forces combated Sinclair's rhetoric by warning of an apocalyptic future if he were elected. The California League against Sinclairism, a group started by Clem Whitaker and Leone Baxter, two of the first political consultants, distributed a series of pamphlets meant to resemble Sinclair's own pamphlets. One, *Plundering the Farmer: An Expose [sic] of Upton Sinclair's 'Epic' Scheme to Russianize California Agriculture and Destroy Independent Farming*, especially warned farmers about Sinclair's crusade. If Sinclair were elected, the pamphlet argued, his "tax confiscation" of independent farms would endanger farmers' "personal security—and the welfare of home and family."[188] There is some evidence that this strategy worked. Farmers in the San Joaquin Valley, worried about "colonies," seem to have flocked to Haight's third-party campaign.[189] The Merriam campaign also distributed a brief article to "working men," which outlined "this novelist's scheme . . . a visionary project which would throw you out of work."[190] The *Times* bemoaned "The Gospel of Hate" allegedly espoused by Sinclair and his supporters, who "destroy the innocent, they divert men's mind from useful service to assaults upon others; they arouse evil passions that wreck vengeance upon the innocent and the helpless."[191] Here was the invasion rhetoric once more at play. While Sinclair pledged to restore supporters' masculinity, his opponents argued that his actions would undermine the gender norms of male labor and familial protection. Breaking down borders, the anti-Sinclair campaign claimed, was dangerous.

Later, Sinclair's remark that "half the unemployed" in America would migrate to California further exposed the debate over the state's future geosocial role. In EPIC *News*, the weekly newspaper distributed by his campaign, Sinclair tried to defend himself in a weekly question-and-answer column, "I Rise to Inquire." In response to the question, "What would you do if 6,000,000 unemployed flocked to California?" Sinclair first outlined his hope that the federal government might help out migrants "in the interim." Once the colonies were self-supporting, however, "Under a system where you are producing for use, you don't have to be afraid of numbers . . . It is only under the profit system where nobody can have a job until the factory owner has made a profit."[192] In October, Sinclair tried to turn the tables on the *Times*, by claiming that the paper was encouraging poverty in California to discourage migration. "The [*Times*'] remedy is very simple . . . Keep the people of California so poor that the rest of the country will not envy their condition, and so will not be moved to come into our state," he argued.[193] Clearly, Sinclair's offhand comment about migration was not just a joke. His campaign centered on California's exceptionalism, connections, and openness. Discouraging migration would admit a flaw in his socialist vision.

Naturally, the *Times* viewed Sinclair's remark as prime oppositional fodder. Among many editorials about domestic migration, two especially stand out for their conceptualization of future invasions. In late September, on its front page the paper mocked "A Sweet Prospect" of domestic migration. Singling out the "Unemployed Influx Menace," the *Times* predicted "the State would be thrown into utter chaos, at the mercy of riotous, Red-incited mobs." "Instead of the 'Epic Plan' we would be under martial law," the newspaper continued. "Sinclair would find himself running errands for a major-general of the United States Army."[194] In this vision, California would endure two invasions: indigent "mobs" would storm the state, and the federal government would violate California's sovereignty. "Sovietization," a proto-invasion of its own, was likely as well. On the day before the election, the *Times* issued its final editorial, a lengthy comparison of the two candidates. "Sinclair, lifelong Socialist, associate and collaborator of radicals . . . self-proclaimed instructor of Communist Russia, proposes to Sovietize California," the editorial claimed. In the interim, another invasion was underway. "[Sinclair's] invitation to the unemployed of the entire country to come here for an easy living at little work and public cost is already bringing in indigents at the rate of 1000 per day," the paper announced.[195] An array of villains threatened California if Sinclair were elected.

Finally, depictions of California's borders solidified the differences between the two campaigns. At different moments, EPIC *News* presented its readers with editorial cartoons that dealt with borders and the Depression. In March EPIC *News* told its readers that California contained "Room for All Who Want to Work." The attached cartoon showed an "EPIC California State Colony," producing for use—the power plant spewed smoke, the laboratory appeared active, and a cart took away "colony produce for [the]

FIG. 9. In March 1934, EPIC *News* portrayed a "California State Colony" as a busy, open place. Upton Sinclair Papers. Courtesy Lilly Library, Indiana University, Bloomington, Indiana.

factory town" (fig. 9).[196] Labeling the town a "California State Colony" implicitly conflated the colony's borders with those of the state. Again, Sinclair did not distance himself from his remark about the unemployed.

On August 6, 1934, another cartoon showed EPIC supporters, "Cooperative Specialists," "Marching Along!" on a bridge over a river titled "The Depression." Road signs announced, "This Is a One-Way Road" and "We Can't Go Back." While the skies were dark and stormy over the bridge, the land beyond was clear and bright. The image not only linked Sinclair's campaign to the New Deal but also evoked California's "golden" qualities so attractive to migrants (fig. 10).[197]

In contrast, the *Times* somewhat jokingly related a conversation between an Angeleno and the Reno, Nevada, chief of police. If migrants came near his district, the chief of police suggested "One Way to Cope with Sinclair

Marching Along!

FIG. 10. In March 1934 EPIC *News* displayed malleable borders as a positive thing, at odds with the ideas of Angeleno elites. Upton Sinclair Papers. Courtesy Lilly Library, Indiana University, Bloomington, Indiana.

Migration" was to build a fence around Reno. "All main entrance [*sic*] will be carefully guarded by mounted police equipped with automatic rifle [*sic*] . . . Searchlights will be used at all gateways and all entrants must show reason for entering city, otherwise will not allow them to pass gates. Assure Sinclair we are prepared for the worst."[198] It may have been a joke, but some Angelenos undoubtedly would have considered the policeman's approach to be proactive.

After suffering a substantial defeat in the general election, Sinclair returned to writing. While his book *I, Candidate for Governor: And How I Got Licked*, a campaign postmortem written in a similar style to *I, Governor of California*, is perhaps best-known, he also wrote a satirical play,

Depression Island, which provides a fitting coda to border discussions. The play opens on three stranded men: Don, a composer; Bing, a taxi driver from Chicago; and Crunk, a real estate executive from Los Angeles. At one point, the three men begin gambling for control of various parts of the island. Bing wins the coconuts, Don wins the bananas, Bing wins the mussels, Don wins the fish, and so on and so forth. Eventually, Crunk, the wealthy Angeleno, has the men roll dice for "the island itself and all that's on it and around it," a bet that he, of course, wins. Crunk quickly tries to put the men to work, a development Don disputes. "Are you a loyal man, Bing?," Crunk asks Bing, who answers affirmatively and forces Don to submit by knocking Don's hat off. "Now, we'll get somewhere, Bing. You and I on my tight little island," Crunk tells his new employee.[199] Sinclair perceptively mocked Los Angeles elites' need for borders in a time of crisis. Of course, Depression Island did not harm the elite Crunk; it only solidified his power. Sinclair recognized that borders were not necessarily permanent. Instead, border protection rhetoric was an effective form of elite activism that generated popular enthusiasm and sustained hierarchy. Similar to the borderlands fortress, Los Angeles's own Depression Island allowed its elites to maintain control over the city by defeating Sinclair.

Debates about migration and Los Angeles's borders did not disappear with the onset of World War II. While much of the venom would be directed at Japanese immigrants, some groups continued to fear the white migrant. In March 1942 the Los Angeles Paper Handlers' Union submitted a resolution to the city council that condemned the chamber of commerce for encouraging migration to California. First, the union laid out its logic regarding "exploitation" of migration. "Tremendous sums of money must be expended by the government and people for this war effort," the group reasoned, and "the moneys used by the Chambers of Commerce . . . devoted to exploitation purposes are expended in efforts to induce people throughout the United States to make their home in California." Migration, the resolution continued, "does not contribute substantially to the further employment of the working people in California."[200] Two messages stand out. First, conceptions of Los Angeles as an island remained popular with the working class long after the worst years of the Depression. Second, the Los Angeles Chamber of Commerce did not discourage migration for long. Only in a moment of crisis did various elites and elite groups need to change their rhetoric to fit the situation.

Depression-era Los Angeles, then, posed a challenge to elites and the politics of connection. Exceptionalism, they found out, could be dangerous. Mediated openness, when restricted to distinct, controllable populations, provided a useful solution. The campaigns to oppose Mexican deportation and domestic migration, present a cosmopolitan image of the city to the world in the Olympics, and defeat Upton Sinclair's insurgent politics demonstrated the remarkable malleability of concepts such as borders and cosmopolitanism. During the Depression, California's eastern border with the United States, in elites' minds, needed to be fortified, but the southern border with Mexico seemed less threatening. As the Depression receded, Los Angeles would again pursue federal infrastructure appropriations and defense contracts. Aviation, the first tendrils of which had so excited and scared Angelenos at the 1910 international aviation meet, would become the next major municipal industry. While the very act of flying threatened to break down all previous boundaries, flight also held the potential to shape more profitable, stronger connections between Los Angeles and the outside world.

SNAPSHOT
LOS ANGELES, 1940

"IN ONE OF THE LIGHTEST ELECTION-DAY TURNOUTS IN THE CITY'S history," reported the *Los Angeles Times* on May 7, 1941, "Los Angeles voters gave a two-thirds indorsement to a proposed bond issue . . . for the $3,500,000 airport bonds."[1] The newspaper's subdued language masked a much larger victory for supporters of a modern airport in Los Angeles. With the passage of the bond issue, three years after a similar proposal failed, the city took its first steps toward creating the Los Angeles International Airport, today one of the ten busiest airports in the world. More importantly, after a lengthy, contested process, Los Angeles embraced its growing identity as a hub of the aircraft industry—the final step in a five decade-long process to secure the city's connections.

Following the 1910 Los Angeles International Air Meet, local interest in air travel remained high. In 1918 famed filmmaker Cecil B. DeMille founded the Mercury Aviation Company and built two airfields west of downtown Los Angeles, adjacent to the current location of the Los Angeles County Museum of Art. Before it closed in 1922, Mercury Aviation offered scheduled flights on a Junkers airplane to Santa Catalina Island, San Diego, and San Francisco.[2] In 1927, after completing the first solo and nonstop transatlantic flight, Charles Lindbergh flew his *Spirit of St. Louis* to Los Angeles as a part of a national aviation tour.[3] Over one million people, the *Times* reported, came out to see Lindbergh, in a city with a population of around 1.2 million. "It was the greatest show Southern California has ever known," exulted the *Times*. "It ran the gamut of human emotion as old men danced and flung their hats into the air in an abandon of joy, as women wept and those in between shrieked and cheered and roared."[4] Lindbergh used the occasion to harp on Los Angeles's need for improved aviation facilities. "If Los Angeles desires to keep the city on the air map," Lindbergh remarked in a live radio address, "it will have to construct a municipal airport."[5]

Lindbergh's message certainly hit home. In May 1928 the city council placed a $6 million bond issue on the ballot for a citywide referendum. If the bond issue passed, the council would use the large sum to buy and develop three potential airport sites within Los Angeles's expanding city limits: Vail Field, located about ten miles southeast of downtown, Sesnon Field in the San Fernando Valley, and Mines Field, a small airfield on a large piece of property in Inglewood, southwest of downtown.[6] Although booster organizations preached the importance of the initiative's passage, it failed to get the needed two-thirds majority of voters.[7] City leaders decided instead to lease and develop Mines Field, which at four hundred acres was twice as large as Vail Field and much closer to the city than Sesnon Field. On October 2, 1928, Los Angeles formally took over Mines Field on a ten-year lease, which cost about $100,000 per year.[8] This did not, however, lead immediately to the successful development of a world-class airport. For example, even when Los Angeles finally purchased Mines Field in 1937, the city was not much closer to a municipal airport to show off to the world than it had been a decade earlier. Other airports in the region—Lockheed Field in Burbank and Grand Central Airport in Glendale, especially—continued to do more business than did Mines Field, which featured one two-thousand-foot runway and a hangar for forty planes but no other amenities.[9] In 1939 city leaders again asked voters to support an expansion of Mines Field, and once again, Angelenos failed to give the initiative a two-thirds majority.[10] A city that had by this time grown to 2.7 million people, sprawled over 450 square miles of land, did not have an airport capable of luring business away from minor local airports.[11]

Undeterred, city leaders kept pressing the issue. In December 1939 the

Los Angeles City Council asked voters to approve a $976,000 bond issue for airport improvements, which, due to its financial structure, would only need a simple majority to pass. As in so many times during the city's history, the federal government agreed to help the city: $476,000 of the bond would go to secure a Works Project Administration grant of $1.5 million for further work on the project.[12] The "yes" campaign used a familiar civic rhetoric, harping on the importance of a modern airport for Los Angeles's prestige and connectedness. "Los Angeles," the *Times* bemoaned, "is the only large city in the United States which does not boast a modern municipal union air terminal. It is a situation beyond the comprehension of outsiders and one of which our own citizenry are painfully obvious."[13] The newspaper asked Angelenos to remember the lessons of Los Angeles's past. "Our union terminal of the air," an editorial surmised, "would be comparable to the harbor we dredged in the swamps and flats early in the century. It would bring here all the commercial airlines now and in future touching this part of the West, even as our ocean port brought the ships."[14] Voters passed the $976,000 bond by a margin of 162,349 to 109,597.[15] In 1941, Angelenos passed another major airport bond issue of $3,5000,000 by the requisite two-thirds majority to purchase more land around Los Angeles Airport, build a large administration building, and provide more hangar space.[16] Finally—after twenty years of failed bond measures and debate about expansion—boosters succeeded. Once, Otis had yearned for port and rail connections. Now, boosters could exult in Los Angeles's port and air connections. 1940, then, found Los Angeles at a pivotal moment in the development of its external connections via aviation.

The year marked a similarly pivotal moment for the Los Angeles aircraft industry. Beginning in the 1920s, the thousands of acres of cheap land available in Southern California had sparked long-term growth in local airplane manufacturing. The industry also benefited from the sheer number of airfields situated near downtown Los Angeles through which companies could transport raw materials, some fifty-three of various sizes in 1929.[17] Accordingly, the city attracted and supported major aircraft manufacturers. In 1921 Donald Wills Douglas Sr., who one year earlier had quit his job as the chief engineer for the Glen L. Martin Company, an Ohio-based aircraft giant, founded Douglas Aviation Company in Los Angeles. Douglas Commercial (DC) jets transformed the industry. In 1927 the Douglas Company opened a large new facility on seven acres of Clover Field, a small airfield in Santa Monica. The DC-3, which was first produced in 1935 and could accommodate fourteen overnight passengers or twenty-eight daytime passengers, became the most important airplane of the 1930s and 1940s.[18] In 1936 James H. "Dutch" Kindelberger, president and general manager of North American Aviation, moved that company from Baltimore to Los Angeles. North American Aviation, a former subsidiary of General Motors, would also grow to become one of the major producers of planes for Britain during World War II.[19]

Douglas's and Kindelberger's narratives illustrate how Los Angeles's newest generation of elites, in growth industries such as aviation manufacturing, sought to use the city's connections during the 1930s and 1940s. In many ways, the two men continued the process Doheny's generation had initiated. Born in 1892 in Brooklyn, Douglas became infatuated with aviation at an early age. After graduating high school in 1909, Douglas saw the Wright brothers display one of their airplanes in Virginia, and three years later he dropped out of the Naval Academy to study aeronautics at the Massachusetts Institute of Technology. "The man who more than any other made commercial aviation possible," in the words of the *Times*, moved to Los Angeles from Ohio in 1920 and set up a small airplane factory in Santa Monica with several other former employees of the Glen L. Martin Company.[20] The company's interest in commercial aviation developed from early work for the American military. Federal investments provided the capital and recognition necessary for Douglas Aircraft to pursue commercial aviation. In 1921 the navy ordered three Douglas planes for early aerial experiments. In 1924 the U.S. Army used three Douglas planes to circumnavigate the globe in six months, a journey that included sixteen days of actual flying time.[21] In the early 1930s Douglas began to produce commercial airplanes. The prototype DC-1 led the company to produce about 130 DC-2s, but the company achieved its major breakthrough with the revolutionary DC-3. "The DC-3 was air-conditioned and soundproofed," remembered the *Times*. "It had reclining seats, hot and cold water, an automatic pilot and night flying instruments. It cut transcontinental flying time in half, and it made people eager to fly. By 1939 it was carrying a phenomenal 90% of the world's airline traffic. The company eventually turned out 11,000 of the craft."[22]

Douglas was both a revolutionary designer and a keen businessman. "As one of his colleagues put it," noted Frank J. Taylor in a 1941 *Times* profile, "Douglas is a man who dips into the future with the mind of a poet and the slide rule of an engineer."[23] In 1919 Douglas thought Los Angeles would provide a perfect center for the future of aviation. "On the Western shore of the continent at Los Angeles in the mind of Donald Douglas there dwelt a panorama of aviation's vast potential," described *Sky Master*, a 1943 Douglas biography.[24] Los Angeles's warm climate allowed for production work to be done in the open air or in lightly insulated factories and for pilots to fly almost every day of the year. The city's history of anti-union activism provided a welcome labor market. Furthermore, aside from Boeing in Seattle, Douglas would not have to immediately compete with any other West Coast airplane manufacturers.

Unsurprisingly, Douglas's journey often fostered a gendered bootstraps discourse. "In Southern California," Taylor noted in his profile, "he is regarded as a sort of symbol of the opportunity America offers men to lift themselves by their own ideas."[25] In the early 1930s Douglas sensed the future of commercial aviation. In the mid-1930s, he made a $2 million investment in an eventually successful effort to win a contract for the American military's next major super bomber. That machine, the XB-19, had a cruising range of 7,500 miles and a wingspan of 212 feet, larger than a modern 747.[26] Though other smaller, lighter bombers quickly overtook the XB-19, Douglas's prior relationship with the military allowed him to gain further defense contracts in the 1940s. "Today the democracies count the minutes as bombers and pursuit planes roll off the assembly lines of the four huge plants in which Douglas directs the top-speed efforts of 30,000 workers," narrated Taylor in 1941.[27] Three of the four plants were in the Los Angeles area—in Santa Monica, Long Beach, and El Segundo, near Los Angeles Airport. The honeymoon period would not last forever: Douglas Aircraft, slow to embrace the era of jetliners, eventually merged with McDonnell Aircraft in 1967, and the new company based its headquarters in St. Louis. Until the end of the 1950s, however, Los Angeles-based Douglas Aircraft built the planes for more than half of all airline seats in the world.[28] Douglas had brought the world to Los Angeles using federal appropriations and the city's growing air connections.

Kindelberger made a similar profitable bet on the future of Los Angeles. As Douglas prepared to leave Glen Martin Aviation in 1920, he offered Kindelberger, one of his promising assistant chief designers, a job in Los Angeles. Kindelberger declined. "Dutch" had taught himself mechanical engineering while working at a steel mill in his home state of West Virginia. He had worked his way to Glen Martin from previous posts in the United States Army Corps of Engineers and as an instructor in the Signal Corps of the U.S. Army during World War I. He was not willing to part with such relative stability.[29] Five years later, Douglas again offered Kindelberger a job, and this time he accepted. After nine years at Douglas Aircraft, Kindelberger, by then promoted to vice president for engineering, struck out on his own and became president of Baltimore-based General Aviation Manufacturing Group, subsequently renamed North American Aviation. He wanted to expand the company, and Los Angeles, with its growing airport at Mines Field, offered cheap land for factory space. To convince his workers to move, Kindelberger called upon Angeleno exceptionalism. "I fed them beer and crab cakes," he remembered in a 1949 *Saturday Evening Post* profile, "and lectured on the marvels of the West."[30] In 1935 North American Aviation entered the increasingly crowded Los Angeles aviation market, and one year later the company's workers began building planes in a new 150,000-square-foot factory adjacent to Mines Field.[31]

Even more than Douglas, Kindelberger based the future of his company on securing defense contracts. Throughout World War II, British and American forces relied on North American Aviation's P-51 Mustang, a single-seat fighter jet. Moreover, North American's B-25 Mitchell bomber was smaller than the Douglas XB-19, but it sold much better. From 1941 to 1945 over ninety-eight hundred B-25s rolled out of the company's Los Angeles, Dallas, and Kansas City factories.[32] In the postwar period, Kindelberger sensed that aircraft business from airlines would not grow as fast as economists were forecasting but that military business might pick up again due to competition with the USSR. "Dutch Kindelberger let other firms have the airline business," noted the *Saturday Evening Post* article. He closed factories in Texas and Kansas, beat a retreat to North American's home plant alongside the Los Angeles Airport, and set engineers to designing new warplanes.[33] By 1962 North American Aviation had weathered the lull. The company employed more than eighty-five thousand people and sold over $1 billion worth of airplanes per year.[34] "Mr. Kindelberger led the nation into wartime superiority over Germany and Japan, and in postwar years retooled the industry for the jet and missile age," summarized the *Times* after Kindelberger's 1962 death.[35] Less of a revolutionary designer than Douglas, Kindelberger was a visionary businessman who sensed coming economic trends and positioned his Los Angeles-based company effectively to meet those changes.

Douglas's and Kindelberger's narratives also illustrate Los Angeles's growing role as an international transportation hub and transcontinental defense center. By 1940 four large aircraft manufacturers—Consolidated Vultee Aircraft, Douglas, Lockheed, and North American Aviation— headquartered their operations and manufacturing plants in Los Angeles. Between them, the four companies employed twenty-five thousand people in factories scattered throughout the Los Angeles area, from Santa Monica to Burbank to Glendale, and made up over 50 percent of the American aircraft industry. In January 1940 the *Times* boasted about the $80 million worth of airplanes Los Angeles manufacturers produced during 1939 and the $160 million in unfilled orders for 1940 at those same companies.[36] One year later, the newspaper reported that for 1940 American airplane sales Douglas ranked fourth—behind first place Curtiss-Wright, a 1929 merger of Curtiss's company and the Wright brothers' company—Lockheed sixth, North American seventh, and Consolidated Vultee twelfth.[37] By February 1940 Los Angeles area plants had over $180 million of unfilled airplane orders on hand.[38] The "Detroit" of the aircraft manufacturing industry, in the words of the *Times*, had arrived.[39]

Aircraft manufacturing companies worked with city leaders to increase connections to and from Los Angeles airports. "Will you please prepare and submit as soon as possible a statement dealing with the growing importance of Los Angeles with respect to transcontinental air passenger travel, air express, and air mail," Los Angeles mayor Fletcher Bowron asked Western Air Express official Tom Wolfe in 1939. "We are anxious to make an effective demonstration of the growing importance of the Los Angeles metropolitan district . . . on the aviation map."[40] Bowron then invited Kindelberger to attend a meeting with other manufacturers and officials from all of the transcontinental airlines, at which they would discuss Los Angeles's airport future as the "western terminal for all of the airlines."[41] By 1940 Pan American Airways carried passengers on round trips to Mexico City, and the *Times* imagined more exotic destinations in the near future. "Soon giant Clipper planes may soar southward from Los Angeles for New Zealand as Southern California for the first time finds a place on a transoceanic schedule," reported the paper in January 1940.[42]

As they had done for the harbor, federal defense appropriations continually spurred business for Los Angeles's aircraft manufacturers in the late 1930s and early 1940s.[43] In September and October 1938—as Germany, the United Kingdom, France, and Italy signed the Munich Agreement permitting Germany to annex the Sudetenland—American leaders ramped up defense plans. In mid-September, at the Western Safety Conference, a federal official outlined a need for the United States to produce more airplanes.[44] One month later, President Franklin Delano Roosevelt unveiled a $2 billion, four-point defense plan, one part of which he devoted to the mass production of airplanes.[45] "Uncle Sam, with 130,000,000 citizens to defend, a Monroe Doctrine to uphold, and 5000 miles of coastline to safeguard . . . last week looked toward Southern California," announced the *Times*. "For within a scant score of miles from Los Angeles' City Hall lay the main vertebrae in the backbone of America's aerial defenses."[46] During the World War I era, Chandler and Hearst had demanded that the city protect itself from federal borderlands inaction; two decades later, the *Times* thought that Los Angeles might defend the nation as a whole.

The federal government certainly fulfilled the *Times*' hopes. In 1939 the government announced that it would require thirteen thousand airplanes in the year ahead, a number that Roosevelt announced would increase to fifty thousand in 1940.[47] In October 1940 the War Department ordered over $140 million worth of bombers and other military aircraft from Douglas, an expenditure that amounted to over 10 percent of the entire 1940 national defense emergency budget.[48] A month later, the company broke ground on a new $11 million plant on two hundred acres in Long Beach, which Douglas designed to employ eighteen thousand people.[49] "We can take the world lead in defense production," maintained Douglas in a January 1941 radio broadcast in conjunction with "Preparedness through Production Week."[50] Chandler and Hearst had used similar terminology during World War I. In many ways 1940 was just the beginning. By 1945 Los Angeles's aircraft manufacturers would help the United States to produce some three hundred thousand airplanes. Federal expenditures set off a regional industrial and demographic boom that lasted for decades.[51]

Granted, entrepreneurs in newer industries benefited from preexisting elite networks. Douglas, for instance, gained the initial $15,000 he needed to start Douglas Aircraft thanks to a meeting with Harry Chandler. Chandler heard Douglas out and gave him a list of nine other Angeleno elites with whom to meet, a list of names sadly lost to history. "The tenth happened to be a banker," Taylor narrated. "Hesitatingly, Douglas asked him if he would put up the $15,000. 'I guess I can do it,' laughed the banker. 'You've got at least $150,000,000 worth of collateral on this piece of paper.'"[52] Still, these local connections were not enough. As Doheny had done, Douglas and Kindelberger consciously tied their companies to broader national and international networks. They pursued capital from eastern banks, appropriations from federal entities, and markets around the world. "These industries were begun or located in Los Angeles because of climate, favorable market conditions, defense contracts . . . a penchant for risk-taking in backing and implementing imaginative schemes . . . and by southern California's increasing influence over American life-styles," notes Jaher in *The Urban Establishment*. "In none of these activities . . . did the Old Guard play an important role."[53] Such trends would continue in the postwar era. Los Angeles's future lay as a modern, hyperconnected, innovative American metropole, a city characterized by elite transience.

Ascendant Los Angeles, however—connected, cosmopolitan,

cutting-edge—would also face a major challenge with American entrance into World War II. "Los Angeles was a city alert yesterday as every man and woman, electrified by the news that Japan had struck at this country 2400 miles westward in the Pacific, took his or her stand solidly for total defense," reported the *Times* on December 8, 1941.[54] The outbreak of war benefited many of Los Angeles's industries. But a powerful Japan, contemporary observers thought, threatened those same connections that elite Angelenos had carefully forged in the previous two decades. Ships streaming in and out of the Port of Los Angeles, airplanes flying in and out of Los Angeles airport, airplane factories churning out planes for the U.S. Army—all might be threatened by an aggressive Pacific neighbor. Japan might also threaten the broader booster project that sought to make Los Angeles a preeminent American city. In reaction to this threat, the doctrine of "total defense" would temporarily defeat even the most progressive proponents of cosmopolitanism.

"THE CENTER OF JAPANESE INTRIGUE
AND ACTIVITY IN AMERICA"

WORLD WAR II BROUGHT IMMENSE BENEFITS TO SOUTHERN CALI-
fornia. Depression-era fears about migration and unemployment
evaporated amid a frenzy of hiring and production. The booming airplane
industry employed 228,000 people. Southern California's shipbuilding
industry gained over $500 million in federal contracts and employed more
than ninety thousand people.[1] Nearly eight hundred thousand people
migrated to Los Angeles from 1900 to 1944, and by 1950 the city had a
population of almost two million, making it the fourth largest in the United
States.[2] As Los Angeles became a major defense site, the city also became
thoroughly enmeshed in the federal infrastructure that imprisoned Japanese Americans without cause. Harkening back to World War I rhetoric,
internment advocates argued that the fruits of Los Angeles's connections
might be damaged without appropriate preparedness.

Shortly after Pearl Harbor, city leaders became some of America's
foremost proponents of interning Nikkei, that is, Japanese immigrants and
their descendants.[3] On February 19, 1942, two months after the Japanese
attack on Hawaii, the board of directors of the Los Angeles Chamber of
Commerce received a report from its Agricultural Committee on the
possibilities for internment. "All Japanese who reside within fifty miles of
the Pacific Coast and Mexican border, or who reside in other areas within
a ten-mile radius of munition plants or military camps," the committee

argued, should be removed to agricultural areas "where housing facilities are available, regardless of whether their labor can immediately be used." Although the board tabled discussion of the document, titled "Control of Japanese in Southern California," because another committee was already working on the issue, the minutes noted that the directors "were in accord completely with the thoughts contained in the report."[4]

Such western support for internment developed in tandem with, and often preceded, federal action. Just two days after Pearl Harbor, Eleanor Roosevelt, Mayor Fiorello La Guardia of New York, and a few federal officials met in Los Angeles with California governor Culbert Olson, Los Angeles mayor Fletcher Bowron, and other local officials.[5] Over the next few months, federal officials—Secretary of War Henry Stimson and Lieutenant General John L. Dewitt, especially—continued to work with West Coast politicians to develop an internment plan.[6] At the cabinet level, Stimson fought for control over policy with Attorney General Francis Biddle, who favored more moderate measures, such as allowing second-generation Nisei to be responsible for the conduct of supposedly less trustworthy first-generation Issei.[7] Western citizens and politicians alike lobbied the White House to pursue internment throughout January and February 1942.[8] Bowron threw his support to the pro-internment camp on February 5, 1942, in a weekly radio address that warned of Japanese "intrigue." "If there is intrigue going on, (and it is reasonably certain that there is), right here is the hotbed, the nerve center . . . of planning for sabotage," Bowron declared.[9] Anti-Japanese figures generally alleged "fifth column" activity by Issei and Nisei to sabotage America from within. Such West Coast lobbying was successful. Ten days after Bowron's speech, the president formally gave the military the authority to pursue internment. On February 19, 1942, Roosevelt signed Executive Order 9066, which cleared the way for internment by authorizing Stimson to create "military areas" from which all 112,000 Nikkei living on the West Coast could be forcibly excluded.[10] Dewitt and Stimson implemented internment plans through the newly created Wartime Civilian Control Administration, later reorganized as the War Relocation Authority (WRA).[11] The WRA first imprisoned Nikkei at "processing centers," one of which federal officials located at the Santa Anita Racetrack, northeast of downtown Los Angeles. Next, the WRA moved internees to one of ten "relocation centers" in Arkansas, Arizona, California, Colorado, Idaho, Utah, and Wyoming. The WRA found the barren Owens Valley, inland in an arid region Los Angeles had stripped of its water, to be an appealing site. In 1942 the WRA leased sixty-two hundred acres of Owens Valley land near Lone Pine, at the foot of the Sierra Nevada mountains, from the City of Los Angeles in order to imprison over ten thousand Nikkei there.[12] The Manzanar War Relocation Center opened on June 1, 1942.

Los Angeles's complicity with the internment policy emerged from past efforts to connect the city to the world. During the 1920s Los Angeles's actions in the Owens Valley had sparked farmers there to rise up in the California Water Wars. Two decades later, the city so dominated the area that it was able to facilitate the placement of a federal prison in the valley with little resistance. When Los Angeles leased part of its land to the federal government for this purpose, Manzanar became both a local symbol of internment writ large and a manifestation of municipal collaboration in anti-Japanese activism. The Owens Valley was both part of Los Angeles and removed from it. Manzanar illustrated city leaders' willingness to aid internment and their real desire to excise Nikkei from the Los Angeles area.

Perhaps unsurprisingly given the city's long history of animosity toward nonwhite groups, Japanese internment united Angelenos regardless of political orientation or social class. Residents of Highland Park, an area in northeast Los Angeles, petitioned Congress to "adopt and to carry out a sensible and realistic program of dealing with the Japanese problem in America, with primary emphasis upon consideration of self protection [sic] and security for America and Americans."[13] The Los Angeles-based California Citizens' Council for the Adoption of a Japanese Exclusion Law sent out a circular to its initial members, all whom had expressed interest "in this vital movement to keep the Japs out of California forever."[14] The Pasadena Chamber of Commerce endorsed indefinite internment.[15] In June 1943 the Women's Club of Hermosa Beach contacted the Los Angeles City Council about Japanese relocation. "Unless the Japanese are entirely uprooted and removed now and forever from this Western Coastal area they will always constitute a menace," the group declared. The government should, the club added, "confine all Japanese in relocation camps under the strict supervision of the United States Army; dispossess all Japanese of land to which they now claim title . . . [and] enact legislation which will deprive them of citizenship."[16] Such sentiments echoed the ideology behind the Alien Land Laws of 1913 and 1920: Japanese were dangerous outsiders who had no place in America.

Los Angeles newspapers, especially the *Times*, added to the campaign.[17] Often, the *Times* sounded very much as it had during World War I—calling on notions of masculine martial virtues to protect the growing city. "As a race, the Japanese have made for themselves a record for conscience-less treachery unsurpassed in history," fulminated one *Times* editorial.[18] "The Japs Are Still Apes," announced the headline of another.[19] In March 1942, after Dewitt formally designated parts of California, Oregon, and Washington as a military area in preparation for internment, the *Times* applauded his actions. "The only sensible method of dealing with the whole problem of protection of the Pacific Coast from alien and native-born Japanese . . . is that ordered into effect yesterday," the paper concluded. "General Dewitt . . . put the Army into position to execute the Presidential order designed to meet the extreme peril of sabotage and fifth-column activity here."[20] In 1943 jingoistic Los Angeles newspapers sounded the alarm at rumors that the federal government might imminently free Nikkei from internment camps.[21] "Neither is there any doubt that the return of these Japanese would constitute the best possible of fifth-column preparation for enemy attacks on our coastal regions," a *Times* editorial surmised.[22] By 1944 the *Times* grudgingly conceded that the federal government would eventually allow Nikkei to return to California, but the paper maintained that such an action would be a "grave mistake . . . predicated on the fact that an enemy invasion of the Pacific Coast on a large scale is no longer a substantial possibility."[23]

In the political sphere, the Los Angeles City Council supported and helped to enact internment. Roy Hampton, a Democratic councilman elected in 1939 from a district in East Hollywood, submitted numerous anti-Japanese resolutions to the council. In 1943 Hampton demanded that internees be put to agricultural work on city-owned land near the Manzanar facility. "Said Japanese are not now engaged in any gainful occupation," Hampton argued, and "an acute shortage of vegetables in this area is imminent . . . unless steps are taken immediately to alleviate the situation."[24] Over the following weeks, the council adopted Hampton's resolution and worked with the DWP to employ Japanese labor to irrigate nearby fields with water siphoned from the aqueduct.[25] In 1943 Hampton authored a resolution about the need for continued internment. "The difference in race, religion, color and thought of the Japanese from our American citizens is such that the ideologies of the Orient are inherently present . . . in the majority of all Japanese in America," Hampton argued.[26] Again, the city council passed Hampton's resolution, and the city clerk forwarded the resolution to the California Congressional Delegation and the War Department.[27]

Los Angeles's political leaders, of course, held the ultimate power to shape the city's relationship with the internment program at Manzanar. The cases of two individuals provide evidence for the way in which internment advocates successfully used the rhetoric of preparedness and progress to support internment: Bowron, a Republican, and Democrat John Anson Ford, a member of the Los Angeles County Board of Supervisors. Both men were relatively cosmopolitan and progressive. In the 1930s they had jointly led a regional reform movement. Yet, after Pearl Harbor, Bowron and Ford emerged as two of the city's most important internment advocates. Their prior political moderation lent them legitimacy in the internment campaign. Historians have tried to distance Bowron in particular from his more belligerent wartime race-baiting—which included a campaign to end Japanese birthright citizenship—but each man's internment position actually emerged from long-term debates about Los Angeles's future connections.[28]

The period from 1941 to 1945 in Los Angeles was not, then, a mysterious outlier sparked by growing racial divisions during wartime. Los Angeles's transformation into the epicenter of the internment movement emerged from a half century focused on the politics of connection. Anti-Japanese activism fit into the broader historical trajectory of social control and the debate about connections from 1890 to 1945. Pro-internment rhetoric paralleled the rhetoric used against both poor white "tramps" in the early twentieth century and the 1930s and the purported Mexican Japanese menace during World War I. Similar to "itinerants," Japanese Americans could be put to work. Similar to potentially violent invaders, Japanese Americans should be moved away from Los Angeles's borders with Mexico and the Pacific Ocean. Bowron's and Ford's remarkable transformation from cosmopolitan reform advocates to bigoted wartime crusaders provides unique insight into the malleable politics of connection. Once again, severing connections in a time of crisis proved to be a seductive ideology.

"The West's Biggest Boom Town"

"Japanese Here Begin Exodus," announced the *Los Angeles Times* on March 22, 1942. "America's greatest mass evacuation began yesterday," the paper continued, "as 86 Japanese aliens and American-born citizens arrived in Manzanar, new evacuees' city in Owens Valley, from Los Angeles."[29] At first, federal authorities used Manzanar as an assembly area, from which they sent one hundred thousand Nikkei to other "inland concentration areas."[30] In March 1942 federal officials hastily secured a workforce of hundreds to build more permanent structures at Manzanar in less than two months. "The West's biggest boom town is rising here with magic swiftness as 400 carpenters' hammers beat a busy tattoo on the walls of 25 city blocks of dwellings that will house 10,000 alien and American-born Japanese from Los Angeles and other Southern California cities," began a *Times* news article on March 20, 1942.[31] In the months and years to follow, the Manzanar internment camp elicited comprehensive coverage by the *Times* and other newspapers. Contemporary newspaper articles illustrate how closely linked the camp was to Los Angeles in the minds of local media outlets.

The initial 180 internees who arrived at the camp on March 23, 1942, soon greeted one thousand new arrivals from the region, all of whom the military insisted had embarked on a "voluntary mass migration" before a March 29 deadline after which Nikkei would be forcibly removed from their homes.[32] "Japs Prepare Desert Home," commented another article in the *Times*, which narrated the first internees' work in the face of a "blustery equinoctial wind."[33] "At reception centers they will be guarded by Army sentries . . . but will govern themselves," optimistically noted the caption on an article in the *Madera Tribune* about the first internees.[34] The WRA paid the first arrivals to erect prefabricated wooden barracks, build furniture, and prepare agricultural fields. Later in March 1942, federal officials decided to nearly double the camp's size from 490 buildings to 912, on an area of about 50 city blocks.[35] The *Highland Park Post-Dispatch* applauded the expansion by quoting one internee, who called the camp "Better Than Hollywood."[36]

By May 1942, after the army had relocated over eighty-five thousand Nikkei from the West Coast, the laborers had completed their work.[37] The WRA used 500 acres of the camp for the "housing station," which was fenced in by barbed wire and featured 504 barracks, each divided up into four twenty-by-twenty-five-foot rooms. Each room housed eight people on straw mattresses. The rough barracks were a far cry from the "pre-fabricated houses of a family type" that the WRA initially promised to build.[38] Internees also shared laundry, toilets, showers, and a mess hall with the other two hundred to four hundred people living in their block, one of thirty-six that made up the housing station.[39] Surrounding the barracks were eight watchtowers, agricultural fields, police housing, and a reservoir. Manzanar housed over ten thousand prisoners until 1944; the camp eventually closed in November 1945.[40] In 1946 Frank Finch profiled the deserted camp. "Except for a few staff buildings left standing," he wrote, "the war-born town of Manzanar which housed 10,000 Japanese internees today is flatter than Hiroshima."[41] The Owens Valley had returned to its barren state.

During Manzanar's operation, the *Times* and other outlets tried to portray it as bucolic and healthy, a vivid illustration of Southern California's riches. "Japanese Get 'Break' in Owens Valley Move: Those Sent to Manzanar Center Find Rich Soil and Fine Scenery instead of Dank Prison Cells," proclaimed a front-page *Times* article as the first internees reached the site.[42] "From this elevation of 3700 feet the Japanese evacuees will enjoy . . . some of the most magnificent scenery in the United

States," argued the *Times'* Manzanar correspondent Tom Cameron before internees arrived.[43] *Life* similarly described the surroundings. "The Japs gasped when they saw Mt. Whitney . . . shrugging its white shoulder above lesser ranges just 15 miles away," a feature noted. "They were gratified to discover no mosquitoes. They tested the soil and found it hard and arid, but potentially fertile."[44] The *Highland Park Dispatch* published an article about the wide variety of vegetables internees were growing for themselves in a community vegetable garden. The article's title, "Gardening Time at the Manzanar Reception Center," made internees' work sound quaint and peaceful.[45] Such articles indicate a desire to shield the public from the reality of conditions; coverage of Manzanar often sounded boosterish in nature. Such articles attempted to gloss over the reality of the situation at the camp. Internees later remembered their imprisonment at Manzanar as anything but bucolic. At thirty-seven hundred feet, Manzanar features extreme wind and weather. The temperature often reaches one hundred degrees in the summer and plummets to forty degrees in the winter.[46] The arid area gets very little rain, and high winds tormented the internees, most of whom had arrived from the Los Angeles area.[47] Living conditions were far from ideal. "We took three or four suitcases, what we could carry," recalled Harry Y. Ueno, who arrived at Manzanar in May 1942. "By the time we got to Manzanar it was already dark," he continued. "Then they gave us a cloth sack to make up a mattress. They said, 'Go and fill up your own mattress from the pile of hay there."[48] Jeanne Wakasuki Houston, who was seven years old when the WRA forced her family to leave their Long Beach fishing business and go to Manzanar, remembered the diminished worldview of Manzanar. "In such a narrowed world," she wrote, "in order to survive, you learn to contain your rage and your despair, and you try to re-create, as well as you can, your normality, some sense of things continuing."[49]

Nevertheless, Nikkei formed a remarkable community at Manzanar. The federal government paid internees to dig canals, grow crops, and complete other menial tasks. Internees pooled their earnings to create a vibrant civil society. They opened schools, a general store, a barbershop, and a bank, as well as volunteer organizations, music groups, and sports leagues. Some former newspaper employees also started a biweekly newspaper, the *Manzanar Free Press*.[50] In its few years of existence, from 1942 to 1945, the moderate paper illustrated how Nikkei rightly perceived that white Americans would judge all Nikkei by their conduct at the camps. In October 1942 an editorial decried Mexican American and Filipino American "Zoot Suiters," youths who wore flamboyant suits featuring long coats and baggy pants as a symbol of youth culture and ethnic pride. "In Los Angeles," the paper noted, "youthful Mexican gangsters, in colorful 'zoot suits' with watch chains that reach their ankles, are terrorizing the population with assaults, murders, and hold-ups."[51] The newspaper most feared that Zoot Suit violence might be used against the Japanese. And indeed, even during internment, police authorities linked the Zoot Suit movement to the Japanese. Internees, Los Angeles County Sheriff Eugene Biscailuz alleged, had "left instructions with these hoodlums." "All of this we know to be untrue," hastily concluded the *Manzanar Free Press* editorial.[52] The newspaper also asked internees to be on their best behavior at Manzanar in preparation for postwar departure. "We must remember that our physical horizon will not always end with these brown Inyo Hills and the snow-capped Sierra Ranges," argued one editorial. "To make Manzanar a real Shangri-La . . . we must forget all former quarrels and personalities."[53]

Though the *Manzanar Free Press* preached intracamp congeniality, younger Manzanar internees grew increasingly frustrated. Some Kibei (Nisei who had traveled back to Japan to complete their education before returning to America) organized themselves in opposition to camp administrators and the Japanese American Citizens League (JACL).[54] During the war, the JACL, a moderate Nisei organization, generally worked with the WRA and federal authorities to promote Nisei assimilation and prove Nisei trustworthiness. Manzanar Kibei, led in part by Harry Ueno, alleged that camp administrators were guilty of various financial improprieties, including selling the camp's sugar on the black market.[55] Tensions between the two groups boiled over on December 5, 1942, when a group of masked men severely beat a JACL member named Fred Tayama for his collaboration with the WRA and allegedly profiting from his position with the JACL.

In the wake of the beating, the FBI investigated, removed, and imprisoned two men suspected of the crime, one of whom was Ueno. "The reaction to Uyeno's [sic] summary disposition [sic] was one of immediate and growing wrath on the part of many segments of the evacuee population," wrote political scientist Morton Grodzins after visiting Manzanar a few months later to report on the incident. "The spiriting away of Harry Ueno was the second large contribution to public wrath. No administrative officer bothered to explain on what basis Uyeno [sic] had been incarcerated."[56] The night after the arrests, internees resisted Ueno's imprisonment and occupied an area of the camp around the jail to prevent him from being removed to an outside prison. When as many as four thousand people rioted, military police fired on the crowd, injuring eleven and killing two. "I heard five or six shots fired nearby and tommy guns or machine guns on the far east side of the police station," Ueno said in a later interview. "I didn't know how many people had been shot."[57] Unsurprisingly, the *Los Angeles Times* used the riot to urge more oppressive internment policies. "The riot at the Manzanar camp . . . seems to show that American kindness to the disloyal does not pay," proclaimed one editorial. "Rioters and troublemakers should be rigorously weeded out and put in close internment."[58] The following week, the Board of Water and Power Commissioners worried about the fate of the aqueduct if dissent continued. The body urged that any potentially disloyal internee be removed to a different site, far away from the aqueduct and the city's water supply.[59] Collectively, the two reactions to the riot indicated the closeness of Los Angeles's connections to the Manzanar concentration camp. Los Angeles had tangible ties to the land, and the camp stood as an image of the city's dedication to the war effort. The Bowron administration recognized these factors and would dedicate itself to internment's success.

The Reformer Mayor

Very little in Bowron's career suggested that he would eventually become one of the West Coast's most rabid internment supporters. Born in San Diego County in 1887, Bowron spent much of his life in and around Southern California politics. He graduated from Los Angeles High School in

1904 and in 1909 enrolled in the University of Southern California Law School after a stint at the University of California-Berkeley. Terminating his full-time education early because of financial difficulties, he worked as a newspaper reporter in San Francisco, Oakland, and Los Angeles while studying on the side. Just as the United States entered World War I, Bowron passed the bar exam and enlisted. He served in the Fourteenth Field Artillery Division and then took a position in military intelligence before moving back to Los Angeles when the war concluded. From there, Bowron used his legal background to move into politics. From 1923 to 1926 he held a minor position in the California Department of Corporations, a now-dissolved body created by Progressive governor Hiram Johnson in 1914 that oversaw business activity in the state. In 1926 Republican governor Friend Richardson (who had previously also been a member of the Progressive Party) appointed Bowron to the California Superior Court, a position Bowron would hold until the pivotal mayoral election of 1938.[60] In 1934 Bowron presided over a grand jury that investigated claims of corruption in the office of District Attorney Byron Fitts. The body eventually indicted Fitts for perjury, though the district attorney escaped conviction.[61] After Bowron's death, the *Times* credited him for work to make the judicial system less onerous.[62] Bowron clearly held progressive tendencies toward making government more accountable and efficient.

Bowron's mayoralty followed upon two decades of corruption allegations and political instability. George Cryer, mayor from 1921 to 1929, focused on public works, public utility ownership, and allying his administration with powerful elites such as Harry Chandler. Cryer's administration also benefited from the help of political boss Kent Parrot, who created a diverse pro-Cryer coalition of businessmen, anti-labor activists, anti-vice activists, and people themselves involved in vice that lasted for the first five years of Cryer's tenure.[63] In 1929, pledging himself to clean up the Cryer regime's purported corruption, John C. Porter won the mayoral election. Evangelical anti-vice activists such as Bob Shuler embraced Porter's populist campaign. Porter, Shuler wrote, could defeat the forces of vice and enforce the will of the people. "If favoritism is shown any man before the bar of justice, it will be the 'little fellow,'" Shuler argued in his 1929 formal endorsement.

"Those who have financed crime in Los Angeles and in return have been rewarded by fabulous fortunes from commercialized iniquity need expect no quarter from Porter."[64] Holding a senior position in the KKK, Porter also capitalized on xenophobia. Los Angeles, Porter pronounced, was "the last stand of native-born Protestant Americans."[65] Though he won the election, Porter's administration sparked immediate opposition, and political opponents led a failed campaign to recall him in 1932.[66]

The 1933 mayoral election, held in the midst of the Great Depression, revolved around unemployment and public works projects. Porter retained his anti-vice evangelical supporters and added support from the business community, which favored the mayor's public spending cuts.[67] Opposing him, Republican Los Angeles County supervisor Frank L. Shaw took up the banner of the New Deal in Los Angeles, uniting a coalition of liberals, public ownership advocates, and members of Parrot's former machine.[68] Shaw perceptively pledged to protect a wide variety of interests: those of union laborers and anti-labor activists, those of businessmen, and those of Angelenos in favor of public projects. Most of all, Shaw tied himself to Franklin Delano Roosevelt.[69] On election night, Shaw's campaign illustrated the New Deal's popularity; he prevailed by about 30,000 votes of 335,000 votes cast.[70]

Even Shaw's support was not to last. Shaw structured his mayoralty around the loose oversight of subordinates whom he asked to court potential supporters in any way possible. Shaw's administration made overtures to minorities, the once-shunned business community, and even criminal groups. Naturally, then, Shaw's political downfall grew out of corruption allegations. In the mid-1930s, Clifford Clinton—an evangelical reformer and founder of the popular Clifton's restaurant chain—led a series of investigations intended to expose Shaw's support for gambling and prostitution. Clinton even created his own independent organization, the Citizen's Independent Vice Investigation Committee (CIVIC), to investigate prostitution and gambling, publicize its findings, and attack the Shaw administration.[71] "We will fight for the Ideals and Sacred Things of the City, both alone and with many," read CIVIC's letterhead, a quotation from the Spartan reformer Lycurgus.[72] Clinton invited liberal and conservative moral reformers to the cause, and many, including Shuler, joined. In the 1937 mayoral election, the anti-Shaw alliance drafted Ford to run against the incumbent mayor. Shaw retaliated through a coordinated red-baiting campaign aimed at the liberal Ford. "Although he holds himself aloof from them, the Communist party and the C.I.O are working for Ford," alleged the *Times* during the campaign. "The reason? Shaw keeps a checkrein on disorder."[73] Shaw's tactics worked. On May 4, 1937, the incumbent mayor prevailed by about 27,000 votes of 305,000 cast.[74]

After the 1937 election, Clinton's CIVIC continued to investigate Shaw. Various CIVIC officials publicly deplored the alleged vice in the city's midst. "Our committee has discovered that we have an organized band of white slavery in the Southern California area, which operates a great number of brothels," alleged the Reverend Joseph J. Cummings in an August 1937 radio address. "This would not be possible if this group did not have the protection of certain public officials."[75] In September 1937, encouraged by Bowron, Clinton released a report alleging that various elected figures close to Shaw, including Fitts and Chief of Police James Davis, were working to protect local vice.[76] In retaliation, the city raised Clinton's real estate taxes by $7,000 and denied permits for the restauranteur to expand his chain. In October 1937, a bomb exploded in the basement of Clinton's home, though the blast did not injure anyone.[77] Three months later, Harry Raymond, a private detective who was investigating vice on Clinton's behalf, nearly died when a car bomb detonated in his garage.[78]

Clinton and CIVIC used the bombings to recall Shaw. First, Clinton alleged that Shaw ordered the LAPD to kill Raymond, a charge that gained credibility when the police arrested several LAPD officials a few days later, including Davis confidant Captain Earl Kynette.[79] Next, Clinton formed the Federation for Civic Betterment (FCB) as a vehicle to pursue recall, which succeeded in gaining enough petitions to put the measure on the ballot. The FCB also needed to nominate its own candidate. Ford declined nomination after the vicious 1937 campaign and instead boosted Bowron, a man with whom Ford had corresponded and who shared Ford's progressive tendencies.[80] "The liberals of Los Angeles want good government," Bowron argued in a 1939 speech meant to once again attract the diverse coalition that had supported his 1938 campaign. "The objectives of liber-alism cannot be attained if Los Angeles politics and the administration of municipal government are to be dominated by any kind of an organization founded on and financed by the products of greed."[81] Unsurprisingly, the recall campaign revolved around corruption allegations. The Bowron campaign launched a variety of attacks on Joe Shaw, the mayor's brother who essentially acted as a chief of staff. Joe Shaw resigned in July 1938, but his removal did little to ease the pressure on the mayor.[82] During the campaign, the *Times* was the only local newspaper to support Shaw, albeit without formally endorsing him.[83] On September 16, 1938, Angelenos overwhelmingly voted to remove Shaw by about 100,000 votes out of about 350,000 votes cast and to elect Bowron in his place by roughly the same margin.[84] Shaw became the first mayor of a large American city to lose his position via recall.

Bowron, then, took power with a mandate to make Los Angeles's government more responsive and upright. "The people of Los Angeles desire honest and decent government," argued Bowron in his inaugural speech.[85] He subsequently served from 1938 to 1953—the longest tenure in Los Angeles history until Tom Bradley's (1973 to 1993)—so he had the opportunity to see his various initiatives blossom.[86] Bowron first asked every city commissioner to resign. He reformed the process by which the city awarded city contracts after an investigation revealed that Shaw's administration had routinely given contracts to friends and political allies. He overhauled the LAPD by replacing the police commission; the new commission forced over twenty prominent officers to resign, Police Chief James Davis among them.[87] "As I believe you know, ever since my election as Mayor of the City of Los Angeles, I have been interested in eliminating the influences that have demoralized the Los Angeles Police Department in the past," Bowron wrote to a Superior Court judge in 1941. "I wanted to stamp out bribery and corruption by the most effective means, which I felt was bringing to justice those who had been responsible for com-mercialized vice in this community."[88] Though Bowron's reform coalition began to crack around 1940—the mayor even had a highly publicized break with Clinton over a contested city attorney general race—Bowron used remnants of the coalition to win reelection easily in 1941.[89] Over three years of governing, Bowron had cemented his power and exhibited his dedication to reshaping the city under a platform of moderate reform.

"A Treacherous, Deceitful and Resourceful Enemy"

Bowron's municipal reform agenda, however, became disrupted by the more pressing concerns of World War II. Immediately after the Japanese attack on Pearl Harbor, the FBI targeted the Japanese fishing community at Terminal Island, which city leaders had built in the nineteenth century as a breakwater for the Port of Los Angeles. Terminal Island housed a community of about three thousand Issei and Nisei, virtually all of whom worked in the fishing industry. Earlier in 1941 the U.S. Navy had opened a shipyard on the island, which gave the FBI further reason to trample the community's rights.[90] Presuming first-generation Japanese to be disloyal, FBI officials initially arrested many Issei fishermen and executed widespread searches of homes throughout the island. "From Fish Harbor, Japanese settlement on Terminal Island . . . Federal authorities hustled more than 300 Orientals to the Immigration Station for identification and questioning," announced the *Times* on December 9, 1941. "Of these an unannounced number won release during the day," the paper added cryptically.[91] One week after Roosevelt issued Executive Order 9066, the WRA forced every other Japanese Terminal Island resident to leave their homes in preparation for internment at Manzanar. After they left, the navy razed the community. The local situation became even more unstable as 1942 progressed. On February 23, 1942, amid rising anti-Japanese hysteria, Japanese submarines patrolled in waters along the Pacific Coast, and one lobbed shells at a desolate area north of Santa Barbara. The next night, during the "Battle of Los Angeles," jittery soldiers fired more than fourteen hundred antiaircraft shells into the air after spotting "unidentified aircraft" in the area.[92]

Sensing a political opportunity, Bowron contributed to wartime hysteria and emerged as one of internment's most radical proponents. When local officials were debating the future of the community on Terminal Island in January 1942, Bowron dismissed any concerns about how cannery closings might affect the local economy. "We must put financial interests of the city in a category of secondary importance," he commented. In late January 1942 Bowron placed all thirty-nine Japanese city employees on leaves of absence.[93] "We found that some of the employees of Japanese blood were in positions where they could secure valuable information which . . . could be most effectively used in an attack upon Los Angeles," Bowron reasoned in his radio address on January 29, 1942.[94] Bowron also took on more of a national role in the internment campaign. In early March 1942, after Dewitt named the Owens Valley a site for a future internment camp, Bowron and other city leaders met with Tom C. Clark—whom Biddle had appointed as the civilian coordinator of the Alien Enemy Control Program—to determine the proper location for a camp in the area.[95] One day later Bowron flew to Washington to give testimony in front of a House of Representatives committee investigating problems coordinating internment. At the hearing, Bowron chastised the FBI for its lack of cooperation with army and navy intelligence services. Poor communication, he alleged, had inhibited efforts to make the West Coast safe from potential sabotage.[96] "I led a vigorous campaign that I hoped was of aid in bringing about the placing of Japanese residents in the coastal area in concentration camps," he wrote to a federal official in October 1942. "I . . . feel that they should be kept where they can do no possible harm."[97]

On the local level, Bowron vociferously defended the internment campaign in a series of radio speeches. The addresses, which Bowron normally delivered live on Thursday evenings on radio station KECA, became the mayor's favorite method of communicating with the public. Each fifteen-minute address, penned by Bowron himself, focused on one or two topics with local implications. In the prewar period, Bowron often sold his political program on Thursday nights.[98] During the war, he focused on preparedness. Even before Bowron embraced anti-Japanese hysteria, he lauded Los Angeles's centrality to national defense. On January 6, 1942, the mayor devoted much of his address to downplaying rampant media rumors that Japan might attack Los Angeles. Los Angeles, Bowron claimed, was "just as safe as the people of any populous area, even tho [sic] we are located on the shores of the Pacific."[99] Bowron's focus on preparedness rhetoric would exacerbate his anti-Japanese feelings in the following months. The radio speeches illustrate how closely the mayor linked Los Angeles's progress to the need for internment.

Beginning in early February 1942, Bowron began castigating Issei and Nisei alike for their alleged disloyalty. The mayor's adviser Alfred Cohn had recently submitted multiple reports to Bowron about the Japanese community in Los Angeles, memos filled with rumored threats and outright racism. Apparently, Bowron took the reports to be factual. After writing multiple private letters to federal officials urging greater action, which had little effect, he made his fears public on February 5, 1942.[100] "While there is no reason for hysteria, I feel that the local situation is much more serious than apparently those in Washington do," he maintained. The threats to Los Angeles, he continued, demanded prophylactic suppression. "Full and adequate protection for the safety of lives and property in this area undoubtedly would work an injustice on many Japanese," he admitted, "but . . . our country comes first. We must win that war and to do it we must take all precautions." It followed in his mind that all Japanese should be removed from the coastal areas, so they could not inform anyone in Japan about troop movements, shipping networks, or munitions production. Again, Bowron seemed most driven to protect Anglo Los Angeles. "All of this may sound harsh and drastic, but we are at war," he concluded. "This is not a time for sentimentality."[101]

Over the next few months, Bowron's ideas about local Japanese grew more racist. His February 19 speech, for instance, focused on the Japanese "menace" in Los Angeles. "With one-fourth of all of the Japanese in California . . . this very area undoubtedly would be the center of activity, the prize objective, if the Japanese hordes should ever attempt to land on American soil," he argued. "The real Japanese problem during the continuance of this war is a Los Angeles problem."[102] Bowron's speech sounded similar to the World War I–era *Patria* and its imagination of a Japanese invasion that would threaten American masculinity. Los Angeles, removed from eastern defense installations, was uniquely threatened. In such an imagined narrative, invading Japanese "hordes" would gain support from Issei and Nisei and then sweep through the region, imposing their martial and sexual will. Bowron then presented his revised plan for internment, one that would put Japanese people to work on "large tracts of land in locations removed from the coastal area, not close to any transcontinental railroad, and where they could observe nothing of military importance."[103] The following week he demanded that Japanese be removed from the coastal "danger zone . . . at least beyond the mountain ranges."[104] In August Bowron applauded local activism for "what we did in Los Angeles in getting every Jap out of this area."[105] Even after the WRA had interned Nikkei, Bowron continued to echo World War I preparedness rhetoric. "Our own city has been threatened and will doubtless yet suffer attack," he argued. "Bombs rained from the skies."[106] Both preparedness and removal privileged Los Angeles's role as a defense hub. To Bowron, Los Angeles's connections, both demographic and economic, had imperiled the city.

The radicalization of Bowron's approach toward Los Angeles's connections might be best seen in his increasing opposition to Japanese birthright citizenship. Bowron's argument rested on a critique of the 1898 Supreme Court case *United States v. Wong Kim Ark*. Ark was born in San Francisco but subsequently denied reentry to the United States under the Chinese Exclusion Act after he returned from a trip to China in 1895.[107] The case hinged on the first clause of the Fourteenth Amendment: "All persons born or naturalized in the United States and subject to the jurisdiction thereof, are citizens of the United States and of the State wherein they reside."[108] The U.S. Government argued that Ark was not a citizen because his parents were "Chinese persons and subjects of the Emperor of China, and the said Wong Kim Ark being also a Chinese person and a subject of the Emperor of China."[109] Ark, Federal lawyers argued, was not "subject to the jurisdiction" of the United States. The court eventually ruled seven to two that the Fourteenth Amendment's language applied to anyone born in the United States. "Subject to the jurisdiction thereof," Justice Horace Gray argued in the majority opinion, should be defined as it would have been defined under English Common Law: including almost everyone born in Britain, with a few minor exceptions, such as ambassadors' children. "And if, at common law, all human beings born within the ligeance of the King . . . were natural-born subjects, and not aliens, I do not perceive why this doctrine does not apply to these United States, in all cases in which there is no express constitutional or statute declaration to the contrary," concluded Gray.[110] Gray's opinion remains constitutional doctrine to this day.

Bowron sided with Chief Justice Melville Fuller's dissenting opinion in *United States v. Wong Kim Ark*. Fuller took issue with Gray's deference to English Common Law. "The tie which bound the child to the Crown was indissoluble," Fuller wrote. "The rule was the outcome of the connection in feudalism between the individual and the soil on which he lived, and the allegiance due was that of liegemen to their liege lord."[111] In 1898, Fuller argued, times were different, and citizenship should be based on the nationality of the parents. "To what nation a person belongs is by the laws of all nations closely dependent on descent; it is almost a universal rule that the citizenship of the parents determines it," he asserted.[112] Therefore, in Fuller's mind, Ark was not a U.S. citizen and could be refused entry to the United States. On May 26, 1943, Bowron briefly informed Angeleno listeners of the case's legal history before outlining his hopes that the Supreme Court might reverse the decision and revoke citizenship from all Nisei. "My answer to the question, 'Do you feel that the Japanese born in this country should be deprived of citizenship' is 'Yes,'" Bowron declared at the end of his address.[113] The following week, Bowron made an even more emphatic argument in favor of revoking Nisei citizenship as a means to restrict Japanese return to the West Coast from internment camps. First, he addressed communications he had received disagreeing with his previous address. "I have not advocated violation of the Bill of Rights, I am not actuated by race prejudice, and am suggesting no action that would be detrimental to any minority group," Bowron claimed. "I have merely pointed out a legal theory that native-born Japanese never were citizens under a proper construction of the provisions of the United States Constitution."[114] Quickly, however, Bowron pivoted to the racist basis for his claims. "We are at war and we are fighting a treacherous, deceitful and resourceful enemy," he thundered. "This also was the center of intrigue. We in Los Angeles ought to know our Japs. We are not going to be fooled, if others are. And those Japanese released through the warm human sympathy of the ... War Relocation Authority had better not come back to Los

Angeles."[115] Of course, Bowron was not alone in decrying Japanese return to Los Angeles. The city's chamber of commerce also passed a resolution in May 1943 that supported internment at least until the end of the war.[116] But Bowron went far beyond many other anti-Japanese actors to advocate for the revocation of Nisei citizenship as a measure to protect Anglo Los Angeles and the gains the city had made.

Still, Bowron was subsequently quick to express remorse for his wartime actions. As World War II wound down and the federal government decided to release internees after the war, Bowron bowed to federal pressure and accepted returning Japanese to the city. On January 14, 1945, he welcomed a returning group at City Hall. In November 1946, Bowron publicly apologized to the JACL.[117] Bowron would serve until 1954 and preside over numerous major projects, such as the expansion of the freeway and public housing and the completion of the Los Angeles International Airport, initiatives that helped distance his mayoralty from internment.[118] In 1967, when John Modell, director of research for the Japanese American Research Project at UCLA, contacted Bowron about his memories related to the internment campaign, Bowron claimed that he did not remember a great deal about the time. "So much was happening during the early days of the war that my personal recollection cannot well be relied on without refreshing my memory," Bowron claimed in one letter.[119] In another letter to Modell, Bowron placed blame on the federal government. "Undeniably a great injustice was done to Japanese residents of this area," he admitted, but "[a]t the time we were acting . . . largely in the dark because of lack of communication as to the results of investigations made by the F.B.I." "Those of use in official position [sic] in state and local government felt that we owed a distinct duty to the people we represented to insure [sic] their protection in time of war," he concluded feebly.[120]

Bowron's legacy is complex. Some contemporary observers noted Bowron's importance to Los Angeles. "He was a man of conscience as he reformed the City of Los Angeles," eulogized pastor Randall C. Phillips at Bowron's funeral. "It was his conscience which maintained the City of Los Angeles, and it is his conscience that sustains the city today."[121] "Few men have served their city so well as did Fletcher Bowron," added the

"THE CENTER OF JAPANESE INTRIGUE"

Times. "The orderly transformation of the city into a metropolis is one of the many tributes to his ability and dedication."[122] Other Angelenos simply forgot the wartime mayor. After Bowron's death in 1981, the *Times* ran a column about the small crowd gathered around Bowron's casket as it lay in state at city hall. "A television crew had to recruit eight youths who had probably never heard of Mr. Bowron to file past the casket for the motion-picture camera," noted the paper. "For a while after that the rotunda was deserted except for a policeman standing at each end of the casket."[123] For their part, when they mention Bowron, modern scholars have generally lauded his later egalitarianism.[124]

Overlooked in these narratives, however, are the origins of Bowron's contributions to Japanese internment. On December 7, 1944, Bowron gave an address in remembrance of Pearl Harbor, a speech that mostly lauded local defense efforts toward internment and preparedness. "Here we were in the center of Japanese intrigue and activity in America," he recalled. "We would not be hasty, but we would at least see that they did nothing." Then, he presented a trite, illuminating summary of wartime lessons learned. "Although we were not attacked," he continued, "the effort was worthwhile. Not only have we had assurance, peace of mind and security during the past three years . . . We have learned how to work together."[125] Again, Bowron placed Los Angeles's progress above all else. The city's role as an internment hub neither developed in a vacuum nor erupted as a historical outlier specific to the World War II sociopolitical environment. Instead, Los Angeles's role in internment emerged from a longstanding discussion of the city's connections to the outside world. Because the city was so important, Bowron felt justified in protecting it from perceived threats.

The Cosmopolitan Supervisor

John Anson Ford presents an even more dramatic case study of the ways in which pro-internment sentiments could overwhelm traditional ideologies. Born in Waukegan, Illinois, in 1883, Ford graduated from Beloit College in Wisconsin in 1907 and then taught history and economics at Beloit High School for several years. He subsequently moved to Chicago, where he wrote for the *Chicago Tribune* and other publications, and then on to Washington, where he worked as a publicist in the Labor and Agriculture Departments. In 1920 he moved to Los Angeles with his wife and young son, relying on his government experience to start a publicity business in the growing city.[126] For the next thirteen years, Ford had some success in that position, until he decided to enter the political sphere, successfully running for Los Angeles County supervisor in 1934. His Third District stretched along the coast from Malibu to Venice and inland to Calabasas, Sherman Oaks, and Hollywood.[127] Ford had first worked in politics for Theodore Roosevelt's Bull Moose Party presidential run in 1912, but his entry into the county supervisor race was not driven by idealism. Mostly, Ford ran in order to earn the supervisor salary of $5,000 per year. "Certainly, as I entered that supervisorial campaign . . . I never dreamed that 24 ½ years later I would be honored at a retirement banquet attended by 1,493 friends," he later recalled, "who presented my wife and me with a Buick sedan, two deluxe round-trip tickets to Copenhagen . . . and many other delightful gifts."[128]

From such relatively inauspicious beginnings, Ford fashioned a lengthy and influential political career, if not with immediate success. After just two years as a county supervisor he ran for mayor, but Shaw's extensive red-baiting eventually led to Democratic defections and doomed Ford's campaign. "I am informed that the margin was about 25,000 votes, which seems to me to be a pretty good showing on the whole. Just why some of our supposedly Democratic friends knifed you in the back, I find it difficult to understand," wrote Democratic congressman Jerry Voorhis to Ford after the 1937 election.[129] After his defeat, Ford refused attempts to draw him into the 1938 recall campaign, boosted Bowron's campaign, and rededicated himself to his work as county supervisor. In the process, he emerged as a major supporter of public institutions in Los Angeles. For example, Ford worked to secure funding to reopen the Hollywood Bowl after funding problems forced the concert venue to close in 1951 and also helped the county acquire the Descanso Gardens, a 150-acre botanical garden northeast of Pasadena.[130]

During his career, Ford promoted three liberal progressive causes:

moral reform, municipal improvement, and minority rights. Often, Ford published newspaper articles to publicize the Los Angeles County Board of Supervisors' efforts to improve Los Angeles's morals. In 1940, for instance, Ford introduced an initiative designed to enforce a dress code at the marriage license bureau. "Bathing girls have their place," he wrote, "but honestly, folks, it isn't in the marriage license bureau! And fish net dresses don't add much to the picture." "Evidently somebody is failing to take marriage seriously," he continued. "This past year this County granted 12,404 divorces and issued 19,366 marriage licenses!"[131] In October 1940 Ford explained his recent board vote against creating another horse-racing track in the county. "I have had men who were neither reformers nor crusaders tell me that thousands of business concerns, large and small, feel a sharp and costly cooling in business every time a betting season comes around," he wrote. "It has been freely predicted that the betting vogue will go just so far and do so much damage to legitimate business, not to say the morals, and then the whole [betting] business will be wiped out by popular demand."[132] In March 1942 Ford decried the content of motion pictures. "Fifty per cent [sic] of the movies I see now days leave me disgusted," he wrote. "The kind of pap some of these pictures dish up for our young people is terrible."[133]

Ford wanted to improve the city because he believed in Los Angeles's potential. In November 1940 he wrote a brief column about his journey to the West Coast, spurred by "Mr. Chandler's gorgeous mid-winter edition of The Times." "When anybody starts in on the migrants and asks impatiently, 'Why they didn't stay where they were?', I rise in protest," he wrote in November 1940. "The urge for change and progress is in us all. That's what made California in the first place."[134] A summary of Ford's 1944 membership dues encapsulates his belief in civic development. He was a member of, among other organizations, the Westlake Chamber of Commerce, the Hollywood Chamber of Commerce, the California Planning & Housing Association, the Friends of Claremont Colleges, and the Southern California Opera Guild.[135]

Finally, Ford held a longstanding commitment to cosmopolitanism and minority rights. He opposed the Chinese Exclusion Act and held membership in the China Society of Southern California, a cultural association seeking to promote understanding between China and America.[136] When Soong Mei-Ling, wife of Chinese nationalist leader Chiang Kai-Shek, visited the China Club in Los Angeles in 1943, Ford attended the dinner and afterward wrote her a glowing letter.[137] "Permit me to add a word of deepest gratitude for the spiritual note in your Los Angeles utterances—a note America so sorely needs to heed," Ford wrote.[138] Ford also tried to promote better relations between Nisei and whites. In August 1938 he answered a series of questions from the editor of *Doho*, a Japanese newspaper based in Los Angeles. In his lengthy written responses, Ford advocated for federal and state expenditures to eliminate racial discrimination and supported the teaching of Japanese in public schools.[139] During the war, Ford corresponded with Biddle, the U.S. attorney general, about Kei Sugahara, a Nisei man who had volunteered his limited Japanese language skills to the U.S. Army and wished to apply for permanent relocation away from the West Coast, out of internment. "I have never had any occasion to think of Mr. Sugahara as anything but an earnest, loyal citizen," Ford wrote in a cover letter to Sugahara's enclosed application.[140] Ford summarized his antidiscrimination stance in a 1942 column. "The way we of the white race treat the colored people, the Mexicans in our midst and the other minorities hinders or helps Hirohito and Hitler," he wrote. "That all men are created with the inherent right to an equal chance in the world . . . is one of the basic principles we are fighting the global war for."[141]

In the postwar period, Ford took on a greater leadership role in local antidiscrimination initiatives. After the Zoot Suit Riots, Ford helped to create the County Human Relations Commission, which worked to improve relationships between whites and African Americans, Japanese Americans, and Mexican Americans. "From the very beginning [the commission] did a very constructive job in helping to interpret the injustices from which Mexican-Americans and other minorities were suffering," Ford later recalled.[142] "We have come a long way since the days of the zoot-suit riots and the road ahead is equally long but in the end people of good will and intelligence will succeed," Ford wrote to the *Times* in 1977.[143] After retiring from his county supervisor position, Ford chaired the California

Fair Employment Practices Commission, a newly formed body intended to police racial discrimination, for eight years.[144] Nevertheless, Ford's anti-racism did have its limits. In February 1947 he received a letter asking that a local African American woman, who taught Chinese culture for Los Angeles junior high schools, be allowed to attend a meeting of the China Society.[145] The society's board, which included Ford, denied the request by ignoring it. "While no members of the Board have prejudice on this matter, their unanimous opinion was that they take no action," the Board's secretary wrote. "Whatever decision might be reached, controversy would arise in an otherwise most harmonious group."[146]

By and large, Ford generated near universal acclaim both during his life and posthumously for his commitment to Southern California. After Ford's retirement from his supervisor position in 1958, he received numerous letters of appreciation from major political figures. "When a region grows as fast as southern California, it demands extraordinary watchfulness on the part of its citizens to insure [sic] that it will progress in the right direction," wrote former California governor and contemporary Supreme Court chief justice Earl Warren. "Your guidance was invaluable in a time of unprecedented change."[147] Ford received similarly complimentary letters from the National Congress of American Indians, the JACL, the National Council of Negro Women, the National Conference of Christians and Jews, and the Anti-Defamation League, among many other organizations.[148] "No cause devoted to better human understanding has found your hand unwilling," read the dedication on the Town Hall Award Ford received for "distinguished service to the Southern California Community."[149] It continued, "Lasting indeed will be the imprint of your services on the cultural and civic life of Southern California."[150] When Ford died in 1983 at the age of one hundred, even the conservative *Times* lauded Ford's career. "We can recall no local official who has done more for this county or whose legacy will outlive that of John Anson Ford," concluded the newspaper's eulogy.[151]

In private and public writings, Ford also promoted a cosmopolitan vision of America. In 1957 Ford returned to Beloit as the commencement speaker. His speech gestured toward humanistic engagement with the outside world. Ford first lauded Beloit, and its natural setting, for inspiring a "lofty yet practical idealism." Then, he moved on to global movements that dimmed his idealism: nuclear proliferation, youth culture's degraded moral standards, even American campaign financing, "a political cancer." "But eventual progress *is* certain," Ford nevertheless told the students, if, as he hoped, young people could "penetrate through the fogs and mists of materialism." "The Orient and the Occident will experience an unprecedented mingling and synthesis in this new day and you are entitled to share in it," he concluded.[152] In his public writings, Ford likewise lauded Los Angeles's cosmopolitanism and progress. His best-known work is *Thirty Explosive Years in Los Angeles County*, a 1961 memoir centering on the region's early twentieth-century history. Ford began the book by arguing that Los Angeles is a "Microcosm of America."[153] In subsequent chapters Ford documented Los Angeles County's history through his own political journey from 1934 to 1960. Along the way he took time to explain the inner workings of the Los Angeles Board of Supervisors and its various initiatives to encourage development, protect the environment, and promote the arts. *Thirty Explosive Years* belongs to the "sunshine" narrative about Los Angeles's rise. Ford was optimistic about Los Angeles's potential, both economic and demographic. In his narrative, for instance, Los Angeles quickly recovered from the Depression because of the city's exceptional qualities. "The traditions and cultures of almost every section of the nation were represented here," he wrote. "Enthusiasm and environment combined to produce a vigorous diversification of industry and an aspiring culture."[154] Ford similarly portrayed the postwar period as a time of cosmopolitan progress. "The happy change in attitude toward the Japanese Americans was not the only example of the community's awakening to the deeper meaning of democracy," he wrote. "A distinct betterment in the feeling of the Anglo-American population towards resident Mexican Americans was equally significant."[155]

"The Principle of Quarantine"

Ford's optimism about Los Angeles's postwar racial environment, however, discounted the significant actions he took during the war to ensure internment's success. In fact, *Thirty Explosive Years* glosses over the Japanese internment program. Ford devoted just three pages at the beginning of chapter 17, "The Problem of Minority Groups," to internment, before he pivoted to improved race relations in the postwar era. "It is to the credit of Los Angeles County that during the 'explosive years' a beneficial evolution took place in the attitude toward these racial groups," he wrote at the beginning of the chapter. "Communities, like individuals, make fearful mistakes, and, also like individuals, may acknowledge their errors and seek to remedy them."[156] In the next three pages, Ford did decry internment and refer to the Japanese as "innocent victims of the war."[157] But he also ignored the work of any local authorities in enacting or encouraging internment. Instead, Ford placed blame on local "racial frictions" and the WRA. Citing *Thirty Explosive Years* and Ford's longstanding commitment to racial harmony, some scholars have portrayed Ford as an internment "dissenter."[158] To be sure, before Pearl Harbor Ford did advocate for the United States to seek Pacific peace through nonmilitary means. In July 1940 Ford wrote an antiwar letter to Secretary of State Cordell Hull. "I write you . . . as a seeker for affirmative antidotes against spreading war," Ford began, before attaching a lengthy letter from an unnamed friend about potentially establishing peace in China and demarcating the Pacific Ocean as "the theater of a combined effort toward international peace."[159] After American entry into the war, however, Ford, like Bowron, became a proponent of internment—or, in his words, "quarantine"—a means to protect Los Angeles.

In the days following Pearl Harbor, after authorities had targeted the San Pedran fishing community and interned many Issei, the county board of supervisors grappled with the problem of Japanese children whose parents had been interned or whose families had lost their primary wage earners. On December 9, 1941, Ford, whose district included a large Japanese population, passed a resolution designed to protect Japanese students in Los Angeles's high schools. "Whereas, children are often among the first ignorantly to display hysterical intolerance," the resolution noted, "BE IT RESOLVED THAT the Board of Supervisors request the office of the Superintendent of Schools to take every step practical to establish in our public schools an attitude of sanity."[160] The following month, Ford began to worry about families whose primary wage earner the WRA had interned. "If kids and women are starving we've got to feed 'em," Ford concisely wrote to Wayne Allen, the county's purchasing agent in early 1942.[161] Afterward, Ford transitioned to favoring internment policies, ostensibly as a means to protect Nikkei.

On January 29, 1942, the board of supervisors passed its most comprehensive resolution supporting internment, a document notable for the reasons the board chose to justify the program. The first few clauses referenced the nearly one hundred thousand Japanese who lived in California, dependents some internees had left behind, and the limited job prospects for those who remained. Quickly, however, the resolution began to sound very much like a more racist version of Great Depression anti-migrant hysteria. "Los Angeles County is without funds to care for the large numbers of Japanese who may become dependent on relief through circumstances arising out of the war," the board argued. "Japanese aliens are a potential source of danger to our security," the resolution continued. "In the event of an invasion of California by forces of Japan, the civil population of California would be unable to cope with the large Japanese population which would constitute a potentially dangerous fifth column enemy." Practitioners of the Shinto religion, the board further felt, might further threaten defense positions, as "the Shinto religion is that of the Emperor of Japan and includes worship of ancestors and the belief that soldiers who die for Japan become spirits to be worshiped." The only solution was internment to points away from the coast, where Japanese "could till the soil far removed from airfields, power and water lines and other strategic defense facilities."[162] Here, then, the board illuminated its racial-economic position that Japanese should be removed because they were a burden and might harm Los Angeles.

Ford seems to have supported and even led the board's work on internment. "I think we are going to get some quick and favorable action," Wayne Allen, the board's chief administration officer, personally wrote to Ford after Allen sent the board's resolution to President Roosevelt, the California congressional delegation, and the FBI.[163] Far from protecting Japanese to whatever extent possible, Ford piloted a program designed to remove them on explicitly racial grounds. Ford defended such a change in his position by highlighting the benefits, in his eyes, of "quarantine" over generalized racism. "The frank recognition of 'the principle of quarantine,' in this situation," he wrote to Biddle on May 4, 1942, "gave the community and nation deserved protection without accusing all who were 'quarantined' of being 'inflected' [sic]."[164] "The principle of 'quarantine' which the Administration has so wisely evolved," Ford wrote in his Sugahara recommendation a few weeks later, "has been justified by public opinion, I believe."[165] Civil defense fears had also not disappeared from Ford's mind. After the war, Ford recalled his justification for internment as a public safety measure for Japanese and white Americans alike. "During the war I approved of their being 'quarantined' for safety's sake," Ford told a member of the Japanese American Community Council in 1948.[166] Ford's rhetoric echoed long-standing racist narratives about the diseases that Asian immigrants purportedly spread due to unsanitary living conditions.[167] Chinese and Japanese immigrants, such logic followed, posed a threat to the public and should be excised from America. In the early twentieth century, Los Angeles authorities even used the "medicalized Yellow Peril," in the words of scholar Natalia Molina, to justify the 1920 Alien Land Law and other anti-Japanese legislation.[168] Ford's defense of "quarantine" as a protective measure, then, belied his real motivations. Far from opposing internment, Ford clearly thought Nikkei were as much of a threat to America as America was to them.

Ford's close work with local civil defense authorities may have sparked his change in tone about internment and the Japanese community. In his capacity as a county supervisor, Ford received significant materials from the Defense Committee of Southern California, a group of two hundred local leaders working under the auspices of the Los Angeles Chamber of Commerce to help state and federal agencies implement a national defense program.[169] Much of the committee's work seems to have gone toward assembling and preparing documents about American defense points on the West Coast for a small set of elites who might advocate for greater defense expenditures. Harry Chandler's son Norman, who became the *Times'* publisher in 1945, held positions on the defense committee's

"Air Boundary" defense team and publishers' committee, and George P. Clements served on the "Site Selection" committee for civilian evacuation.[170] In 1940 the committee collated the information into a handbook and sent a copy to each member, including Ford. "Preparedness is as necessary today as it was for us when was war declared in 1917, and we find ourselves in practically the same condition," began an introductory page taken from an article written by John J. Pershing. "The very life of this Republic depends on the energy and determination with which our people undertake the task of placing the United States in a state of thorough preparation in both men and equipment."[171] Much of the following material summarized the American defense system: army and navy organization, training facility locations, troop levels, armament production, and future appropriation plans. Another document disseminated by the committee detailed America's Pacific vulnerabilities. "Our Fleet is ready for the next year, but it can't fight without bases, and the greatest dearth of this vital element of seapower is in the Pacific," concluded one passage copied from a *Los Angeles Times* article, "where the menace of Japanese aggression is more real, despite the war in Europe, than at any time in our national history."[172]

In his personal papers, Ford also collected various articles and resolutions about defending Los Angeles. One, a 1945 *Times* article titled "It Can Happen Here Right Now," told Angelenos to expect future Japanese air raids. "If they happen while the general public is serenely, obstinately and stupidly sure they won't happen, consequences will be all the more terrible and all the more costly," declared the author as he tried to rouse a spirit of masculine preparedness.[173] In his civil defense files, Ford even kept an advertisement for the "Scream-Master," an air raid siren the company billed as "the Modern Paul Revere."[174] Ford, then, was attuned to Los Angeles's perceived vulnerabilities and familiar with preparedness rhetoric. His journey seems similar to that of Bowron. Both men began the war as relatively moderate and sane figures who preached rationality. Yet, after Pearl Harbor, defense trumped their progressive tendencies. Bowron advocated more publicly and vociferously for internment, but both men willingly participated in the internment campaign.

Still, at the end of World War II, Ford renewed his campaign for Japanese rights. In January 1945 Ford authored a county board of supervisors' resolution that asked the WRA to release one Japanese American Los Angeles County employee who had demonstrated "unquestioned loyalty."[175] He also began to argue for an expansion of Japanese citizenship. "The fortitude and lack of recrimination or subversiveness displayed by these people offered further evidence of their fitness to serve as American citizens," wrote Ford in January 1948.[176] "I feel that is [*sic*] is truly contrary to basic American principle to exclude the small minorities from citizenship because of Oriental origin," he wrote to a Senate committee deliberating a bill to expand naturalization criteria in 1948.[177] One year later, Ford opposed Karl Bendetsen's appointment as assistant secretary of the army because Bendetsen had worked closely with Dewitt on the internment program. "Direct quotations from Mr. Bendetsen seem to give strong evidence of the distinct lack of qualifications for a position often involving delicate international relations," wrote Ford to President Harry Truman.[178] In 1950 Ford would work to overturn the 1920 California Alien Land Law.[179] Even in these cases, however, Ford predicated many of his arguments on Japanese "loyalty," mistrust of which he had previously used to justify internment. He had not changed his viewpoints; external circumstances had changed the level of threat he felt that Los Angeles faced.

Internment, Remembered

The distance between Bowron's and Ford's actions and true anti-internment activism can be best seen through the story of William C. Carr, a real estate agent who emerged as one of the city's few white anti-internment advocates. Unlike Ford or Bowron, Carr did not hesitate to fight internment, especially in his often-caustic letters to officials at all levels of government. "You continue to make America unsafe for democracy," Carr told California governor Earl Warren in December 1943, addressing a man who held national political ambitions and had recently given a pro-internment speech to a U.S. governors' meeting in Columbus, Ohio.[180] He continued, "Glad they knocked your ears back in Columbus and wrecked a race baiter's chance to head our country."[181] Carr held similar contempt for Bowron. "Do you think 'the people' are so dumb as not to know that of all Los Angeles politicians you have tried hardest to make political capital from the plight of these evacuees of Japanese descent," Carr wrote the mayor in December 1944, after Bowron had begun to soften his stance toward internees. "We are already laying plans to cooperate with the thousands of others who regret their honest mistake in electing a bigot and hypocrite."[182] "If the World War III is the colored races fighting for justice from the Saxon how will you feel about your record?," Carr asked Bowron in a separate letter.[183] Carr did not accept the excuses made by internment advocates.

So outraged was he by Japanese internment, in 1944 Carr founded the Friends of the American Way, an organization that tried to restore Japanese American civil rights.[184] Similar to the JACL, the Friends of the American Way often used the stories of Nikkei in battle to oppose internment. "Earned by Japanese Americans in Italy: Over 1,000 Purple Hearts, 46 Silver Stars, 31 Bronze Stars, 9 Distinguished Service Crosses, 3 Legion of Merit Medals," announced one circular. On the same page, the association somberly gave notice of a military funeral set to be held for one Nisei soldier who had died in battle and whose family would mourn him "Behind the Barbed Wire of Heart Mountain Relocation Center, Wyoming."[185] Another Friends of the American Way document made a case for internees to return, in part because Angelenos should pay attention to "all that is involved in goodwill and friendly relations with a billion people across the Pacific Ocean—highly important even in trade with that half of the world."[186] Carr realized how to use the politics of connection for his cause. Elites should foster future connections, he maintained, not through preparedness but through cosmopolitan goodwill.

Carr's postwar correspondence with Ford more fully illustrates the distance between their worldviews. In August 1945 Carr asked Ford to investigate a racial discrimination complaint from a Japanese woman against Los Angeles County, which had hired only one person of Japanese ancestry. After introducing the case, Carr moved on to the broader reasons for investigation. "We feel that the evacuation gives proof to the Orient that, like the Germans, we believe in master-race treatment," Carr wrote, "and that we distinguish and discriminate between both our own citizens and the enemy on the basis of race." "We do ask you to watch so that in the future there is not unaccountable coincidence of 'lack of qualification' and of Japanese ancestry in those rejected by your department heads," he concluded.[187] In his response, Ford tried to avoid Carr's broader claims and instead spent much of his time apologizing for a bureaucratic mistake that had hindered the investigation. "I am quite in accord with your comments about beginning the practice of real democracy here and home and recognize that there may be some in positions of County influence who are not in accord with the ideals that you express" is all Ford could muster.[188] Carr believed in sustained, aggressive anti-racism campaigns. Ford preferred to keep controversy out of the public eye. After all, Ford had big plans for the city and did not wish to harm its public image. The last chapter of *Thirty Explosive Years* explored "The County's Purpose." "It is more than a poetic figure to note that 'Westward the course of empire takes its way,'" Ford argued. "Steadily economic power and culture have been increasing in the West. Perhaps tardily, nevertheless surely, the Los Angeles megalopolis . . . is awakening to the decisive role it can and must play in America's future."[189]

Four decades later, as the federal government considered legislation to pay reparations to former internees, Angelenos seemed similarly anxious to distance the city from the internment campaign. To its credit, the *Times* fervently advocated the reparations bill, the Civil Liberties Act of 1988, which paid each surviving internee $20,000. "The Issue Is National Honor," proclaimed one editorial in August 1989, as Congress debated implementation of the program. "The forced relocation to remote areas of the ethnic Japanese . . . was an example of wartime hysteria at worst," continued the article, "a wholly unnecessary response to a wholly unfounded fear that saw resident Japanese Americans as potential spies and saboteurs."[190] "This gross violation of an entire community's civil liberties arose from war-induced hysteria fanned by decades of regional racism," admitted another editorial three months later.[191] Readers certainly recognized the paper's stance. "I want to applaud The Times for its advocacy on behalf of the 117,000 Japanese Americans who were forcibly interned by the American government during World War II," wrote Jonathan T. Kaji in a letter to the editor.[192] In August 1988 the newspaper even showcased the stories of individual internees in a three-page article, "Reparations Awaken Painful Recollections." The article detailed the experiences of local Japanese Americans who were taken from their homes to the Santa Anita racetrack and on to camps across the United States. "Sumi Seo Seki remembers entering the expansive grandstands of Santa Anita in Arcadia, with their magnificent view of the San Gabriel Mountains," the article began. "But Seki, 17, felt as if she were going into a dungeon, into a deep dark hole."[193]

Yet, notably, much of the *Times'* coverage of the reparations bill sought to discount Los Angeles's prominent role in the internment program. Though the paper admitted the "Painful Recollections" of Santa Anita, articles detailed neither Los Angeles's ties to the Owens Valley and Manzanar nor Bowron's emphatic denunciations of Japanese Americans. In fact, a front-page retrospective about Southern California during World War II, published in September 1989, largely glossed over internment. Subtitled "Sleeping Giant Awakens," the article, the last in a five-part series on the global effects of World War II, sought to show how the war "would loom as large as the ocean and as threatening as the night sky for Southern Californians, because of the proximity of Japanese forces in the Pacific." Over three pages, the article detailed local preparedness, demographic change, and racial unrest, including the Zoot Suit Riots. Much of the text portrayed World War II as a beneficial economic catalyst for the city, which allowed it to emerge from the "tailspin" of the Great Depression and transform into a "recession proof" dynamo. Journalist Alan Citron did briefly mention internment in two places, but he placed internment in the context of the "pivotal role" played by Japanese Americans in the region's modern economic development. "It was a tidal wave of change that impacts our economy to this day," concisely commented business analyst Larry J. Kimbell.[194] Citron's narrative sounded similar to Ford's *Thirty Explosive Years in Los Angeles County*. In both, the boosterish narrative of long-term prosperity obscured the steps that Los Angeles elites took to ensure that growth against imagined threats.

Progressive internment activism in Los Angeles reveals how definitively connective discourse had pervaded elite discourse by 1940. So consuming had discussions about the city's connections become that it easily swept away Bowron's and Ford's prior progressive ideals and led them to support internment. Carr's battle against internment was a lonely, isolated exception. Of course, Bowron and Ford also emerged from World War II relatively unscathed by their wartime actions. They continued to win elections and wield power, as postwar optimism and development propelled Los Angeles even higher in the hierarchy of American cities. Temporary disconnection via preparedness was yet another tool for elites to use in moments of crisis. Nikkei—like Owens Valley farmers and internal migrants before them—became quickly forgotten casualties, people tossed aside so Los Angeles elites could continue their work. While many Angelenos tried to forget the city's centrality to Japanese imprisonment, internment was inextricable from the narrative of vitality and vulnerability that had dominated city culture and civic rhetoric for the previous fifty years. In the postwar era, city elites would see the fruits of their past work. But, often, they would not like what they saw.

CODA

"Where They All Are Headed"

DODGER STADIUM OPENED ON APRIL 10, 1962, A SYMBOL OF LOS Angeles's growing prestige and the immense power Los Angeles elites still held to forge new connections for the city. Nine years earlier, the business community had propelled Republican Norris Poulson into the mayor's office, and over the next decade he set about justifying its support. Most notably, Poulson purchased the Chavez Ravine area, originally acquired by Fletcher Bowron to build a public housing project, and gave the land to the Brooklyn Dodgers' owner Walter O'Malley, who in turn moved his team west in 1957.[1] In 1958 Angelenos approved the controversial land deal after city elites waged a scare campaign to warn voters that the Dodgers might leave Los Angeles if citizens did not approve the contract. Efforts to remake Chavez Ravine devastated the Mexican American community that had lived there, though its battle against eviction lay forgotten ten years later. "O'Malley's Mammoth Miracle . . . is an eyepopper, the most glamorous baseball park in history," crowed the *Times* on the stadium's opening-day. "Sprawled across an area which only a short time ago was a mountainous goat pasture, it truly is an artistic and engineering marvel."[2]

The effort to build Dodger Stadium illustrates the continuing power of a civic language in Los Angeles that emphasized the importance of mediated connectivity and masculinity to urban development. Los Angeles's elites had carefully crafted such rhetoric over the previous seven decades—from the Free Harbor Fight to the California Water Wars to the 1932 Olympics campaign. In each instance, elites had disseminated a distinctive narrative about Los Angeles's growth being dependent on the outside world, even as they hoped to triumph over other cities and sometimes sought to temporarily sever connections during times of crisis. With the opening of Dodger Stadium, city leaders could exult in one more success. Luring one of the most prominent American baseball teams to the West Coast illustrated the city's growing cultural power. Not only did Los Angeles have a significant place in the professional sports landscape but Poulson had also taken a team from New York: Collis Huntington's city and the traditional node of America's economy. The *Times'* depiction of a transformed "goat pasture," therefore, reveals that Los Angeles's connective rhetoric remained powerful.

Under the surface, however, lurked cracks in elite Angeleno power. In 1961 Poulson lost the mayoral election to populist Sam Yorty, a conservative Democrat who ran against Poulson's subservience to the business community. Poulson's defeat signaled that Los Angeles elites no longer held nearly unfettered power over the city's development. As the *Times* celebrated Dodger Stadium's opening, for instance, it also felt the need to reassure readers about the city's prospects under Yorty. "Dodger Stadium is another of those things that help to give the city a living heart," commented the paper. "It is additional insurance that the central city will not wither."[3] Seven decades after the paper had compared Los Angeles's prospects to those of Wichita in the wake of the 1890s housing crash, fears about the city's future had not dissipated.

As the 1960s progressed, Los Angeles's developing connections further demonstrated erosions in elite control. Beginning in the 1940s, Los Angeles became a much more diverse place. Lured by plentiful jobs in wartime industries, African Americans arrived in droves to Los Angeles during the second Great Migration. At the beginning of World War II, about sixty-three thousand African Americans lived in the city, a number that increased to over seven hundred fifty thousand by 1970.[4] As Black migrants experienced local segregation and white supremacy, they fought for greater rights. In the aftermath of the 1965 Watts Rebellion, one *Times* article located the roots of the "horror unprecedented in this state's history" in the Great Migration. "The huge migration of unskilled rural Negroes from the far different culture of the South to the big cities of the North and West," maintained one editorial, "and the frustrating gap between the possibilities of a prosperous society and the harsh limitations of the nation's poor—black and white alike—all must be considered."[5] The rebellion challenged notions of the city as a pristine Pacific metropolis at a time when Los Angeles also became a hub for Asian and Latin American immigration. In the 1950s and 1960s, Japanese and Mexican Americans created diverse neighborhoods in Boyle Heights, Monterey Park, and Montebello. Such demographic change accelerated when the Immigration and Naturalization Act of 1965 removed racial and national quotas.[6] "For 'Huddled Masses,' L.A. Is Ellis Island," the *Times* told its readers in 1980. "Los Angeles is the first city among immigrants," an immigration official told the newspaper. "This city, this office, is where they all are headed."[7]

Los Angeles's shifting power dynamics in the postwar era were perhaps best reflected in the city's flagship newspaper, the *Times*. Harry Chandler died in 1944 and left the paper to his son Norman. Norman would eventually transform the *Times* into a global media company, but, in discussing Southern California, Norman's *Times* often continued the paper's conservative, boosterish legacy. By 1960 boosters could indeed be pleased about the city's progress. Los Angeles was more "vital" than Harrison Gray Otis, Norman's grandfather, could have ever imagined. At the same time, Poulson's 1961 mayoral defeat, the Watts Rebellion, and Los Angeles's changing demographics suggested some challenges to elites' vision of the city as a peaceful, prosperous Anglo metropolis. A reading of the *Times* in the first few decades after World War II reveals an elite media outlet struggling to adapt to new circumstances. The newspaper modified its previous rhetorical strategies to try to maintain a semblance of control over Los Angeles's changing cultural and political atmosphere. The *Times* still preached boosterism and preparedness, of course, but often in ways that revealed a city escaping its grasp.

In order to build Dodger Stadium and gain a professional baseball team for Los Angeles, Poulson leveraged the full power of Los Angeles's economic and political elites. His career had prepared him well to be a conduit for elite power.[8] Born in Oregon in 1895, Poulson migrated to Los Angeles at age twenty-eight. By taking night classes, Poulson became a certified public accountant before pursuing a political career and winning election to the California State Assembly in 1938. Four years later, he successfully ran for Congress, a position he held until 1953, with the exception of the two years following a defeat in 1944. A conservative Republican, Poulson's views meshed with those of his constituents in California's Thirteenth District, which included the communities of Eagle Rock, Highland Park, and Silver Lake, north of downtown.[9] His views also coincided with those of the conservative *Times*, which formally endorsed him in 1942 and would continue to support his career in the years ahead.[10] In Congress Poulson vociferously supported projects central to Los Angeles's rise. During the early 1950s he became increasingly involved in the legal and political battle between Arizona and California over apportioning Colorado River water. The fight had festered since Los Angeles began to build the Colorado River Aqueduct in 1933: Arizona alleged that California was taking an unfair share of the water. In 1952 Arizona formally filed suit against California in federal court. The case would last more than a decade, but Poulson seized the moment to declare the importance of protecting California.[11] "What southern California wants is to keep the water that belongs to it," Poulson wrote to the *Washington Post* in 1952.[12] "Water is the lifeblood of Southern California," he concluded in a 1966 letter to the *Los Angeles Times*, sounding very much like Mulholland.[13]

In 1953 Los Angeles's business community drafted Poulson to run against Bowron, who was finishing his fourth term in office. The officially nonpartisan election—with an initial vote held on April 7 and a runoff between the two men held on May 26—revolved around Bowron's and Poulson's different visions of Los Angeles's future. Their debate especially centered on public housing. In 1950, with the aid of the National Housing Act of 1949, Bowron and the Los Angeles City Council had embarked on a plan to build ten thousand public housing units. The project included over three thousand units on land in the Chavez Ravine, a Mexican American neighborhood close to downtown, to be renamed Elysian Park Heights.[14] In pursuing the public housing development, Bowron demolished the neighborhood and pushed out the eighteen hundred mostly Mexican American families living there, a set of actions that came to be known as The Battle of Chavez Ravine. Through buyouts, eminent domain, and promises that residents could return to the area after the development was finished, the city had removed many of the families by 1952, though the Aréchiga family would last until 1959, living in a tent next to their razed home.[15] By 1953 the Los Angeles City Housing Authority (CHA) had built about two thousand public housing units. Due to the controversial evictions, however, work had not yet started on Elysian Park Heights.[16]

Disturbed by the initial popularity of the public housing project, its elite opponents attempted to brand public housing as socialist. In August 1951 the *Times* published an editorial titled "A New Look at Public Housing," which solidified anti-housing rhetoric. "This is Socialism that no longer creeps," the article maintained. It was a "threat to Los Angeles taxpayers."[17] In the context of McCarthyism and the ongoing Red Scare, the paper's argument held cultural currency. In September 1950 the Los Angeles City Council had even passed an ordinance mandating that "communists and other subversives" register with the Los Angeles Police Department.[18] Yet again in Los Angeles's history, the city needed to be protected from inimical interests. In addition to its public opinion campaign, the *Times* began a political campaign to defeat public housing supporters. By the end of 1951, the newspaper and its allies had convinced the public to replace eight pro-housing members of the city council. The new anti-housing majority then voted to end Los Angeles's contract with the CHA. Although the California Supreme Court would later hold that the city council could not legally terminate the contract, the council asked the public to ratify its action in a referendum. On election day, the vote held no binding power, but the anti-housing campaign turned out enough voters to emerge victorious.

The subsequent 1953 mayoral election also centered on the future of public housing in Los Angeles. "A vote for Poulson will be a vote against the public housing program," the *Times* argued succinctly a few days before the runoff.[19] During the Depression, the *Times* had warned voters that electing Upton Sinclair would amount to a communist takeover of the state. In the postwar era, the newspaper portrayed Bowron in a similar light. Sometimes, *Times* articles merely gestured towards Bowron's purported leftist tendencies, often portraying him as a dangerous dictator. "Mayor Bowron has hardened in office," one editorial maintained. "He has come very near to proclaiming, 'I am the city.'"[20] "He has grown crotchety and dictatorial," another surmised.[21] "Mayor Bowron has equated leadership with dictatorship," argued the newspaper in its official endorsement of Poulson.[22] Similar to its attacks on Sinclair, the newspaper claimed that Bowron was an anti-democratic politician who would not hesitate to pervert the city's capitalist ideals in pursuit of his radical agenda. Bowron tried to respond to the attacks by framing the election as a choice between himself and a pro-*Times* puppet. "This is not just an ordinary election," Bowron thundered in a televised speech in early May. "It is an attempt by a small, immensely wealthy, incredibly powerful group to force you to elect as your Mayor a man who will represent them—not you—a man who will do their bidding, not yours."[23] Naturally, the newspaper responded with indignation, again using Bowron's rhetoric to paint him as a would-be dictator. "The Times and I personally have been made the target of one of the most venal and vicious attacks in the history of local politics," Norman Chandler wrote in a front-page editorial a few weeks later. "Backed to the wall by indications of an overwhelming defeat, this man . . . now has become a demagogue of the worst type."[24]

As the campaign crept on, the *Times* grew more explicit in its red-baiting. Bowron, the paper maintained, had once been a good mayor—one the newspaper proudly endorsed. Now, however, something had changed. "Yesterday's edition of the Daily People's World, spokesman of the Communist Party, carried an article advocating that Mayor Bowron attack the Los Angeles Times as a means of defeating Rep. Norris Poulson for Mayor at the coming election," the *Times* reported on May 7.[25] Two days before the runoff election, the newspaper published its most obvious red-baiting attack on Bowron, titled "Strange Case of Mayor Bowron." "The alliance with the public housers was in fact the first step in the change that brought

Mayor Bowron to ally himself with the 'liberal' and leftist elements," the article claimed. "The public housing program brought him to bed with some characters who were dubious indeed."[26] Through such constant references to Bowron's "strange changes," the editorial positioned Bowron as something of a Manchurian candidate, beholden to dangerous, leftist influences. Poulson echoed such charges in his own speeches, decrying Bowron's "apathy" toward communist threats.[27] Through the *Times*, Poulson sold an image of himself as an upstanding citizen who would maintain the city's respectable, conservative identity. Collectively, then, the anti-Bowron campaign relied on preparedness ideals: Los Angeles was in danger, and Angelenos needed to awaken to the threat posed should they grant the incumbent mayor another term.

To further its preparedness rhetoric, the *Times* also claimed that Bowron did not possess the masculine characteristics necessary to make him a good leader in the years to come. Poulson was only eight years younger than Bowron—fifty-seven years old to the mayor's sixty-five—but the newspaper argued that he lacked masculinity and vigor. Bowron had a "very weak head for figures," the newspaper told its readers, whereas Poulson was a "hardheaded economist."[28] After the election, the paper told its readers that the incumbent had been "bleating weekly swan songs on the radio, telling them how well he has served them all these years."[29] Of course, the newspaper's portrayals of Bowron as a dangerous demagogue clashed with those of him as aging and weak, but the *Times* did not dwell on the paradox. On Poulson's first day in office, the *Times* informed its readers that Poulson was up to the job. "Mayor Poulson Breezes through Crowded First Day in City Hall," it reported. Even after a lengthy set of obligations, Poulson was "still looking fresh and relaxed" as he made his way into the office for the first time.[30] Poulson, in the *Times*' depictions, was energized and virile. He was well-equipped to ensure the city's future prosperity, an "era of good feeling" in Los Angeles.[31]

As in 1934 the *Times*' smear campaign succeeded in swaying voters. On election day, Poulson ousted Bowron by about 35,000 votes out of 540,000 cast.[32] In his victory statement, Poulson rushed to assure Angelenos that city elites did not control him—he was "not the beholden slave of anyone or of any group."[33] Of course, the newspaper printed the message in its entirety and showered the new mayor with positive coverage in the weeks following the election. "Los Angeles has had a revolution, which is no less arresting because no blood was shed," exulted the *Times*. Poulson, in the newspaper's mind, won because he planned to defeat Bowron's public housing plan, which "aims at establishing a government landlordism to control the community."[34] Poulson and the *Times* viewed public housing as more than an effective campaign issue; defeating it was central to the identity of Los Angeles. By pledging himself to "get out of public housing," Poulson assured white Angelenos that he would protect the city from radical left-wing schemes.[35]

Upon taking office, Poulson further established his conservative credentials. In October he vetoed a city council proposal to grant raises to fourteen thousand city employees.[36] He worked to cut taxes and slash government spending. Poulson also had a keen eye for flamboyant publicity. "As Mayor he was expected to be a timid and unimaginative mouthpiece for the community's conservative elements," the *New York Times* told its readers in 1959. "He has not tangled with any millionaires, but his unpredictableness keeps people reading their newspapers." "Mayor Poulson's pixyish qualities—he has slid into home plate in a clean white shirt and posed for photographers recumbent on a motorized reducing couch," the article continued, "are a fixture in the nation's third largest city."[37] Though the *New York Times* seemed to think that Poulson's "pixyishness" clashed with his pro-business mindset, the two qualities were complimentary. Poulson would vividly display his eye for business opportunities and public acclaim in the ensuing "Dodger War." At that very moment, in Brooklyn, the Dodgers' owner Walter O'Malley was dueling with city authorities over a new baseball stadium, and Chavez Ravine lay empty. In a single stroke, Poulson would defeat public housing and demonstrate Los Angeles's newfound power.

"A Titanic Struggle"

In its time, Ebbets Field was a jewel of America's baseball landscape. Located in the heart of Brooklyn, it grew to hold thirty thousand Brooklynites who flocked to the stadium, "dodging" trolley cars along the way.

As work neared completion on the $600,000 facility in February 1913, the *New York Times* called it the "Most Modern in Baseball Circuits."[38] One month later, Ebbets Field opened, hosting an exhibition game between the Dodgers and the Yankees. The *New York Times* marveled at the occasion, telling readers how "the upper and lower tiers of boxes held the galaxy of Brooklyn's youth . . . it was just like the ceremony at the opening of a world's fair."[39] Over the next four decades, the park continued to attract enormous crowds. In 1947 over 1.8 million people attended Dodgers' games at Ebbets Field, the second-largest attendance number of the sixteen teams in the major leagues.[40] While Ebbets Field may have seemed modern in 1913, however, it was ill-equipped to handle the postwar suburban boom. In the opinion of the team's new owner, the Dodgers had outgrown their surroundings.

Walter O'Malley became an infamous figure for his decision to move the team to Los Angeles. In October 1957, after he announced the team's impending move west, the *Baltimore Sun* interviewed Dodgers' fans as to their opinion of the executive. Calling him a "snake in the grass," the article's author informed readers that O'Malley "better stay out of [Brooklyn] if he wants to live to see the Los Angeles Dodgers in action."[41] O'Malley's decision, however, should not have surprised anyone. By moving his team to Los Angeles, O'Malley demonstrated the capitalist drive that had propelled his life. The future owner of the Dodgers was born in the Bronx in 1903 to Edwin O'Malley, a connected Tammany Hall politician. After spending his formative years in New York City, Walter attended high school at Culver Military Academy in northwestern Indiana. There, he prospered in a system designed to foster leadership skills, masculinity, and morality in its all-male student body.[42] "Well, that was the worst four hours of drill that I ever had," O'Malley wrote to his parents in 1922. "We went out on the drill field with full equipment, went into action, fired a few rounds and then had to change our position. Fun, yes, but awfully tiresome and HARD."[43] After Culver, O'Malley attended the University of Pennsylvania and then law school at Fordham University. By 1930 he was practicing as a business attorney in New York City.[44] Thirteen years later, he became the counsel for the Dodgers, a position from which he slowly began to consolidate power. In 1944 he bought an ownership share, and six years later took a controlling interest in the team. To do so, he won a power struggle with renowned executive Branch Rickey, who in 1947 had broken baseball's color barrier by signing Jackie Robinson.[45] "Branch Rickey, baseball's 69-year-old wizard, 'resigned' the presidency of the Brooklyn Dodgers yesterday and Walter F. O'Malley, 47-year-old Brooklyn lawyer, was elected to succeed him," the New York Times reported skeptically on October 27, 1950.[46] As he gained wealth, O'Malley embraced an elite lifestyle. "He liked material comforts, was a frequent diner at a gourmet restaurant and smoked a reported 20 expensive cigars a day," the Boston Globe reported after his death. "His hobbies were golf and big game hunting."[47]

To purchase a controlling stake in the team, O'Malley had to sell his other investments, so the Dodgers became his foremost business interest. Early in his tenure as owner, he expressed concerns about Ebbets Field's outdated infrastructure and limited parking facilities. Increasing suburbanization had reduced attendance at Dodgers' games, given that many fans now arrived by automobile. The Dodgers' attendance peaked in 1947 and fell to just over one million in 1955, eighth in the league, behind Cleveland, Detroit, and Kansas City, among other teams.[48] In 1953 the Boston Braves moved to Milwaukee, drawn by a new stadium (County Stadium) built for the team, which could hold over forty-four thousand fans. In the 1954 season over two million people attended games at County Stadium, numbers that, O'Malley concluded, illustrated baseball's future economic trajectory.[49] In 1957, after announcing his team's move to Los Angeles, O'Malley explained his reasoning to the Los Angeles Times. "Ebbets Field park accomodate [sic] approximately 700 cars," the article informed readers. "Contrasted to that, Milwaukee is able to provide space for 10,000 to 12,000 cars."[50] However, Ebbets Field could not easily be expanded given its central location. In 1953 O'Malley approached city and state leaders about building the Dodgers a new stadium in Brooklyn, at the intersection of Atlantic and Flatbush Avenues. While O'Malley pledged to pay for construction of the new stadium, he asked the city to condemn the land using eminent domain.[51] In this effort, he ran up against the power of

New York City planning czar Robert Moses, who proposed a different site in Queens, near the eventual location of Shea Stadium.[52] For four years, Moses and O'Malley negotiated privately and sparred publicly over the fate of the Dodgers. Moses, at the height of his powers in New York City, continually resisted O'Malley's entreaties to help build a new stadium in Brooklyn. Moses and O'Malley's debate became public knowledge in 1955, when O'Malley announced that the Dodgers would play seven home games in Jersey City in 1956 and demanded a new stadium project be approved by the city in the next two years.[53]

On the West Coast, Los Angeles's leaders saw O'Malley's dissatisfaction as an opportunity to cement their city's ascent. Six days after O'Malley's public announcement, the Los Angeles City Council approved a resolution declaring the city's intent to pursue either the Dodgers or the New York Giants.[54] The resolution, forwarded to O'Malley, invited him to visit Los Angeles for "a serious conference and 'look-see' at our facilities."[55] Nine days later, when O'Malley had not yet responded to the letter, City Councilwoman Rosalind Wyman wrote to O'Malley to inform him that she would be in New York in late September on business and available to meet to discuss a move.[56] Poulson similarly viewed the Dodgers as a priority; he likely contacted O'Malley during the 1956 World Series.[57] In February 1957 the mayor asked the president of the Los Angeles City Council to fly with him to Florida on short notice to meet with O'Malley about the move.[58] He also wrote to John Anson Ford, chairman of the County Board of Supervisors, to ask him to attend the Florida meetings and support the project.[59] After he returned to Los Angeles, Poulson informed the *Los Angeles Times* that he was "confident" of success in bringing the Dodgers west at the end of the 1957 season.[60]

Whatever O'Malley's initial motives may have been for announcing his dissatisfaction, he began to seriously consider moving as Moses remained recalcitrant in 1956 and 1957. First, O'Malley sold Ebbets Field and announced that the season would be the Dodgers' final one in the stadium.[61] In January he asked one of his co-owners, James Mulvey, to examine Elysian Park during a trip to Los Angeles.[62] In February O'Malley purchased the Los Angeles Angels, a minor league baseball team, and the team's Wrigley Field, located in South Central Los Angeles.[63] Though Los Angeles's Wrigley Field was too small to function as a long-term stadium for the Dodgers, the team could theoretically play games there while a new stadium was being built in Los Angeles. "Walter F. O'Malley, who throws baseball bombshells the way Walter Johnson used to throw his fast ball, fired another one into the Brooklyn picture today," commented *New York Times* writer Roscoe McGowen. "This surprising action may have moved the Brooklyn Dodgers a little closer to becoming the Los Angeles Dodgers."[64] For the next few months, negotiations between O'Malley and New York City leaders, including Moses and Mayor Robert Wagner, remained at an impasse.[65] In early May O'Malley traveled to Los Angeles, ostensibly to visit his newly acquired baseball team.[66] On May 28, 1957, National League owners approved the Dodgers' move to Los Angeles. Finally, after months of further negotiations, O'Malley announced that he was moving the team to Los Angeles on October 9, 1957. "Los Angeles, the Dodgers' Home," proclaimed the *Los Angeles Times*.[67]

Unlike the effort to defeat public housing at Elysian Park, the plans to build a stadium on the land encountered significant resistance.[68] Critical to O'Malley's move was a new ballpark on a chosen site in the Chavez Ravine. He envisioned a fifty-five-thousand-seat stadium with ample parking space surrounding it, either built by the city or built by the Dodgers on land given to him by the city. After his election in 1953, Poulson had formally ended the public housing project on the site and negotiated with the federal government to instead develop a project there that would suit "public purposes." In 1956 Poulson asked a city commission to draw up plans for a stadium in the Chavez Ravine, and Los Angeles allocated $2 million in the 1957 city budget to begin improving the area. On October 7 the city council passed an ordinance codifying the land transfer: essentially, Los Angeles would give O'Malley Chavez Ravine and pay to improve the land, in exchange for Wrigley Field. During the meeting leading up to the vote, Poulson declared that the ordinance would mark another transformative moment in the city's history. Directly comparing the Chavez Ravine deal to the creation of the Port of Los Angeles and the completion of the Owens Valley and Colorado aqueducts, he demanded that the city council ratify another connection in the city's favor. "This too," he argued, "is a deal in which we are going to do something for this great city of ours."[69]

Not everyone agreed with the mayor. Early city council debates about the land deal presaged two further years of political and legal battles over the future of Chavez Ravine. Los Angeles's agreement with the federal government stipulated that any project needed to be in the public's interest, and Poulson quickly ran into difficulties defending a private baseball stadium as a public entity. Still, Poulson was determined to shape an agreement that would pass legal and popular muster. "To save the day for the Dodgers," he later recalled, "there were strings that quietly had to be pulled. As Mayor of Los Angeles at the time, I pulled them."[70] Opponents of the stadium deal—including minor league baseball owners and movie executives, both of whom feared entertainment competition—fought on two fronts: a lawsuit to prevent the land transfer and a referendum petition to veto it.[71] O'Malley, therefore, had announced the team's move but could not begin construction on his new stadium. The Dodgers began their West Coast tenure by playing in Los Angeles Coliseum, constructed for the 1932 Olympics, which usually hosted football games. To O'Malley, the son of a Tammany politician, the challenges exposed the excesses of democracy. "I never anticipated a referendum," he would later recall. "Very few places have it. Very peculiar . . . no boss."[72] As the court case wound its way through the legal system, the public would vote on the deal on June 3, 1958.

The Chavez Ravine referendum, officially titled "Proposition B," again hinged on the politics of connection. As they had done in the 1934 gubernatorial election and again in the 1953 mayoral election, elites harped on the dangers Los Angeles faced if the public voted incorrectly. Poulson warned voters that the Dodgers would leave Los Angeles if the referendum failed to produce a positive vote.[73] In May 1958, at a state hearing about the deal, the mayor told a skeptical assemblyman that if the measure failed to pass, "There is no other thing they can do."[74] The "yes" campaign, then, returned to the civic rhetoric of beneficial connections. If the city failed to pass the land deal, it would lose a prized baseball team lured from America's most powerful city. The "no" campaign, in contrast, merely claimed that the agreement was not in the public interest; trading hundreds of acres in the Chavez Ravine for the small Wrigley Field was a bad deal for the city.[75] City Councilman Edward Roybal, an advocate for low-income housing and minority rights, led the charge.[76] Roybal, the only Latino member of the city council, asked voters to remember the inhabitants of Chavez Ravine. Hundreds of people were evicted to build public housing for thousands. "Today," he argued, "these people find their property was taken . . . to be turned over to a big business concern."[77] Roybal was fighting, then, for a logical conception of the "public interest." Poulson, meanwhile, was employing the long-standing elite idea—present from the Free Harbor Fight onward—that the "public interest" was any project that might improve Los Angeles's economic prospects and prestige.

On election day, the politics of connection prevailed again. In a surprisingly close vote, Proposition B passed, 345,435 to 321,142.[78] In an editorial after the referendum, the *Times* crowed about the victory. "The city is finding itself . . . we shall have a sports center that will be the envy of the nation," the newspaper proclaimed. Over the next few paragraphs, the editorial outlined the project's benefits and the need to safeguard them from the "guardhouse litigants" who opposed the project.[79] Once again, Los Angeles had achieved an important project that was simultaneously susceptible to sabotage. The victory was complete: though the court case contesting the deal would last until October 1959, the California Supreme Court upheld the land deal on the basis that the city had the right to define the "public interest," and the United States Supreme Court concurred.[80] After the city evicted the Aréchiga family, the last residents of Chavez Ravine, the Dodgers began construction on September 17, 1959.[81]

When it opened in 1962, Dodger Stadium manifested all of O'Malley's hopes. Costing $18 million to build, it could seat fifty-six thousand fans and the spacious parking lots surrounding it could hold sixteen thousand cars. In the decades to come, Dodger Stadium would prove to be an enormous success. During the 1978 season, before O'Malley's death in August 1979, the Dodgers drew over 3.3 million fans to Chavez Ravine.[82] On Opening Day in 1962, the *Times* expounded on the resources that had gone into its construction. "There are more than 40,000 cubic yards of concrete in the edifice," one article detailed, "13 million pounds of reinforcing steel, 375,000 board feet of northern elm wood from 250 acres of forest land in the seats, 550 tons of cast iron in the chairs and 80,000 tons of asphalt on the parking lots and roads."[83] Similar to the "taming" of the Colorado River, Los Angeles had conquered nature to construct a great sporting arena. In the same vein, the radical reshaping of the environment in Chavez Ravine indicated a growing architectural modernism in Los Angeles, which continually displaced minority populations.[84] Furthermore, the stadium's opening illustrated the extent of elite power in the city. As Poulson remembered, elites emerged victorious in a "Titanic Struggle."[85] Poulson and his allies had routed local opposition, a popular long-term mayor, and a New York power broker. They had triumphed in the courts. And they had convinced the public to ratify their conception of the "public interest." In June 1962 *Los Angeles Times* columnist Jack Smith attended a game at Dodger Stadium. His article, "The Rapture of Chavez Ravine," attested to the degree of public acclaim for O'Malley's project. "It may well be that Mr. Walter O'Malley has constructed one of the wonders of the modern world," he wrote. "It seems unique and marvelous to me because it couldn't have happened at any other time or place in civilization."[86] Smith had a point. Los Angeles elites seemed to be at the height of their powers.

"America's Own Boat People"

On Opening Day 1962, however, Poulson was an ex-mayor. After two terms in office, he ran for reelection in 1961 against Sam Yorty, a nominal Democrat who had supported Republican Richard Nixon in the 1960 presidential election. As Bowron had done in his own first successful election eight years earlier, Yorty sought to exacerbate public opinion against Poulson's ties to Los Angeles elites. Shortly after the initial election, when Poulson and Yorty advanced to the May 31 runoff, the *Times* commented on the "hectic campaigning" of both men. Yorty, the paper claimed, "repeated charges that Poulson was in the toils of some sort of a city hall political octopus from which he could not extricate himself." Poulson tried to turn the attack back on Yorty. "I might reply that Mr. Yorty is backed by an underworld machine," he snidely responded.[87] For the next two months, the mayoral campaign revolved around such issues. Poulson charged that Yorty was the corrupt tool of vice interests, and Yorty charged that Poulson was the corrupt tool of Los Angeles elites. As he had in his previous mayoral campaigns, Poulson could rely on the staunch support of the *Los Angeles Times*. The newspaper's official endorsement of the incumbent mayor portrayed him as a "statesman" who had advanced the city's interests by luring the Dodgers west, among other accomplishments. "Mr. Poulson . . . is irreplaceable," the editorial maintained.[88]

As the runoff campaign progressed, Yorty effectively manipulated popular antipathy toward Los Angeles elites. Ironically, Yorty also succeeded using some of the gendered strategies Poulson had used against Bowron. Poulson was sidelined with persistent laryngitis, and Yorty so criticized the incumbent's health that Poulson submitted to a full physical six days before the election.[89] On entering the hospital, Poulson decried Yorty's "ugly and insidious whispering campaign," one not so different from the aspersions he had once cast against Bowron's age and vigor. On election day, Yorty defeated Poulson by about sixteen thousand votes out of over five hundred thousand cast.[90] "This is the first real people's victory in the 35 years that I have lived here," announced the elated Yorty on election night. "I don't blame you for your shouting," he told his supporters. "We have been silenced for so long that we deserve to shout."[91] Though Yorty would often make life worse for working-class Angelenos of all races in the years to come, his shocking election exposed cracks in elite domination over city politics. During the ensuing decade, such cracks would widen, especially as Yorty deepened racial animosity in the city. Through the Watts Rebellion and accelerating demographic change, the powerful men who had connected Los Angeles to the world would increasingly see the city escaping their grasp.

Founded as an independent municipality in 1907, Watts was originally settled by Mexican laborers who worked for Henry Huntington's Pacific Electric Railway, which operated a major station nearby at the confluence of two its lines. Los Angeles annexed the area in 1926, and for two decades it housed a working-class community of African Americans, Mexicans, and whites. With the advent of the second Great Migration, Watts and South

Central Avenue became landing spots for the masses of African Americans who made their way west to work in industrial plants and at the nearby port.[92] Similar to Mexican migrants of the past, African Americans did not choose Watts; local housing segregation forced them to settle in the underserviced community.[93] Generally, their arrival in the area sparked racial violence and white flight. In 1948, after the Supreme Court ruled restrictive covenants unconstitutional in *Shelley v. Kraemer*, the *Los Angeles Sentinel*, the city's Black-owned newspaper, detailed whites' efforts "To Force Negroes to Stay in Ghettoes." Among the listed crimes were three arson attempts aimed at a home newly occupied by a Black woman and her two grandchildren, in a white neighborhood.[94] Another article a few months later detailed how the "lily white families" in one white section of Watts "have been flooding the local real estate offices listing their homes for sale . . . the result of just one Negro family that bought a home in the area."[95] By 1953 the *Chicago Tribune* remarked with some surprise that Angelenos, and Los Angeles's businesses, were "flocking" to the suburbs, at the expense of areas such as Watts-Wilmington-San Pedro. "The move to locate industry on the perimeter of the city is an excellent one," blithely commented Los Angeles Chamber of Commerce president Roy Hagen. "It means better housing for workers, less congestion in the central area and generally more freedom of movement."[96]

As white Angelenos deserted Watts, its residents became increasingly isolated from the surrounding city. Only one fire company served the area, for instance, and Watts's business district lacked sufficient street lighting and traffic signals.[97] The Black community had initially sought industrial jobs nearby, but those plants largely moved to the suburbs. The 1952 completion of the elevated Harbor Freeway, which linked downtown to the Port of Los Angeles, signaled a new era in urban infrastructure, one that would largely cut off minority communities from the city and decimate public transit systems.[98] Though the *Sentinel* and other community organizations tried to foster community advocacy and pride, by 1965 Watts was plagued by dilapidated housing, high unemployment, and pervasive poverty.[99] "The palm-loving rats of Los Angeles are at home in the slums, where holes in the walls allow them to share the families' food or eat the uncollected garbage," noted *Nation* writer Charles Adams in 1950. "Though the houses they occupy range from creaking wooden tenements to makeshift shacks and converted chicken coops, these slum-dwellers have one problem in common: they are hemmed in."[100]

The Los Angeles Police Department, meanwhile, paid excessive, often violent, attention to Watts's residents.[101] Roughly 75 percent of those arrested during the eventual rebellion had prior arrest records.[102] William H. Parker, who served as the chief of the LAPD from 1950 to 1966, fought with great success for the department's autonomy from city authorities. Parker then used his independence to enforce a vision of city order grounded in white supremacy. During Parker's tenure, the LAPD was over 95 percent white, arrest rates in minority communities were significantly higher than those in white neighborhoods, and police abuse ran rampant.[103] "Chief Parker: He who lives by the sword shall die by the sword," read picket signs carried by police brutality protesters in May 1964.[104] "Suppose we cut down police work in the Negro community?," replied Parker to his critics. "A reign of terror would ensue."[105] In such moments, Parker echoed the preparedness rhetoric of World War I and World War II.

Watts residents had been speaking out against police inequities for twenty years by the time of the rebellion. In 1947 the LAPD singled out Watts for its second blockade in two weeks. Police barricaded all five roads leading into the community, stopped every car, roughly searched each car with a Black driver, and arrested over seventy people in a campaign directed at "crime in general." "Is this the Gestapo regime or democratic America?," wondered one resident.[106] In April 1964 groups of Black Angelenos attacked policemen on multiple occasions. "Been Coming for Years," commented the *Sentinel*.[107] Moreover, though Yorty was elected in part due to Black support, he wholeheartedly supported Parker's LAPD.[108] It should not have been surprising, then, that a minor traffic offense set off the Watts Rebellion. "The Watts uprising drew strength from a legacy of frustration with racism, employment discrimination, and residential segregation," argues historian Max Felker-Kantor. "Yet racist policing was ultimately the uprising's trigger."[109]

The rebellion erupted on Wednesday August 11, 1965, after two Los

Angeles policemen pulled over two Black men, Marquette and Ronald Frye, in Watts for a suspected DUI. As the police tried to take Marquette Frye away, a crowd of 250 to 300 people assembled around the group, including Frye's mother. She likely tried to prevent Marquette's arrest, at which point violence broke out between the officers and the group. Sparked by accusations of police brutality, the crowd grew to around fifteen hundred people and forced the LAPD to vacate the area under a hailstorm of bottles and rocks.[110] From there, violence spread more widely. On the evening of August 11, Watts's pent-up anger at racism and the violence of the LAPD erupted, and neither Black community leaders nor politicians were able to quell it. Protests only grew after the LAPD sent large contingents of officers into the area to try to crush the rebellion. Parker castigated the "meddlers" who, in his mind, had sparked the rebellion through allegations of police brutality.[111] Yorty blamed the "criminal element" and seemingly tried to ignore the massive numbers of people in the streets. For the next four nights, thousands of people fought the police, looted, and rioted; thirty-four people died and over one thousand were wounded during the uprising.[112] Though the LAPD eventually arrested almost four thousand people, the rebellion only ceased after the State of California dispatched fourteen thousand National Guardsmen to the area.[113] "Watts' main business thoroughfare . . . looked like a battleground Friday morning," commented one *Times* article. "Stores had burned. The street was dotted with the hulks of cars that had been overturned and burned. Shattered glass and rubble were everywhere."[114]

As the rebellion grew in scope, the *Los Angeles Times* became increasingly worried about its effect on the city's orderly appearance and image. "Bands of Negro youths and adults roamed the turbulent neighborhoods," an article told readers. "Hundreds of householders telephoned police seeking protection."[115] Los Angeles's "fortress" demands had returned. On August 14 a front-page article depicted "The Face of Violence—A City's Agony."[116] That same day, the newspaper seemed shocked by Black antipathy toward white Angelenos, noting the "Spirit of Hate Underlying Violent Rioting" that lent the riots an "ugly, almost hopeless, sickening," mood. "It's too late, white man," commented one rioter. "You had your chance.

Now it's our turn." "This is a grass roots thing, white devil," commented another.[117] Overall, the *Times* seemed to despair about Los Angeles's racial climate and the implications of the events for the city's future and global image. Indeed, Watts quickly became national news. An August 14 *New York Times* article included large pictures and took up much of the front page. "2,000 Troops Enter Los Angeles on Third Day of Negro Rioting," proclaimed the headline. "Youths Run Wild," read the first subheading.[118] For Los Angeles elites, then, the Watts Rebellion was an exponentially worse California Water Wars: a nationally publicized vision of Angeleno chaos, disorder, and oppression. The Watts Rebellion had demonstrated the real issues festering under the surface of the city's seemingly placid hierarchy. Elite control was not absolute.

In the years following the Watts Rebellion, the *Times* often featured writers who sought to reevaluate Los Angeles's urban environment. Generally, these visions agreed that the city's future lay in a hypersegregated set of distinct neighborhoods—a process already well underway. Fears about Black mobs threatening white neighborhoods lay behind such ideas. Watts might be improved, then, but it also would not be integrated into the white city. Debates about the city's connections resurfaced, as the *Times* urged new forms of mediated connections between Watts and white Los Angeles. In March 1966, for instance, the LAPD suppressed a minor uprising in the community, one that the *Times* feared was similar to the rebellion. Arguing that "a gathering mob of jobless Negroes with hate in their hearts" threatened civic disorder, the newspaper appreciated that "This Time It Was Contained." The idea of "containing" Watts, similar to American policy toward the USSR, presupposed that the Watts community was malicious and threatening. The editorial urged Angelenos to remain "vigorously on guard against fresh outbreaks," while also continuing to try to provide jobs for residents. Here, then, was the newspaper's philosophy: Watts needed to be supported but separated. Its rhetoric harkened back to the "medicalized Yellow Peril" that justified segregating the city's Asian communities. One year later, the newspaper presented similar ideas with a much more optimistic gloss. Extolling "Incredible Los Angeles," John L. Chapman foresaw that Los Angeles would be "the first of several enormous super-cities destined to dominate our environment in the 21st century." To Chapman, super-cities would be distinguished by a kind of connected sprawl, which he termed "the cellular approach." "The basic area-wide pattern—that of a growing multitude of contiguous cells which feed partly on each other and partly on a central hub (Los Angeles)—has been established more or less by happenstance," he wrote, "and probably couldn't work any better if it had been planned that way." At the end of the article, Chapman tried to link his ideas to cosmopolitanism. "In spite of Watts," he argued, the city was on a positive trajectory. "It resists . . . the shoals of bigotry," he concluded. "Its window on life is true, unwarped, untinted."[119] Chapman's "cellular super-city" was just another way for Los Angeles to segregate communities such as Watts. City leaders could claim to help one "cell" while also isolating it from the white organism. The *Times* may have urged economic development in Watts, then, but its real message was of mediated connection: the one-way transfer of capitalist values to the area under a broader banner of quarantine.

Communities, however, are not static. Beginning in the 1980s, Watts saw an exodus of Black inhabitants and an influx of Latino residents. Today, Watts is over 60 percent Latino.[120] One 1980 *Times* article depicted the "strains" between Black and Latino residents, many of whom were undocumented. "Because they are unable to blend into the existing social fabric," the authors argued, "the new immigrants run the risk of interacting with blacks primarily as the victims of crime."[121] Here, again, lay notions of Watts as unchanging, as a hotspot of crime isolated from the rest of Los Angeles. But the article also gestured toward the other process that undermined elite control: post-1965 immigration. With the passage of the 1965 Immigration Act, also called the Hart-Celler Act, Congress ended forty-one years of U.S. immigration policy designed to privilege immigration from northern and western Europe, as well as essentially eliminate immigration from Asia. The 1965 bill did not completely open up the United States, but it gave preference to professional workers and relatives of American citizens at the expense of immigrants from Latin and South America. In short order, the United States experienced two "unexpected" developments: massive increases in both documented Asian immigration and undocumented immigration from the Western Hemisphere.[122] While not as immediately explosive as Watts, post-1965 immigration streams would profoundly impact Los Angeles in the years to come.[123]

By imposing uniform worldwide quotas of twenty thousand immigrants per country, historian Mae Ngai argues, the Hart-Celler Act embodied the ideals of a postwar "liberal nationalism" that emphasized both cultural pluralism and American exceptionalism.[124] The *Times*' coverage of the act was positive. "Thus the antiquated system of racial immigration quotas, with its ugly overtones of racial prejudice, will at last go by the board," argued Joseph Alsop in one article.[125] Even if some American officials foresaw an increase in Asian immigration, Chinese and Japanese immigrants were increasingly seen as positive assets to America's plural society. As historian Ellen Wu has shown, the "model minority" myth upheld Chinese and Japanese immigrants as hardworking members of American society, definitively "not black." In the mid-1960s Wu writes, "not-blackness eclipsed not-whiteness as a signal characteristic of Asian American racialization as African American freedom movements took center stage in the life of the nation."[126]

After 1965 the effects of the Hart-Celler Act became quickly apparent. The 1960 census listed approximately seventy thousand Japanese and twenty thousand Chinese residents of Los Angeles County. By 1970 those numbers had risen to 104,000 and 40,000, respectively. By 1980 they grew to 116,000 and 94,000.[127] The conclusion of the Vietnam War in 1975, moreover, would force hundreds of thousands of Vietnamese to flee the country in the next two decades. The exodus of these "boat people" came to a head in 1978, as the Vietnamese regime increased its political persecution of former South Vietnamese officials and supporters. In the context of rising Asian immigration, the Vietnamese migration crisis sparked a renewed conversation in Los Angeles about the city's connections. Once again, a variety of editorials in the *Times* called upon America to accept Vietnamese refugees in the name of American exceptionalism and cultural pluralism.[128] Four years later, as the refugee crisis grew worse, another editorial called the situation a "moral imperative" for America to solve. "What began as a flow from refugees from Vietnam has now become a hemorrhage," it began; in response, the United States, in the newspaper's mind, should increase its admission of refugees from seven thousand to ten thousand per month.[129] The image of a "hemorrhage," of course, was not entirely benign: it echoed the long history of the "medicalized Yellow Peril."

As immigration increased, the *Times* featured nascent anxieties about demographic change in Los Angeles. The "model minority" myth had privileged Chinese and Japanese immigrants for the purported ease with which they assimilated and achieved economic independence. The Vietnamese refugees of the late 1970s, on the other hand, were significantly more impoverished. One editorial, amid a discussion of the need for residents to be "good neighbors," pondered the changing demographic landscape. "And so what was once a remote world problem," the paper maintained, "is now a neighborhood problem that the county's residents can see."[130] Immigration seemed significantly more tangible than it had in the past. In 1980 the newspaper even published a report on growing nativist sentiment in America in response to the "seemingly endless flood of refugees coming into America from Cuba, Haiti, Vietnam and God knows where else." Its author, Ernest Conine, urged America to alleviate poverty in nations experiencing mass emigration. "Surely it makes more sense to spend x-millions of dollars today on foreign economic assistance . . . than to spend triple-x-millions tomorrow to cope with the urban overload created by the arrival of too many refugees in this country," he concluded.[131] After the Watts Rebellion, the *Times* had assured readers that Watts might be isolated and quarantined. After the 1965 Immigration Act, the newspaper had similarly predicted that America might attract only upstanding, "model" immigrants instead of impoverished refugees and undocumented immigrants. Occasionally, the *Times* even connected the Black experience to the refugee experience in Los Angeles. In 1979 it published a remarkable editorial, "America's Own Boat People," which urged greater employment for Black youth. "These youngsters are boat people within our own country," it concluded, "and they should be brought ashore."[132] The paper failed to note that it had often desired to separate Watts from the city writ large, pushing such young people out to sea.

Though the *Times* continued to urge federal refugee aid in the 1970s, it clearly did not expect the 1965 immigration bill to transform Los Angeles so substantively. In 1981 the newspaper published an editorial about the 1980 census and Southern California. The article noted with some surprise that whites were now a minority in the region, that the Latino and Asian populations had grown significantly, and that Southern California's nine hundred thousand Black residents had spread out beyond the "ghettos of South-Central Los Angeles." Long gone was any idea of Los Angeles as a "Borderlands Fortress." "There are people who will see in such large statistics something vaguely troubling, perhaps even threatening," the paper noted, but "we prefer to see them as exciting and challenging."[133] *Times* coverage of the census demonstrated the extent to which Los Angeles had changed. No longer was it an Anglo outpost mostly dominated by a cadre of elites who sought to transform the city into a global economic power. Instead, Los Angeles was a global economic power in which whites were a minority. In the face of this new reality, the newspaper could not even complain. Instead, it urged Angelenos to aid assimilation, to ensure the city's future character by transforming potentially dangerous Asian immigrants into successful members of the "model minority" and African American "boat people" into exemplars of Angeleno pluralism.

"The Engineering Wonder of the World"

For six decades, Los Angeles elites achieved a vision of their city, in the words of Eric Avila, as the "Nation's White Spot." Los Angeles was a utopia for eastern and midwestern migrants who could purchase inexpensive homes on substantial tracts of land and find jobs in the city's growing industries.[134] To be fair, Anglo elites also were not necessarily as parochial as Avila's characterization might imply; they were remarkably forward-looking. In the early twentieth century, men such as Harrison Gray Otis and Henry Huntington realized Los Angeles's very real limitations and sought to overcome them through federal appropriations, East Coast funding, and local activism. Later, men such as Edward Doheny, Donald Douglas, and James Kindelberger realized Los Angeles's potential as both an industrial hub and a consumer's market. They directed global capital through Southern California. To these men, the politics of connections entailed a delicate balancing act between ensuring municipal progress and maintaining elite Anglo control.

Indeed, Los Angeles's elite connective project was fabulously successful. The prewar era provided a sociopolitical atmosphere particularly conducive to the transformation of the metropolis via elite activism and discourse mandating both preparedness and progress. During the 1890s Otis and his Los Angeles Chamber of Commerce successfully fought for a notion of the public interest mediated by a local elite vision instead of eastern prerogatives—a set of ideals that would continue to guide the city's growth. The World War I–era elite preparedness project demanding that the city be protected from a dual Japanese-Mexican menace similarly positioned elites against eastern power. It also culminated in victory, with a city fortified against future invasion threats and positioned to take advantage of postwar global trading currents. The 1920s Los Angeles water saga—the California Water Wars, the construction of the Colorado River Aqueduct—was more regional but just as successful, temporarily ensuring the future of a city utterly dependent on natural resources plucked from other areas. Even the St. Francis Dam disaster did not derail the city's imperial ambitions. The one million Angelenos who attended the city's exuberant "tribute to electricity" when it began receiving power from the Hoover Dam were assuredly not dwelling on the past. The Depression witnessed the most significant challenge to elite power before World War II. Federal efforts to deport the city's controllable agricultural labor source, dramatic increases in national migration, and Upton Sinclair's popular socialist gubernatorial campaign might have undercut traditional hierarchical norms. However, men such as George Clements, William Garland, and Louis Mayer banded together to shore up the status quo. They then presented a utopian vision of the city to the world during the 1932 Olympic Games. Finally, during World War II, elites' connective rhetoric had its most profound, and ugliest, success. The transformation of Fletcher Bowron and John Anson Ford—two cosmopolitan, progressive politicians—into internment advocates indicates that elite ideals had thoroughly permeated the municipal political spectrum.

In their work, Los Angeles elites also mandated and enforced specific notions of masculine identity for the city and vituperated those who stood in their way. They composed a specific notion of masculinity that centered on the value of capitalist labor and vigilance to reinforce a gendered hierarchy. Otis's martial legacy carried over into the *Times'* coverage of preparedness during World War I, elite discussions of the value of Mexican migrants versus "tramps" during the Depression, and internment activism focused on purported "fifth column" disloyalty by Issei and Nisei. Similarly, elites projected masculine norms on their campaigns to "tame" the wilderness. The creation of the Los Angeles Harbor out of a mud swamp was the first in a long line of actions illustrating how the elite men of Los Angeles meant to chisel a metropolis out of an allegedly unforgiving wilderness and then advertise their efforts to the world. *The Winning of Barbara Worth* vividly demonstrated how the proponents of infrastructure projects could unite with the leaders of other local industries, such as motion pictures, in constructing and broadcasting Los Angeles's masculine image.

Painstakingly, then, elites created an intensely hierarchical city, intricately connected to the outside world. The California Water Wars, Japanese internment campaign, and the Watts Rebellion are as much a part of these men's connective legacy as the Port of Los Angeles, the Hoover Dam, and Los Angeles International Airport. Connections were also constantly negotiated. Elites shaped a metropolis that could both act as an epicenter for Japanese internment and then become a global immigration conduit twenty years later. If anything, then, modern Los Angeles is bigger than its boosters ever thought possible and beset by more significant issues—homelessness, resource usage, traffic—than they could have imagined. Los Angeles's morally muddy expansion has presented a problem for modern Angelenos, who, using familiar rhetoric, generally prefer to focus on ensuring the city's future. In November 1988, as the seventy-fifth anniversary of the Los Angeles Aqueduct approached, the *Times* published a lengthy reminiscence of the work that lay behind the aqueduct. Marc Reisner, the article's author, had two years previously published *Cadillac Desert: The American West and Its Disappearing Water*, a critical account of western, and especially Southern Californian, water development. Rather remarkably given his *Times* byline, Reisner highlighted how the aqueduct fostered risky, exponential municipal growth. Even Reisner, however, could not resist a dose of Angeleno exceptionalism. "The city fathers, the ones who plotted and schemed for the aqueduct . . . deified growth," argued Reisner, "perhaps because Los Angeles had made such titans out of them. There were Harrison Gray Otis, who had been an unremarkable printer, . . . until he founded the Los Angeles Times." Reisner continued, describing "Harry Chandler, a New Hampshire refugee with a tubercular cough and a gambler's heart . . . And William Mulholland, a gruff Irish castoff from a merchant ship who began as a well digger and built the engineering wonder of the world."[135] Still, growth worried Reisner. Further water projects seemed untenable, and water for Southern California would need to be siphoned from agricultural interests. "If Los Angeles can neither stop growth nor find a new source of water, what will it do?" he pointedly asked readers at the end of the article.[136]

Of course, Reisner was just one in a long line of commentators who had juxtaposed municipal growth with the need for connections. In the aftermath of the 1890 real estate crash, the *Times* had bemoaned that Los Angeles was not among the "most rare cases of cities which are fortunately located at points where railroad and deep-water ocean traffic meet."[137] In 1952 political activist and city booster Marshall Stimson extolled the city's future expansion. "I think in the future, we'll find people living just where they like; on a farm, at a lake, at the ocean, on mountains or on the desert, coming to their work in downtown Los Angeles on helicopters they will park on the roofs of office buildings," he forecast. "Or thousands of them may be coming to work at 100 miles an hour or faster by monorail rapid transit." The end of Stimson's futuristic prediction focused on water connections as well. "Los Angeles will be limited in size only by the supply of water we'll have available," he argued. "But by that time," Stimson hoped, "science probably will have found the way to get water from the ocean as cheaply as we now get it from streams and lakes."[138]

The connections that loomed large throughout Los Angeles's history continue to haunt the city's boosters today. In 2013, on the hundredth anniversary of the opening of the Los Angeles Aqueduct, city leaders gathered to reenact the occasion. In front of five hundred people—a small crowd compared to the forty thousand who had swarmed the southern terminus of the aqueduct a century before—Los Angeles mayor Eric Garcetti gave a speech that outlined the city's development, the factors that threatened it, and its future potential. As only the third Latino mayor in the city's history, Garcetti himself demonstrated the scope of Los Angeles's transformation. His words, however, might have been recited at any moment in the previous 125 years. "Los Angeles can, must and will protect its destiny," he proclaimed. "In a span of a century, we have not only changed the course of water, but of history itself." "So as we might have said in the past, 'Here it is. Take it!,'" he continued, echoing Mulholland's speech at the aqueduct's opening, "I say to you today: Here it still is. Let us treasure it. Let us conserve it. Let us share it. It our legacy. It is our right. But it is also our responsibility. Let us continue to build great things. Let us build a great L.A."[139]

NOTES

INTRODUCTION

1. Roger Butterfield, "Los Angeles Is the Damnedest Place," *Life*, November 22, 1943, 102.
2. Butterfield, "Los Angeles Is the Damnedest Place," 103.
3. On Chicago, see Cronon, *Nature's Metropolis*; on Kansas City see Glaab, *Kansas City and the Railroads*; on Seattle see Lee, *Claiming the Oriental Gateway*.
4. Sandul, *California Dreaming*, 117.
5. Needham, *Power Lines*, 7–9.
6. For a summation of "sunshine" versus "noir" from which I drew this analysis, see Culver, *Frontier of Leisure*, 4–5. For the "sunshine" narrative, one could look to the Kevin Starr series Americans and the California Dream, in particular, Starr, *Inventing the Dream*. For the "noir" narrative, see Davis, *City of Quartz*. "Sunshine or Noir" is also the title of chapter 1 of *City of Quartz*.
7. Jaher, *Urban Establishment*, 685.
8. Baltzell, *Philadelphia Gentlemen*, 6.
9. The Merchants and Manufacturers Association was founded in 1893 as a trade group to promote the city. With Otis's help, it quickly became devoted to the open shop movement in the city and to anti-labor policies more generally. The organization still exists, under a different name: Employers Group.
10. Stansell, *City of Women*, xiv.
11. See, for instance, Kwolek-Folland, *Engendering Business*.
12. See Bederman, *Manliness and Civilization*, 4–17; Kasson, *Houdini, Tarzan, and the Perfect Man*, 8–19.
13. Kimmel, *Manhood in America*, 72.
14. Rico, *Nature's Noblemen*, 17.

15. Hoganson, *Fighting for American Manhood*, 150–51. See also Rotundo, *American Manhood*, 222–46.
16. See Connell and Messerschmidt, "Hegemonic Masculinity," 829–59.
17. Connell and Wood, "Globalization and Business Masculinities," 348.
18. Chauncey, *Gay New York*, 26.
19. Chauncey, *Gay New York*, 25–26.
20. Davis, *Company Men*, 146.
21. For works on racial formation in Los Angeles in the twentieth century see Brilliant, *Color of America*; Brooks, *Alien Neighbors, Foreign Friends*; Garcia, *World of Its Own*; González, *Labor and Community*; Kurashige, *Shifting Grounds of Race*; Ruíz, *Cannery Women, Cannery Lives*; Sanchez, *Becoming Mexican American*.
22. Molina, *Fit to Be Citizens?*, 1.
23. Carpio, *Collisions at the Crossroads*, 5–6.
24. Avila, *Popular Culture*, 20.
25. Molina, *Fit to Be Citizens?*, 18.
26. Smith, *City Water, City Life*, 8.
27. Smith, *City Water, City Life*, 2–4
28. Jaher, *Urban Establishment*, 5.
29. For more on the functioning of the elite class, see Mills, *Power Elite*.
30. The "Great Men" theory is generally attributed to the nineteenth-century Scottish scholar Thomas Carlyle and his 1840 lecture collection, *On Heroes, Hero-Worship, and the Heroic in History*. For an analysis of his work, see Atwood, "'Leading Human Souls to What Is Best.'"
31. Beckert, *Monied Metropolis*, 333.
32. Caro, *Power Broker*, 19–20.
33. For the legal mechanisms used to create borders, see Lee, *At America's Gates*; Hernández, *Migra*; Ngai, *Impossible Subjects*.
34. Yu, "Los Angeles and American Studies," 531–43.
35. See also Azuma, "Japanese Immigrant Settler Colonialism," 255–76.
36. The dimensions and scale of the "Pacific World" are hotly debated historiographical topics, but scholars at least agree that the Pacific World tied the American West to East Asian nations. For conceptual pieces on the Pacific World, see Banner, *Possessing the Pacific*, 1–13; Dirlik, "Pacific Contradictions"; Hau'ofa, "Our Sea of Islands"; Igler, "Diseased Goods"; Jones, *Empire of Extinction*; Melillo, *Strangers on Familiar Soil*; Matsuda, *Pacific Worlds*.
37. For works on this trend nationally in the nineteenth century, see Chang, *Pacific Connections*; Jacobson, *Barbarian Virtues*; Kaplan, *Anarchy of Empire*.
38. Bolton, *Spanish Borderlands*.
39. Anzaldúa, *Borderlands/La Frontera*, 3.
40. See Castillo-Muñoz, "Beyond Red-Light Districts."

41. See Truett, *Fugitive Landscapes*, 1–10, 55–77; Ruiz, *People of Sonora*.

42. Kim, *Imperial Metropolis*, 20.

43. See Roth, "Concrete Utopia."

44. Gish, "Growing and Selling Los Angeles," 397–99.

45. "Tourist Rush for Winter On," *Los Angeles Times*, October 29, 1925.

46. For broader Los Angeles histories, see McWilliams, *Southern California*; Gottlieb and Wolt, *Thinking Big*; Fogelson, *Fragmented Metropolis*; Torres-Rouff, *Before L.A*; Starr, *Material Dreams*. For works on the cultural mythology of Los Angeles see Deverell, *Whitewashed Adobe*; McClung, *Landscapes of Desire*. For works on Los Angeles as a built environment, see Fulton, *Reluctant Metropolis*; Axelrod, *Inventing Autopia*.

47. Kurashige, *Shifting Grounds of Race*, 8. Historical monographs that describe Los Angeles as a "global city" include Abu-Lughod, *New York, Chicago, Los Angeles*; Gottlieb, *Reinventing Los Angeles*; Hamilton and Chinchilla, *Seeking Community*.

48. Butterfield, "Los Angeles Is the Damnedest Place," 114.

49. Sandoval-Strausz, "Latino Landscapes."

50. Fletcher Bowron, radio address, March 17, 1943, 1, LAMRB, 1943, box C-2021.

51. Avila, *Popular Culture*, 20.

52. "Los Angeles, CA," Census Reporter, accessed November 9, 2017, https://censusreporter.org/profiles/16000us0644000-los-angeles-ca/.

53. Harrison Gray Otis to A. B. Henderson, July 29, 1900, LAT, box 209, folder 9.

SNAPSHOT, LOS ANGELES, 1890

1. "Wichita and Los Angeles," *Los Angeles Times*, May 24, 1890.

2. "Historical General Population: City and County of Los Angeles, 1850–2010," Los Angeles Almanac, accessed October 26, 2017, http://www.laalmanac.com/population/po02.php; "Largest U.S. Cities By Population—Year 1890," Biggest US Cities, accessed October 26, 2017, https://www.biggestuscities.com/1890.

3. Newmark, *Sixty Years in Southern California*, 569–70.

4. "'Yankee Enough,'" *New York Times*, January 3, 1888.

5. Torres-Rouff, *Before L.A*, 220–22; 226.

6. For a full treatment of the incident, see Zesch, *Chinatown War*.

7. Molina, *Fit to Be Citizens?*, 16.

8. Torres-Rouff, *Before L.A.*, 223, 230–39.

9. "City of Los Angeles Annexations-Index," accessed February 22, 2018, Los Angeles pw.lacounty.gov/sur/nas/SMPM_AnnexationCityPDFs/Los_Angeles_Index.pdf; Fogelson, *Fragmented Metropolis*, 137. See also H. J. Stevenson, "Map of the City of Los Angeles, California, 1884," Los Angeles Public Library, accessed February 22, 2018, http://www.lapl.org/collections-resources/visual-collections/map-city-los-angeles-california-1884.

10. Torres-Rouff, *Before L.A.*, 240–49.

11. "The Progressive March of Los Angeles," *Los Angeles Times*, December 16, 1890.

12. Torres-Rouff, *Before L.A.*, 36.

13. For a full narrative of the development of the ranchero elite, see Torres-Rouff, *Before L.A.*, 23–54.

14. See Jaher, *Urban Establishment*, 583–96; Fogelson, *Fragmented Metropolis*, 1–23.

15. Demographic data from Jaher, *Urban Establishment*, 588–89.

16. "About USC: The Era of the Founders," University of Southern California, accessed August 25, 2017, https://about.usc.edu/history/founders.

17. "John G. Downey: Sudden Demise of the Ex-Governor," *Los Angeles Times*, March 2, 1894.

18. "Death Claims I. W. Hellman," *Los Angeles Times*, April 10, 1920.

19. "O. W. Childs: Sudden Death of an Old Los Angeles Pioneer," *Los Angeles Times*, April 18, 1890.

20. "Front Feet: A Glance at the Los Angeles Real-Estate Market," *Los Angeles Times*, January 1, 1888.

21. "Progress of the Boom," *Los Angeles Times*, May 6, 1888.

22. "Confidence Men: Their Manner of Working Los Angeles," *Los Angeles Times*, April 2, 1888.

23. Statistic from Jaher, *Urban Establishment*, 618.

24. "M. L. Wicks: Cheap and Desirable Real Estate of all Descriptions," *Los Angeles Daily Herald*, January 14, 1887.

25. "Letters to the Times: Financial Embarrassments of M. L. Wicks," *Los Angeles Times*, March 29, 1889.

26. "Fell with the Boom: Goodall, Perkins & Co.'s San Diego Agent Short," *Los Angeles Times*, November 1, 1889.

27. "The New and the Old," *Los Angeles Times*, January 1, 1890.

28. "Our Greatest Need—A Suggestion," *Los Angeles Times*, May 10, 1890.

29. "Largest US Cities By Population—Year 1890."

30. "The Population of Los Angeles," *Los Angeles Times*, June 29, 1890.

31. "Our Future," *Los Angeles Times*, December 6, 1890.

32. "Population of Los Angeles."

1. COMMAND POST OR OUTPOST

1. Mike Davis, "The Ghost of Wrath," *Los Angeles Review of Books*, July 15, 2011, https://lareviewofbooks.org/article/the-ghost-of-wrath.

2. Harrison Gray Otis to A. B. Henderson, LAT, July 29, 1900, box 209, folder 9.

3. "The Southern Pacific Company," *Los Angeles Times*, August 17, 1900.

4. Resolution of the Los Angeles Chamber of Commerce, October 16, 1912, LACOC, carton 006, series 1, box 6 (May 1912–February 1913), 196–97.

5. The United States took over the Panama Canal project from France in 1904 and did not complete the project until 1914.

6. Walter Lindley, Report to the Los Angeles Chamber of Commerce, May 22, 1912, LACOC, carton 006, series 1, box 6 (June 1911–April 1912), 31–32.

7. "1910 Los Angeles International Aviation Meet, 1909–1999" collection, California State University, Dominguez Hills, accessed April 20, 2017, http://www.oac.cdlib.org/findaid/ark:/13030/kt4m3nc8jw/.

8. "Yes. Bring the Aviators!" *Los Angeles Times*, November 16, 1909.

9. "Men or Money May Soon Fly," *Los Angeles Times*, November 16, 1909.

10. "Serious Problem of Defending Los Angeles May Be Solved by Men and Ships of the Air," *Los Angeles Times*, December 25, 1910.

11. Background for the biographical sketch of Otis is from Gottlieb and Wolt, *Thinking Big*, 17–31.

12. Shortly after the conclusion of the Hartford Convention, Andrew Jackson's forces won a sweeping victory over British forces at the Battle of New Orleans. Jackson's success, and the war's end, led to the demise of the Federalist Party.

13. "Resignation of Col. Otis," *Los Angeles Times*, April 25, 1882.

14. Eliza Ann Otis to Harrison Gray Otis, June 27, 1879, 1–2, LAT, box 209, folder 4.

15. "Desperate Folly," *Los Angeles Times*, January 14, 1890.

16. For more on Boyce's story after he left Los Angeles, see "Gen. H. H. Boyce Killed by Car," *Los Angeles Herald*, October 15, 1903.

17. Gottlieb and Wolt, *Thinking Big*, 23.

18. Ed. T. Gadden, "TO THE PHALANX: STEREOTYPING DEPARTMENT," October 1, 1912, LAT, box 209, folder 18.

19. Hoganson, *Fighting for American Manhood*, 7.

20. Harrison Gray Otis, "Order by the General Manager," January 23, 1917, LAT, box 209, folder 18.

21. Harrison Gray Otis, "The Untouched Eagle," *Los Angeles Times*, October 3, 1910.

22. "Mr. Otis and the Los Angeles 'Times,'" Los Angeles, Publicity Committee of Los Angeles Typographical Union no. 174, 1915, pages 1 and 24, LAT, box 209, folder 25.

23. McDougal, *Privileged Son*, 43.

24. *Advertiser's Rate Book*, 12–13.

25. The *Examiner*'s numbers were 77,782 daily and 143,422 on Sundays. *Advertiser's Rate Book*, 12–13.

26. Gottlieb and Wolt, *Thinking Big*, 28.

27. "A Letter from Harrison Gray Otis," University of California, n.d: likely 1917, 8–9, https://babel.hathitrust.org/cgi/pt?id=uc2.ark:/13960/t20c4vd5s&view=1up&seq=5.

28. Many different scholarly works address the *Times* and boosterism. See, for instance, Gottlieb and Wolt, *Thinking Big*, 25–117; McDougal, *Privileged Son*, 7–45; Davis, *City of Quartz*, 24–30; Starr, *Inventing the Dream*, 64–98.

29. Copy of letter from Harrison Gray Otis to *Los Angeles Star*, May 1, 1875, LAT, box 213, folder 7.

30. See Willard, *History of the Chamber of Commerce*, 7.

31. Willard, *History of the Chamber of Commerce*, 21. For more on Willard, see Culton, "Charles Dwight Willard."

32. Harrison Gray Otis to Kate Tannatt Woods, January 24, 1906, LAT, box 209, folder 14.

33. Frederick Jackson Turner's "frontier thesis," for instance, posited that "the wilderness masters the colonist. It finds him a European in dress, industries, tools, modes of travel, and thought. It takes him from the railroad car and puts him in the birch canoe. It strips off the garments of civilization and arrays him in the hunting shirt and the moccasin. It puts him in the log cabin of the Cherokee and Iroquois and runs an Indian palisade around him. Before long he has gone to planting Indian corn and plowing with a sharp stick; he shouts the war cry and takes the scalp in orthodox Indian fashion. In short, at the frontier the environment is at first too strong for the man. He must accept the conditions which it furnishes, or perish, and so he fits himself into the Indian clearings and follows the Indian trails." Turner, "Significance of the Frontier," 201.

34. Background for this sketch taken from Lavender and Lavender, *Great Persuader*, 1–8.

35. "Millionaires Were Feddlers: Such Men as Astor, Huntington, Gould and Russell Sage Began Small," *Los Angeles Times*, June 16, 1907.

36. Background for this paragraph taken from Lavender and Lavender, *Great Persuader*, 9–110.

37. "C. P. Huntington Dies in Woods: Millionaire Succumbs to Heart Disease while on an Outing in New York State," *Chicago Daily Tribune*, August 15, 1900.

38. "Collis Potter Huntington Papers, Biographical History," Syracuse University Libraries, accessed January 23, 2017, https://library.syr.edu/digital/guides/h/huntington_cp .htm.

39. For a lively account of Huntington's personality and work, see Lewis, *Big Four*, 211–82.

40. Lewis, *Big Four*, 224–25.

41. "The Dead Huntington: Strong Friends and Bitter Foes in Life," *Los Angeles Times*, September 16, 1900.

42. There are many accounts of the creation of the transcontinental railroad. See, for instance, Bain, *Empire Express*.

43. "Mr. Huntington's Estate: Family Decides to Offer the Will for Probate," *New York Times*, August 24, 1900.

44. "H. E. Huntington Arrives: Record Breaking Trip to His Uncle's Funeral, Which Takes Place Today," *New York Tribune*, August 17, 1900.

45. Collis Potter Huntington to James Spreyer, December 6, 1899, 18, CPH, box 130.

46. Huntington to Spreyer, December 6, 1899, 21.

47. For greater background on the Southern Pacific's actions in California, see Orsi, *Sunset Limited*.

48. Orsi, *Sunset Limited*, 20.

49. Orsi, *Sunset Limited*, 163.

50. Collis Potter Huntington to William H. Mills, July 19, 1898, Collis P. Huntington Papers [microform] (Sanford NC: Microfilming Corp. of America, 1978), series II, reel #34.

51. Orsi, *Sunset Limited*, 143.

52. For background on this story in the 1870s, see Deverell, *Railroad Crossing*, 34–60.

53. For a look at how Californians overstated the Southern Pacific's power, see Williams, *Democratic Party and California Politics*, 206–32; Orsi, "'The Octopus' Reconsidered."

54. Norris, *Octopus*, 69–70.

55. See, for instance, "The End of Uncle Collis: C. P. Huntington a Dead Man," *Los Angeles Times*, August 15, 1900.

56. "The Dead Huntington."

57. "The Dead Huntington."

58. Mills to Huntington, December 28, 1898, 3, CPH, box 129.

59. For a more specific breakdown of the Southern Pacific's actions at Santa Monica, see Deverell, *Railroad Crossing*, 96–99.

60. For detailed investigation of Phineas Banning's life and work, see Sitton, *Grand Ventures*, 25–117.

61. "Port of Los Angeles: Cabrillo's Legacy," Port of Los Angeles, accessed June 23, 2016, https://www.portoflosangeles.orghistory/cabrillo.asp; Fogelson, *Fragmented Metropolis*, 109.

62. Gottlieb and Wolt, *Thinking Big*, 57.

63. Gottlieb and Wolt, *Thinking Big*, 58.

64. Willard, *History of the Chamber of Commerce*, 132.

65. N. O. Anderson, "San Pedro's Day: A Clear-Cut Argument in Her Behalf," *Los Angeles Times*, September 2, 1892.

66. "Letters to The Times: 'God Is on the Side of the Heaviest Battalions,'" *Los Angeles Times*, June 2, 1894.

67. "The Harbor Question Is On," *Los Angeles Times*, August 27, 1892.

68. "Let Us Have a Deep-Sea Harbor for the People," *Los Angeles Times*, April 5, 1894.

69. "Huntington's Man," *Los Angeles Times*, November 24, 1897.

70. Background for this paragraph taken from Deverell, *Railroad Crossing*, 93–122 and Fogelson, *Fragmented Metropolis*, 108–15. Many historians have offered their analyses of the Free Harbor Fight. See also Gottlieb and Wolt, *Thinking Big*, 58–64; Lavender and Lavender, *Great Persuader*, 365–74; Willard, *Free Harbor Contest at Los Angeles*. For a broader take on development in Los Angeles during this time period see Erie, *Globalizing L.A.*, 45–60.

71. Willard, *History of the Chamber of Commerce*, 136–37.

72. Willard, *History of the Chamber of Commerce*, 139.

73. For the full testimony, see *Deep Water Harbor in Southern California*.

74. Willard, *History of the Chamber of Commerce*, 138.

75. "Stephen Mallory White," *Los Angeles Times*, February 22, 1901.

76. "Stephen M. White," *Los Angeles Herald*, December 12, 1908.

77. For a brief history of the statue, see Roger M. Grace, "Statue Goes from Broadway to Hill to Storage Yard to Grand . . . to San Pedro," *Metropolitan News-Enterprise*, October 30, 2006, http://www.metnews.com/articles/2006/perspectives103006.htm.

78. Willard, *History of the Chamber of Commerce*, 141.

79. Fogelson, *Fragmented Metropolis*, 115–17.

80. Los Angeles City Council Minutes, August 17, 1909, LACC, vol. 78 (April 1, 1909–August 17, 1909), 597–98.

81. Los Angeles City Council Minutes, August 24, 1909, LACC, vol. 79 (August 24, 1909–December 14, 1909), 28.

82. Resolution on January 31, 1900, LACOC, carton 002, series 1, box 2 (September 1899–June 1909), 72. For the chamber's support of the canal see a resolution on January 11, 1899. LACOC, carton 002, series 1, box 2 (September 1898–August 1899), 100.

83. "Port of Los Angeles: Cabrillo's Legacy." For a summation of the many legal maneuverings involved around this time, see Tejani, "Dredging the Future," 28–37; Tejani, "Harbor Lines."

84. W. C. Peterson and the Los Angeles Area Chamber of Commerce Committee on Commerce to the Los Angeles Area Chamber of Commerce Board of Directors, December 8, 1897, LACOC, carton 002, series 1, box 2 (July 1897–September 1898), 99–100.

85. Los Angeles Chamber of Commerce Resolution, April 20, 1898, LACOC, cartoon 002, series 1, box 2 (July 1897–September 1898), 200–201.

86. Los Angeles Chamber of Commerce Harbor Committee Resolution, December 12, 1906, LACOC, carton 004, series 1, box 4 (April 1906–July 1907), 148.

87. Report of the Committees on Fortification and Military and Naval Affairs to the Board of Directors, November 15, 1911, LACOC, carton 006, series 1, box 6 (June 1911–April 1912), 127–28.

88. Report of the Committees on Fortification and Military and Naval Affairs, 128.

89. Los Angeles Chamber of Commerce Resolution, January 11, 1899, LACOC, carton 002, series 1, box 2 (September 1898–August 1899), 100.

90. Lindley, Report to the Los Angeles Chamber of Commerce, 31.

91. "Panama Canal Tolls," Los Angeles Chamber of Commerce, March 12, 1912, LACOC, carton 006, series 1, box 6 (June 1911–April 1912), 252–53.

92. "Action of the Chamber of Commerce in Favor of Free Tolls on American Ships through the Panama Canal, and in Opposition to Railway Owned Ships Engaging in Coastwise Trade through the Panama Canal," July 17, 1912, LACOC, carton 006, series 1, box 6 (May 1912–February 1913), 106.

93. For a summation of the meet and its effects on western aviation and popular interest see Launius and Embry, "1910 Los Angeles Airshow." For more on the culture of prewar

aviation, see Bilstein, "Airplane and the American Experience"; Corn, *Winged Gospel*, 3–28; Courtwright, *Sky as Frontier*, 3–88; Wohl, *Spectacle of Flight*.

94. "1910 Los Angeles International Aviation Meet Research Collection, 1909–1999: Background," Online Archive of California, accessed April 20, 2017, http://www.oac.cdlib .org/findaid/ark:/13030/kt4m3nc8jw/.

95. "Aeroplanes Are Completed for Aviation Week Trials," *Los Angeles Times*, November 7, 1909.

96. Don Berliner, "The Big Race of 1910: How the First U.S. Air Race Launched an Aviation Tradition," *Air and Space Magazine*, January 2010, https://www.smithsonianmag.com /air-space-magazine/the-big-race-of-1910-9075126/.

97. Copy of the *Los Angeles Express*, January 14, 1910, LAAM, box 1, folder 49.

98. For a biography of Curtiss see Hatch, *Glenn Curtiss*; Roseberry, *Glenn Curtiss*.

99. "Glenn H. Curtiss," *Washington Post*, July 25, 1930.

100. "Glenn H. Curtiss," *Time* 4, no. 5 (October 13, 1924): cover page.

101. Pattillo, *Pushing the Envelope*, 11–12.

102. For an interesting, accessible history of the rivalry between Curtiss and the Wright brothers, see Goldstone, *Birdmen*.

103. Steven M. Spencer, "How to Avoid Sudden Death," *Saturday Evening Post*, July 16, 1955.

104. Marvel Mills Logan speaking on H. R. 11980, on February 25, 1933, 72nd Congress, Calendar no. 1414: S.rp.1305.

105. "American Flies Off with Grand Prize," *Los Angeles Times*, August 29, 1909.

106. The Second Gordon Bennett Trophy was awarded in 1910 to the English aviator Claude Grahame-White, who had also completed the first night flight earlier that year.

107. Curtiss and Post, *Curtiss Aviation Book*, 86–87.

108. Background in this paragraph taken from Friedricks, *Henry E. Huntington*, 30–47.

109. In his belongings, Huntington held the Citizens' Alliance Constitution and By-Laws. HEH, box 38/8–2, folder 4.

110. Letter from Southern California Edison Company to stockholders, September 26, 1921, HEH, box 38/8–2, folder 4.

111. *Etiquette of Yacht Colors* (Roseland NJ: Annin, 1902), HEH, box 38/8–2, folder 7.

112. "What Is the Sunset Club?: By Its Presidents, Past and Present," *Sunset Club of Los Angeles, 1895–1905, Volume I* (Los Angeles: Sunset Club, 1905), 5, SCA, box 001, item 002.

113. "What Is the Sunset Club?," 6.

114. "Oriental Night" announcement, December 30, 1910, SCA, box 001, item 004.

115. Rotundo, *American Manhood*, 222–46.

116. "To the Memory of Henry Edwards Huntington," *Annals of the Sunset Club: Volume III* (Los Angeles: Sunset Club, 1927), 132, SCA, box 001, item 004.

117. Collis Potter Huntington to Henry Edwards Huntington, November 4, 1897, HEH, box 11/4/1/, folder: Los Angeles and Pasadena Electric Railways, 1897–1902.

118. See Friedricks, *Henry E. Huntington*, 48–67, for the trolley network's development; see pages 87–92 for a discussion of land development; see page 99 for details on Huntington's deal to sell his Pacific Electric shares.

119. "Los Angeles Offers $150,000 for Meet," *Aeronautics* 5, no. 6 (December 1909): 215.

120. 1910 aviation meet ticket, LAAM, box 1, folder 6.

121. "Aviation Week," LACOC, carton 005, series 1, box 5, July 1909–July 1910, 81.

122. "Aviation Week Means Millions," *Los Angeles Times*, December 15, 1909.

123. F. J. Zeehandelaar, "Citizens of Los Angeles Asked to Do Their Duty," *Los Angeles Times*, January 7, 1910.

124. Berliner, "Big Race of 1910," 2.

125. "Fortunes for Big Aviators," *Los Angeles Times*, December 19, 1909.

126. Berliner, "Big Race of 1910," 1.

127. "1910 Los Angeles International Aviation Meet Research Collection, 1909–1999: History," Online Archive of California, accessed April 20, 2017, http://www.oac.cdlib.org/findaid/ark:/13030/kt4m3nc8jw/admin/#bioghist-1.2.3.

128. "We Have the Playground; Get the Plays," *Los Angeles Times*, January 16, 1910.

129. "Young Aviators Fly Ships of Their Own Clever Mark," *Los Angeles Times*, February 20, 1910.

130. "Teach Youth to Fly: Novelty for Public Schools," *Los Angeles Municipal News*, May 22, 1912, Los Angeles City Archives, Los Angeles CA.

131. For a brief discussion of the gender dynamics of aviation before World War II, see Meyer, *Weekend Pilots*, 7–10.

132. Bilstein, "Airplane and the American Experience, " 22.

133. Corn, *Winged Gospel*, 9.

134. Postcards referenced in this paragraph taken from LAAM, box 9.

135. Hamilton Wright, "With the Bird-Men at Los Angeles," *World Today*, March 1910, page 270, LAAM, box 2, folder 18.

136. Charlton Lawrence Edholm, "The Noble Sport Of Aviation," *OutWest*, 33, no. 1 (January 1910): 11, LAAM, folder 15.

137. Edholm, "Noble Sport of Aviation," 7.

138. Michael Sherry in particular downplays measured early twentieth-century ideas about military uses of the airplane. See Sherry, *Rise of American Air Power*, 1–21.

139. "We Fly," *Los Angeles Times*, January 13, 19130.

140. "Curtiss Proves Efficacy of Aeroplane in Warfare," *Los Angeles Times*, July 13, 1910.

141. "Permanent Station Is Assured Los Angeles," *Los Angeles Times*, December 15, 1910.

142. "Harkness Flies Over the Line," *Los Angeles Times*, February 8, 1911.

143. "To Harbor and Over Fortifications Site Paulhan Makes an Astonishing Flight," *Los Angeles Times*, January 15, 1910.

144. "To Harbor and Over Fortifications."
145. "To Harbor and Over Fortifications."
146. "Serious Problem of Defending Los Angeles May Be Solved."
147. "Fortifications for Defense," *Los Angeles Times*, December 9, 1910.
148. 1910 Los Angeles International Air Meet poster, LAAM, box 6.
149. Dayton, Ohio, aviation meet poster, June 17–18, 1909, LAAM, box 6.
150. Grande semaine d'aviation poster, June 19–26, 1910, LAAM, box 6.
151. "Teach Youth to Fly."
152. "Teach Youth to Fly."
153. "Aviation Mysteries Bared to Japanese," *Los Angeles Times*, November 8, 1909.
154. Curtiss and Post, *Curtiss Aviation Book*, 149.
155. "Teach Youth to Fly."

2. BORDERLANDS FORTRESS

1. For a recent treatment of the Yellow Peril narrative in American culture at the turn of the twentieth century, and the limits to the narrative when nativists tried to apply it to Chinese students, see Hsu, *Good Immigrants*, 23–54.
2. After the Plan of San Diego was discovered, Mexican raids into the United States were stopped only after violent intervention into Mexico by the Texas Rangers. See Johnson, *Revolution in Texas*; Sandos, *Rebellion in the Borderlands*; Harris and Sadler, "The Plan of San Diego." The Zimmerman Telegram was intercepted by the British and used as propaganda to enjoin U.S. citizens to support U.S. entry into the war. For a recent reexamination, see Boghardt, *Zimmermann Telegram*.
3. Contemporary actors used this term; it should not be associated with progressivism. Though some national preparedness advocates, such as Theodore Roosevelt, were progressives, Chandler and Hearst generally opposed progressivism. They belonged to the special interest groups—which sought to influence policy through direct influence on politicians—demonized by progressives as agents of political corruption. For the actions that Californian progressives took to remake the political process, see Putnam, "Progressive Legacy in California." For limits on progressivism in Southern California, see Rogin, "Progressivism and the California Electorate." For a lively discussion of the Progressive movement as a whole see McGerr, *Fierce Discontent*.
4. The law was strengthened in 1920 and remained in effect until a California Supreme Court decision in 1952. For a discussion of the effect of the 1913 Alien Land Law see Kurashige, *Shifting Grounds of Race*, 66–69.
5. Scherer, *Japanese Crisis*, 41.
6. For more on the story of Ricardo Magón and his followers, see MacLachlan, *Anarchism and the Mexican Revolution*; Raat, *Revoltosos*.
7. Pearlman, *To Make Democracy Safe for America*, 121. See also Capozzola, *Uncle Sam Wants You*; Finnegan, *Against the Specter of a Dragon*.

8. In fact, as Frederic Jaher has argued, most of the members of the Los Angeles upper class from 1885 onward were recent immigrants. See Jaher, *Urban Establishment*, 577–709.

9. In contrast, middle- and upper-class women in Los Angeles used traditional ideas about their roles as mothers and wives to urge wartime mobilization through voluntarist organizations. See Dumenil, "Women's Reform Organizations."

10. Gottlieb and Wolt, *Thinking Big*, 232.

11. For more on Chandler and Otis's dual efforts, see Joan Didion, "Letter from Los Angeles," *New Yorker*, February 26, 1990.

12. Gottlieb and Wolt, *Thinking Big*, 121–25.

13. Harry Chandler, "Progress—In The Northwest: An Open Letter," *Los Angeles Times*, November 28, 1937.

14. See Harrison Gray Otis to Harry Chandler, September 30, 1905, and March 31, 1911, LAT, box 215, folder 16.

15. Otis to Chandler, September 30, 1905.

16. Otis to Chandler, March 31, 1911.

17. Harry Chandler, "Harry Chandler, 'Oldest Employee,' Has Seen This City Transformed," copy of article from *Los Angeles Times*, December 4, 1931, LAT, box 215, folder 9.

18. Gottlieb and Wolt, *Thinking Big*, 125.

19. The newspaper mogul's secrecy extended even into the archives. He ordered his papers burned after suffering a heart attack in 1944.

20. The land companies were: Big Conduit Land Company, California-Mexico Land and Cattle Company, Imperial Valley Farm Lands Association, Los Angeles Suburban Homes Company, Mission Land Company, Rowland Land Company, and Tejon Ranch Company. The mortgage firm was Bond and Mortgage Insurance Company. The oil company was Columbia Oil Producing Company. The water company was Interurban Water Company. See "From March 1, 1915, form letter: H. D. Walker, publisher of *Manual of Calif. Securities*, and a directory of company directors," LAT, box 215, folder 15.

21. H. J. Whitley, sample letter in reply to a request for information, 1910, LAT, box 215, folder 14.

22. W. D. Davis to Harry Chandler, April 7, 1920, LAT, box 215, folder 6.

23. See "Translation: First Testimonie [*sic*] of the instrument of lease executed by the representative of the Colorado River Land Co., S.A., in favor of Messrs. Tom Quong Ning and Ng. Hawk Nun," April 22, 1919, LAT, box 215, folder 6.

24. O. F. Brant to Harry Chandler, November 23, 1920, LAT, box 215, folder 6.

25. Nasaw, *The Chief*, 41–60; 95–99; 255–59.

26. He had developed this jingoistic rhetoric in the pages of his first newspaper, the *San Francisco Examiner*. Nasaw, *The Chief*, 73–81.

27. Hamilton Basso, "From the Stacks: 'Mr. Hearst's Apostolic Creed,'" *New Republic*, May 8, 1935, republished August 14, 2013, https://newrepublic.com/article/114292

/william-randolph-hearsts-dangerous-patriotism-stacks. Part of the circulation battle between Hearst and Pulitzer famously revolved around "yellow journalism" and their dual advocacy for U.S. intervention into Cuba, the conflict that became the Spanish-American War.

28. "Hearst Castle: Facts and Stats," Hearst Castle, accessed April 18, 2017, http://hearstcastle .org/history-behind-hearst-castle/facts-and-stats/.

29. "Sale of Spanish Art From Ruiz Collection Brings $189, 326," *New York Herald Tribune*, May 11, 1924.

30. Duncan Aikman, "A Renaissance Palace in Our West," *New York Times*, July 21, 1929.

31. Andrew Leckey, "Castles That Even the Rich Can't Afford," *Chicago Tribune*, May 4, 1989, http://articles.chicagotribune.com/1989-05-04/business/8904090761_1_hearst -castle-buildings-san-simeon.

32. For a fuller description of Hearst's land holdings in Mexico see Nasaw, *The Chief*, 248. For a more detailed description of Harry Chandler's land holdings in Mexico, see McDougal, *Privileged Son*, 74. For an analysis of Chandler's action to incite a revolt to protect his property in Mexico see Blaisdell, "Harry Chandler and Mexican Border Intrigue."

33. McDougal, *Privileged Son*, 81.

34. Frank J. Taylor, "It Costs $1000 to Have Lunch with Harry Chandler," *Saturday Evening Post*, December 16, 1939.

35. "Midas of California," *Newsweek*, October 2, 1944, 80–81.

36. For instance, "In July and then again in October of 1912, the Hearst ranch was placed under siege by Mexican peasant revolutionists and only rescued, at the last minute, by the Mexican army." Nasaw, *The Chief*, 229. Chandler's estate in Baja California was threatened throughout this period, beginning in 1911 when the anarchist PLM, the Mexican Liberal Party, took over the area. Baja California would continue to be a contested region throughout the Mexican Revolution.

37. "Constitution of Mexico," Organization of American States, accessed March 30, 2014, http://www.oas.org/juridico/mla/en/mex/en_mex-int-text-const.pdf. The historian Alan Knight has emphasized the fundamental radicalism of the many Revolutionary groups: "The metamorphosis of despised plebeians into capable *politicos* . . . implied a democratization of the Mexican polity . . . The trend of Porfirio politics towards narrow, self-perpetuating oligarchies was decisively reversed." Knight, *Mexican Revolution*, 2:217.

38. Gottlieb and Wolt, *Thinking Big*, 296.

39. Azuma, "Japanese Immigrant Settler Colonialism."

40. K. K. Kawakami, "Will Japan Fight?," *Los Angeles Times*, November 8, 1916.

41. The Grand Army of the Republic was an organization of veterans of the U.S. Civil War. It functioned as an advocacy group for veterans' causes.

42. The reader should also remember that Japan was in the process of asserting more direct control over China. "SEES JAPAN AS REAL MENACE: Grand Army's Chaplain Says

America Must Prepare; Canal, Railway Termini and Fuel Bases Weak Spots; Thinks Coast's Fate Hangs on Control of Pacific," *Los Angeles Times*, December 19, 1915.

43. "Jap. Invasion Is Predicted," *Los Angeles Times*, January 30, 1916.

44. Harry Carr, "Mighty Agitation Is Needed to Get Protection for Southern California," *Los Angeles Times*, September 10, 1916.

45. "OUR DUTY IN MEXICO," *Los Angeles Times*, June 30, 1916.

46. "An American Protectorate," *Los Angeles Times*, June 27, 1916.

47. "COLUMN FORWARD!" *Los Angeles Times*, April 17, 1917.

48. "Exposes Carranza's Plot to Seize Border States," *Los Angeles Times*, December 9, 1919.

49. "When the Time Comes Be Ready All of You with Shields on Your Arms and Swords in Your Hands to Face the Foe and Win the Victory," *Los Angeles Examiner*, March 2, 1917.

50. "When the Time Comes Be Ready."

51. Shah, "Race-ing Sex." See also Marchetti, *Romance and the "Yellow Peril."*

52. "Mrs. Vernon Castle as 'Patria,'" *Los Angeles Examiner*, January 14, 1917.

53. There is very little information about the film, and there may be no existing copies of the complete film, but *Patria* does have a brief entry in the International Movie Database, online at http://www.imdb.com/title/tt0008411/ (accessed January 20, 2015).

54. Woodrow Wilson letter to Jacques A. Berst, June 4, 1917. In Link et al., eds., *Papers of Woodrow Wilson*, 42:447.

55. "Mrs. Vernon Castle as 'Patria,'" *Los Angeles Examiner*, April 22, 1917.

56. "Japanese Spies Busy near Our Important Forts and Harbors," *Los Angeles Examiner*, February 11, 1917.

57. "Japanese Spies Busy."

58. McDougal, *Privileged Son*, 94.

59. "COLUMN FORWARD!," *Los Angeles Times*, December 13, 1913.

60. "How L.A. Is Being Defended at Fort MacArthur," *Los Angeles Examiner*, April 14, 1917.

61. "$12,000,000 Harbor Plan in Council Hearing on Huge Project This Week," *Los Angeles Examiner*, April 15, 1917.

62. The plan would eventually pass, and shipping through the Port of Los Angeles would grow throughout the twentieth century.

63. "IMPREGNABLE BY LAND AND SEA," *Los Angeles Times*, October 25, 1915.

64. Carr, "Mighty Agitation Is Needed."

65. "Is Los Angeles in Real Danger of a German-Mexican Attack by Land? No; From Japan? No; From Spies within? Yes," *Los Angeles Times*, April 8, 1917.

66. "PREPAREDNESS," *Los Angeles Times*, November 23, 1915.

67. When Woodrow Wilson decided to withdraw support from Pancho Villa and recognize Venustiano Carranza, Villa's ally-turned-enemy, Villa attacked Columbus. In response, Wilson sent a "punitive force," with the tentative acquiescence of Carranza, into Mexico to capture Villa. The Punitive Expedition, which lasted from February 1916 to

March 1917, ended in failure after the U.S. military failed to capture Villa and Carranza threatened to declare war against the United States if the expedition continued.

68. "Failure of Militia in Mexico Crisis Shows Need of Universal Military Training," *Los Angeles Examiner*, January 12, 1917.

69. "The Feminine Heart Loves a Uniform," *Los Angeles Examiner*, September 25, 1917.

70. For a description of camp life, see Pearlman, *To Make Democracy Safe for America*, 58–81.

71. Pearlman, *To Make Democracy Safe for America*, 58–60; 148.

72. "Failure of Militia in Mexico Crisis."

73. Testi, "Gender of Reform Politics," 1522.

74. For an examination of contemporary frontier values see, for instance, Richard Slotkin's examination of Frederick Jackson Turner and Theodore Roosevelt's frontier myths in the late nineteenth century. Slotkin, *Gunfighter Nation*, 29–62. For an examination of the difficulties elite men sometimes had in sustaining their masculine traditions, such as dueling, on the antebellum frontier, see Dearinger, "Violence, Masculinity, Image," 26–55.

75. Slotkin, *Gunfighter Nation*, 51.

76. "COME ON!," *Los Angeles Times*, March 3, 1914. The International Workers of the World (IWW) are a radical labor group that enjoyed prominence in the United States in the 1910s. Coxey's Army was a group of unemployed people who marched on Washington in 1893 and again in 1914. Both marches were populist protests against economic depression and inequality.

77. Hernández, "Hobos in Heaven."

78. "PREPARE!," *Los Angeles Times*, June 14, 1916.

79. "When the Time Comes Be Ready."

80. "America Is Effeminate," *Los Angeles Times*, April 23, 1917.

81. "Wilsonian Stupidity," *Los Angeles Times*, August 7, 1913.

82. "Shirt-Sleeve Diplomacy," *Los Angeles Times*, June 29, 1917.

83. "Will Mr. Wilson Change His Mind about Mexico? The 'Examiner' Hope So," *Los Angeles Examiner*, December 29, 1916.

84. von Hintze, *Murder and Counterrevolution*, 60.

85. von Hintze, *Murder and Counterrevolution*, 60.

86. For a fuller narrative of Wilson's actions see Blasier, "United States and Madero," 207–37.

87. Cooper, *Woodrow Wilson*, 239–40.

88. Cooper, *Woodrow Wilson*, 240.

89. Turner, "Anti-Americanism in Mexico," 512. Turner traces a long history of anti-American sentiment in Mexico during the Mexican Revolution; he especially cites Mexican antipathy toward Hearst.

90. Lind to Washington, March 6, 1914, MMP, frame 00193, roll 4.

91. Lind to Wilson, January 10, 1914, MMP, frame 00454, roll 3.

92. Lind to Washington, December 5, 1913, MMP, frame 00070, roll 3.

93. For a concise summary of Wilson's various policies toward leaders such as Villa and Carranza, see Katz, *Secret War in Mexico*, 298–314.

94. Woodrow Wilson, "Address to a Joint Session of Congress on Mexican Affairs," August 27, 1913, American Presidency Project, http://www.presidency.ucsb.edu/ws/?pid= 65371.

95. Harris and Sadler, *Archaeologist Was a Spy*, 14.

96. Cooper, *Woodrow Wilson*, 244.

97. von Hintze, *Murder and Counterrevolution*, 93.

98. von Hintze, *Murder and Counterrevolution*, 99.

99. Cooper, *Woodrow Wilson*, 245.

100. Cooper, *Woodrow Wilson*, 321.

101. Harris and Sadler, *Great Call-Up*, 7.

102. In his first annual message, Wilson declared that "we shall not . . . be obliged to alter our policy of watchful waiting. And then, when the end comes, we shall hope to see constitutional order restored in distressed Mexico by the concert and energy of such of her leaders as prefer the liberty of their people to their own ambitions." Woodrow Wilson, "First Annual Message," December 2, 1913, American Presidency Project, http://www.presidency.ucsb.edu/ws/?pid=29554. For a detailed account of border intrigue during the Mexican Revolution see Harris and Sadler, *Secret War in El Paso*.

103. For a revisionist account of the Plan of San Diego, see Harris and Sadler, *Plan de San Diego*.

104. Harris and Sadler, *Archaeologist Was a Spy*, 16.

105. See Harris and Sadler, *Plan de San Diego* for a full development of this term.

106. In effect it further subjugated the Chinese, as it allowed for foreign "spheres of influence" in China.

107. For a fuller discussion of diplomacy between the United States and Japan during this period, see Beers, *Vain Endeavor*. Beers argues that the Lansing-Ishii Agreement was a statement of divergent aims: Japan sought to control China while the United States wanted to continue "spheres of influence."

108. Lansing became secretary of state when Bryan resigned in 1915. Bryan left office after Wilson issued a note in response to the sinking of the Lusitania that Bryan viewed as overly bellicose. Kawamura, *Turbulence in the Pacific*, 16.

109. For a full account of the Japanese Crisis of 1913, see Braisted, *United States Navy in the Pacific*, 123–40.

110. Harris and Sadler, *Archaeologist Was a Spy*, 25. In 1913 the War Department even created plans to defend Pearl Harbor and Honolulu from Japanese attack, but it did so without "ostentatiously violating the wishes of the President." Braisted, *United States Navy in the Pacific*, 135.

111. John Lind, "Report of Investigation," n.d. (1916?), MMP, roll 7, frame 00006–00007. Offutt was a gambling bookmaker.

112. Lind, October 9, 1916, public speech, MMP, roll 7, frame 00396–00397. Lind probably gave the speech to an audience of parishioners. He began by stating that "your pastor has asked me to discuss the subject of 'Peace and War' this evening." Lind, October 9, 1916, MMP, roll 7, frame 00392.

113. "1916 an Epochal Year," *Los Angeles Examiner*, December 27, 1916, "Preparedness and Progress Edition."

114. "The United States Is Mexico's Friend," *Los Angeles Times*, June 23, 1917.

115. "Probable Exodus of Carranza," *Los Angeles Times*, November 28, 1917.

116. "Wake! Los Angeles; Do NOT Let the NAVAL BASE Drift Away," *Los Angeles Examiner*, May 26, 1917.

117. "Our Harbor a Great Link with All the World's Commerce," *Los Angeles Examiner*, November 7, 1917.

118. "Article no. 3: Feeding the People," *Los Angeles Examiner*, September 4, 1918.

119. "Article no. 6: Bringing the World's Shopping Here," *Los Angeles Examiner*, September 19, 1918.

120. "California Preparedness and Progress Edition," *Los Angeles Examiner*, December 27, 1916. The woman and her oil lamp may also be a reference to Matthew 25, the Gospel parable of the ten virgins, five of whom prepared to meet the bridegroom by bringing oil for their lamps, and five who did not and were subsequently denied entry to the wedding banquet.

121. "How a Critical Situation Was Changed into Safety," *Los Angeles Examiner*, June 17, 1917.

122. "America and the Allies Must Have Access to Mexican Oil," *Los Angeles Examiner*, September 10, 1918.

123. "The Hope for Mexico," *Los Angeles Times*, June 3, 1920.

124. "Mexico's New Opportunities," *Los Angeles Times*, December 3, 1920.

125. "Recognition of Mexico," February 9, 1922, LACOC, carton 014 (January 9, 1922–January 10, 1923), 323.

126. "Recognition of Mexico," resolution on March 2, 1922, LACOC, carton 014 (January 9, 1922–January 10, 1923), 442.

127. Kurashige, *Shifting Grounds of Race*, 24. The law was strongly supported in Los Angeles.

128. Flowers, *Japanese Conquest of American Opinion*, vii.

129. Flowers, *Japanese Conquest of American Opinion*, vii.

130. "Largest US Cities by Population—Year 1920," Biggest US Cities, accessed April 18, 2017, https://www.biggestuscities.com/1920.

131. "Lower California's Unusual Charms," *New York Times*, December 17, 1916.

1. "Production," *Los Angeles Times*, January 1, 1920.

2. William Earl Perry, "Los Angeles," *Los Angeles Times*, July 7, 1920.

3. "The City of Wonder," *Los Angeles Times*, July 20, 1919.

4. *Los Angeles Today*, 2.

5. "Largest US Cities by Population—Year 1920 (see ch. 2, n. 130).

6. "City of Los Angeles Annexations-Index."

7. For a map of the growing city, see Fogelson, *Fragmented Metropolis*, 224–25.

8. Gibson and Jung, *Historical Census Statistics on Population Totals*. Notably, the 1920 census had a category for "Japanese," but census takers did not record any people in this category—likely rendering them "other." The 1930 census, the first and only census to include "Mexican" as a racial category, identified 7.8 percent of Los Angeles's population as Mexican.

9. Ross, "How Hollywood Became Hollywood," 262. For the early development of Hollywood, see the same chapter at 255–76; Starr, *Inventing the Dream*, 283–308.

10. Hughes, *Souls for Sale*. See also Eaton, "What Price Hollywood?"; Roger Ebert, "Souls for Sale," July 29, 2009, Roger Ebert.com, http://www.rogerebert.com/reviews/souls -for-sale-1923.

11. Term taken from Jonaki Mekha and Sonari Glinton, "Before Hollywood, the Oil Industry Made LA," *All Things Considered*, April 5, 2016, NPR, http://www.npr.org/2016/04 /05/473107378/before-hollywood-the-oil-industry-made-la.

12. "The Great Southwest," *Los Angeles Times*, January 1, 1921.

13. For opposition to drilling, see Quam-Wickham, "'Cities Sacrificed.'"

14. The 2007 film *There Will Be Blood* is in part based on *Oil!*

15. Sinclair, *Oil!*, 6.

16. See Jaher, *Urban Establishment*, 654–57.

17. Jaher, *Urban Establishment*, 685.

18. "Doheny's Colorful Rise to Oil Fame Outlined," *Los Angeles Times*, September 9, 1935; Davis, *Dark Side of Fortune*, 21–33.

19. Indicating the national scope of Doheny's power, he played a leading role in the 1921 Teapot Dome scandal, when investigators discovered that Doheny and fellow oil tycoon Harry Sinclair had bribed Interior Secretary Albert Fall to secure favorable leases for developing oil fields on federal lands. Davis, *Dark Side of Fortune*, 128.

20. "E. L. Doheny, Oil Man, Dies of Long Illness," *Los Angeles Times*, September 9, 1935.

21. Edward L. Doheny, "The Perpetuity of Our Vast Petroleum Yield," *Los Angeles Times*, January 1, 1925.

22. "E. L. Doheny, Oil Man, Dies of Long Illness."

23. "Edward L. Doheny," *Los Angeles Times*, September 10, 1935.

24. "Looking Ahead," *Los Angeles Times*, December 31, 1920.

25. "Our Greatest Need—A Suggestion."

26. Scott Harrison, "When Rail Reigned; L.A. Had Several Grand Train Depots," *Los Angeles Times*, March 28, 2016, http://www.latimes.com/local/california/la-me-train -stations-retrospective-20160328-story.html.

27. "The Pacific Electric RAILWAY: *Comfort, Speed, Safety*," American Railways, accessed September 1, 2017, http://www.american-rails.com/pacific-electric-railway.html.

28. "The Great Southwest."

29. "Miss Lura Anson Thinks a Buick and Los Angeles Is Hard Combination to Beat," *Los Angeles Times*, July 11, 1920.

30. P. H. Dowling, "Streets a Disgrace," *Los Angeles Times*, November 17, 1922.

31. Jonathan S. Dodge, "Keeping Up Los Angeles County Roads," *Los Angeles Times*, January 6, 19191.

32. Roth, "Concrete Utopia," 73–74.

33. See Bottles, *Los Angeles and the Automobile*, 64–91; "To Solve the Traffic Problem by Eliminating Traffic," *Los Angeles Times*, January 23, 1920. In 1922 city leaders asked Frederick Law Olmsted Jr., the son of famed city planner Frederick Law Olmsted, and two other consultants to prepare a road-building plan that might alleviate traffic and provide for future growth. The Major Traffic Street Plan proposed to build a series of parkways and widen existing streets to accommodate public transportation and impose order on Los Angeles's fragmentation and sprawl. While voters passed the plan in 1924, city leaders only allotted it $5 million in bonds, and many of the consultants' major ideas never came to fruition. Roth, "Concrete Utopia," 129–77.

34. The IWW disseminated the radical ideal of "One Big Union," whereby all workers could unite and take over the means of production.

35. Laslett, *Sunshine Was Never Enough*, 70–72.

36. American business leaders and politicians viewed the IWW promotion of class and racial equality as especially dangerous, and the federal government cracked down on IWW agitation during World War I. For more on the federal anti-IWW policies, see Dubofsky, *We Shall Be All*, 215–54.

37. "To the Citizens of Los Angeles," *Los Angeles Times*, June 12, 1919; "Harbor Strike a Failure," *Los Angeles Times*, July 15, 1919; "Day of Union Boss Is Gone," *Los Angeles Times*, November 11, 1919.

38. "To the Citizens of Los Angeles."

39. See Laslett, *Sunshine Was Never Enough*, 70–72. For an insightful history of 1920s activism in the Los Angeles business community see Davis, "Sunshine and the Open Shop."

40. "The Tenth Industrial City; Why?," *Los Angeles Times*, August 25, 1920.

41. "Obstructing Industries," *Los Angeles Times*, June 9, 1919.

3. "VIRTUALLY ON THE EDGE OF A DESERT"

1. For more on development and boosterism as catalysts for the rise of 1920s Los Angeles, see Starr, *Material Dreams*, 65–119.

2. For more on demographic changes in 1920s Los Angeles, see Fogelson, *Fragmented Metropolis*, 75–84.

3. "Historical Resident Population: City and County of Los Angeles, 1850–2010," *Los Angeles Almanac*, accessed February 20, 2017, http://www.laalmanac.com/population/po02.htm.

4. Tygiel, "Introduction, Metropolis in the Making," 2.

5. "Harbor Goal Realized: Sea-Borne Commerce for 1929 at Los Angeles Port Attains Grand Total of $1,070,683,931," *Los Angeles Times*, January 1, 1930; Edgar Lloyd Hampton, "The Great Migration: And Where It Will Lead," *Los Angeles Times*, January 2, 1930; "Unprecedented Growth in All Branches of Southern California Economic Activity," *Los Angeles Times*, January 2, 1930; "Vegetables," *Los Angeles Times*, January 2, 1930.

6. Hampton, "The Great Migration."

7. Gottlieb and Wolt, *Thinking Big*, 131–43.

8. Kahrl, *Water and Power*, 367. The power structure of water services changed a good deal in Los Angeles in the early twentieth century. In 1903 the city created a five-person board of water commissioners to oversee the water department. This was followed, in 1911, by the creation of the Department of Public Service, consisting of the Bureau of Water Works and Supply (Mulholland's department, the water department renamed) and the Bureau of Power and Light. In 1937 the Bureau of Water Works and Supply and the Bureau of Power and Light merged to become the Los Angeles Department of Water and Power. To avoid confusion, I have termed Mulholland's department the Los Angeles Department of Water and Power (DWP) throughout this chapter. For more information, see "Water in Early Los Angeles," from Water and Power Associates, accessed March 14, 2017, http://waterandpower.org/museum/Water_in_Early_Los_Angeles.html. For more on DWP as an institutional force, see Starr, *Material Dreams*, 155–63.

9. William Mulholland, "The Proposed Aqueduct from the Colorado River," draft of speech given before the California Section Meeting, 1926, 2, LADWP, Los Angeles City Archives, box C-1501.

10. Mulholland, "Proposed Aqueduct from the Colorado River."

11. For a recent, critical appraisal of the St. Francis Dam disaster, see Hundley Jr. and Jackson, *Heavy Ground*.

12. For an alternative view—that economic elites expressed limited influence over city politics in 1920s Los Angeles—see Sitton, "Did the Ruling Class Rule at City Hall."

13. Historians have debated Mulholland's culpability for two events discussed later in this chapter: the Owens Valley Water Wars and the St. Francis Dam disaster. For a positive account of Mulholland's work, see Catherine Mulholland, *William Mulholland and the Rise of Los Angeles*; for more critical appraisals of Mulholland's, and other city leaders', actions in the Owens Valley see Hoffman, *Vision or Villainy*; Kahrl, *Water and Power*; Nadeau, *Water Seekers*; for a more general history of water in Los Angeles,

which includes important analysis of and primary sources relating to the Owens Valley and the Boulder Dam project, see Deverell and Sitton, *Water and Los Angeles*; for two more popular-oriented books that touch on Mulholland's contributions to Los Angeles water and power development see Reisner, *Cadillac Desert*, 52–103, 120–44 and Standiford, *Water to the Angels*.

14. For the argument behind the Cross analysis see Felicity Barringer, "The Water Fight That Inspired 'Chinatown,'" *New York Times*, April 25, 2012, https://green.blogs.nytimes .com/2012/04/25/the-water-fight-that-inspired-chinatown/; for the argument behind the Mulwray and Mulvihill analyses, see Brook, *Land of Smoke and Mirrors*, 129–46.

15. Resolution of the Los Angeles Water and Power Employees' Association, July 22, 1935, CMC, series II, box 43, folder 12.

16. Background taken from Mulholland, *William Mulholland and the Rise of Los Angeles*, 3–29.

17. "William Mulholland: Father of the Los Angeles Municipal Water System" (Los Angeles: City of Los Angeles Department of Water and Power Publicity Division, 1939), LADWP, box C-1502, Bound Volume: Pamphlets, Booklets, Leaflets, etc. Issued by Publicity Division from May 1933 to January 1940.

18. Richard Prosser, "The Maker of Los Angeles," *Western Pipe and Steel News*, 2, no. 1 (January 1925): 11, LADWP, box C-1501.

19. See Mulholland, *William Mulholland and the Rise of Los Angeles*, 5.

20. For a well-researched brief post on Mulholland's homes, see "William Mulholland, Longtime Boyle Heights Resident," Boyle Heights History Blog, accessed April 20, 2017, http://boyleheightshistoryblog.blogspot.com/2013/11/william-mulholland -longtime-boyle.html.

21. For a map of the Mulholland family holdings in the San Fernando Valley, see CMC, series II, box 114, folder 3.

22. In 1909 cement finishers made $0.5625 per hour in Los Angeles for a forty-eight-hour work week. Mulholland's hourly rate, when translating his salary, for a forty-eight-hour work week would have been just over $6 per hour. See U.S. Bureau of Labor Statistics, "Union Scale of Wages and Hours of Labor, 1907 to 1912: Bulletin of the United States Bureau of Labor Statistics, no. 131," 75, accessed August 30, 2017, https://fraser .stlouisfed.org/scribd/?item_id=476865&filepath=/files/docs/publications/bls/bls _0131_1913.pdf; Mulholland, *William Mulholland and the Rise of Los Angeles*, 181.

23. William Mulholland, "Bureau of Water Works and Supply: Report of the Chief Engineer," July 1, 1919, Eighteenth Annual Report of the Board of Public Service Commissioners, 8, LADWP, box C-1503.

24. William Mulholland, "A Brief Historical Sketch of the Growth of the Los Angeles City Water Department," *Public Service* 4, no. 6 (June 1920): 1, LADWP, box C-1501, *Public Service*, vol. 1–45 (1917–21).

25. The history of negotiations between the city and water company is complex; see Mulholland, *William Mulholland and the Rise of Los Angeles*, 61–79, for a detailed account.

26. On the more general engineering culture in 1920s Los Angeles, see Roth, "Mulholland Highway."

27. William Mulholland, "The Near Completion of the Los Angeles Aqueduct," *Real Estate News*, May 29, 1912, draft from CMC, series II, box 43, folder 16.

28. For a negative view of Mulholland's aqueduct activism, see Hoffmann, *Vision or Villainy*, 47–173; Kahrl, *Water and Power*, 26–229; Reisner, *Cadillac Desert*, 52–89; for a positive view, see Mulholland, *William Mulholland and the Rise of Los Angeles*, 100–248.

29. "William Mulholland: Father of the Los Angeles Municipal Water System."

30. William Mulholland and J. B. Lippincott, "Third Annual Report of the Bureau of the Los Angeles Aqueduct," November 30, 1908, LADWP, box C-1502.

31. "Official Program: The Los Angeles Aqueduct and Exposition Park Celebration," LADWP, box C-1502.

32. "Resistance to the Aqueduct," Los Angeles Aqueduct Digital Platform, accessed October 26, 2017, http://digital.library.ucla.edu/aqueduct/scholarship/resistance-aqueduct.

33. The development lay on sixteen thousand acres of parched land in the San Fernando Valley the group had purchased in 1904, in a partnership named the San Fernando Mission Land Company. After the aqueduct's construction, Otis and Chandler used excess water from the aqueduct to irrigate the acres they had bought and transformed a near-desert into a viable development site.

34. *Communication to the California Legislature Relating to the Owens Valley Water Situation* (Sacramento: California State Printing Office, 1931), 5, reprint of *Gridiron*, April 21, 1931, LADWP, box C-1508, folder: Printed Matter, California Political Issues, Miscellaneous Campaign Literature, 1919–58.

35. "A Great Public Fraud," *Los Angeles Taxpayer*, August 19, 1924, LADWP, box C-1508, folder: Printed Matter, California Political Issues, Miscellaneous Campaign Literatures, 1919–58.

36. For a summary of the *Times'* activism around the aqueduct, see Gottlieb and Wolt, *Thinking Big*, 131–43.

37. "Stupendous Aqueduct Project Will Make Los Angeles Great," *Los Angeles Times*, June 23, 1907.

38. "The Water Is Coming," *Los Angeles Times*, September 17, 1907.

39. Mulholland to W. J. Washburn, June 5, 1905, 2, CMC, series II, box 44, folder 2.

40. William Mulholland, "'We Must Start Now,'" in May 1925 pamphlet, *Our Water Supply Must Not Fail*, LADWP, box C-1509, folder: Printed Matter, Election Ephemera-Department of Water and Power, Related Issues, 1922–29.

41. William Mulholland, "Report of the Chief Engineer," *Twenty First Annual Report of the Board of Public Service Commissioners, for the Fiscal Year Ending June 30, 1922*" (Los Angeles, 1922), 5, LADWP, box C-1503.

42. Louis C. Hill, J. B. Lippincott et. al, to Los Angeles Board of Public Service, August 14, 1924, 3, CMC, series II, box 44, folder 3.

43. Kahrl, *Water and Power*, 262.

44. Mulholland, *William Mulholland and the Rise of Los Angeles*, 274–75; Libecap, *Owens Valley Revisited*, 54–56.

45. Kahrl, *Water and Power*, 278–80.

46. "Statement of Inyo Country Land Purchases—1923—In Connection with McNally Ditch," John Randolph Haynes papers (Collection 1241), UCLA Library Special Collections, Charles E. Young Research Library, http://digital.library.ucla.edu/aqueduct/archives /statement-inyo-county-land-purchases-1923-connection-mcnally-ditch.

47. Kahrl, *Water and Power*, 284.

48. Kahrl, *Water and Power*, 288–310.

49. "Aqueduct Is Seized; Los Angeles Water Turned into River," *New York Times*, November 17, 1924.

50. "Aqueduct Is Seized."

51. "Owens River Valley Situation," July 1, 1924, LACOC, carton 015 (December 20, 1923–October 16, 1924), 220–21.

52. "Owens Valley Water Situation," December 4, 1924, LACOC, carton 015 (October 18, 1924–August 27, 1925), 46.

53. "Owens Valley Situation," August 24, 1927, LACOC, carton 017 (August 11, 1927–May 31, 1928), 16–17.

54. For a brief summary of the muckraking, see Mulholland, *William Mulholland and the Rise of Los Angeles*, 270–72.

55. Kahrl, *Water and Power*, 320.

56. Andrae B. Nordskog, "Water Bureau Power-Drunk," *Gridiron*, June 3, 1927, Andrae B. Nordskog Collection, Special Collections and Archives, Oviatt Library, California State University, Northridge, http://digital-library.csun.edu/cdm/singleitem/collection /Gridiron/id/2/rec/14.

57. Andrae B. Nordskog, "Civil War Threatened: L.A. Faces Water Famine," *Gridiron*, June 17, 1927, Andrae B. Nordskog Collection, Special Collections and Archives, Oviatt Library, California State University, Northridge, http://digital-library.csun.edu/cdm /singleitem/collection/Gridiron/id/59/rec/15.

58. Andrae B. Nordskog, "Aqueduct Dynamited: Water Board Stubborn," *Gridiron*, June 24, 1927, Andrae B. Nordskog Collection, Special Collections and Archives, Oviatt Library, California State University, Northridge, http://digital-library.csun.edu/cdm /singleitem/collection/Gridiron/id/75/rec/16.

59. Andrae B. Nordskog, "Dynamite Suspect Taken: L.A. Refuses to Abritrate [*sic*]," *Gridiron*, July 1, 1927, Andrae B. Nordskog Collection, Special Collections and Archives, Oviatt Library, California State University, Northridge, http://digital-library.csun .edu/cdm/singleitem/collection/Gridiron/id/69/rec/18.

60. Nordskog, "Dynamite Suspect Taken."

61. Andrae B. Nordskog, "Owens Valley Suffers Loss: L.A. Officials Make Profit," *Gridiron*, July 8, 1927, Andrae B. Nordskog Collection, Special Collections and Archives, Oviatt Library, California State University, Northridge, http://digital-library.csun.edu/cdm /singleitem/collection/Gridiron/id/65/rec/19. Mulholland did own land in the San Fernando Valley and earned a high salary from the city, but, William Kahrl argues, he did not belong to the "world" of social clubs and luxurious accommodations inhabited by other San Fernando land syndicate members such as Chandler and Huntington. See Kahrl, *Water and Power*, 232.

62. Nordskog, "Owens Valley Suffers Loss," 1–2.

63. "Owens Valley and the Los Angeles Aqueduct," January 1925 (Los Angeles: Los Angeles Department of Water and Power Publicity Department), 1, LADWP, box C-1501, folder: Printed Matter, Department of Water and Power Publications: Water Supply-Owens Valley, 1924–25.

64. "Owens Valley and the Los Angeles Aqueduct"

65. For descriptive information on Whitsett, see "W. P. Whitsett Endowment, California State University-Northridge," accessed March 10, 2017, http://www.csun.edu/~jsides /whitsett.htm.

66. W. P. Whitsett, "Straight Ahead for the Owens Valley: An Address by W. P. Whitsett Before the Directors of the Los Angeles Chamber of Commerce, November 6, 1924" (Van Nuys: Issued by the Bank of Van Nuys, 1924), LADWP, box C-1508, folder: Printed Matter, California Political Issues, Miscellaneous Campaign Literature, 1919–58.

67. Whitsett, "Straight Ahead for the Owens Valley."

68. "Owens Valley as Recreation Center," November 6, 1924, LACOC, carton 015 (October 18, 1924–August 27, 1925), 19.

69. "Inyo-Mono: The Open Sesame to Nature's Treasure House" (pamphlet produced by the Bishop Mono Lake Stage Line, Bishop Calif., n.d.), LADWP, box C-1508, folder: Printed Matter, Los Angeles Water Issues, Los Angeles Aqueducts/Owens Valley Controversy, 1912–41.

70. "Our Own Little Grand Canyon," *Intake* 3, no. 6 (June 1926): cover page, LADWP, box C-1504.

71. See Kahrl, *Water and Power*, 306–11.

72. "History of LADWP Land Purchases," LA Aqueduct Centennial 2013, accessed March 10, 2017, http://www.laaqueduct100.com/our-legacy/history-of-ladwp-land-purchases/.

73. On tourism in the Owens Valley, see Vanessa Gregory, "Rugged Country, Rugged History in California's Owens Valley," *New York Times*, May 6, 2010, http://www.nytimes .com/2010/05/07/travel/07owens.html.

74. For more information on the Hoover Dam, see Arrigo, *Imaging Hoover Dam*; Hiltzik, *Colossus*; Moeller, *Phil Swing and Boulder Dam*; Stevens, *Hoover Dam*. For more on the development of American water systems, and the ideas behind them, see Worster,

Rivers of Empire. For more on the capital behind modern developments in the American West, including the Hoover Dam, see Wiley and Gottlieb, *Empires in the Sun.*

75. Background from Hiltzik, *Colossus*, 52–120.

76. For more on this effort, see Starr, *Material Dreams*, 20–44.

77. Eventually, the Boulder Dam would incorporate power facilities and an aqueduct.

78. William Mulholland, "Water from the Colorado," reprint of March 1928 article in *Community Builder*, LADWP, box C-1508.

79. "Hoover Dam: Frequently Asked Questions and Answers," U.S. Bureau of Reclamation, accessed March 14, 2017, https://www.usbr.gov/lc/hooverdam/faqs/powerfaq.html.

80. For a brief summary of early interest in the Boulder Dam Project and Chandler's opposition to it, see Kahrl, *Water and Power*, 263–70.

81. See "'The Times' and Boulder Dam," *Los Angeles Times*, March 11, 1924.

82. "A Staggering Scheme," *Los Angeles Times*, May 22, 1923.

83. "Building of Boulder Dam by Government Assailed," *Los Angeles Times*, October 24, 1916.

84. For more on Haynes and municipal ownership see Sitton, *John Randolph Haynes*, 51–65, 150–80. Also see John R. Haynes, "Letter to City Council, *Twenty Ninth Annual Report of the Board of Public Service Commissioners, for the Fiscal Year Ending June 30, 1930*" (Los Angeles, 1930), 3–4, LADWP, box C-1503.

85. "Are the Power Interests Interested," *Boulder Dam Association Bulletin*, no. 101 (November 7, 1927), LADWP, box C-1508.

86. Hiltzik, *Colossus*, 118.

87. William Mulholland, "Municipal Hydro-Electric Power System" (Los Angeles: City of Los Angeles Department of Water and Power Publicity Division, 1921), LADWP, box C-1501, folder: Printed Matter, Department of Water and Power Publications: Power Supply—General and Hydro, 1921–82.

88. William Mulholland, "Report of the Chief Engineer," *Twenty Fourth Annual Report of the Board of Public Service Commissioners, for the Fiscal Year Ending June 30, 1925*" (Los Angeles, 1925), 7–8, LADWP, box C-1503.

89. William Mulholland, "We Must Start Now," pamphlet issued by Los Angeles Department of Public Service (Los Angeles, 1925), LADWP, box C-1509, folder: Printed Matter, Election Ephemera-Department of Water and Power, Related Issues, 1922–29.

90. "Prepare for the Next Million Population," pamphlet issued by Los Angeles Department of Water and Power (Los Angeles: May 1929), LADWP, box C-1509, folder: Printed Matter, Election Ephemera-Department of Water and Power, Related Issues, 1922–29.

91. "The Builder, the Task, the Inspiration," *Intake* 2, no. 11 (November 1925), LADWP, box C-1504.

92. "Wishing You All a Merry Christmas," *Intake* 2, no. 12 (December 1925), LADWP, box C-1504.

93. "Water," *Intake* 7, no. 5 (May 1930), LADWP, box C-1504.

94. "Los Angeles Chamber of Commerce Urges Congress to Act Promptly in the Matter of Colorado River Control and Utilization," copy of statement made by Richard W. Pridham, October 27, 1925, LADWP, box C-1508.

95. Herbert Corey, "Boulder Dam: A National Opportunity to Turn a Menace into an Asset," reprint of article published in *American Legion Weekly*, May 11, 1923, LADWP, box C-1508, folder: Printed Matter, Boulder Canyon Project (Hoover Dam), 1923–28.

96. Corey, "Boulder Dam."

97. "Boulder Dam Opens New Era: Great American Desert About to be Conquered, Says Secretary Wilbur Signalizing Start of Dam Construction," *Intake* 7, no. 8 (May 1930): 31, LADWP, box C-1504.

98. See, for instance, Heslop, "Making the Desert Blossom."

99. For the historical relationship between masculinity and irrigation, see Margreet Zwarteveen, "Questioning Masculinities in Water," *Economic and Political Weekly* 46, no. 18 (April 30–May 6, 2011): 40–48.

100. For the associations between bureaucracy and masculinity, see Ferguson, *Feminist Case against Bureaucracy*, 3–29.

101. Film summary and all quotes from *The Winning of Barbara Worth*.

102. Berg, *Goldwyn*, 157–58.

103. Berg, *Goldwyn*, 158.

104. "Columbia," *Washington Post*, February 14, 1927.

105. "Winning the West," *Los Angeles Times*, October 10, 1926.

106. "The Last Act," *Los Angeles Times*, October 27, 1926.

107. For this background, see Hundley, Jackson, and Patterson, *Heavy Ground*, 18–19.

108. Hundley, Jackson, and Patterson, *Heavy Ground*, 34–36.

109. For a detailed account of the site selection, design, and construction, see Hundley, Jackson, and Patterson, *Heavy Ground*, 37–98.

110. Hundley, Jackson, and Patterson, *Heavy Ground*, 107.

111. Hundley, Jackson, and Patterson, *Heavy Ground*, 112–200; "St. Francis Dam Inquest Set Here on Wednesday," *Los Angeles Times*, March 18, 1928.

112. "Rebuilders Follow Rescuers in St. Francis Dam Tragedy," *Los Angeles Times*, March 15, 1928.

113. See Mulholland, *William Mulholland and the Rise of Los Angeles*, 319–32.

114. "Report of Committee Appointed by the City Council of Los Angeles to Investigate and Report the Cause of the Failure of the St. Francis Dam," April 11, 1928, LACC, box B-135.

115. "The Disaster Verdict," *Los Angeles Times*, April 13, 1928.

116. "Comment and Opinion," *Bob Shuler's Magazine* 8, no. 8 (October 1929): 187, Los Angeles Public Library, Central Library, Los Angeles CA. For more on Shuler, see Johnson, "'Truth Is the Keenest Weapon.'"

117. "Ready for Hoover Dam Power Rites: Great Lights to Flood City at Hoover Dam Power Fete," *Los Angeles Times*, October 4, 1936.

118. "Millions Give Wild Ovation as Hoover Dam Lights City: First Power Flashed to Los Angeles," *Los Angeles Times*, October 10, 1936.

119. "Millions Give Wild Ovation."

120. Roger M. Andrews, "Los Angeles in the Industrial Mirror," March 27, 1924, speech before the Optimists Club (reprinted by the Los Angeles Chamber of Commerce), LADWP, box C-1511, folder: Printed Matter, Los Angeles Civic Organizations, Los Angeles Chamber of Commerce, 1922–29.

4. THE PERILS OF EXCEPTIONALISM

1. T. A. Sloan, "Letter to The Times: Must Organize for Defense," *Los Angeles Times*, January 30, 1931.

2. For the substantial cultural and economic impact of the Depression on the working class of Chicago and the decline of "welfare capitalism," see Cohen, *Making a New Deal*, 213–50.

3. The evangelist minister Aimee Semple McPherson built and founded the Angelus Temple in Echo Park in 1923.

4. Alma Whitaker, "Temple Helps Deserving Poor," *Los Angeles Times*, May 2, 1932.

5. Report of the Los Angeles Department of Social Services in the "Annual Message of Mayor of the City of Los Angeles for Year Ending December 31, 1932," LACA, box C-2021.

6. Report of the Los Angeles Department of Social Services, in the "Annual Message of Frank L. Shaw, Mayor of the City of Los Angeles, January 2, 1934," LACA, box C-2021.

7. In 1932 the department had spent $447,471.48 on similar efforts. Report of the Los Angeles Department of Social Services in the "Annual Message of Mayor of the City of Los Angeles for Year Ending December 31, 1932."

8. Welburn Mayock, "Statement of Expenditures Made from $6,000 City Fund Appropriations by the Unemployed Cooperative Relief Council of Los Angeles," February 21, 1933; for the number of people helped by the council see Mayock to the City Council, December 18, 1933; for the city's later $10,000 appropriation see the Los Angeles City Council to John C. Porter, February 23, 193; for the city's later $20,000 appropriation see the Los Angeles City Council to Thos. R. Murchison, July 24, 1933. All information from LACC file 6336 (1932).

9. Statistic from Gregory, *American Exodus*, 13.

10. Gregory, *American Exodus*, 41.

11. For more on the impact of the Great Depression on California, see Gregory, *American Exodus*, 3–138; Leader, *Los Angeles and the Great Depression*; Hartley, Sheffrin, and Vasche, "Reform during Crisis"; Starr, *Endangered Dreams*, 61–274; Stein, *California and the Dust Bowl Migration*.

12. Darwin Tate, proposed resolution to Los Angeles City Council, October 25, 1934, LACC file 4557 (1934).

13. See note on Los Angeles City Council Public Welfare Committee to Los Angeles City Council. November 1, 1934, LACC file 4557 (1934).

14. Franklin Delano Roosevelt created the Works Progress Administration in 1935; the WPA would eventually employ 8.5 million people before it was dissolved in 1943. See "WPA Pays Up and Quits," *New York Times*, July 1, 1943.

15. Los Angeles City Council Resolution, December 19, 1935, LACC file 4099 (1935).

16. Howard O. Hunter to Los Angeles City Council. January 16, 1938, LACC file 4099 (1935).

17. Gregory, *American Exodus*, 80.

18. Stein, *California and the Dust Bowl Migration*, 71–108.

19. Statistic from Gregory, *American Exodus*, 42.

20. Hoffman, "Stimulus to Repatriation," 207. Also see Hoffman's longer monograph, *Unwanted Mexican Americans*. Camille Guerin-Gonzales puts Mexican labor in California into a longer trajectory in *Mexican Workers and American Dreams*. See pages 77–94 for discussion of Mexican deportation efforts in California. For a look at the Depression's impact on the Mexican American community in Los Angeles, see Sánchez, *Becoming Mexican American*, 209–26.

21. Hoffman, "Stimulus to Repatriation," 218.

22. George P. Clements, letter to California Congressmen and Senators, December 27, 1927, GPC, box 80. At this time, Congress was considering a bill to place all Western Hemisphere nations under the quotas legislated by the Immigration Act of 1924.

23. Los Angeles Chamber of Commerce letter to G. J. Brunske, December 18, 1936, GPC, box 64, Folder: "Subcommittee Hearing and Minutes."

24. For a look at the Community Development Association and its previous attempt to build the Los Angeles Coliseum, see Riess, "Power without Authority."

25. William May Garland, "A Sincere and Hearty Welcome," Official Program of the 1932 Olympics, July 30, 1932, pg. 13, SOC, box 2, folder 1.

26. *Xth Olympiad Official Report*, published by the Xth Olympiade Committee of the Games of Los Angeles (Los Angeles CA, 1933), 236, available at LA 84 Foundation, accessed April 8, 2022, http://library.la84.org/6oic/OfficialReports/1932/1932spart2.pdf.

27. Lee, *Claiming the Oriental Gateway*, 12. For an enlightening discussion of cosmopolitanism, transnational communities, and the Pacific World in the early twentieth century, see 1–18. The historiography of cosmopolitanism—how historical actors mediated, negotiated and upheld transcultural connections and differences—is vast. See, for instance, Appiah, *Cosmopolitanism*; Hollinger, "Ethnic Diversity, Cosmopolitanism"; Vaughan, "Cosmopolitanism, Ethnicity."

28. For instance, Robert W. Rydell has argued that African exhibits at America's nineteenth- and twentieth-century world's fairs, 1893–1940, "served the purpose of ideological repair . . . at the expense of people of color." Rydell, "'Darkest Africa',," 135. For further discussions on the ways in which world's fairs allowed organizers and participants to

present mediated cosmopolitanism, see Miller, "Incoherencies of Empire"; Nelson, "When Modern Tourism Was Born"; Trennert, "Selling Indian Education."

29. Sinclair won the primary election by almost 150,000 votes, or just over 17 percent. "Our Campaigns: 1934 CA Governor—D Primary," Our Campaigns, accessed April 13, 2017, http://www.ourcampaigns.com/RaceDetail.html?RaceID=103765.

30. "Cast Every Honest Vote!," *Los Angeles Times*, November 4, 1934.

31. For a captivating, and extremely detailed, look at this contest see Mitchell, *Campaign of the Century*. See also Starr, *Endangered Dreams*, 121–55. For a briefer and broader treatment of the Republican Party's relation to Hollywood in the 1930s and the Sinclair campaign see Critchlow, *When Hollywood Was Right*, 7–41.

32. "Heavy Rush of Idles Seen By Sinclair: Transient Flood Expected," *Los Angeles Times*, September 27, 1934.

33. Haight ran as a liberal centrist on the Progressive Party ticket and garnered 302,519 votes, or 12.99 percent.

34. Hailey Giczy's superb article "The Bum Blockade," which won the American Historical Association Raymond J. Cunningham Prize for best undergraduate thesis, provides a good look into the "Bum Blockade" and Los Angeles history. Also Wild, "If You Ain't Got That Do-Re-Mi."

35. The CDA was a private, nonprofit booster society created first to gain and then to organize the 1932 Olympic Games for Los Angeles.

36. "Sinclair Invites Mob Rule in California," *Los Angeles Times*, October 11, 1934.

37. "Biography of Dr. George P. Clements."

38. Frank J. Taylor, "A Heretic in the Promised Land," *Saturday Evening Post*, December 21, 1940.

39. "Dr. G. P. Clements Dies, Long Friend of Farmers," *Los Angeles Times*, August 8, 1958.

40. "Dr. G. P. Clements Dies."

41. "Dr. G. P. Clements Dies."

42. In part, one can see both interests as related to Democratic Party ideology. Franklin Delano Roosevelt, for instance, addressed both conservation and Native American affairs in the New Deal. The Civilian Conservation Corps hired three hundred thousand men to implement environmental public works projects, and the 1934 Indian Reorganization Act (sometimes termed the "Indian New Deal") sought to return some sovereign power to Native American tribes.

43. George P. Clements, "Lo the Poor Indian," *Los Angeles Times*, July 25, 1930.

44. George P. Clements, "Butchering California's Landscape," *Los Angeles Times*, April 12, 1931.

45. Byron B. Blotz, "Letters to the Times—Philosophical," *Los Angeles Times*, September 7, 1958.

46. Taylor, "Heretic in the Promised Land," 62.

47. Taylor, "Heretic in the Promised Land," 27.

48. Taylor, "Heretic in the Promised Land," 62.

49. Taylor, "Heretic in the Promised Land," 64.

50. Taylor, "Heretic in the Promised Land," 27.

51. Clements to A. C. Arnoll, October 8, 1935, GPC, box 64, folder: "Special Subcommittee Hearing and Minutes."

52. Clements to Thomas Barker, August 12, 1937, GPC, box 62, folder 1, part 2.

53. For more on the dynamics of race in Californian farm labor communities, see Cruz, "Racialized Fields"; Garcia, *World of Its Own*; González, *Labor and Community*.

54. C. P. Visel to Crime and Unemployment Committee, Los Angeles Chamber of Commerce, January 7, 1931, GPC, box 62, folder 1, part 1.

55. C. P. Visel to Crime and Unemployment Committee.

56. Rosales, *Chicano*, 50.

57. "Fugitive Aliens Seized in Drive," *Los Angeles Times*, February 15, 1931.

58. Hoffman, *Unwanted Mexican Americans*, 48.

59. J. A .H. Kerr, Statement of the Los Angeles Chamber of Commerce, May 7, 1931, GPC, box 62, folder 1, part 1.

60. Los Angeles Chamber of Commerce to C. P. Visel, January 29, 1931, GPC, box 62, folder 1, part 1.

61. See Hoffman, *Unwanted Mexican Americans*, 79–81, for the denouement of deportation in Los Angeles.

62. For a summation of the county repatriation effort see Hoffmann, *Unwanted Mexican Americans*, 86–90.

63. George P. Clements to A. C. Arnoll, August 17, 1931, GPC, box 62, folder 1, part 1.

64. Clements to Arnoll, August 17, 1931.

65. George P. Clements, title unknown, December 2, 1927, pg. 1, GPC, box 62, folder 1, part 1.

66. For a long trajectory of the rhetoric surrounding Puerto Ricans and American citizenship, see Thomas, *Puerto Rican Citizen*.

67. At this time in the United States, "Porto" was the common spelling.

68. George P. Clements, "Notes for talk before the Annual Conference of 'Friends of the Mexicans' under the auspices of Pomona College, Claremont California," November 13, 1926, GPC, box 64, folder: "Labor 1," 5.

69. The letter uses identical language to an undated speech Clements gave to the Ladies of the Pasadena Women's Civic League. On page 7 of that speech, Clements lauded the contributions of Mexican labor and deplored "Porto-Rican negroes" who "tainted" the nation. See GPC, box 62, folder 1, part 1.

70. Los Angeles Chamber of Commerce to Wm. Butterworth, pg. 3, September 15, 1929, GPC, box 62, folder 1, part 2.

71. George P. Clements, "Mexican Immigration and Its Bearing on California's Agriculture," speech for Lemon Men's Club, p. 6, dated October 2, 1929, GPC, box 62, folder 1, part 2.

72. McGreevey, *Borderline Citizens*, 93–117.

73. "Unemployment Situation," September 17, 1931, LACOC, carton 023 (March 6, 1931–February 4, 1932), 181–82.

74. The chamber demanded that a rock pile be included in any transient labor camp on both October 22, 1931, and November 27, 1931. See "Work Camp and Rock Pile," October 22, 1931, LACOC, carton 023 (March 6, 1931–February 4, 1932), 216; "Border Patrol and Rock Pile," November 27, 1931, LACOC, carton 023 (March 6, 1931–February 4, 1932), 247.

75. Blackburn, Fowler, and Pollock, eds., *Prisons: Today and Tomorrow*, 30. For a history of the rise of chain gangs and their rhetorical import, see Colvin, *Penitentiaries, Reformatories, and Chain Gangs*, 201–25.

76. Prison authorities sometimes use chain gangs and rock piles in conjunction with each other. In 1995 Alabama brought rock piles to some of its prisons to supplement chain gang labor. "Alabama to Make Prisoners Break Rocks," *New York Times*, July 28, 1995.

77. Hernández, "Hobos in Heaven," 444.

78. For a summation of the change to "punishment without labor," and other post–World War I prison reform, see McLennan, *Crisis of Imprisonment*, 417–68.

79. "Bums," *Los Angeles Times*, March 8, 1931.

80. Abelson, "'Women Who Have No Men to Work for Them'."

81. "Border Patrol and Rock Pile," November 27, 1931.

82. "Border Patrol and Rock Pile," November 27, 1931.

83. "Work Camp and Rock Pile," October 22, 1931.

84. "Border Patrol to Keep Out Undesirables," October 28, 1931, LACOC, carton 023 (March 6, 1931–February 4, 1932), 227.

85. "Registration and Work Test Ordinance," February 4, 1932, LACOC, carton 023 (March 6, 1931–February 4, 1932), 314.

86. "Unemployed Transients," October 19, 1933, LACOC, carton 024 (February 9, 1933–March 22, 1934), 197.

87. "Indigent Transients," March 28, 1934, LACOC, carton 025 (March 29, 1934–May 9, 1935), 282–83.

88. Edward C. Krauss, "Light on Transient Problem," *Los Angeles Times*, November 12, 1935.

89. George P. Clements to Jerry Voorhis, August 18, 1937, GPC, box 64.

90. George P. Clements to Harrison S. Robinson, November 20, 1939, GPC, box 80.

91. See "Border Patrol to Keep Out Undesirables."

92. Starr, *Endangered Dreams*, 177.

93. "Davis Tells Need of War on Indigents," *Los Angeles Times*, February 5, 1936.

94. "The Border Patrol," *Los Angeles Times*, March 23, 1936.

95. "Indigent Transient Problem and Border Patrol," March 12, 1936, LACOC, carton 025 (March 16, 1935–June 18, 1936), 225.

96. "Indigent Transient Problem and Border Patrol."

97. "Border Patrol—Attorney General's Opinion as to Legality," March 19, 1936, LACOC, carton 025 (March 16, 1935–June 18, 1936), 232.

98. "Border Patrol against Indigent Transients," October 29, 1936, LACOC, carton 026 (June 25, 1936–August 5, 1937), 89.

99. "Indigent Problem," September 28, 1939, LACOC, carton 027 (July 13, 1939–July 3, 1941), 63.

100. McWilliams, *Factories in the Field*, 65.

101. McWilliams, *Factories in the Field*, 65.

102. George P. Clements, review of *Factories in the Field* (unknown if this piece was published), 16–19, November 29, 1939, GPC, box 64, folder: "Clements' Reaction to *Factories in the Field*, Roy Pike: Review of *Factories in the Field*."

103. The games also seem to have provided opportunities for marginalized groups, especially Japanese Americans and women athletes, to find inspiration. See Yamamoto, "Cheers for Japanese Athletes" and Pieroth, *Their Day in the Sun*.

104. Zimmerman, *Los Angeles: The Olympic City*, 2.

105. Zimmerman, *Los Angeles: The Olympic City*, 3.

106. *Xth Olympiad Official Report*, 108; Zimmerman, *Los Angeles: The Olympic City*, 4.

107. "Japan Triumphs before 100,000: Olympic Games End as Thousands Sing 'Aloha,'" *Los Angeles Times*, August 15, 1932.

108. "Tell of Games, Writers Urged," *Los Angeles Times*, March 13, 1932.

109. Al Stump, *Reaching Olympian Heights—When the Bottom Fell Out* (American Heritage Publishing, 1984), 21, LA84.

110. "EASTERNERS!," *Los Angeles Times*, December 4, 1941.

111. Union Pacific Program and Brochure, SOC, box 6, folder 5.

112. Stump, *Reaching Olympian Heights*, 22.

113. For a fuller description of boosters' work on the Olympics, see White, "Los Angeles Way."

114. "Things Are Looking Up," *Los Angeles Times*, July 21, 1932.

115. *Touring Topics*, July 1932, SOC, box 3, folder 10.

116. "A Village of All Nations," *Los Angeles Times*, fiftieth anniversary edition, December 4, 1931, SOC, box 3, folder 4.

117. For one of the luncheon invites see "Invitation to luncheon and tour at MGM Studios, August 6, 1932," SOC, box 5, folder 3.

118. Zimmerman, *Los Angeles: The Olympic City*, 4.

119. William May Garland, *Story of the Origin of the Xth Olympiad held in Los Angeles, California, in 1932, as Written by William May Garland* (Undated and unpublished manuscript), 2, LA84.

120. *Xth Olympiad Official Report*, 40.

121. Riess, "Power without Authority," 54–56.

122. Garland, *Story of the Origin of the Xth Olympiad*, 24.

123. Biographic information from "Civic Leader W. M. Garland Dies at 82," *Los Angeles Times*, September 27, 1948.

124. "To Open Addition at Beverly Hills," *Los Angeles Herald*, June 29, 1912.

125. "To Open Addition at Beverly Hills."

126. Garland to Pierre de Coubertin, November 14, 1924, LA84, OLY COL GV 721.2.C583 L651 [Letters].

127. "Civic Leader W. M. Garland Dies at 82."

128. Garland to Coubertin, May 4, 1923, LA84, OLY COL GV 721.2.C583 L651 [Letters].

129. William May Garland, "Aloha!," *Los Angeles Times*, August 14, 1932.

130. William May Garland, "Securing the Tenth Olympiad For Los Angeles," *World Affairs Interpreter* (January 1933): 10.

131. The background material on the Village comes from White, "Los Angeles Way."

132. *Xth Olympiad Official Report*, 256–60.

133. White, "Los Angeles Way," 79.

134. Braven Dyer, "Turbaned Tornadoes Hit Olympic Village as Indian Men Arrive," *Los Angeles Times*, July 10, 1932.

135. Braven Dyer, "Olympic Odds and Ends," *Los Angeles Times*, June 28, 1932; Muriel Babcock, "Second Squad of Japanese Arrives," *Los Angeles Times*, July 19, 1932.

136. "Army of German Athletes Here Today," *Los Angeles Times*, July 21, 1932.

137. Terrel DeLapp, "Father: Son on Team," *Los Angeles Times*, July 23, 1932; "Purple Patent Leather Shoes for Australians," *Los Angeles Times*, July 15, 1932.

138. Hazel Moffett, "Welcome, Country Men!," *Los Angeles Times*, July 31, 1932.

139. *Official Report of the Xth Olympiad*, 30.

140. *Official Report of the Xth Olympiad*, 99–100. Olympic tickets do seem relatively reasonably priced. In comparison, USC sold football season tickets that August for $15.40—all games cost below three dollars except for the California and Notre Dame home games, which cost $3.30 and $4.40 respectively. "Trojan Football Seats Will Go On Sale Today," *Los Angeles Times*, August 17, 1932.

141. "Mayor Asks Children Be Let in Free," *Los Angeles Times*, August 11, 1932; *Official Report of the Xth Olympiad*, 100.

142. Pierre de Coubertin, speech at the Opening Session of the 1932 Olympics, 8, SOC, box 6, folder 3.

143. "Souvenir Book—Official Pictorial," 4, SOC, box 4, folder 3.

144. The concept of the "Olympic Movement" as a creator of cosmopolitan sportsmanship had a lengthy history before and after the 1932 Olympics. See Barney, Wenn, and Martyn, *Selling the Five Rings*, 18–40, Congelio, "An Odyssey," and Senn, *Power Politics, and the Olympic Games*, 1–64.

145. Garland to de Coubertin, May 4, 1923.

146. Maynard McFie, "The Story of the Olympic Games," *Los Angeles Times*, December 4, 1931.

147. Robert Gordon Sproul, "The Same Great Pattern," Official Program of the 1932 Olympics, July 30, 1932, 19, SOC, box 2, folder 1.

148. Background information from Arthur, *Radical Innocent*, 3–24.

149. Arthur, *Radical Innocent*, 4.

150. Sinclair, *Brass Check*, 197.

151. Sinclair, *Brass Check*, 202

152. Sinclair, *Brass Check*, 203.

153. Sinclair, *Brass Check*, 213.

154. Sinclair, *Brass Check*, 214.

155. Sinclair, *Lie Factory Starts*.

156. Sinclair, *Brass Check*, 197.

157. Mitchell, *Campaign of the Century*, 207. In 1942 Sinclair and Mary Craig moved to Monrovia, nine miles north of Pasadena, where they settled in a large, neo-Mediterranean home that Sinclair also used as his writing center.

158. Starr, *Endangered Dreams*, 124–25.

159. At one point, Gillette kept Sinclair on retainer in hopes that Sinclair would help him write a monograph on reforming the global economy toward a version of private socialism. Starr, *Endangered Dreams*, 125.

160. For a discussion of American communism, the Depression-era "Popular Front," and its relationship to EPIC, see Denning, *Cultural Front*, 3–50.

161. Upton Sinclair, "Address of Upton Sinclair KNX, Shrine Auditorium," August 27, 1934, USP, Sinclair MSS Series 3, box 36.

162. Sinclair, *I, Governor of California*, 47

163. Sinclair, *I, Governor of California*, 47–58.

164. Sinclair, *I, Governor of California*, 61–62.

165. Background information from Eyman, *Lion of Hollywood*, 17–59.

166. Eyman, *Lion of Hollywood*, 3–6.

167. Louis B. Mayer, "Traits Needed to Rise Told," *Los Angeles Times*, August 24, 1930.

168. Cecil Smith, "Throngs Pay Tribute at Louis B. Mayer Rites," *Los Angeles Times*, November 1, 1957.

169. Edwin Shallert, "Films' Global Influence Laid to Mayer's Vitality," *Los Angeles Times*, October 40, 1957.

170. Ross, *Hollywood Left and Right*, 51.

171. Ross, *Hollywood Left and Right*, 65–69.

172. Critchlow, *When Hollywood Was Right*, 27.

173. Mitchell, *Campaign of the Century*, 304.

174. Critchlow, *When Hollywood Was Right*, 25.

175. Mitchell, *Campaign of the Century*, 359.

176. "Studio Plan Awaits Vote: Warner Brothers to Suspend Building Program for Election Result," *Los Angeles Times*, October 14, 1934.

177. Starr, *Endangered Dreams*, 148.

178. Mitchell, *Campaign of the Century*, 298.

179. Mitchell, *Campaign of the Century*, 484.

180. Hearst published the *Examiner* in the morning and the *Herald-Express* in the afternoon. Information on newspaper activism from Starr, *Endangered Dreams*, 143.

181. "Is This Still America?," *Los Angeles Times*, August 30, 1934.

182. Upton Sinclair, "Address by Upton Sinclair Over KFI," August 2, 1934, USP, Sinclair MSS series 3, box 36.

183. Upton Sinclair, "Upton Sinclair over Radio KNX," August 13, 1934, USP, Sinclair MSS series 3, box 36.

184. For the image, see Oliver Thornton to C. W. Anderson, November 2, 1934, USP, Sinclair MSS series 1, box 29.

185. J. Lee Austin, "When We Elect Sinclair," USP, Sinclair MSS series 1, box 29, Correspondence 1934, October 7–November 8.

186. Untitled Song, USP, Sinclair MSS series II, box 1, Misc f.2 EPIC Songs.

187. Pendergast, "'Horatio Alger Doesn't Work Here Any More'." For other analyses of gender in the Great Depression, see Dickstein, *Dancing in the Dark*, 507–21; Hanson, "Feminine Image."

188. *Plundering the Farmer!* (California League against Sinclairism, 1934), 1, "Upton Sinclair's End Poverty in California Campaign: Campaign pamphlets & periodicals," University of Washington: Upton Sinclair's End Poverty in California Campaign, accessed March 1, 2018, https://depts.washington.edu/epic34/pamphlets.shtml.

189. For a summation of Haight's influence, see Donald L. Singer, "Going Negative: The Smear Campaign Against Upton Sinclair," paper delivered at the Fortnightly Club, October 19, 2000, http://www.redlandsfortnightly.org/papers/singer00.htm.

190. "Bulletin to Working Men of California," undated, 2, USP, Sinclair MSS series II, box 1, misc. f3.

191. "The Gospel of Hate," *Los Angeles Times*, November 1, 1934.

192. "I Rise to Inquire," *EPIC News*, July 9, 1934, 8, USP, EPIC News Set no. 1.

193. Upton Sinclair, "Don't Joke with The Times!" USP, *EPIC News*, October 1, 1934.

194. "A Sweet Prospect," *Los Angeles Times*, September 28, 1934.

195. "The Choice of California," *Los Angeles Times*, November 4, 1934.

196. "Room for All Who Want to Work," USP, *EPIC News*, March 1934.

197. "Marching Along," USP, *EPIC News*, August 6, 1934.

198. "Here's One Way to Cope with Sinclair Migration," *Los Angeles Times*, October 13, 1934.

199. Upton Sinclair, script of *Depression Island*, USP, Sinclair MSS series III, box 30, folder 2, 62–63–65.

200. Los Angeles City Council File #10869, March 27, 1942, LACC, box A-802.

1. "Bowron Re-Elected Mayor: Airport Bonds Voted; School Contest Close," *Los Angeles Times*, May 7, 1941.

2. "Aviation History of the Miracle Mile," accessed September 7, 2017, Miracle Mile Residential Association, https://miraclemilela.com/the-miracle-mile/aviation-history-of-the-miracle-mile/.

3. For a short summary of reaction to his flight, see Berg, *Lindbergh*, 1–10.

4. "Los Angeles Thunders Greeting to Lindbergh," *Los Angeles Times*, September 21, 1927.

5. "Los Angeles Thunders Greeting."

6. Nathan Masters, "From Mines Field to LAX: The Early History of L.A. International Airport," KCET, July 25, 2012. https://www.kcet.org/shows/lost-la/from-mines-field-to-lax-the-early-history-of-la-international-airport.

7. "Drive for Bond Issue Growing: Radio Talks This Week Will Urge 'Yes," *Los Angeles Times*, April 23, 1928; "Airports Held Necessary: Council to Continue Efforts for Aero Facilities; Lease of Field Probably for Present," *Los Angeles Times*, May 3, 1928.

8. "City Takes Over Airport," *Los Angeles Times*, October 2, 1928.

9. "From Mines Field to LAX."

10. "Council 'Purge' Partial Success: Vote Recount Looming in Three Races," *Los Angeles Times*, May 3, 1939.

11. "Historical Census Racial/Ethnic Numbers in Los Angeles County, 1850–1980," *Los Angeles Almanac*, accessed February 22, 2018, http://www.laalmanac.com/population/po20.php; "City of Los Angeles Annexations-Index."

12. "Making One Job of It," *Los Angeles Times*, December 7, 1939.

13. "For a Real Airport," *Los Angeles Times*, December 3, 1939.

14. "A Good Investment," *Los Angeles Times*, December 10, 1939.

15. "Pin-Ball Games and Bus Plan Rejected," *Los Angeles Times*, December 13, 1939.

16. "Early Start on Airport Development Assured by Victory of Bond Proposal," *Los Angeles Times*, May 7, 1941.

17. Graham, "Blueprinting the Regional City," 248–52.

18. "DC-3 Commercial Transport," Boeing, accessed September 9, 2017, http://www.boeing.com/history/products/dc-3.page.

19. "James H. Kindelberger, N. American Board Chairman, Dies at His Home," *Los Angeles Times*, July 28, 1962.

20. "Aviation Giant Donald Douglas Is Dead at 88," *Los Angeles Times*, February 3, 1981.

21. "Aviation Giant Donald Douglas."

22. "Aviation Giant Donald Douglas."

23. Frank J. Taylor, "Master of the Skies," *Los Angeles Times*, June 8, 1941.

24. Cunningham, *Sky Master*, 102.

25. Cunningham, *Sky Master*, 99.

26. Taylor, "Master of the Skies"; Tyler Rogoway, "America's Real WWII Flying Fortress Was the Massive Douglas XB-19," *Jalopnik*, September 11, 2014, http://foxtrotalpha .jalopnik.com/americas-real-wwii-flying-fortress-was-the-massive-doug-1632864365.

27. Taylor, "Master of the Skies."

28. "Aviation Giant Donald Douglas."

29. Wesley Price, "Merchant of Speed," *Saturday Evening Post*, February 19, 1949.

30. Price, "Merchant of Speed."

31. Harold Walsh, "Key Posts in L.A.: J. H. Kindelberger," *Los Angeles Times*, May 17, 1941.

32. "North American B-25B Mitchell," National Museum of the US Air Force, April 14, 2015, http://www.nationalmuseum.af.mil/Visit/Museum-Exhibits/Fact-Sheets/Display /Article/196310/north-american-b-25b-mitchell/.

33. Price, "Merchant of Speed."

34. "(Dutch) Kindelberger Dies," *New York Tribune*, July 28, 1962.

35. "James H. Kindelberger, N. American Board Chairman, Dies at His Home."

36. James Bassett, "Aviation's Powerhouse," *Los Angeles Times*, January 2, 1940.

37. Wesley Smith, "March of Finance," *Los Angeles Times*, November 19, 1941.

38. "Unfilled Airplane Orders Total Nearly $200,000,000," *Los Angeles Times*, February 12, 1940,.

39. "For a Real Airport."

40. Fletcher Bowron to Tom Wolfe, October 19, 1939, FBP, box 1, folder: Extra Copies of Letters: 1930–1940–1941, The Huntington Library, San Marino CA.

41. Fletcher Bowron to J. H. Kindelberger, November 10, 1939, FBP, box 1, folder: Extra Copies of Letters: 1930–1940–1941.

42. Bassett, "Aviation's Powerhouse."

43. See Lotchin, *Fortress California*, 64–130; Nash, *World War II and the West*, 67–90.

44. "Aerial Defense Need Related," *Los Angeles Times*, September 15, 1938.

45. "Vast Program for Defense Being Prepared in Capital," *Los Angeles Times*, October 15, 1938.

46. "Heart of Air Defense Here," *Los Angeles Times*, October 2, 1938.

47. James Bassett, "Wings for America," *Los Angeles Times*, January 22, 1939; "Roosevelt Asks 50,000 Planes," *Stanford Daily Mail*, May 17, 1940, http://stanforddailyarchive .com/cgi-bin/stanford?a=d&d=stanford19400517-01.2.15.

48. "Douglas Gets Huge Contract," *Los Angeles Times*, October 4, 1940.

49. "Ground Broken for New Douglas Plane Plant at Beach," *Los Angeles Times*, November 23, 1940.

50. "Douglas Says Nation's Planes Second to None in World," *Los Angeles Times*, January 25, 1941.

51. Matthew H. Hersch, "Equitable Growth and Southern California's Aerospace Industry," report of the Washington Center for Equitable Growth, November 18, 2015, http://

equitablegrowth.org/report/equitable-growth-and-southern-californias-aerospace
-industry.

52. Taylor, "Master of the Skies."

53. Jaher, *Urban Establishment*, 666.

54. "City Springs to Attention," *Los Angeles Times*, December 8, 1941.

5. "THE CENTER OF JAPANESE INTRIGUE"

1. Verge, *Paradise Transformed*, 97–98.

2. Verge, *Paradise Transformed*, 88; "Largest US Cities by Population—Year 1950," Biggest US Cities, accessed September 23, 2017, https://www.biggestuscities.com/1950.

3. I continue to use Nikkei to refer to the broader group of Japanese Americans throughout this chapter.

4. "Control of Japanese in Southern California," February 19, 1942, LACOC, carton 029 (July 17, 1941–January 14, 1944), 96–97.

5. Hoffman, "Conscience of a Public Official," 246.

6. For more on Roosevelt and internment, see Robinson, *By Order of the President* and Reeves, *Infamy*.

7. See Daniels, *Decision to Relocate the Japanese Americans*, 21–30. For more on the American West and its influence on internment see Grodzins, *Americans Betrayed*; Kurashige, *Shifting Grounds of Race*, 115–16.

8. Robinson, *By Order of the President*, 89–93.

9. Fletcher Bowron, radio broadcast, February 5, 1942, LMRB, 1942, box C-2021.

10. Robinson, *By Order of the President*, 105–8.

11. For clarity, I refer to the work of both organizations as that of the WRA in the rest of this chapter.

12. For information on site selection and federal power see tenBroek et al., *Prejudice, War, and the Constitution*, 99–142.

13. Undated [1943?] petition "now circulating in Highland Park," Japanese American Research Project collection about Japanese in the United States, 1893–1973: WCC, box 53, folder 17.

14. Undated circular from California Citizens Council for the Adoption of a Japanese Exclusion Law, WCC, box 53, folder 17.

15. William Carr to Pasadena Chamber of Commerce, May 23, 1943, WCC, box 53, folder 17.

16. Women's Club of Hermosa Beach to Los Angeles City Council, June 23, 1943, LACC, file #15199.

17. For the *Examiner*'s role, see Hoffman, "Conscience of a Public Official," 262.

18. "Stupid and Dangerous," *Los Angeles Times*, April 22, 1943.

19. "The Japs Are Still Apes," *Los Angeles Times*, October 12, 1943.

20. "Editorials: The Army 'Takes Over' on Coast," *Los Angeles Times*, March 4, 1942.

21. For a summary of the campaign, see Hoffman, "Conscience of a Public Official," 261–62.

22. "Stupid and Dangerous."

23. "We Shan't Pretend to Like It," *Los Angeles Times*, December 19, 1944.

24. Roy Hampton, resolution submitted to the Los Angeles City Council, March 22, 1943, LACC, file #14539.

25. See H. A. Van Norman to the Honorable Board of Water and Power Commissioners, April 21, 1943, LACC, file #14539.

26. Roy Hampton, Resolution submitted to the Los Angeles City Council, May 28, 1943, LACC, file #15011.

27. See LACC, file #15011 for all correspondence related to the resolution.

28. For background on Bowron's role see Hoffman, "Conscience of a Public Official"; Sitton, *Los Angeles Transformed*, 51–80.

29. "Japanese Here Begin Exodus," *Los Angeles Times*, March 22, 1942.

30. "Santa Anita Track to Be Alien Station," *Los Angeles Times*, March 21, 1942.

31. Tom Cameron, "Construction of Huge Alien City Rushed," *Los Angeles Times*, March 20, 1942.

32. Tom Cameron, "Auto Caravan and Train Take 1000 Japs in Voluntary Mass Migration to Manzanar," *Los Angeles Times*, March 24, 1942. For more on the experience of Nikkei at Manzanar, see Ueno et al., *Manzanar Martyr*; Houston and Houston, *Farewell to Manzanar*; Molden, "Seven Miles from Independence; Takaki, *Double Victory*, 137–79.

33. Tom Cameron, "Japs Prepare Desert Home," *Los Angeles Times*, March 25, 1942.

34. "New Life for Evacuees," *Madera Tribune*, March 27, 1942.

35. "Manzanar Camp Will Be Doubled," *Los Angeles Times*, March 26, 1942.

36. "Better Than Hollywood," *Highland Park Post-Dispatch*, April 30, 1942.

37. "Shift of Japs Near End," *Los Angeles Times*, May 24, 1942.

38. "Army Begins Work on Jap Camp Site," *Madera Tribune*, March 9, 1942.

39. "Japanese Americans at Manzanar," National Park Service: Manzanar National Historic Site, accessed September 25, 2017, https://www.nps.gov/manz/learn/historyculture/japanese-americans-at-manzanar.htm.

40. "Manzanar Center for Nisei Closed," *Los Angeles Times*, November 22, 1945.

41. Frank Finch, "Manzanar, War-Born Jap Town Dismantled," *Los Angeles Times*, December 2, 1946.

42. "Japanese Get 'Break' in Owens Valley Move," *Los Angeles Times*, March 30, 1942.

43. Cameron, "Construction of Huge Alien City Rushed."

44. "Coast Japs Are Interned in Mountain Camp," *Life*, April 6, 1942, 15.

45. "Gardening Time at the Manzanar Reception Center," *Highland Park Post-Dispatch*, May 14, 1942.

46. "Weather," *National Park Service: Manzanar National Historic Site*, accessed September 25, 2017, https://www.nps.gov/manz/planyourvisit/weather.htm.

47. "Japanese Americans at Manzanar."

48. Ueno et al., *Manzanar Martyr*, 24.

49. Houston and Houston, *Farewell to Manzanar*, 89.

50. "Manzanar Free Press (Newspaper)," Densho Encyclopedia, accessed September 27, 2017, http://encyclopedia.densho.org/Manzanar_Free_Press_%28newspaper%29/.

51. "'Zoot Suit' Gangsters," *Manzanar Free Press*, October 15, 1942, JIC. In the Zoot Suit Riots of June 1943, white servicemen in Los Angeles attacked those who wore the outfits. The Zoot Suit issue would also disturb Japanese communities in the Midwest, when young people who had migrated to Chicago from California began to don the outfits. See Wu, *Color of Success*, 16–42.

52. "'Zoot Suit' Gangsters."

53. "For a True Shangri La," *Manzanar Free Press*, July 31, 1942.

54. For more on the JACL's attempts to work with the federal government, especially regarding promoting American Nisei soldiers, and the organization's relationship to the Japanese American community more broadly, see Wu, *Color of Success*, 72–110. For a summary of tensions at Manzanar, see Reeves, *Infamy*, 117–23.

55. "Harry Ueno Dies at 97," *New York Times*, December 18, 2004, http://www.nytimes.com/2004/12/18/us/harry-ueno-dies-at-97-exposed-corruption-in-war.html.

56. Morton Grodzins, "The Manzanar Shooting," January 10, 1943, The Japanese American Evacuation and Resettlement: A Digital Archive, http://digitalassets.lib.berkeley.edu/jarda/ucb/text/cubanc6714_b210o10_0004.pdf.

57. Ueno et al., *Manzanar Martyr*, 58–62.

58. "Kindness to Alien Japs Proves Poor Policy," *Los Angeles Times*, December 8, 1942.

59. "Removal of Alien Japs Near Aqueduct Urged," *Los Angeles Times*, December 15, 1942.

60. Background from Dick Main, "Former Mayor Bowron Dies," *Los Angeles Times*, September 12, 1968.

61. Sitton, *Los Angeles Transformed*, 13.

62. Main, "Former Mayor Bowron Dies."

63. See Sitton, "The 'Boss' without a Machine."

64. "John C. Porter," *Bob Shuler's Magazine* 8, no. 4 (June 1929): 77.

65. Cecilia Rasmussen, "A Mayor Who Stood for Reform," *Los Angeles Times*, November 16, 1997, http://articles.latimes.com/1997/nov/16/local/me-54428.

66. Rogers, "Attempted Recall," 416–19. The recall petition also cited municipal corruption and inefficiency.

67. "Porter for Mayor," *Los Angeles Times*, April 23, 1933; "An American for Mayor," *Los Angeles Times*, May 31, 1933.

68. Sitton, *Los Angeles Transformed*, 8–11.

69. Sitton, *Los Angeles Transformed*, 11.

70. "Los Angeles Mayoral Election, 1933," Wikiwand, accessed October 3, 2017, http://www.wikiwand.com/en/Los_Angeles_mayoral_election,_1933.

71. Sitton, *Los Angeles Transformed*, 9–16.

72. Undated letterhead, CEC, box 001, folder 9.

73. "The Mayoralty Race," *Los Angeles Times*, May 2, 1937.

74. "Los Angeles Mayoral Election, 1937," Wikiwand, accessed October 3, 2017, http://www.wikiwand.com/en/Los_Angeles_mayoral_election,_1937.

75. Joseph J. Cummings, radio address, August 27, 1937, CEC, box 001, folder 9.

76. Sitton, *Los Angeles Transformed*, 16.

77. Buntin, *L.A. Noir*, 72–73.

78. "Frank Shaw—First U.S. Mayor Successfully Recalled from Office," *Los Angeles Almanac*, accessed October 2, 2015, http://www.laalmanac.com/history/hi06f.htm.

79. Kynette would later be convicted. Buntin, *L.A. Noir*, 73–75; Sitton, *Los Angeles Transformed*, 16–17.

80. Sitton, *Los Angeles Transformed*, 16–24.

81. Fletcher Bowron, "Government by Mayor Fletcher Bowron," November 10, 1939, FBP, box 1, folder: Extra Copies of Letters, 1939–1940–1941.

82. "Joe Shaw Quits Secretary Post," *Los Angeles Times*, July 24, 1938.

83. Sitton, *Los Angeles Transformed*, 22. I have not found an endorsement of Shaw in the pages of the *Times* from 1938.

84. "1938 L.A. Mayoral Recall Results," accessed October 2, 2017, Los Angeles City Clerk, accessed October 2, 2017, https://www.documentcloud.org/documents/701201-bowron-wins-recalls.html.

85. "City Seats Bowron as New Mayor," *Los Angeles Times*, September 27, 1938.

86. "Bowron, 81, Dies," *Los Angeles Times*, September 15, 1968.

87. Sitton, *Los Angeles Transformed*, 32–35.

88. Bowron to Clarence L. Kincaid, November 6, 1941, FBP, box 1, folder: Extra Copies of Letters, 1939–1940–1941.

89. See Rena M. Vale, "A New Boss Takes Los Angeles," *American Mercury*, March 1941, 299–306, for a contemporary article that critiqued Clinton's power over Bowron and led to a split between the two men.

90. "Terminal Island, California," *Densho Encyclopedia*, accessed October 4, 2017, http://encyclopedia.densho.org/Terminal_Island%2c_California/.

91. "Citizens Gird for Defense," *Los Angeles Times*, December 9, 1941.

92. Daniels, *Decision to Relocate the Japanese Americans*, 24.

93. Hoffman, "Conscience of a Public Official," 252.

94. Fletcher Bowron, radio broadcast, January 29, 1942, LMRB, 1942, box C-2021.

95. "Army Picks Alien Reception Centers," *Los Angeles Times*, March 6, 1942.

96. "Mayor Criticizes F.B.I in War," *Los Angeles Times*, March 7, 1942.

97. Bowron to Drew Pearson, October 23, 1942, FBP, box 1, folder: Extra Copies of Letters, 1942.

98. Hoffman, "Conscience of a Public Official," 246–47.

99. Bowron, radio address, January 13, 1942, 1, LMRB, 1942, box C-2021.

100. Hoffman, "Conscience of a Public Official," 248–54.

101. Fletcher Bowron, radio address, February 5, 1942, 2, LMRB, 1942, box C-2021.

102. Fletcher Bowron, radio address, February 19, 1942, 1; 3–4; 9, LMRB, 1942, box C-2021.

103. Fletcher Bowron, radio address, February 19, 1942, 4.

104. Fletcher Bowron, radio address, February 19, 1942, 5, LMRB 1942, box C-2021.

105. Fletcher Bowron, radio address, August 13, 1942, 4, LMRB, 1942, box C-2021.

106. Fletcher Bowron, radio address, August 13, 1942, 3.

107. Syllabus, United States v. Wong Kim, Ark, 169 U.S. 649 (1898), accessed October 5, 2017, https://www.law.cornell.edu/supremecourt/text/169/649#writing-ussc_cr_0169_0649_zo.

108. U.S. Const. amend XIV. Sec. 1, accessed October 5, 2017, http://constitutionus.com/#rl4.

109. Syllabus, United States v. Wong Kim, Ark.

110. Horace Gray, Majority Opinion, *U.S. v. Wong Kim Ark*.

111. Melville Fuller, Dissenting Opinion, *U.S. v. Wong Kim Ark*.

112. Fuller, Dissenting Opinion, *U.S. v. Wong Kim Ark*.

113. Fletcher Bowron, radio address, May 26, 1942, 9, LMRB, 1942, box C-2021.

114. Fletcher Bowron, radio address, June 2, 1943, 3–4, LMRB, 1943, box C-2021.

115. Bowron, radio address, June 2, 1943, 7–8.

116. "Return of Japanese to Pacific Coast Areas," May 13, 1943, LACOC, carton 029 (July 17, 1941–January 13, 1944), 281–82.

117. For a summary of his postwar sentiments, see Hoffman, "Conscience of a Public Official," 261–69.

118. Sitton, *Los Angeles Transformed*, 81–164

119. Fletcher Bowron to John Modell, July 12, 1967, FBP, box 52, folder: Japanese-Americans.

120. Fletcher Bowron to John Modell, August 16, 1967, 2, FBP, box 52, folder: Japanese-Americans.

121. John Kendall, "Civic Leaders Hear Bowron Eulogizes as 'Man of Conscience,'" *Los Angeles Times*, September 15, 1968.

122. "Fletcher Bowron and His City," *Los Angeles Times*, September 13, 1968.

123. Richard West, "Only a Few Honor Ex-Mayor Bowron at City Hall Rotunda," *Los Angeles Times*, September 14, 1968.

124. See Sitton, *Los Angeles Transformed*, 63–66. Hoffman's "The Conscience of a Public Official" is more balanced.

125. Fletcher Bowron, radio address, December 7, 1944, 3–5, LMRB, 1944, box C-2021.

126. Ted Vollmer, "Former Supervisor John Anson Ford Dies," *Los Angeles Times*, November 4, 1983.

127. The boundaries have changed slightly over time, but for a modern map, see "3rd Supervisorial District Map Los Angeles County," *Los Angeles Almanac*, accessed October 18, 2017, http://www.laalmanac.com/government/gl01d3map.php.

128. Vollmer, "Former Supervisor John Anson Ford Dies."

129. Voorhis would later suffer the effects of red-baiting in a bitter 1946 loss to Richard Nixon, in which Nixon dislodged the incumbent by alleging extensive ties between Voorhis and the Communist Party. Jerry Voorhis to John Anson Ford, May 13, 1947, JAF, box 2, folder A V (2), The Huntington Library, San Marino CA.

130. "John Anson Ford's Legacy," *Los Angeles Times*, November 6, 1983.

131. John Anson Ford, "Straight from the Shoulder," undated (1940), newspaper unknown, JAF, box 2, folder AVI 1 (1).

132. John Anson Ford, "Straight from the Shoulder," October 24, 1940, newspaper unknown, JAF, box 2, folder AVI 1 (1).

133. John Anson Ford, "Straight from the Shoulder," March 9, 1942, newspaper unknown, JAF, box 2, folder AVI 1 (2).

134. John Anson Ford, "Straight from the Shoulder," November 4, 1940, newspaper unknown, JAF, box 2, folder AVI 1 (1).

135. 1944 Membership Dues and Charitable Donations, JAF, box 3, folder A VIX.

136. "Repeal Chinese Exclusion Now," undated, JAF, box 74, folder AA (8); Theodore H. E. Chen to Ford, October 20, 1942, JAF, box 74, folder AA (7).

137. For the dinner acceptance, see John Anson Ford to T. K. Chang, March 26, 1943, JAF, box 74, folder AA (8).

138. John Anson Ford to Madame Chiang Kai-shek, April 8, 1943, JAF, box 74, folder AA (8).

139. John Anson Ford to Shuji Fujii, August 19, 1938, JAF, box 74, folder BB (1).

140. John Anson Ford to Francis Biddle, May 28, 1942, JAF, box 74, folder BB (8). Ford's efforts had a happy conclusion. Sugahara later worked for the Office of Strategic Service on propaganda in India and made a fortune after the war by building tankers in Japan for American oil companies. Liz Nakahara, "Millionaire's Mission," *Washington Post*, October 8, 1981.

141. John Anson Ford, "Straight from the Shoulder," October 6, 1942, JAF, box 2, folder AVI 1 (3).

142. *John Anson Ford and Los Angeles County Government Oral History Transcript.*

143. John Anson Ford, "Letters to The Times: L.A.'s 'Long History of Intolerance," *Los Angeles Times*, December 4, 1988.

144. Vollmer, "Former Supervisor John Anson Ford Dies."

145. Stephanie Holton to the China Society Board of Directors, February 9, 1947, JAF, box 74, folder AA (12).

146. Helen F. Faries to Stephanie Holton, May 28, 1947, JAF, box 74, folder AA (12).

147. Earl Warren to Ford, April 1, 1957, JAF, box 3, folder A VIII.

148. See all of these letters in JAF, box 3, folder A VIII.

149. "Town Hall Award Presented to John Anson Ford," May 12, 1959, JAF, box 3, folder A VIII.

150. "Town Hall Award Presented to John Anson Ford."

151. "John Anson Ford's Legacy."

152. John Anson Ford, "Wilson and Palomar: The Commencement Address," 1957 Beloit College Commencement, 4–6, JAF, box 2, folder A IV (2).

153. Ford, *Thirty Explosive Years*, 3.

154. Ford, *Thirty Explosive Years*, 16.

155. Ford, *Thirty Explosive Years*, 133.

156. Ford, *Thirty Explosive Years*, 129.

157. Ford, *Thirty Explosive Years*, 132.

158. The full quote, from Sitton: "Dissenters such as County Supervisor John Anson Ford accepted internment to protect the internees from the rest of California Society." *Los Angeles Transformed*, 65.

159. John Anson Ford to Cordell Hull, July 9, 1940, JAF, box 74, folder BB (6).

160. John Anson Ford, Los Angeles County Board of Supervisors' Resolution, December 9, 1941, JAF, box 74, folder BB (8).

161. John Anson Ford to Colonel Wayne Allen, January 29, 1942, JAF, box 74, folder BB (8).

162. Los Angeles County Board of Supervisors Resolution, January 29, 1942, JAF, box 74, folder BB (8).

163. Handwritten note from Wayne Allen to John Anson Ford, bottom of copied, printed letter from Allen to the California Congressional delegation, January 29, 1942, JAF, box 74, folder BB (8).

164. John Anson Ford to Francis Biddle, May 4, 1942, JAF, box 74, folder BB (8).

165. Ford to Biddle, May 28, 1942.

166. John Anson Ford to William R. Burke, January 19, 1948, JAF, box 74, folder BB (14).

167. See, for instance, Molina, *Fit to Be Citizens?*, 46–74.

168. Molina, *Fit to Be Citizens?*, 55–60.

169. John Anson Ford's copy of the "Handbook of Information Prepared for Defense Committee of Southern California," July 11, 1940, JAF, box 76, folder AA.

170. "Handbook of Information Prepared for Defense Committee."

171. John J. Pershing, "Preparedness," in "Handbook of Information Prepared for Defense Committee."

172. Waldo Drake, "Strong and Weak Points of U.S. Defense Detailed," 5–6, JAF, box 76, folder AA.

173. Kyle Palmer, "It Can Happen Here Right Now," *Los Angeles Times*, February 14, 1945, JAF, box 74, folder BB (9).

174. "Scream-Master," print advertisement, JAF, box 76, folder AA.

175. John Anson Ford, Los Angeles Board of Supervisors' Resolution, January 15, 1945, JAF, box 74, folder BB (10).

176. Ford to Burke, January 19, 1948.

177. John Anson Ford to Senate Subcommittee on Immigration and Naturalization, September 30, 1948, JAF, box 74, folder BB (14).

178. John Anson Ford to Harry S. Truman, October 17, 1949, JAF, box 74, folder BB (15).

179. See John Anson Ford to J. Rupert Mason, October 26, 1950, JAF, box 74, folder BB (16).

180. William C. Carr to Earl Warren, December 23, 1943, WCC, box 53, folder 1; Robinson, ed., *Pacific Citizens*, 241.

181. Carr to Warren, December 23, 1943.

182. William C. Carr to Fletcher Bowron, December 29, 1944, WCC, box 53, folder 1.

183. William C. Carr to Fletcher Bowron, August 24, 1944, WCC, box 53, folder 1.

184. "William C. Carr Papers, 1941–1962: Abstract," Online Archive of California, accessed October 18, 2017, http://www.oac.cdlib.org/findaid/ark:/13030/tf6g50073j/entire_text/.

185. The Friends of the American Way, undated circular, WCC, box 53, folder 5.

186. "Considerations Favoring the Release of Japanese Americans from Relocation Centers with Complete Freedom to Reestablish Themselves," undated, WCC, box 53, folder 5.

187. William C. Carr to John Anson Ford, August 6, 1945, JAF, box 54, folder BB (11).

188. John Anson Ford to William C. Carr, August 9, 1945, JAF, box 54, folder BB (11).

189. Ford, *Thirty Explosive Years*, 220.

190. "The Issue Is National Honor," *Los Angeles Times*, August 15, 1989.

191. "For Redress at Last," *Los Angeles Times*, October 3, 1989.

192. "Reparations for Japanese Internees," *Los Angeles Times*, October 14, 1989.

193. Berkley Hudson, "Reparations Awaken Painful Recollections," *Los Angeles Times*, August 18, 1988.

194. Alan Citron, "S. California in WWII—Sleeping Giant Awakens," *Los Angeles Times*, September 1, 1989.

CODA

1. For an insightful look at this series of events, see Avila, *Popular Culture*, 145–84.

2. "Newest Stadium Baseball Marvel," *Los Angeles Times*, April 10, 1962.

3. "At Last: The New Ball Park," *Los Angeles Times*, April 9, 1962.

4. Kelly Simpson, "The Great Migration: Creating a New Black Identity in Los Angeles, KCET, February 5, 2012, https://www.kcet.org/history-society/the-great-migration-creating-a-new-black-identity-in-los-angeles.

5. "Watts: A Time for Action," *Los Angeles Times*, October 17, 1965.

6. See Wendy Cheng, "Is Los Angeles a City of Immigrants?," KCET, June 12, 2016, https://www.kcet.org/shows/artbound/demographics-of-los-angeles-immigrantion.

7. "INS Swamped," *Los Angeles Times*, October 19, 1980.

8. Background for this biographical sketch taken from "A Pixyish Mayor: Norris Poulson," *New York Times*, September 21, 1959.

9. The district would change over time through redistricting. In 1951, for instance, the redistricting process made Poulson the representative from California's Twenty-Fourth District, similar to the Thirteenth but with the addition of conservative South Pasadena. T. Anthony Quinn, "Redrawing the Lines: 1951—A Study of the Redistricting

Process in California" (Claremont CA: The Rose Institute of State and Local Government, n.d): 44–47, accessed June 10, 2020, http://ccdl.libraries.claremont.edu/cdm/compoundobject/collection/ric/id/1658.

10. "These Men Recommended for Election as Representatives," *Los Angeles Times*, August 23, 1942.

11. In 1963 the U.S. Supreme Court slightly adjusted state water claims. See "Arizona v. California, 373 U.S. 546 (1963)," accessed June 10, 2020, https://supreme.justia.com/cases/federal/us/373/546/.

12. Norris Poulson, "Deserts in Retreat," *Washington Post*, February 28, 1952.

13. Norris Poulson, "The Water Issue," *Los Angeles Times*, September 1, 1966.

14. For a summary of these events and the proposed public housing development see Hines, "Housing, Baseball, and Creeping Socialism."

15. "Arechigas Pull Down Tent and Leave Chavez," *Los Angeles Times*, May 19, 1959.

16. Hines, "Housing, Baseball, and Creeping Socialism," 137–40.

17. "A New Look at Public Housing," *Los Angeles Times*, August 9, 1951.

18. "Red Sign-Up Ordered by City Council," *Los Angeles Times*, September 14, 1950.

19. "Yes for Poulson, No for Housing," *Los Angeles Times*, April 1, 1953.

20. "Yes for Poulson, No for Housing."

21. "Now the Grapes Are Sour," *Los Angeles Times*, May 5, 1953.

22. "Norris Poulson for Mayor," *Los Angeles Times*, February 20, 1953.

23. "Bowron Attacks The Times in His Bid for Re-election," *Los Angeles Times*, May 6, 1953.

24. Norman Chandler, "This Is Where We Stand," *Los Angeles Times*, May 24, 1953.

25. "Bowron Attack on Times Asked in Reds' Paper," *Los Angeles Times*, May 7, 1953.

26. "The Strange Case of Mayor Bowron," *Los Angeles Times*, May 24, 1953."

27. Norma H. Goodhue, "Poulson Cites Apathy Danger," *Los Angeles Times*, May 15, 1953.

28. "Norris Poulson for Mayor."

29. "Mayor Bowron Takes His Revenge," *Los Angeles Times*, June 25, 1953.

30. "Bowron Turns Over Key to Office," *Los Angeles Times*, July 2, 1953.

31. "Strange Case of Mayor Bowron."

32. "Our Campaigns: Los Angeles Mayor," Our Campaigns, accessed June 11, 2020, https://www.ourcampaigns.com/RaceDetail.html?Raceid=230943.

33. "Vote Victory Statement by Rep. Poulson," *Los Angeles Times*, May 27, 1953.

34. "Now Is the Time for a Good Man," *Los Angeles Times*, May 28, 1953.

35. "Poulson's Career Started on Farm," *Los Angeles Times*, May 27, 1953.

36. "The Mayor Faces the Facts," *Los Angeles Times*, October 8, 1953.

37. "A Pixyish Mayor."

38. "Brooklyn Ball Park Nearly Completed," *New York Times*, February 21, 1913.

39. "Ebbets Field Opening Victory for Superbas," *New York Times*, April 6, 1913.

40. Mitchell, *Baseball Goes West*, 108.

41. Bob Maisel, "Dodger Fans Claim O'Malley Real Culprit," *Sun*, October 9, 1957.

42. For more on O'Malley's early years, see D'Antonio, *Forever Blue*, 5–20.

43. Walter O'Malley to Edwin J. O'Malley, April 28, 1922, WOP.

44. William Stanfield, "Obituaries: Walter O'Malley, 75, Owner of L.A. Dodgers," *Boston Globe*, August 10, 1979.

45. For more on O'Malley's ownership maneuvers, see Podair, *City of Dreams*, 1–23.

46. Roscoe McGowen, "O'Malley Elected to Succeed Rickey as Dodger President," *New York Times*, October 27, 1950.

47. Stanfield, "Obituaries: Walter O'Malley."

48. "1950–1959 Ballpark Attendance," Ballparksofbaseball.com, accessed June 23, 2020, https://www.ballparksofbaseball.com/1950–1959-mlb-attendance/.

49. "1950–1959 Ballpark Attendance." For more on the Braves' move and O'Malley's fears see Avila, *Popular Culture*, 145–52.

50. "O'Malley Tells Reason for Moving," *Los Angeles Times*, October 9, 1957.

51. Fetter, "Revising the Revisionists," 60–64.

52. For more on Moses's actions, see Sullivan, *Dodgers Move West*, 45–57.

53. Fetter, "Revising the Revisionists," 60.

54. The Giants would move to San Francisco in 1957. See Mitchell, *Baseball Goes West*, 115–29.

55. Walter Peterson to Walter O'Malley, August 22, 1955, WOP.

56. Rosalind Wiener Wyman to Walter O'Malley, September 1, 1955, WOP.

57. Henderson, "Los Angeles and the Dodger War, 1957–1962," 264.

58. Norris Poulson to John S. Gibson, Jr., February 25, 1957, WOP.

59. Norris Poulson to Ford, February 25, 1957, WOP.

60. "Poulson Confident Dodgers to Move," *Los Angeles Times*, March 9, 1957.

61. Henderson, "Los Angeles and the Dodger War," 263.

62. Walter O'Malley to James A. Mulvey, January 8, 1957, WOP.

63. Avila, *Popular Culture*, 156.

64. Roscoe McGowen, "Dodgers Buy Los Angeles Club, Stirring Talk of Shift to Coast," *New York Times*, February 22, 1957.

65. For a good summary of the various plans proposed and rejected, see Sullivan, *Dodgers Move West*, 107–36.

66. "O'Malley Due for Routine Visit Today," *Los Angeles Times*, April 30, 1957.

67. "Los Angeles, the Dodgers' Home," *Los Angeles Times*, October 9, 1957.

68. Background from Henderson, "Los Angeles and the Dodger War," 264–86.

69. Paul Zimmerman, "Deal for Dodgers Gets L.A. Council Approval," *Los Angeles Times*, September 17, 1957.

70. John C. Waugh, "Ball Park 'Titanic Struggle' Disclosed: Poulson 'Confesses,'" *Christian Science Monitor*, April 11, 1962.

71. For more on the opposition campaign, see Podair, *City of Dreams*, 51–89.

72. Penelope McMillan, "Walter O'Malley, Owner of Dodgers, Dies at 75," *Los Angeles Times*, August 10, 1979.

73. Henderson, "Los Angeles and the Dodger War," 278.

74. "Mayor Poulson Assails Critics of LA. Land Deal," *Washington Post*, May 17, 1958.

75. For more on the referendum campaign, see Podair, *City of Dreams*, 90–126.

76. For more on Roybal's activism, see Avila, *Popular Culture*, 147–49; Sánchez, "Edward R. Roybal and the Politics of Multiracialism"; Underwood, "Pioneering Minority Representation."

77. "Mayor Poulson Assails Critics of L.A. Land Deal."

78. "24,293-Vote Victory Won for Baseball," *Los Angeles Times*, June 6, 1958.

79. "The City Is Finding Itself," *Los Angeles Times*, June 5, 1958.

80. Henderson, "Los Angeles and the Dodger War," 280. For more on the legal battle, see Podair, *City of Dreams*, 127–51.

81. For more on resistance to the Chavez Ravine evictions, see López, "Community Resistance and Conditional Patriotism." For more on the negative reaction to the evictions, see Parson, *Making a Better World*, 173–80.

82. "Man Who Moved the Dodgers: Walter O'Malley Dies at 75," *Sun*, August 10, 1979.

83. Park, "Here It Is—Ready," *Los Angeles Times*, April 10, 1962.

84. See Estrada, "If You Build It, They Will Move"; Parson, "'This Modern Marvel'."

85. Waugh, "Ball Park 'Titanic Struggle' Disclosed."

86. Jack Smith, "The Rapture of Chavez Ravine," *Los Angeles Times*, June 25, 1962.

87. Carlton Williams, "Battle Shapes Up for Mayor," *Los Angeles Times*, April 6, 1961.

88. "Poulson Should Be Re-Elected," *Los Angeles Times*, March 19, 1961.

89. Carlton Williams, "Poulson to Undergo Health Check to Silence 'Whispering Campaign," *Los Angeles Times*, April 30, 1961.

90. For an analysis of the issues involved, see Mayo, "1961 Mayoralty Election in Los Angeles."

91. "Yorty Hails Election as People's Victory," *Los Angeles Times*, June 1, 1961.

92. For a brief historical background to the area, see Abu-Lughod, *Race, Space, and Riots*, 199–203. For more on World War II and demographic change, see Verge, "Impact of the Second World War on Los Angeles."

93. See Fogelson, *Fragmented Metropolis*, 186–204, for a discussion of this trend in the city as a whole.

94. "Arson, Death Threat Terrorize Watts Family," *Los Angeles Sentinel*, June 10, 1948.

95. "Watts Whites Try to Sell Homes," *Los Angeles Sentinel*, October 7, 1948.

96. Seymour Korman, "Los Angeles Citizens Flock to the Suburbs," *Chicago Daily Tribune*, November 16, 1953.

97. "On Watts Transportation," *Los Angeles Sentinel*, July 17, 1947; "Watts Citizens Demand More Traffic and Street Lights," *Los Angeles Sentinel*, April 22, 1948.

98. Abu-Lughod, *Race, Space, and Riots*, 200–201.

99. For a description of Watts at the time of the rebellion, see Fogelson, "White on Black," in *The Los Angeles Riots*. For efforts to improve the community, see "Letters to the Editor: The Watts Citizens Welfare Committee," *Los Angeles Sentinel*, February 20, 1947; "Our Watts Good Neighbors" series in the *Sentinel* in 1946.
100. Charles Adams, "Rats among the Palm Trees," *Nation*, February 25, 1950, 178.
101. For an earlier response to racist policing in Los Angeles, see Lytle Hernández, *City of Inmates*, 158–92.
102. Fogelson, "White on Black," 136.
103. Felker-Kantor, *Policing Los Angeles*, 19–42.
104. "Pickets Favor, Blast Parker," *Los Angeles Times*, May 3, 1964.
105. "Police Chief Parker States His Views," *Los Angeles Times*, May 17, 1962.
106. "Watts Citizens Seethe over 2nd Police Raid," *Los Angeles Sentinel*, March 27, 1947.
107. Stanley G. Robertson, "L.A. Confidential: The Minority Community and Messrs. Parker and Yorty," *Los Angeles Sentinel*, April 30, 1964.
108. See, for instance, Erwin Baker, "Police Board, Yorty, Council Back Parker," *Los Angeles Times*, May 7, 1964; Robertson, "L.A. Confidential."
109. Felker-Kantor, *Policing Los Angeles*, 19.
110. The exact sequence of events leading to the rebellion are contested. For a summary of the different accounts, see Abu-Lughod, *Race, Space, and Riots*, 204–13.
111. "Parker Raps 'False' Negro Leadership," *Los Angeles Times*, August 15, 1965.
112. Jack Jones, "Yorty Raps Shrived over Poverty Funds," *Los Angeles Times*, August 19, 1965. For statistics on the devastation, see "Violence in the City—An End of a Beginning?," in *Fogelson, Los Angeles Riots*, 1.
113. See Felker-Kantor, *Policing Los Angeles*, 26–34 for a summary of the rebellion.
114. Charles Davis Jr., "Anatomy of a Riot: Minor Incident Ignited Violence," *Los Angeles Times*, August 15, 1965.
115. Art Berman and Mack McCurdy, "New Rioting," *Los Angeles Times*, August 13, 1965.
116. Art Berman, "Eight Men Slain; Guard Moves In," *Los Angeles Times*, August 14, 1965.
117. Charles Hillinger, "Burning Buildings Symbolize Spirit of Hate Underlying Violent Riots," *Los Angeles Times*, August 14, 1965.
118. Peter Barts, "2,000 Troops Enter Los Angeles on Third Day of Negro Rioting," *New York Times*, August 14, 1965.
119. John L. Chapman, "Incredible Los Angeles," *Los Angeles Times*, February 5, 1967.
120. "Mapping L.A.: Watts," *Los Angeles Times*, accessed July 2, 2020, http://maps.latimes.com/neighborhoods/neighborhood/watts/.
121. Marita Hernandez and Austin Scott, "Latino Influx: New Strains Emerge as Watts Evolves," *Los Angeles Times*, August 24, 1980.
122. See Wong, *Lobbying for Inclusion*, 44–63.
123. See Waldinger, "Not the Promised City"; Widener, "Another City Is Possible."
124. See Ngai, *Impossible Subjects*, 227–64.

125. Joseph Alsop, "Immigration Reform May Crown Admirable Record of Congress," *Los Angeles Times*, July 16, 1965. See also "Revising the U.S. Immigration Law," *Los Angeles Times*, January 17, 1965.

126. Wu, *Color of Success*, 149–50.

127. "Historical Census Racial/Ethnic Numbers in Los Angeles County, 1850–1980."

128. See, for instance, "About Those Refugees," *Los Angeles Times*, April 29, 1975.

129. "The Refugees—A Moral Imperative," *Los Angeles Times*, June 22, 1979.

130. "Our Problem Now," *Los Angeles Times*, July 15, 1979.

131. Ernest Conine, "'Please, No More of Your Huddled Masses,'" *Los Angeles Times*, June 9, 1980.

132. "America's Own Boat People," *Los Angeles Times*, July 31, 1979.

133. "The Magic of Numbers," *Los Angeles Times*, April 14, 1981.

134. Avila, *Popular Culture*, 20–64.

135. Marc Reisner, "Looking Back: Water Power," *Los Angeles Times*, November 13, 1988.

136. Reisner, "Looking Back: Water Power."

137. "Our Greatest Need—A Suggestion."

138. Stimson is quoted in Campbell, "In Memory: Marshall Stimson," 85. Campbell does not give the exact date of the quotation, but says it was Stimson's "latest peek into the future," before Stimson's 1952 death.

139. Dana Bartholomew, "LA Re-enacts the Opening of Its Aqueduct, 100 Years Later," *Los Angeles Daily News*, November 5, 2013, https://www.dailynews.com/2013/11/05/la-re-enacts-the-opening-of-its-aqueduct-100-years-later/.

BIBLIOGRAPHY

ARCHIVES/MANUSCRIPT MATERIALS

CEC. Clifford E. Clinton Papers (Collection 2018). UCLA Library Special Collections. Charles E. Young Research Library.

CMC. Catherine Mulholland Collection. Special Collections. California State University, Northridge.

CPH. Collis Potter Huntington Papers. Special Collections Research Center, Syracuse University Libraries.

FBP. Fletcher Bowron Papers. The Huntington Library, San Marino CA.

GPC. George Pigeon Clements Papers (Collection 118). UCLA Library Special Collections. Charles E. Young Research Library.

HEH. Henry Edwards Huntington papers. The Huntington Library, San Marino CA.

JAF. John Anson Ford Papers. The Huntington Library, San Marino CA.

JIC. Japanese Internment collection, Collection no. 0296. Regional History Collection, Special Collections, USC Libraries, University of Southern California.

LA84. LA84 Foundation Archive. Los Angeles.

LAAM. 1910 Los Angeles International Aviation Meet Research Collection. Gerth Archives and Special Collections, California State University, Dominguez Hills.

LACA. Los Angeles City Archives. City Archives and Records Center, Los Angeles.

LACC. Los Angeles City Council Files. City Archives and Records Center, Los Angeles.

LACOC. Los Angeles Area Chamber of Commerce Board of Directors' Minutes. Special Collections. Doheny Memorial Library, University of Southern California.

LADWP. Los Angeles Department of Water and Power papers. City Archives and Records Center, Los Angeles.

LAMRB. Los Angeles Mayor Radio Broadcasts. City Archives and Records Center, Los Angeles.

LAT. *Los Angeles Times* records. The Huntington Library, San Marino CA.

MMP. Mexican Mission Papers, 1913–1931 [microform]. St. Paul: Minnesota Historical Society, 1971.

SCA. Sunset Club Archives. The Huntington Library, San Marino CA.

SOC. 1932 Olympics Collection. Seaver Center for Western History Research, Natural History Museum of Los Angeles County.

USP. Upton Sinclair Papers. Sinclair mss. Lilly Library, Indiana University, Bloomington.

WCC. William C. Carr Papers. Japanese American Research Project Collection (Collection 2010). UCLA Library Special Collections. Charles E. Young Research Library, University of California, Los Angeles.

WOP. Walter O'Malley Papers. https://www.walteromalley.com/en/historic-documents /Business-Correspondence.

PUBLISHED WORKS

Abelson, Elaine S. "'Women Who Have No Men to Work for Them': Gender and Homelessness in the Great Depression, 1930–1934." *Feminist Studies* 29, no. 1 (Spring 2003): 105–27.

Abu-Lughod, Janet L. *New York, Chicago, Los Angeles: America's Global Cities.* Minneapolis: University of Minnesota Press, 1999.

——. *Race, Space, and Riots in Chicago, New York, and Los Angeles.* New York: Oxford University Press, 2007.

Advertiser's Rate Book: Including a Catalog of Newspapers, Magazines and Periodicals which Have a Circulation of 5,000 and Over. Chicago: Nelson Chesman, 1916.

Anzaldúa, Gloria. *Borderlands/La Frontera: The New Mestiza.* San Francisco: Spinsters, 1987.

Appiah, Kwame Anthony. *Cosmopolitanism: Ethics in a World of Strangers.* Issues of Our Time. New York: W. W. Norton, 2010.

Arrigo, Anthony F. *Imaging Hoover Dam: The Making of a Cultural Icon.* Reno: University of Nevada Press, 2014.

Arthur, Anthony. *Radical Innocent: Upton Sinclair.* New York: Random House, 2007.

Atwood, Sara. "Leading Human Souls to What Is Best." In Carlyle, *On Heroes, Hero-Worship, and the Heroic in History,* 247–59.

Avila, Eric. *Popular Culture in the Age of White Flight: Fear and Fantasy in Suburban Los Angeles.* Berkeley: University of California Press, 2004.

Axelrod, Jeremiah B. C. *Inventing Autopia: Dreams and Visions of the Modern Metropolis in Jazz Age Los Angeles.* Berkeley: University of California Press, 2009.

Azuma, Eiichiro. "Japanese Immigrant Settler Colonialism in the U.S.-Mexican Borderlands and the U.S. Racial-Imperialist Politics of the Hemispheric 'Yellow Peril.'" *Pacific Historical Review* 83, no. 2 (May 2014): 255–76.

Bain, David Haward. *Empire Express: Building the First Transcontinental Railroad.* New York: Penguin, 2000.

Baltzell, E. Digby. *Philadelphia Gentlemen: The Making of a National Upper Class.* New York: Free Press, 1958.

Banner, Stuart. *Possessing the Pacific: Land, Settlers, and Indigenous People from Australia to Alaska.* Cambridge MA: Harvard University Press, 2009.

Barney, Robert Knight, Stephen R. Wenn, and Scott G. Martyn. *Selling the Five Rings: The International Olympic Committee and the Rise of Olympic Commercialism.* Salt Lake City: University of Utah Press, 2002.

Beckert, Sven. *The Monied Metropolis: New York City and the Consolidation of the American Bourgeoisie, 1850–1896.* Cambridge UK: Cambridge University Press, 2001.

Bederman, Gail. *Manliness and Civilization: A Cultural History of Gender and Race in the United States, 1880–1917.* Chicago: University of Chicago Press, 1996.

Beers, Burton Floyd. *Vain Endeavor: Robert Lansing's Attempts to End the American-Japanese Rivalry.* Durham NC: Duke University Press, 1962.

Berg, A. Scott. *Goldwyn: A Biography.* New York: Simon and Schuster, 2013.

———. *Lindbergh.* New York: Simon and Schuster, 2013.

Bilstein, Roger. "The Airplane and the American Experience." In *The Airplane in American Culture,* edited by Dominick A. Pisano, 16–38. Ann Arbor: University of Michigan Press, 2003.

"Biography of Dr. George P. Clements." In *History of Riverside County California with a Biographical Review,* 553–54. Los Angeles: Historic Record Company, 1912.

Blackburn, Ashley G., Shannon K. Fowler, and Joycelyn M. Pollock, eds. *Prisons: Today and Tomorrow.* Burlington MA: Jones and Bartlett Learning, 2014.

Blaisdell, Lowell L. "Harry Chandler and Mexican Border Intrigue, 1914–1917." *Pacific Historical Review* 35, no. 4 (November 1966): 385–93.

Blasier, Cole. "The United States and Madero." *Journal of Latin American Studies* 4, no. 2 (November 1972): 207–31.

Boghardt, Thomas. *The Zimmermann Telegram: Intelligence, Diplomacy, and America's Entry into World War I.* Annapolis MD: Naval Institute Press, 2012.

Braisted, William Reynolds. *The United States Navy in the Pacific, 1897–1909.* Annapolis MD: Naval Institute Press, 2008.

Brilliant, Mark. *The Color of America Has Changed: How Racial Diversity Shaped Civil Rights Reform in California, 1941–1978.* New York: Oxford University Press, 2010.

Brook, Vincent. *Land of Smoke and Mirrors: A Cultural History of Los Angeles.* Piscataway NJ: Rutgers University Press, 2013.

Brooks, Charlotte. *Alien Neighbors, Foreign Friends: Asian Americans, Housing, and the Transformation of Urban California.* Chicago: University of Chicago Press, 2009.

Browne, Francis Granger, ed. *The Games of the Xth Olympiad, Los Angeles, 1932: Official Report.* Los Angeles: Xth Olympiade Committee of the Games of Los Angeles, 1932.

Buntin, John. *L.A. Noir: The Struggle for the Soul of America's Most Seductive City.* New York: Harmony Books, 2009.

Campbell, John B. T. "In Memory: Marshall Stimson." *Historical Society of Southern California Quarterly* 34, no. 1 (March 1952): 81–86.

Capozzola, Christopher. *Uncle Sam Wants You: World War I and the Making of the Modern American Citizen*. New York: Oxford University Press, 2010.

Carlyle, Thomas. *On Heroes, Hero-Worship, and the Heroic in History*. Edited by David R. Sorensen and Brent E. Kinser. With essays by Sarah Atwood, Owen Dudley Edwards, Christopher Harvie, Brent E. Kinser, Terence James Reed, David R. Sorensen, and Beverly Taylor. New Haven: Yale University Press, 2013.

Caro, Robert A. *The Power Broker: Robert Moses and the Fall of New York*. New York: Knopf, 1974.

Carpio, Genevieve. *Collisions at the Crossroads: How Place and Mobility Make Race*. Berkeley: University of California Press, 2019.

Castillo-Muñoz, Verónica. "Beyond Red-Light Districts: Regional and Transnational Migration in the Mexican-U.S. Borderlands, 1870–1912." In *Globalizing Borderlands Studies in Europe and North America*, edited by John W. I. Lee and Michael North, 193–218. Lincoln: University of Nebraska Press, 2016.

Chang, Kornel. *Pacific Connections: The Making of the U.S.-Canadian Borderlands*. Berkeley: University of California Press, 2012.

Chauncey, George. *Gay New York: Gender, Urban Culture, and the Makings of the Gay Male World, 1890–1940*. New York: Basic Books, 1994.

Cohen, Lizabeth. *Making a New Deal: Industrial Workers in Chicago, 1919–1939*. Cambridge UK: Cambridge University Press, 1990.

Colvin, Mark. *Penitentiaries, Reformatories, and Chain Gangs: Social Theory and the History of Punishment in Nineteenth-Century America*. New York: St. Martin's, 1997.

Congelio, Brad J. "An Odyssey: The City of Los Angeles and the Olympic Movement, 1932–1984." *Southern California Quarterly* 97, no. 2 (Summer 2015): 178–212.

Connell, R. W., and James W. Messerschmidt. "Hegemonic Masculinity: Rethinking the Concept." *Gender and Society* 19, no. 6 (December 2005): 829–59.

Connell, R. W., and Julian Wood. "Globalization and Business Masculinities." *Men and Masculinities* 7, no. 4 (April 2005): 347–64.

Cooper, John Milton. *Woodrow Wilson: A Biography*. New York: Vintage Books, 2011.

Corn, Joseph J. *The Winged Gospel: America's Romance with Aviation*. Baltimore: Johns Hopkins University Press, 2002.

Courtwright, David T. *Sky as Frontier: Adventure, Aviation, and Empire*. College Station: Texas A&M University Press, 2004.

Critchlow, Donald T. *When Hollywood Was Right: How Movie Stars, Studio Moguls, and Big Business Remade American Politics*. New York: Cambridge University Press, 2013.

Cronon, William. *Nature's Metropolis: Chicago and the Great West*. New York: W. W. Norton, 1992.

Cruz, Adrian. "Racialized Fields: Asians, Mexicans, and the Farm Labor Struggle in California." PhD diss., University of Illinois at Urbana-Champaign, 2010.

Culton, Donald R. "Charles Dwight Willard: Los Angeles' 'Citizen Fixit', City Booster and Progressive Reformer." *California History* 57, no. 2 (July 1978): 158–71.

Culver, Lawrence. *The Frontier of Leisure: Southern California and the Shaping of Modern America*. New York: Oxford University Press, 2012.

Cunningham, Frank. *Sky Master: The Story of Donald Douglas*. Ebook: Pickle Partners, 2016.

Curtiss, Glenn Hammond, and Augustus Post. *The Curtiss Aviation Book*. New York: Frederick A. Stokes, 1912.

Daniels, Roger. *The Decision to Relocate the Japanese Americans*. Philadelphia: J. B. Lippincott, 1975.

D'Antonio, Michael. *Forever Blue: The True Story of Walter O'Malley, Baseball's Most Controversial Owner, and the Dodgers of Brooklyn and Los Angeles*. New York: Penguin, 2009.

Davis, Clark. *Company Men: White-Collar Life and Corporate Cultures in Los Angeles, 1892–1941*. Baltimore: Johns Hopkins University Press, 2000.

Davis, Margaret Leslie. *Dark Side of Fortune: Triumph and Scandal in the Life of Oil Tycoon Edward L. Doheny*. Berkeley: University of California Press, 1998.

Davis, Mike. *City of Quartz: Excavating the Future in Los Angeles*. New York: Verso, 1998.

——. "Sunshine and the Open Shop: Ford and Darwin in 1920s Los Angeles." In Sitton and Deverell, *Metropolis in the Making*, 96–122.

Dearinger, Ryan L. "Violence, Masculinity, Image, and Reality on the Antebellum Frontier." *Indiana Magazine of History* 100, no. 1 (March 2004): 26–55.

Deep Water Harbor in Southern California: Port Los Angeles vs. San Pedro: Full Report of Oral Testimony at Public Hearings in Los Angeles, December 1896. Los Angeles: Evening Express Company Printers, 1897.

Denning, Michael. *The Cultural Front: The Laboring of American Culture in the Twentieth Century*. London: Verso, 1996.

Deverell, William. *Railroad Crossing: Californians and the Railroad, 1850–1910*. Berkeley: University of California Press, 1996.

——. *Whitewashed Adobe: The Rise of Los Angeles and the Remaking of Its Mexican Past*. Berkeley: University of California Press, 2005.

Deverell, William, and Tom Sitton. *Water and Los Angeles: A Tale of Three Rivers, 1900–1941*. Berkeley: University of California Press, 2016.

Deverell, William, and Tom Sitton, eds. *California Progressivism Revisited*. Berkeley: University of California Press, 1994.

Dickstein, Morris. *Dancing in the Dark: A Cultural History of the Great Depression*. New York: W. W. Norton, 2010.

Dirlik, Arif. "Pacific Contradictions." In *What Is in a Rim?: Critical Perspectives on the Pacific Region Idea*, edited by Arif Dirlik, 3–14. 2nd edition. Lanham MD: Rowman and Littlefield, 1998.

Dubofsky, Melvyn. *We Shall Be All: A History of the Industrial Workers of the World*. Edited by Joseph A. McCartin. Champaign-Urbana: University of Illinois Press, 2000.

Dumenil, Lynn. "Women's Reform Organizations and Wartime Mobilization in World War I-Era Los Angeles." *Journal of the Gilded Age and Progressive Era* 10, no. 2 (April 2011): 213–45.

Eaton, Mark. "What Price Hollywood?" In *A Companion to the Modern American Novel, 1900-1950*, edited by John T. Matthews, 466–95. Oxford: Wiley-Blackwell, 2009.

Erie, Steven P. *Globalizing L.A.: Trade, Infrastructure, and Regional Development*. Palo Alto CA: Stanford University Press, 2004.

Estrada, Gilbert. "If You Build It, They Will Move: The Los Angeles Freeway System and the Displacement of Mexican East Los Angeles, 1944–1972." *Southern California Quarterly* 87, no. 3 (Fall 2005): 287–315.

Eyman, Scott. *Lion of Hollywood: The Life and Legend of Louis B. Mayer*. New York: Simon and Schuster, 2008.

Felker-Kantor, Max. *Policing Los Angeles: Race, Resistance, and the Rise of the LAPD*. Chapel Hill: University of North Carolina Press, 2018.

Ferguson, Kathy E. *The Feminist Case against Bureaucracy*. Philadelphia: Temple University Press, 1984.

Fetter, Henry D. "Revising the Revisionists: Walter O'Malley, Robert Moses, and the End of the Brooklyn Dodgers." *New York History* 89, no. 1 (Winter 2008): 54–74.

Finnegan, John Patrick. *Against the Specter of a Dragon: The Campaign for American Military Preparedness, 1914–1917*. Westport CT: Greenwood Press, 1974.

Flowers, Montaville. *The Japanese Conquest of American Opinion*. New York: George H. Doran, 1917.

Fogelson, Robert M. *The Fragmented Metropolis: Los Angeles, 1850–1930*. Berkeley: University of California Press, 1993.

——. *The Los Angeles Riots*. New York: Arno Press, 1969.

Ford, John Anson. *Thirty Explosive Years in Los Angeles County*. San Marino CA: Huntington Library, 1961.

Ford, John Anson, Lynn Craig Cunningham, and Elizabeth I. Dixon. *John Anson Ford and Los Angeles County Government Oral History Transcript*. Los Angeles: Oral History Program, University of California, Los Angeles, 1967.

Fox-Genovese, Elizabeth, and Eugene D. Genovese. *The Mind of the Master Class: History and Faith in the Southern Slaveholders' Worldview*. Cambridge UK: Cambridge University Press, 2005.Friedricks, William B. *Henry E. Huntington and the Creation of Southern California*. Columbus: Ohio State University Press, 1992.

Fulton, William. *The Reluctant Metropolis: The Politics of Urban Growth in Los Angeles*. Baltimore: Johns Hopkins University Press, 2001.

Garcia, Matt. *A World of Its Own: Race, Labor, and Citrus in the Making of Greater Los Angeles, 1900–1970*. Chapel Hill: University of North Carolina Press, 2001.

Gibson, Campbell, and Kay Jung. *Historical Census Statistics on Population Totals by Race, 1790 to 1990, and by Hispanic Origin, 1970 to 1990, for Large Cities and Other Urban Places in the United States.* Washington DC: U.S. Census Bureau, 2005.

Giczy, Hailey. "The Bum Blockade: Los Angeles and the Great Depression." *Voces Novae: Chapman University Historical Review* 1, no. 1 (2009). https://digitalcommons.chapman.edu/vocesnovae/vol1/iss1/6.

Giddens, Anthony. *The Class Structure of the Advanced Societies.* New York: Hutchinson, 1981.

Gish, Todd. "Growing and Selling Los Angeles: The All-Year Club of Southern California, 1921–1941." *Southern California Quarterly* 89, no. 4 (Winter 2007–8): 391–415.

Glaab, Charles Nelson. *Kansas City and the Railroads: Community Policy in the Growth of a Regional Metropolis.* Madison: State Historical Society of Wisconsin, 1962.

Goldstone, Lawrence. *Birdmen: The Wright Brothers, Glenn Curtiss, and the Battle to Control the Skies.* New York: Ballantine Books, 2015.

González, Gilbert G. *Labor and Community: Mexican Citrus Worker Villages in a Southern California County, 1900–1950.* Champaign-Urbana: University of Illinois Press, 1994.

Gottlieb, Robert. *Reinventing Los Angeles: Nature and Community in the Global City.* Cambridge MA: MIT Press, 2007.

Gottlieb, Robert, and Irene Wolt. *Thinking Big: The Story of the Los Angeles Times, Its Publishers, and Their Influence on Southern California.* New York: Putnam, 1977.

Graham, Wade. "Blueprinting the Regional City: The Urban and Environmental Legacies of the Air Industry in Southern California." In *Blue Sky Metropolis: The Aerospace Century in Southern California,* edited by Peter J. Westwick, 247–73. Berkeley: University of California Press, 2012.

Gregory, James Noble. *American Exodus: The Dust Bowl Migration and Okie Culture in California.* New York: Oxford University Press, 1991.

Grodzins, Morton. *Americans Betrayed: Politics and the Japanese Evacuation.* Chicago: University of Chicago Press, 1974.

Guerin-Gonzales, Camille. *Mexican Workers and American Dreams: Immigration, Repatriation, and California Farm Labor, 1900–1939.* Piscataway NJ: Rutgers University Press, 1994.

Hamilton, Nora, and Norma Stoltz Chinchilla. *Seeking Community in a Global City: Guatemalans and Salvadorans in Los Angeles.* Philadelphia: Temple University Press, 2001.

Hanson, Philip. "The Feminine Image in Films of the Great Depression." *Cambridge Quarterly* 32, no. 2 (June 2003): 113–41.

Harris, Charles H., III, and Louis R. Sadler. *The Archaeologist Was a Spy: Sylvanus G. Morley and the Office of Naval Intelligence.* Albuquerque: University of New Mexico Press, 2003.

———. *The Great Call-Up: The Guard, the Border, and the Mexican Revolution.* Norman: University of Oklahoma Press, 2015.

———. *The Plan de San Diego: Tejano Rebellion, Mexican Intrigue.* Lincoln: University of Nebraska Press, 2013.

——. "The Plan of San Diego and the Mexican-United States War Crisis of 1916: A Reexamination." *Hispanic American Historical Review* 58, no. 3 (August 1978): 381–408.

——. *The Secret War in El Paso: Mexican Revolutionary Intrigue, 1906–1920.* Albuquerque: University of New Mexico Press, 2009.

Hartley, James E., Steven M. Sheffrin, and J. David Vasche. "Reform during Crisis: The Transformation of California's Fiscal System during the Great Depression." *Journal of Economic History* 56, no. 3 (September 1996): 657–78.

Hatch, Alden. *Glenn Curtiss: Pioneer of Aviation.* New York: Rowman and Littlefield, 2007.

Hau'ofa, Epeli. "Our Sea of Islands." *Contemporary Pacific* 6, no. 1 (Spring 1994): 148–61.

——. *We Are the Ocean: Selected Works.* Honolulu: University of Hawaii Press, 2008.

Henderson, Cary S. "Los Angeles and the Dodger War, 1957–1962." *Southern California Quarterly* 62, no. 3 (Fall 1980): 261–89.

Hernández, Kelly Lytle. *City of Inmates: Conquest, Rebellion, and the Rise of Human Caging in Los Angeles, 1771–1965.* Chapel Hill: University of North Carolina Press, 2017.

——. "Hobos in Heaven: Race, Incarceration, and the Rise of Los Angeles, 1880–1910." *Pacific Historical Review* 83, no. 3 (August 2014): 410–47.

——. *Migra!: A History of the U.S. Border Patrol.* Berkeley: University of California Press, 2010.

Heslop, Katherine. "Making the Desert Blossom: Spreading the Gospel of Irrigation." *Journal of the Southwest* 56, no. 1 (Spring 2014): 29–51.

Hiltzik, Michael. *Colossus: Hoover Dam and the Making of the American Century.* New York: Free Press, 2010.

Hines, Thomas S. "Housing, Baseball, and Creeping Socialism: The Battle of Chavez Ravine, Los Angeles, 1949–1959." *Journal of Urban History* 8, no. 2 (February 1982): 123–43.

Hintze, Paul von. *Murder and Counterrevolution in Mexico: The Eyewitness Account of German Ambassador Paul von Hintze, 1912–1914.* Edited and with an introduction by Friedrich E. Schuler. Lincoln: University of Nebraska Press, 2017.

Hoffman, Abraham. "The Conscience of a Public Official: Los Angeles Mayor Fletcher Bowron and Japanese Removal." *Southern California Quarterly* 92, no. 3 (Fall 2010): 243–74.

——. "Stimulus to Repatriation: The 1931 Federal Deportation Drive and the Los Angeles Mexican Community." *Pacific Historical Review* 42, no. 2 (May 1973): 205–19.

——. *Unwanted Mexican Americans in the Great Depression: Repatriation Pressures, 1929–1939.* Tucson: University of Arizona Press, 1974.

——. *Vision or Villainy: Origins of the Owens Valley-Los Angeles Water Controversy.* College Station: Texas A&M University Press, 1981.

Hoganson, Kristin L. *Fighting for American Manhood: How Gender Politics Provoked the Spanish-American and Philippine-American Wars.* New Haven: Yale University Press, 2000.

Hollinger, David A. "Ethnic Diversity, Cosmopolitanism and the Emergence of the American Liberal Intelligentsia." *American Quarterly* 27, no. 2 (May 1975): 133–51.

Houston, Jeanne Wakatsuki, and James D. Houston. *Farewell to Manzanar: A True Story of Japanese American Experience during and after the World War II Internment.* Boston: Houghton Mifflin Harcourt, 2002.

Hsu, Madeline Y. *The Good Immigrants: How the Yellow Peril Became the Model Minority.* Princeton: Princeton University Press, 2015.

Hundley, Norris, Jr., and Donald C. Jackson. *Heavy Ground: William Mulholland and the St. Francis Dam Disaster.* Berkeley: University of California Press, 2016.

Igler, David. "Diseased Goods: Global Exchanges in the Eastern Pacific Basin, 1770–1850." *American Historical Review* 109, no. 3 (June 2004): 693–719.

Jacobson, Matthew Frye. *Barbarian Virtues: The United States Encounters Foreign Peoples at Home and Abroad, 1876–1917.* New York: Hill and Wang, 2000.

Jaher, Frederic Cople. *The Urban Establishment: Upper Strata in Boston, New York, Charleston, Chicago, and Los Angeles.* Champaign-Urbana: University of Illinois Press, 1982.

Johnson, Benjamin Heber. *Revolution in Texas: How a Forgotten Rebellion and Its Bloody Suppression Turned Mexicans into Americans.* New Haven: Yale University Press, 2005.

Johnson, Maxwell. "'Truth Is the Keenest Weapon Ever Drawn': 'Fighting Bob' Shuler's Crusade to Expose Los Angeles's Sins." *California History* 98, no. 2 (Summer 2021): 50–73.

Jones, Ryan Tucker. *Empire of Extinction: Russians and the North Pacific's Strange Beasts of the Sea, 1741–1867.* New York: Oxford University Press, 2017.

Kahrl, William L. *Water and Power: The Conflict over Los Angeles Water Supply in the Owens Valley.* Berkeley: University of California Press, 1983.

Kaplan, Amy. *The Anarchy of Empire in the Making of U.S. Culture.* Cambridge MA: Harvard University Press, 2005.

Kasson, John F. *Houdini, Tarzan, and the Perfect Man: The White Male Body and the Challenge of Modernity in America.* New York: Hill and Wang, 2001.

Katz, Friedrich. *The Secret War in Mexico.* Palo Alto: Stanford University Press, 2003.

Kawamura, Noriko. *Turbulence in the Pacific: Japanese-U.S. Relations during World War I.* Westport CT: Praeger, 2000.

Kennedy, David M. *The American People in the Great Depression: Freedom from Fear, Part One.* New York: Oxford University Press, 2003.

Kim, Jessica M. *Imperial Metropolis: Los Angeles, Mexico, and the Borderlands of American Empire, 1865–1941.* Chapel Hill: University of North Carolina Press, 2019.

Kimmel, Michael. *Manhood in America: A Cultural History.* 3rd edition. New York: Oxford University Press, 2011.

Knight, Alan. *The Mexican Revolution.* Lincoln: University of Nebraska Press, 1990.

Kurashige, Scott. *The Shifting Grounds of Race: Black and Japanese Americans in the Making of Multiethnic Los Angeles.* Princeton: Princeton University Press, 2010.

Kwolek-Folland, Angel. *Engendering Business: Men and Women in the Corporate Office, 1870–1930.* Baltimore: Johns Hopkins University Press, 1994.

Laslett, John H. M. *Sunshine Was Never Enough: Los Angeles Workers, 1880–2010.* Berkeley: University of California Press, 2012.

Launius, Roger D., and Jessie L. Embry. "The 1910 Los Angeles Airshow: The Beginnings of Air Awareness in the West." *Southern California Quarterly* 77, no. 4 (Winter 1995): 329–46.

Lavender, David. *The Great Persuader: The Biography of Collis P. Huntington.* Boulder: University Press of Colorado, 1998.

Leader, Leonard Joseph. *Los Angeles and the Great Depression.* New York: Garland, 1991.

Lee, Erika. *At America's Gates: Chinese Immigration during the Exclusion Era, 1882–1943.* Chapel Hill: University of North Carolina Press, 2004.

Lee, Shelley Sang-Hee. *Claiming the Oriental Gateway: Prewar Seattle and Japanese America.* Philadelphia: Temple University Press, 2011.

Lewis, Oscar. *The Big Four: The Story of Huntington, Stanford, Hopkins, and Crocker, and of the Building of the Central Pacific.* New York: Knopf Doubleday, 2012.

Libecap, Gary D. *Owens Valley Revisited: A Reassessment of the West's First Great Water Transfer.* Palo Alto: Stanford University Press, 2007.

Lindfors, Bernth, ed. *Africans on Stage: Studies in Ethnological Show Business.* Bloomington: Indiana University Press, 1999.

Link, Arthur S., et al., eds. *The Papers of Woodrow Wilson.* 69 vols. Princeton: Princeton University Press, 1966.

López, Ronald W. "Community Resistance and Conditional Patriotism in Cold War Los Angeles: The Battle For Chavez Ravine." *Latino Studies* 7, no. 4 (Winter 2009): 457–79.

Los Angeles Today. Los Angeles: Los Angeles Chamber of Commerce, 1922. The Huntington Library, Rare Book #31039.

Lotchin, Roger W. *Fortress California, 1910–1961: From Warfare to Welfare.* New York: Oxford University Press, 1992.

MacLachlan, Colin M. *Anarchism and the Mexican Revolution: The Political Trials of Ricardo Flores Magón in the United States.* Berkeley: University of California Press, 1991.

Marchetti, Gina. *Romance and the "Yellow Peril": Race, Sex, and Discursive Strategies in Hollywood Fiction.* Berkeley: University of California Press, 1993.

Matsuda, Matt K. *Pacific Worlds: A History of Seas, Peoples, and Cultures.* Cambridge UK: Cambridge University Press, 2012.

Mayo, Charles G. "The 1961 Mayoralty Election in Los Angeles: The Political Party in a Nonpartisan Election." *Political Research Quarterly* 17, no. 2 (June 1964): 325–37.

McClung, William Alexander. *Landscapes of Desire: Anglo Mythologies of Los Angeles.* Berkeley: University of California Press, 2002.

McDougal, Dennis. *Privileged Son: Otis Chandler and the Rise and Fall of the L.A. Times Dynasty.* Boston: Da Capo Press, 2009.

McGerr, Michael. *A Fierce Discontent: The Rise and Fall of the Progressive Movement in America, 1870–1920.* New York: Simon and Schuster, 2010.

McGreevey, Robert C. *Borderline Citizens: The United States, Puerto Rico, and the Politics of Colonial Migration*. Ithaca: Cornell University Press, 2018.

McLennan, Rebecca M. *The Crisis of Imprisonment: Protest, Politics, and the Making of the American Penal State, 1776–1941*. Cambridge UK: Cambridge University Press, 2008.

McWilliams, Carey. *Factories in the Field: The Story of Migratory Farm Labor in California*. Berkeley: University of California Press, 2000.

——— . *Southern California: An Island on the Land*. New York: Duell, Sloan and Pierce, 1946.

Melillo, Edward Dallam. *Strangers on Familiar Soil: Rediscovering the Chile-California Connection*. New Haven: Yale University Press, 2015.

Meyer, Alan. *Weekend Pilots: Technology, Masculinity, and Private Aviation in Postwar America*. Baltimore: Johns Hopkins University Press, 2016.

Miller, Bonnie. "The Incoherencies of Empire: The 'Imperial' Image of the Indian at the Omaha World's Fairs of 1898–99." *American Studies* 49, no. 3/4 (Fall/Winter 2008): 39–62.

Mills, C. Wright. *The Power Elite*. New York: Oxford University Press, 2000.

Mitchell, Greg. *The Campaign of the Century: Upton Sinclair's Race for Governor of California and the Birth of Media Politics*. New York: Random House, 1992.

Mitchell, Lincoln Abraham. *Baseball Goes West: The Dodgers, the Giants, and the Shaping of the Major Leagues*. Kent OH: Kent State University Press, 2018.

Moeller, Beverley Bowen. *Phil Swing and Boulder Dam*. Berkeley: University of California Press, 1971.

Molden, Danny Toshio. "Seven Miles from Independence: The War, Internee Identity and the Manzanar Free Press." PhD diss., University of Minnesota, 1998.

Molina, Natalia. *Fit to Be Citizens?: Public Health and Race in Los Angeles, 1879–1939*. Berkeley: University of California Press, 2006.

Mulholland, Catherine. *William Mulholland and the Rise of Los Angeles*. Berkeley: University of California Press, 2002.

Nadeau, Remi A. *The Water Seekers*. Garden City NY: Doubleday, 1950.

Nasaw, David. *The Chief: The Life of William Randolph Hearst*. Boston: Houghton Mifflin Harcourt, 2013.

Nash, Gerald D. *World War II and the West: Reshaping the Economy*. Lincoln: University of Nebraska Press, 1990.

Needham, Andrew. *Power Lines: Phoenix and the Making of the Modern Southwest*. Princeton: Princeton University Press, 2014.

Nelson, David. "When Modern Tourism Was Born: Florida at the World Fairs and on the World Stage in the 1930s." *Florida Historical Quarterly* 88, no. 4 (Spring 2010): 435–68.

Newmark, Harris. *Sixty Years in Southern California, 1853–1913, Containing the Reminiscences of Harris Newmark*. Edited by Maurice H. Newmark and Marco R. Newmark. New York: Knickerbocker Press, 1916.

Ngai, Mae M. *Impossible Subjects: Illegal Aliens and the Making of Modern America*. Princeton: Princeton University Press, 2014.

Norris, Frank. *The Octopus: A Story of California*. Garden City NY: Doubleday, Page, 1901.

Orsi, Richard J. "'The Octopus' Reconsidered: The Southern Pacific and Agricultural Modernization in California, 1865–1915." *California Historical Quarterly* 54, no. 3 (Fall 1975): 197–220.

——. *Sunset Limited: The Southern Pacific Railroad and the Development of the American West, 1850–1930*. Berkeley: University of California Press, 2007.

Parson, Don. "Los Angeles' 'Headline-Happy Public Housing War.'" *Southern California Quarterly* 65, no. 3 (Fall 1983): 251–85.

——. *Making a Better World: Public Housing, the Red Scare, and the Direction of Modern Los Angeles*. Minneapolis: University of Minnesota Press, 2005.

——. "'This Modern Marvel': Bunker Hill, Chavez Ravine, and the Politics of Modernism in Los Angeles." *Southern California Quarterly* 75, no. 3/4 (Fall/Winter 1993): 333–50.

Pattillo, Donald M. *Pushing the Envelope: The American Aircraft Industry*. Ann Arbor: University of Michigan Press, 1998.

Pearlman, Michael David. *To Make Democracy Safe for America: Patricians and Preparedness in the Progressive Era*. Champaign-Urbana: University of Illinois Press, 1984.

Pendergast, Tom. "'Horatio Alger Doesn't Work Here Any More': Masculinity and American Magazines, 1919–1940." *American Studies* 38, no. 1 (Spring 1997): 55–80.

Pieroth, Doris Hinson. *Their Day in the Sun: Women of the 1932 Olympics*. Seattle: University of Washington Press, 1996.

Podair, Jerald. *City of Dreams: Dodger Stadium and the Birth of Modern Los Angeles*. Princeton: Princeton University Press, 2019.

Putnam, Jackson K. "The Progressive Legacy in California: Fifty Years of Politics, 1917–1967." In Deverell and Sitton, *California Progressivism Revisited*, 247–68.

Quam-Wickham, Nancy. "'Cities Sacrificed on the Altar of Oil': Popular Opposition to Oil Development in 1920s Los Angeles." *Environmental History* 3, no. 2 (April 1998): 189–209.

Raat, W. Dirk. *Revoltosos: Mexico's Rebels in the United States, 1903–1923*. College Station: Texas A&M University Press, 2000.

Reeves, Richard. *Infamy: The Shocking Story of the Japanese American Internment in World War II*. New York: Henry Holt, 2015.

Reisner, Marc. *Cadillac Desert: The American West and Its Disappearing Water*. New York: Penguin, 1993.

Rico, Monica. *Nature's Noblemen: Transatlantic Masculinities and the Nineteenth-Century American West*. New Haven: Yale University Press, 2013.

Riess, Steven A. "Power without Authority: Los Angeles' Elites and the Construction of the Coliseum." *Journal of Sport History* 8, no. 1 (Spring 1981): 50–65.

Robinson, Greg. *By Order of the President: FDR and the Internment of Japanese Americans*. Cambridge MA: Harvard University Press, 2009.

Robinson, Greg, ed. *Pacific Citizens: Larry and Guyo Tajiri and Japanese American Journalism in the World War II Era*. Champaign-Urbana: University of Illinois Press, 2012.

Rogers, Stanley. "The Attempted Recall of the Mayor of Los Angeles." *National Municipal Review* 21, no. 7 (July 1932): 416–19.

Rogin, Michael. "Progressivism and the California Electorate." *Journal of American History* 55, no. 2 (September 1968): 297–314.

Rosales, F. Arturo. *Chicano! The History of the Mexican American Civil Rights Movement*. Houston: Arte Público Press, 1997.

Roseberry, Cecil R. *Glenn Curtiss: Pioneer of Flight*. Syracuse: Syracuse University Press, 1972.

Ross, Steven J. *Hollywood Left and Right: How Movie Stars Shaped American Politics*. New York: Oxford University Press, 2011.

———. "How Hollywood Became Hollywood: Money, Politics, and Movies." In Sitton and Deverell, *Metropolis in the Making*, 255–76.

Roth, Matthew William. "Concrete Utopia: The Development of Roads and Freeways in Los Angeles, 1910–1950." PhD diss., University of Southern California, 2007.

———. "Mulholland Highway and the Engineering Culture of Los Angeles in the 1920's." In Sitton and Deverell, *Metropolis in the Making*, 47–76.

Rothkopf, David. *Superclass: The Global Power Elite and the World They Are Making*. New York: Farrar, Straus and Giroux, 2008.

Rotundo, E. Anthony. *American Manhood: Transformations in Masculinity from the Revolution to the Modern Era*. Reprint edition. New York: Basic Books, 1994.

Ruiz, Ramón Eduardo. *The People of Sonora and Yankee Capitalists*. Tucson: University of Arizona Press, 2017.

Ruíz, Vicki L. *Cannery Women, Cannery Lives: Mexican Women, Unionization, and the California Food Processing Industry, 1930–1950*. Albuquerque: University of New Mexico Press, 1987.

Russell, Ann Marie, and Susan T. Fiske. "Power and Social Perception." In *The Social Psychology of Power*, edited by Ana Guinote and Theresa K. Vescio, 231–50. New York: Guilford Press, 2010.

Rydell, Robert W. "'Darkest Africa': African Shows at America's World's Fairs, 1893–1940." In Lindfors, *Africans on Stage*, 135–55.

Sánchez, George J. *Becoming Mexican American: Ethnicity, Culture, and Identity in Chicano Los Angeles, 1900–1945*. New York: Oxford University Press, 1995.

———. "Edward R. Roybal and the Politics of Multiracialism." *Southern California Quarterly* 92, no. 1 (Spring 2010): 51–73.

Sandos, James A. *Rebellion in the Borderlands: Anarchism and the Plan of San Diego, 1904–1923*. Norman: University of Oklahoma Press, 1992.

Sandoval-Strausz, A. K. "Latino Landscapes: Postwar Cities and the Transnational Origins of a New Urban America." *Journal of American History* 101, no. 3 (December 2014): 804–31.

Sandul, Paul J. P. *California Dreaming: Boosterism, Memory, and Rural Suburbs in the Golden State*. Morgantown: West Virginia University Press, 2014.

Scherer, James Augustin Brown. *The Japanese Crisis*. New York: Frederick A. Stokes, 1916.

Senn, Alfred Eric. *Power, Politics, and the Olympic Games*. Urbana IL: Human Kinetics, 2018.

Shah, Nayan. "Race-ing Sex." *Frontiers: A Journal of Women Studies* 35, no. 1 (2014): 26–36.

Sherry, Michael S. *The Rise of American Air Power: The Creation of Armageddon*. New Haven: Yale University Press, 1987.

Sinclair, Upton. *The Brass Check: A Study of American Journalism*. Urbana-Champaign: University of Illinois Press, 1928.

———. *I, Candidate for Governor: And How I Got Licked*. Self-published, 1935.

———. *I, Governor of California, and How I Ended Poverty: A True Story of the Future*. Chicago: W. B. Conkey, 1933.

———. *The Lie Factory Starts*. Los Angeles: End Poverty League, 1934.

———. *Oil!* New York: Penguin, 2007.

Sitton, Tom. "The 'Boss' without a Machine: Kent K. Parrot and Los Angeles Politics in the 1920s." *Southern California Quarterly* 67, no. 4 (Winter 1985): 365–87.

———. "Did the Ruling Class Rule at City Hall in 1920's Los Angeles?" In Sitton and Deverell, *Metropolis in the Making*, 302–18.

———. *Grand Ventures: The Banning Family and the Shaping of Southern California*. San Marino CA: Huntington Library, 2010.

———. *John Randolph Haynes, California Progressive*. Stanford CA: Stanford University Press, 1992.

———. *Los Angeles Transformed: Fletcher Bowron's Urban Reform Revival, 1938–1953*. Albuquerque: University of New Mexico Press, 2005.

Sitton, Tom, and William Francis Deverell, eds. *Metropolis in the Making: Los Angeles in the 1920s*. Berkeley: University of California Press, 2001.

Slotkin, Richard. *Gunfighter Nation: The Myth of the Frontier in Twentieth-Century America*. Norman: University of Oklahoma Press, 1998.

Smith, Carl. *City Water, City Life: Water and the Infrastructure of Ideas in Urbanizing Philadelphia, Boston, and Chicago*. Chicago: University of Chicago Press, 2013.

———. *Souls for Sale*. Directed by Rupert Hughes. 1923; Burbank CA: Warner Bros. Archive Collection, 2009.

Standiford, Les. *Water to the Angels: William Mulholland, His Monumental Aqueduct, and the Rise of Los Angeles*. New York: Harper Collins, 2015.

Stansell, Christine. *City of Women: Sex and Class in New York, 1789–1860*. Urbana-Champaign: University of Illinois Press, 1987.

Starr, Kevin. *Endangered Dreams: The Great Depression in California*. New York: Oxford University Press, 1997.

———. *Inventing the Dream: California through the Progressive Era*. New York: Oxford University Press, 1986.

——. *Material Dreams: Southern California through the 1920s*. New York: Oxford University Press, 1991.

Stein, Walter J. *California and the Dust Bowl Migration*. Westport CT: Greenwood Press, 1973.

Stevens, Joseph E. *Hoover Dam: An American Adventure*. Norman: University of Oklahoma Press, 2014.

Sullivan, Neil. *The Dodgers Move West*. New York: Oxford University Press, 1989.

Takaki, Ronald. *Double Victory: A Multicultural History of America in World War II*. Boston: Little, Brown, 2001.

Tejani, James. "Dredging the Future: The Destruction of Coastal Estuaries and the Creation of Metropolitan Los Angeles, 1858–1913." *Southern California Quarterly* 96, no. 1 (Spring 2014): 5–39.

——. "Harbor Lines: Connecting the Histories of Borderlands and Pacific Imperialism in the Making of the Port of Los Angeles, 1858–1908." *Western Historical Quarterly* 45, no. 2 (Summer 2014): 124–46.

tenBroek, Jacobus, Edward N. Barnhart, and Floyd W. Matson. *Prejudice, War, and the Constitution: Causes and Consequences of the Evacuation of the Japanese Americans in World War II*. Berkeley: University of California Press, 1954.

Testi, Arnaldo. "The Gender of Reform Politics: Theodore Roosevelt and the Culture of Masculinity." *Journal of American History* 81, no. 4 (March 1995): 1509–33.

Thomas, Lorrin. *Puerto Rican Citizen: History and Political Identity in Twentieth-Century New York City*. Chicago: University of Chicago Press, 2010.

Torres-Rouff, David Samuel. *Before L.A.: Race, Space, and Municipal Power in Los Angeles, 1781–1894*. New Haven: Yale University Press, 2013.

Trennert, Robert. "Selling Indian Education at World's Fairs and Expositions, 1893–1904." *American Indian Quarterly* 11, no. 3 (Summer 1987): 203–20.

Truett, Samuel. *Fugitive Landscapes: The Forgotten History of the U.S.-Mexico Borderlands*. New Haven: Yale University Press, 2008.

Turner, Frederick C. "Anti-Americanism in Mexico, 1910–1913." *Hispanic American Historical Review* 47, no. 4 (November 1967): 502–18.

Turner, Frederick Jackson. "The Significance of the Frontier in American History." In *Annual Report of the American Historical Association for the Year 1893*, 197–227. Washington DC: U.S. Government Printing Office, 1894.

Tygiel, Jules. "Introduction, Metropolis in the Making: Los Angeles in the 1920's." In Sitton and Deverell, *Metropolis in the Making*, 1–10.

Ueno, Harry Yoshio, Sue Kunitomi Embrey, and Betty Kulberg Mitson. *Manzanar Martyr: An Interview with Harry Y. Ueno*. Oral History Program, California State University, Fullerton, 1986.

Underwood, Katherine. "Pioneering Minority Representation: Edward Roybal and the Los Angeles City Council, 1949–1962." *Pacific Historical Review* 66, no. 3 (August 1997): 399–425.

Vaughan, Leslie J. "Cosmopolitanism, Ethnicity and American Identity: Randolph Bourne's 'Trans-National America.'" *Journal of American Studies* 25, no. 3 (December 1991): 443–59.

Verge, Arthur C. "The Impact of the Second World War on Los Angeles." *Pacific Historical Review* 63, no. 3 (August 1994): 289–314.

——. *Paradise Transformed: Los Angeles during the Second World War.* Dubuque IA: Kendall/Hunt, 1993.

Waldinger, Roger. "Not the Promised City: Los Angeles and Its Immigrants." *Pacific Historical Review* 68, no. 2 (May 1999): 253–72.

White, Jeremy. "The Los Angeles Way of Doing Things: The Olympic Village and the Practice of Boosterism in 1932." *Olympika: The International Journal of Olympic Studies* 11 (2002): 79–116.

Widener, Daniel. "Another City Is Possible: Interethnic Organizing in Contemporary Los Angeles." *Race/Ethnicity: Multidisciplinary Global Contexts* 1, no. 2 (Spring 2008): 189–219.

Wild, H. Mark. "If You Ain't Got That Do-Re-Mi: The Los Angeles Border Patrol and White Migration in Depression-Era California." *Southern California Quarterly* 83, no. 3 (Fall 2001): 317–34.

Wiley, Peter Booth, and Robert Gottlieb. *Empires in the Sun: The Rise of the New American West.* New York: Putnam, 1982.

Willard, Charles Dwight. *The Free Harbor Contest at Los Angeles: An Account of the Long Fight Waged by the People of Southern California to Secure a Harbor Located at a Point Open to Competition.* Los Angeles: Kingsley-Barnes & Neuner, 1899.

——. *A History of the Chamber of Commerce of Los Angeles, California: From Its Foundation, September 1888, to the Year 1900.* Los Angeles: Kingsley-Barnes & Neuner, 1899.

Williams, R. Hal. *The Democratic Party and California Politics, 1880–1896.* Stanford CA: Stanford University Press, 1973.

The Winning of Barbara Worth. Directed by Henry King. 1926; Beverly Hills CA: MGM Movie Legends, 2007.

Wohl, Robert. *The Spectacle of Flight: Aviation and the Western Imagination, 1920–1950.* New Haven: Yale University Press, 2005.

Wong, Carolyn. *Lobbying for Inclusion: Rights Politics and the Making of Immigration Policy.* Stanford CA: Stanford University Press, 2006.

Worster, Donald. *Rivers of Empire: Water, Aridity, and the Growth of the American West.* New York: Oxford University Press, 1985.

Wu, Ellen D. *The Color of Success: Asian Americans and the Origins of the Model Minority.* Princeton: Princeton University Press, 2013.

Yamamoto, Eriko. "Cheers for Japanese Athletes: The 1932 Los Angeles Olympics and the Japanese American Community." *Pacific Historical Review* 69, no. 3 (August 2000): 399–430.

Yu, Henry. "Los Angeles and American Studies in a Pacific World of Migrations." *American Quarterly* 56, no. 3 (September 2004): 531–43.

Zesch, Scott. *The Chinatown War: Chinese Los Angeles and the Massacre of 1871.* New York: Oxford University Press, 2012.

Zimmerman, Paul. *Los Angeles: The Olympic City.* Edited by Delmar Watson. Self-published by Delmar Watson, 1984.

INDEX

on, 93; psychological effects of, 9–10; and relations with Mexico, 86–87; socialist approach to, 142, 170–74; and transcontinental migration, 146–47

Boston Braves, 232

Boston Globe, 232

Boulder Dam, 108, 121–24, 125, 275n77. *See also* Hoover Dam

Boulder Dam Association, and *Boulder Dam Association Bulletin*, 123

Bowron, Fletcher: about, 196–97; attitudes toward, 217–18; on aviation, 183–84; and Japanese-Americans, 12, 188, 191–92, 201–6, 207, 216, 220, 221; and Japanese internment, 247; legacy of, 206–7; as mayor, 197, 199–201, 223, 226–27; media on, 228–30; on wartime Los Angeles, 14

Boyce, H. H., 32

The Brass Check (Sinclair), 162–63

Braves, 232

Bryan, William Jennings, 85, 266n108

Bureau of Power and Light, 270n8

Bureau of Reclamation, 122

Bureau of Water Works and Supply, 270n8

Butterfield, Roger, 1, 13–14

"calamity howlers," 93, *94*

California: government actions of, 94–95, 122, 197, 226, 227, 236, 241, 261n4; as invasion target, 46, 66–67, 82–83, 214; and migration, 149–54, 173–74

California Aviation Society, 53

California Citizens' Council for the Adoption of a Japanese Exclusion Law, 189

California Department of Corporations, 197

California Fair Employment Practices Commission, 210–11

California League against Sinclairism, 169

California Real Estate Association, 167

California Superior Court, 197

California Supreme Court, 227, 236, 261n4

California Water Wars, 116–21, 189

Calle de los Negros (Los Angeles CA), 20

Cameron, Tom, 193–94

canals, international, 29, 46–47, 103, 255n5

canals, local, 20, 121, 122–23, 126

capitalism, 4–5, 139, 164, 243, 248

Cardenas, Francisco, 84

Caro, Robert, *The Power Broker*, 8

Carpio, Genevieve, 6

Carr, Harry, 75–76, 80

Carr, William C., 217–19, 221

Carranza, Venustiano, 74, 86, 87, 88, 90, 93, 264n67

cartoons, editorial, 91–93, *92, 94*, 124–25, *128*, 170–71, *171, 172*, 267n120

Cartwright (fictional character), 127, 129

Casa Grande (Hearst estate), 72

CDA (Community Development Association), 141, 154, 157, 279n35

cement finishers, 111, 271n22

census, 99–100, 244, 246, 268n8

Central Pacific Railroad, 37, 39

CHA (City Housing Authority), 227

Chaffey, George, 121

chain gangs, 149, 281n76

Chamber of Commerce (California), 151

Chamber of Commerce (Los Angeles): about, 35; and aviation meet, 53; and defense, 29, 45–47, 215; global reach of, 13–14; and harbor decision, 43; and international relations, 94; and Japanese internment, 187–88, 206; and labor issues, 144–46, 148; and migration, 140–41, 149, 150–53, 173–74, 281n74; political activism of, 167; power of, 3; and railroad industry, 39–40; and tourism, 119–20; and water supply, 116–17, 119, 125

Chamber of Commerce (Pasadena), 189

Chamber of Commerce (United States), 147

Chandler, Harry: about, 68–70, 262n19; and aviation industry, 185; business dealings of, 70–71, 262n20; and international relations, 73–75, 86, 88–89, 263n36; land ownership of, 10; in newspaper business, 34, 65, 68, 225; and Olympic Games, 142; political views of, 141, 166, 261n3; and preparedness, 89, 93–94, 95, 96; and water supply, 113–14, 123, 124

Chandler, Marian Otis, 34, 69

Chandler, Norman, 215–16, 225, 228

Chapman, John L., 242–43

Chauncey, George, 5

Chavez Ravine, 223, 227, 230, 234–37

Chesapeake and Ohio Railroad, 37–38

Chicago Daily Tribune, 36

Chicago Tribune, 239

children, 138, 213–14

Childs, Ozro W., 21–22

China, in international relations, 65, 83, 87, 209–10, 213, 263n42, 266nn106–7

China Society of Southern California, 209–10, 211

Chinatown (film), 109

Chinatown (Los Angeles CA), 20

Chinese Exclusion Act (1882), 66, 204, 209

Chinese immigrants, 20, 66, 204, 209–10, 215, 244, 245

Citizen's Alliance of Los Angeles, 51

citizenship, American, 140, 146, 147–48, 189–90, 191, 204–6, 217

Citizen's Independent Vice Investigation Committee, 198–99

Citron, Alan, 220

City Housing Authority (Los Angeles), 227

City Water, City Life (Smith), 6–7

CIVIC (Citizen's Independent Vice Investigation Committee), 198–99

Civilian Conservation Corps, 279n42

Civil Liberties Act (1988), 219

Civil War, 31, 263n41

Clark, Tom C., 202

Claude Mulvihill (fictional character), 109

Clements, George P., 140–41, 142–45, 146–49, 151, 153–54, 216, 247, 280n69

Clinton, Clifford, 198–99, 200

Colman, Ronald, 127

Colorado River: about, 121; aqueducts and dams on, 122–26, 226; media on, 126–30

Colorado River Aqueduct, 122, 124–25, 226

Colorado River Flood (1908), 129–30

Colorado River Land Company, 71

communism, 166, 199, 227–29, 293n129

Community Builder, 122

Community Development Association. *See* CDA (Community Development Association)

Conine, Ernest, 245

connectivity: about, 3–4, 6–8, 246–50; from aviation, 177, 179, 182; changes in, 185–86; elites influencing, 11, 13, 223–24, 235–36; and extractive interests, 115, 119, 124, 130, 133–34; and Japanese internment, 187, 189, 190–91, 207, 218, 220–21; levels of, 8–9; local, 109; and masculinity, 5; of media, 117; political, 47–48; and racism, 242–43, 244; selectivity in, 142–43, 153–54, 174; and tourism, 120; transcontinental, 154, 158, 161, 182; transnational, 64; as war disadvantage, 204; and West, 129

Connell, R. W., 4–5

conservation activities, 143, 144, 279n42

Consolidated Vultee Aircraft, 183

Coolidge, Calvin, 122

Cooper, Gary, 127

Corey, Herbert, 125

cosmopolitanism: malleability of, 174; in Olympic Games, 141, 154, 155–56, 159, 161, 283n144; promotion of, 209–10, 211–12

Coubertin, Pierre de, 157, 158, 160

County Human Relations Commission (Los Angeles County), 210

County Stadium (Milwaukee WI), 232

Coxey's Army, 265n76

Creel, George, 141–42

Criminal Syndicalism Act (California, 1919), 105

Crocker, Charles, 35, 37

Crunk (fictional character), 173

Cryer, George, 197

Cuba, intervention in, 72, 262n27

Cummings, Joseph J., 199

Curtiss, Glenn, 30, 49–50, 57, 59, 61; *The Curtiss Aviation Book*, 50, 61

The Curtiss Aviation Book (Curtiss and Post), 50, 61

Curtiss-Wright, 183

dams, 51, 108, 121–24, 125, 130–35, 144, 247, 275n77

Davis, Clark, 5

Davis, James, 142, 151–52, 199, 200

Davis, W. D., 71

DC-3 jets, 180–81

defense, *94*; aviation involved in, 56–59, 181, 182–83, 184–86; harbor in, 29, 79–80; and Japanese internment, 12; media on, 65–68, 75–77; military training for, 80–83; in Pacific area, 45–46, 87–88, 266n110. *See also* preparedness

Defense Committee of Southern California, 215–16

DeMille, Cecil B., 177

Democratic Party, 85, 141–42, 143, 164–65, 208, 279n42

Department of Public Service, 270n8

Depression Island (Sinclair), 172–73

desert environment, 108, 125, 126–30, *128*

Dewitt, John L., 188, 190, 217

Díaz, Porfirio, 74, 90

diseases, and racist paranoia, 215

displacement of minority groups, 223, 227, 237

Dodge, Jonathan, 104

Dodgers, 223, 230–37

Dodger Stadium, 223–24, 234–37

Doheny, Edward L., 101–3, 246–47, 268n19

Doho (Japanese newspaper), 210

Dominguez, Manuel, 110

Don (fictional character), 173

Douglas, Donald Wills, Sr., 179–82, 185, 246–47

Douglas Aircraft, 179–80, 181–82, 183, 185

Downey, John G., 22

DWP (Department of Water and Power), *128*; accusations toward, 117, 118; influence of, 130; influences on, 121; and masculinity, 126; organizational position of, 270n8; projects of, 115, 131, 191; public relations efforts of, 109, 114, 119, 124–25; water sources pursued by, 108; and William Mulholland, 112, 132, 134

East and West. *See* West: East compared with

Eaton, Fred, 110–11, 111–12, 113, 130–31, 132

Ebbets Field, 230–31, 232, 233

Edison Electric Company, 121

electric railways, 11, 22, 52–53, 103, 238

elites: about, 2–3, 10–13, 14–15; Anglos as, 21–22; and baseball stadium, 223–24,

Mulholland, William: about, 109–12, 274n61; influence of, 121; and masculinity, 126; media on, 117–19; and St. Francis dam disaster, 130–35; and water supply, 8, 108–9, 112–15, 122, 124–25

Munich Agreement (1938), 184

National Housing Act (1949), 226–27

Native Americans, 143, 279n35

Nave, Orville J., 75

Navy, 88, 91, 180, 201

Needham, Andrew, *Power Lines*, 2

New Deal, 171, 198

New England Women's Press Association, 35

Newmark, Harris, 19

Newport News Shipbuilding and Drydock Company, 38

New Republic, 72

Newsweek, 74

New Woman ideal, 4

New York Evening Journal, 72

New York Journal, 71

New York NY, 3, 9, 91, 233–34

New York Times, 19–20, 38, 73, 96, 116, 230–31, 232, 234, 242

New York Tribune, 38, 72–73

New York World, 71–72

Ngai, Mae, 244

Nicaragua Canal, 46–47

Nikkei, 187, 188–89, 190, 192–93, 194–95, 214, 215, 218, 221

Nisei, 188, 195, 201, 203–4, 205–6, 210, 218, 248

Nixon, Richard, 293n129

Noah Cross (fictional character), 109

Noble, Phineas, 36

Nordskog, Andrae B., 117–18, 164–65

Norris, Frank, *The Octopus*, 40

North American Aviation, 180, 182–83

Oakland Tribune, 167

Obregón, Álvaro, 93–94, 144

The Octopus (Norris), 40

Oil! (Sinclair), 101

oil industry, 100–103, 268n19

Okies, 138, 150, 153

Olmsted, Frederick Law, Jr., 269n33

Olson, Culbert, 188

Olympiad Committee of the Games, 157

Olympic Games (Los Angeles, 1932): about, 154–55; economic aspects of, 160, 283n140; and elite activism, 142–43, 154; ideals of, 160–61; inclusivity of, 158–60, 282n103; as Los Angeles promotion, 139–40, 141; solicitation of, 155–58, 279n35

Olympic Movement, 283n144

O'Malley, Edwin, 231

O'Malley, Walter, 223, 230, 231–34, 235, 236, 237

Open Door Policy, 87, 266n106

Orr, E. C., 33

Otis, Eliza Wetherby, 31–32, 34

Otis, Harrison Gray: about, 30–35; business dealings of, 70, 113–14; family connections of, 69–70; influence of, 27–29; and labor issues, 251n9; as land owner, 10; legacy of, 246–47, 248; on Los Angeles, 14–15; as newspaper magnate, 11; and tramp panic, 82; and transportation issues, 40–41, 42–44; western outlook of, 64

Otis, Harrison Gray (Federalist), 30

Otis, Sara Dyer, 30

Otis, Stephen, 30

Outdoor Life, 83

OutWest, 56

Owens Valley CA, 8, 108–9, 112, 113–14, 115–21, 189, 193, 202

Owens Valley Herald, 117

P-51 Mustang jets, 182
Pacific Electric Railway, 11, 22, 52–53, 103, 238
Pacific World, 8–9, 14, 252n36
Panama Canal, 29, 46–47, 103, 255n5
Pan American Airways, 184
Pan American Petroleum and Transport Company, 102
Parker, William H., 240, 241
Parker Dam, 122
Parrot, Kent, 197
Patria (film), 77–79, *78*, 91, 95
Patria Channing (fictional character), 77–79
Paulhan, Louis, 57–58, 59
Pearl Harbor, legacy of, 187, 191, 201, 207, 213, 216
Pearlman, Michael, 81
Pershing, John, 87, 216
Philadelphia Gentlemen (Baltzell), 2
Phillips, Randall C., 206
Plan of San Diego (1915), 65–66, 76, 87, 261n2
Plattsburgh NY, and Plattsburgh training camp, 81
PLM (Mexican Liberal Party), 67, 263n36
Plundering the Farmer, 169
Porter, John C., 160, 197–98
Port of Los Angeles, 79, 103, 104, 264n62. *See also* harbor
Post, Augustus, *The Curtiss Aviation Book* (Curtiss and Post), 50, 61
Poulson, Norris, 223, 225, 227–30, 233, 234–36, 237–38, 295n9
The Power Broker (Caro), 8
Power Lines (Needham), 2
preparedness, *92*; border protection in, 75; and connectivity, 204; during Great Depression, 153; infrastructure helped by, 79–80; and Japanese

internment, 187, 191, 202–3, 207, 216; and masculinity, 77, 82–83, 84; media on, 12, 77–79; military role in, 80–82; progress enabled by, 66, 89–93, 95–96; resistance to, 88–89; variation in, 67–68. *See also* defense
Pridham, Richard W., 125
prisons, 149–50, 189, 281n76
Proposition B (Chavez Ravine referendum), 235–36
public housing, 226–29, 230, 234, 236
public mobilization, 10, 11–12
Public Service, 111
Public Service Commission, 111, 113, 123
Puerto Rico and Puerto Ricans, 147–49, 280n69
Pulitzer, Joseph, 71–72, 262n27
Punitive Expedition, 80, 87, 264n67
Pure Food and Drug Act (1906), 162

racism: against African Americans, 224–25, 238–44; against Asians, 82–83; against Chinese, 20; efforts against, 209–11, 216–19; of elites, 6; in films, 77–79; and Hawaiian annexation, 45; against Japanese, 66–67, 77–79, 190–92, 203, 212–15; against Latinos, 243–44; against Mexicans, 20, 67, 146–47; migrants as targets of, 150, 153–54; in post-war era, 12–13; against Puerto Ricans, 148–49; during World War II, 4
railroads: advertising by, 155–56; antagonism toward, 39–40, 44, 47–48; and boosterism, 27–29; and harbor interests, 41–42; management of, 35, 37–39, 50–51, 52; and migration policy, 151; and oil industry, 102; urban need for, 9, 10–11, 24, 103, 249
raincrop (term), 143

socialists and socialism, 162–64, 166–72, 227, 284n159

Sommerfeld, Felix, 84

Soong Mei-Ling, 210

Souls for Sale (film), 100

Southern California Edison Company, 51

Southern Pacific Railroad, 9, 24, 28–29, 37–38, 39–42, 44, 50–51, 52

Spanish-American War, 262n27

The Spanish Borderlands (Bolton), 9

Spirit of St. Louis (airplane), 177

sportsmanship, 159, 160, 283n144

Sproul, Robert, 161

Stanford, Leland, 35, 37–38, 42

Stansell, Christine, 3

St. Francis Dam disaster, 108, 130–33

Stimson, Henry, 188

Stimson, Marshall, 149

strikes, labor, 104–5

Stump, Al, 155–56

Suárez, José María Pino, 84

Sugahara, Kei, 210, 215, 293n140

Sunset, 39

Sunset Club, 51–52

super-cities concept, 242–43

Swing, Phil, 122, 134

Swing-Johnson Bill (1927), 122, 123

Symons, William, 115

Tate, Darwin, 138

Tayama, Fred, 195

Taylor, Frank J., 144, 181, 185

Teapot Dome Scandal, 268n19

Terminal Island, 201–2

Texas Rangers, 261n2

Thalberg, Irving, 165–66

Thirty Explosive Years in Los Angeles County (Ford), 212–13, 219

Thomas, Chauncey, 83

Time, 49

Touring Topics, 156

tourism, 24, 119–20

transients, 138–39, 149, 150–52, 153–54, 156, 281n74

transportation, 10–11, 183. *See also* aviation; railroads; shipping industry

Treaty of Amity, Commerce, and Navigation (1888), 85

Truman, Harry, 217

Turner, Frederick Jackson, 256n33

Typographical Union (Los Angeles), 33

Ueno, Harry Y., 194, 195–96

Unemployed Cooperative Relief Council of Los Angeles, 138

Union Pacific Railroad, 37, 155–56

unions, 33, 104–5, 173, 181, 269n34. *See also* anti-unionism

United States Supreme Court, 204–5, 236, 239, 296n11

United States v. Wong Kim Ark, 204–5

University of Southern California, 22, 102

The Urban Establishment (Jaher), 2, 185

Vail Field (Los Angeles CA), 178

Van Nuys, Isaac Newton, and Van Nuys CA, 70–71

Veracruz incident, 86–87

veterans, military, 263n41

Vietnam and Vietnamese immigrants, 244–45

Villa, Pancho, 80, 86, 87, 264n67

Visel, Charles P., 140, 145–46

Voorhis, Jerry, 151, 208, 293n129

wages, 111, 271n22

Wagner, Robert, 234

War Department, 185, 266n10

Warner Brothers, 167

Printed in the USA
CPSIA information can be obtained
at www.ICGtesting.com
LVHW041209191223
766481LV00026B/141